AF352674

INTRODUCTION to PHILOSOPHY

INTRODUCTION TO PHILOSOPHY

Martin Heidegger

Translated by William McNeill

Indiana University Press

This book is a publication of

Indiana University Press
Office of Scholarly Publishing
Herman B Wells Library 350
1320 East 10th Street
Bloomington, Indiana 47405 USA

iupress.org

Originally published in German as Martin Heidegger
Gesamtausgabe 27: Einleitung in die Philosophie
© Vittorio Klostermann GmbH, Frankfurt am
Main, 1996. 2nd, revised print run 2001.
English translation © 2024 by Indiana University Press

Manufactured in the United States of America

First Printing 2024

Library of Congress Cataloging-in-Publication Data

Names: Heidegger, Martin, 1889-1976, author. | McNeill, William, 1961-
   translator.
Title: Introduction to philosophy / Martin Heidegger ; translated by
   William McNeill.
Other titles: Einleitung in die Philosophie. English
Description: Bloomington, Indiana : Indiana University Press, [2024] |
   Series: Studies in continental thought | Includes bibliographical references.
Identifiers: LCCN 2023054585 (print) | LCCN 2023054586 (ebook) | ISBN
   9780253069207 (hardback) | ISBN 9780253069214 (ebook)
Subjects: LCSH: Philosophy. | BISAC: PHILOSOPHY /
   Movements / Phenomenology | PHILOSOPHY / Logic
Classification: LCC B3279.H48 E3613 2024 (print) | LCC B3279.H48 (ebook)
   | DDC 190—dc23/eng/20240123
LC record available at https://lccn.loc.gov/2023054585
LC ebook record available at https://lccn.loc.gov/2023054586

Contents

Translator's Foreword   *xi*

Introduction   *1*

The Task of an Introduction to Philosophy   3

§1. *To be human already means to philosophize*   3

§2. *To introduce means: To get philosophizing underway*   5

§3. *The preunderstanding of philosophy*   6

§4. *How does philosophy relate to science, Weltanschauung,
     and history?*   8

Division 1 Philosophy and Science   *11*

1. What Is Philosophy?   13

§5. *Is philosophy a science?*   13

§6. *Ancient and modern conceptions of philosophy*   16

§7. *The expression "philosophy"*   17

2. The Question Concerning the Essence of Science   21

§8. *Provisional question concerning the essence of science
     in terms of the crisis of science*   21

     a) The crisis in the relationship of the individual to science   22

     b) The crisis of science with regard to its position in the
         whole of our historical and social existence   24

     c) The crisis within the inner structure of the essence of
         science itself   27

§9. *A new reflection on the essence of science*   30

     a) Science as methodological, systematic, exact,
         and universally valid knowledge   32

     b) Science and truth—*Adaequatio intellectus ad rem*   33

§10. *Truth as propositional truth*   34

     a) The traditional concept of truth   36

b) Truth as feature of a proposition: The connecting of
subject and predicate   *37*

c) The approach to the problem of truth in antiquity   *41*

§11. *On the problem of the subject-object relation.*
Predicative and veritative relation   *45*

3. Truth and Being   *49*
On the Original Essence of Truth as Unconcealment

§12. *The original essence of truth*   *49*

a) Going back behind the subject-object relation:
Being alongside . . .   *50*

b) Being alongside . . . as a determination of Dasein's
existence   *52*

c) Beings as they make themselves known in contexts of
involvement   *54*

d) Truth as unconcealment. Various ways in which
beings are manifest   *55*

§13. *Manner of being and manifestness. Diverse manners of*
being pertaining to beings   *59*

a) Being present at hand together—Being with one another   *61*

b) Being with one another: Several comporting themselves
toward the same   *63*

c) Sameness   *66*

d) The same as common   *69*

e) Is partaking something common?   *72*

f) Of the letting be of things   *72*

§14. *We share in the unconcealment of beings*   *75*

a) Being with one another is a sharing in truth   *76*

b) The unconcealment of what is present at hand   *78*

c) The belonging of truth to Dasein does not declare
truth to be something "subjectivistic"   *80*

d) Being alongside what is present at hand and being with one
another belong equiprimordially to the essence of Dasein   *83*

e) The being uncovering of Dasein. The truth of what is
present at hand and ready to hand as uncoveredness   *85*

4. Truth—Dasein—Being-With   87

§15. *Being uncovering in early human and early childhood Dasein*   87

§16. *The uncoveredness of what is present at hand and the manifestness of Dasein*   89

§17. *The manifestness of Dasein qua Da-sein*   93

§18. *Dasein and being-with*   97

§19. *Leibniz's* Monadology *and the interpretation of being with one another*   100

§20. *Community on the grounds of the with-one-another*   102

5. The Realm of the Essence of Truth and the Essence of Science   105

§21. *Summary of the interpretation of truth*   105

§22. *Determining the essence of science in terms of the originary concept of truth*   110

    a) Science as a kind of truth?   111

    b) Prescientific and scientific Dasein   112

    c) Scientific truth   116

§23. *Science as a possible fundamental stance of human existence.* Βίος θεωρητικός—Vita contemplativa   117

§24. *The original belonging together of theory and praxis in* θεωρεῖν *as making beings manifest*   121

§25. *Construction of the essence of science*   125

    a) Being-in-the-truth for the sake of truth   125

    b) The originary action. The letting be of beings   127

§26. *The change in the understanding of being in the scientific projection. The new determination of beings as nature*   128

    a) How the understanding of being precedes every conceptual comprehending   132

    b) The change in our understanding of being: An example from physics   134

    c) The positivity of science. The antecedent, nonobjective projection of the constitution of being that demarcates a field   136

6. On the Difference between Science and Philosophy ... 138

§27. *The projection of the constitution of being pertaining to beings as the inner enabling of positivity, that is, of the essence of science. Preontological and ontological understanding of being* ... 138

§28. *Ontic and ontological truth. Truth and transcendence of Dasein* ... 141

§29. *Philosophizing as transcending belongs to the essence of human Dasein* ... 149

§30. *The different realms of questioning in philosophy and science* ... 151

§31. *A summary of what has been presented. The understanding of being as the primordial fact of Dasein: The possibility of the ontological difference. The ontological difference and the distinction between philosophy and science* ... 154

Division 2 Philosophy and Weltanschauung ... 159

1. Weltanschauung and the Concept of World ... 161

§32. *What is Weltanschauung?* ... 161

    a) The word *Weltanschauung* ... 161

    b) Interpretations of Weltanschauung: Dilthey—Jaspers—Scheler ... 165

§33. *What is meant by world?* ... 168

    a) The concept of world in ancient philosophy and in early Christianity ... 169

    b) The concept of world in Scholastic metaphysics ... 171

§34. *Kant's concept of world* ... 174

    a) Kant's concept of world in the *Critique of Pure Reason* ... 177

    b) Excursus: Kant's laying the ground for metaphysics ... 180

        α) *The main theses* ... 181

        β) *The execution* ... 184

    c) Excursus: Kant's Dialectic ... 192

    d) Kant's concept of 'idea' ... 194

    e) World as the idea of the totality of appearances: Correlate of finite human knowledge ... 201

f) Idea and ideal. The full determination of the concept
of world as a transcendental ideal — 202

g) The existentiell signification of the concept of world — 207

2. Weltanschauung and Being-in-the-World — 212

§35. *Dasein as being-in-the-world* — 212

§36. *World as "play of life"* — 215

a) Being-in-the-world as the original play of transcendence — 216

b) Transcendence qua understanding of being as play — 219

c) The correlation of being and thinking. Its narrowing in the
"logical" interpretation of the understanding of being — 220

§37. *Achieving a more concrete understanding of transcendence* — 225

a) Selfhood (for the sake of oneself) as determining the
being of Dasein. Exposure as an intrinsic determination
of being-in-the-world — 225

b) Exposure as thrownness — 228

c) Facticity and thrownness. The nihilative character and
finitude of Dasein. Dissemination and individuation — 230

d) The lack of hold pertaining to being-in-the-world — 234

§38. *The structural character of transcendence* — 235

a) Retrospect on the structural character of
being-in-the-world attained — 235

b) Weltanschauung as holding oneself in being-in-the-world — 237

3. The Problem of Weltanschauung — 239

§39. *Fundamental questions regarding the principle problem of
Weltanschauung* — 239

a) Weltanschauung as factically engaged being-in-the-world — 239

b) The concept of Weltanschauung in Dilthey — 241

§40. *How does Weltanschauung relate to philosophizing?* — 246

a) The ordinary form of the problem: Can and should
philosophy construct a scientific Weltanschauung? — 246

b) On the historicality of Weltanschauungen — 247

§41. *Two fundamental possibilities of Weltanschauung* — 248

a) Weltanschauung in myth: Shelter as a hold amid overwhelming beings themselves   248

b) The degeneration of shelter: Weltanschauung that has become busyness   252

§42. *The other fundamental possibility: Weltanschauung as held bearing*   254

a) Weltanschauung as held bearing and the confrontation with beings arising from it   254

b) Weltanschauung as held bearing and the transformation of truth as such   257

c) Forms of degeneration of Weltanschauung as held bearing   258

§43. *On the inner relationship between Weltanschauung as a held bearing and philosophy*   261

a) On the problematic of this relationship   261

b) Philosophy is Weltanschauung as held bearing in an exceptional sense   263

§44. *In Weltanschauung as held bearing the problem of being irrupts*   265

a) The awakening of the problem of being from Weltanschauung within myth as sheltering   266

b) Historical forms of development of philosophy from Weltanschauung as sheltering and held bearing   268

4. The Connection between Philosophy and Weltanschauung   272

§45. *The problem of being and the problem of world*   272

a) The question of being as a question concerning ground and the problem of world   272

b) In the problem of being and the problem of world, transcendence brings itself to conceptual unfolding   274

§46. *Philosophy as held bearing in relation to ground: Letting transcendence happen from out of its ground*   276

Editors' Epilogue   281

German–English Glossary   283

English–German Glossary   291

Translator's Foreword

THE PRESENT TEXT offers a translation of the lecture course *Einleitung in die Philosophie*, which Martin Heidegger delivered in the winter semester of 1928–29 at the University of Freiburg, where he had just been appointed to the chair in philosophy vacated by his mentor Edmund Husserl. Published as volume 27 of the *Gesamtausgabe*, the course represents an important bridge between the last course Heidegger offered at Marburg in the summer semester of 1928, the Metaphysical Foundations of Logic,[1] and the seminal winter semester 1929–30 course, the Fundamental Concepts of Metaphysics.[2]

It will come as no surprise to those familiar with Heidegger's work and teaching that the course is anything but a schematic introduction to an academic discipline labeled philosophy. It is designed instead as a veritable initiation into philosophical thinking, with the stated aim of "getting philosophizing underway." Aside from the two major themes treated in the course—namely, the relation between philosophy and science and that between philosophy and Weltanschauung—a number of topics emerge as especially significant. These include the analysis of truth as our sharing in unconcealment, with particular attention to being with one another and community; further development of themes from the 1928 course, such as transcendence, world, the neutrality of Dasein, nihilation, dissemination, and dispersion; and comments on so-called primitive or mythic Dasein and early childhood Dasein. Also of particular importance are the consideration of world and transcendence in terms of "play" (*Spiel*) and the analyses of the "letting be" (*Seinlassen*) of things and of "release-ment" (*Gelassenheit*), while the theme of "world-formation" (*Weltbildung*) anticipates the more extensive treatment of that issue in the 1929–30 course.

The most recent, second edition of the *Gesamtausgabe* text (2001) was used as the basis for this translation. Minor errors or inconsistencies in the German edition have been corrected. The German *Sein* has been translated as "being," while

---

1. Martin Heidegger, *Metaphysische Anfangsgründe der Logik im Ausgang von Leibniz*, Gesamtausgabe Band 26 (Frankfurt: Klostermann, 1978), translated as *The Metaphysical Foundations of Logic* by Michael Heim (Bloomington: Indiana University Press, 1984).
2. Martin Heidegger, *Die Grundbegriffe der Metaphysik: Welt—Endlichkeit—Einsamkeit*, Gesamtausgabe Band 29/30 (Frankfurt: Klostermann, 1983), translated as *The Fundamental Concepts of Metaphysics: World, Finitude, Solitude* by William McNeill and Nicholas Walker (Bloomington: Indiana University Press, 1995).

das Seiende has been rendered as "beings" or "a being." Other translation choices are indicated in the glossaries. The translation of two word families in particular, those built on the roots *Teil* and *Halt,* proved especially challenging; some of the difficulties are discussed in translator's notes at the appropriate points. Translator's notes are indicated by "Trans." All other notes stem from the source texts or from the German editors. See the editor's epilogue for details on the sources used to compile the German edition. Occasional words in Heidegger's manuscript that proved illegible or uncertain are marked by [?], as in the *Gesamtausgabe* volume. Corresponding pagination in the German edition is indicated in square brackets in the running heads.

There are various stylistic inconsistencies in the German volume. Since the translation is meant to be an accurate reflection of the *Gesamtausgabe* volume (which is supposed to accurately reflect Heidegger's original manuscript, although I have not had the opportunity to consult the manuscript to check this), I have generally reproduced these inconsistencies in the translation. One prominent instance of such inconsistency concerns the use of single versus double (or no) quotation marks. Often this occurs in relation to instances where a word or term is not used functionally but is referred to as the word or term itself. For example, in sections 5 through 7, we find the following: the expression "scientific philosophy" (§5); the expression 'philosophy' (§6); the expression philology (§7). Rather than impose consistency where none exists in the German text, I have simply reproduced the inconsistencies of the *Gesamtausgabe* volume in this regard, except where the term is a foreign word (in which case I have set it in italics with no quotation marks).

Section 34 of the text, on Kant's concept of world, cites extensively from Kant's *Critique of Pure Reason* (as well as from other works of Kant). In translating passages from the *Critique,* I have consulted the existing English translation by Norman Kemp Smith, frequently adopting his solutions but often with modification or revision.[3]

My thanks are due to the College of Liberal Arts and Social Sciences at DePaul University for a summer research grant that supported final preparation and revision of this translation. I also wish to thank my colleagues Avery Goldman and Sean Kirkland, each of whom provided valuable input at the final stage. My gratitude is due also to the anonymous reviewer for Indiana University Press who made numerous helpful suggestions for improvement.

---

3. Immanuel Kant, *Critique of Pure Reason,* trans. Norman Kemp Smith (New York: St. Martin's, 1965).

INTRODUCTION

The Task of an Introduction to Philosophy

§1. *To be human already means to philosophize*

The task of this lecture course is an introduction to philosophy. If your intention is to let yourself be led into philosophy, then this is based on the presupposition that we initially stand "outside" of philosophy. A path is therefore required that leads from this position outside of philosophy over and into the field of philosophy.

This seems to be such a straightforward state of affairs that one need only point it out in order to understand it as a self-evident way of approaching the introduction to philosophy. The path taken by the introduction is supposed to lead into the field of philosophy. If we are not to go astray in the direction of our path, however, we must know the destination in advance. Before the introduction, therefore, and for it, we already need an idea in advance of what philosophy is. With this, a difficulty enters our entire undertaking, yet only apparently; for after all, we are not altogether cut off from the field of philosophy. We have a certain acquaintance with what today counts as philosophy, and we can gain a rough orientation from the philosophical literature as to what philosophy signifies. In addition, reference books about the history of philosophy provide us with a means of procuring information about this or that philosopher, this or that system. Admittedly, our task becomes difficult once more when we face the decision as to which of the philosophers is to be authoritative: Kant or Hegel, Leibniz or Descartes, Plato or Aristotle. Yet even this can be remedied by our attempting to provide an overview of all the philosophers and the entire history of philosophy, at least in its main traits—and this is precisely what an introduction is supposed to do.

However, we do not simply want some historiographical knowledge of what philosophy has been. Rather, we want to become acquainted with the "problems" in the field of philosophy, the various problem areas of the philosophical disciplines—logic, epistemology, ethics, aesthetics—not in depth, of course, but at least in outline, so that we can see how these disciplines are ordered among themselves, how they cohere, how they form a system of philosophy. In addition to the historiographical side, the introduction to philosophy must have a systematic side, and the two can complement one another in the most perfect way.

If at the end of the semester we have gone through such a historiographical and systematic introduction, we shall be the fortunate possessors of knowledge of the historiographical and systematic field of philosophy. Certainly, the impression will not entirely disappear that this field is indeed very varied yet equally uncertain and changing; above all, however, the feeling, which we more or less concede, will become reinforced, namely, that we really don't know where to start with what we have heard. We leave it to "professional philosophers" to occupy themselves with it and to believe they have finally eliminated the confusing mishmash of opinions.

If such reflection stirs, it is certainly a lot already. But for the most part, nothing at all stirs any more. One has also once heard a lecture course on philosophy—in the end, one should not neglect one's general education entirely, even if today it is much more important to know about the newest types of race car or the most recent efforts in the field of cinematic art.

Such is the situation with regard to philosophy, and to a certain degree, it will always remain so, despite the many introductions. Yet why is it like this in general, despite the many introductions? Because an introduction to philosophy of the kind discussed merely leads out of philosophy—not only that, but in addition it gives rise to the opinion that one has now been introduced to philosophy. And why must the usual introduction to philosophy that we have depicted necessarily fail? Because in its approach, it rests on a fundamental illusion. The approach proceeds from the presupposition that we who are supposed to be introduced into philosophy initially have our position outside of philosophy and that philosophy itself is a field into which a path is supposed to be taken (cf. p.152).

Yet we are not at all "outside" of philosophy, and not because, for instance, we perhaps bring with us certain bits of knowledge about philosophy. Even if we know nothing of philosophy explicitly, we are already in philosophy, because philosophy is in us and belongs to us ourselves and, indeed, in the sense that we are always already philosophizing. We are philosophizing even when we know nothing of it, even when we do not "pursue philosophy." We do not philosophize now and then but constantly and necessarily, insofar as we exist as human beings. To be there as a human being means to philosophize. The animal cannot philosophize; God does not need to philosophize. A God who philosophized would not be a God, because the essence of philosophy is to be a finite possibility of a finite being.

To be human already means to philosophize. Human Dasein as such by its very essence stands already within philosophy, not sometimes and sometimes not. However, because being human has different possibilities, manifold levels, and degrees of wakefulness, the human being can stand within philosophy in various ways. Correspondingly, philosophy as such can remain concealed or manifest itself in myth, in religion, in poetry, or in the sciences without it being recognized as philosophy. Now, because philosophy as such can develop itself explicitly and independently, it looks as though those who do not participate in explicit philosophizing stand outside of philosophy.

Yet if human Dasein already stands essentially within philosophy, then an introduction in the sense depicted, as leading one into the field of philosophy from a position outside of it, becomes meaningless. What point does an "introduction to philosophy" still have, then, in general? Why not then break with this custom?

§2. To introduce means: To get philosophizing underway

If we nevertheless make it our task to provide an introduction to philosophy, then it must have a different character. It indeed looks as though we initially stood outside of philosophy. The question is: What are the grounds for this appearance and semblance? If philosophy already lies within our Dasein as such, then that semblance can only arise from the fact that philosophy is, as it were, asleep in us. It lies within us, albeit fettered and entangled; it is not yet free, not yet in motion in the manner possible for it. Philosophy is not happening within us in the way that it ultimately could and should happen.

This is why an introduction is required. However, introduction now no longer means: leading into the field of philosophy from a position outside; rather, introducing now means: getting philosophizing underway, letting philosophy happen within us. Introduction to philosophy means: introducing philosophizing (getting it underway). Yet how should we bring this about? Surely, we cannot be transposed into the state of philosophizing through some trick or other, a technique or some kind of magic.

Philosophy is to become free in us, that is, it is to become an inner necessity of our ownmost essence, in such a way that it gives this essence its ownmost dignity. Yet whatever is to become free within us in this manner is something that we must take up into our freedom; we ourselves must freely take hold of and awaken philosophizing within us.

Yet to do this, we must surely already be familiar with it once again; we require a preunderstanding of philosophy. Thus, it could be that we have to keep to the history of philosophy. Perhaps history, yet not only the history found in philosophical literature, is in a much more originary sense essential for philosophizing. For reasons that we have yet to see, it would be a grave mistake to think that we could ever cultivate philosophy while completely casting aside the historical tradition.

Yet it does not follow from all this that the usual path of a historiographical overview of the history of philosophy could accomplish anything essential for our intent to introduce philosophizing. Acquiring bits of knowledge, even comprehensive and erudite knowledge of what and how philosophers have thought, may have its uses, only not for philosophizing. To the contrary, possessing bits of knowledge about philosophy is the chief cause of the illusion that one would in this way have arrived at philosophizing.

Yet how else can a preunderstanding of philosophy be attained, which we require if philosophizing is not to be a blind process but to be an action taken hold of in freedom? Manifestly, we must seek this preunderstanding of philosophy in the way that is already prefigured for us by the essence of philosophizing. For now, we know about this only in the sense of an assertion: philosophizing belongs to human Dasein as such. Within human Dasein as such, it happens and has its history (cf. p.157).

Philosophizing is to get underway in Dasein. Yet human Dasein, after all, never exists in some general way; rather, each Dasein exists, if it exists, as itself. Philosophizing is to be brought to happen within our Dasein itself. Within our Dasein—yet this too not in some general way, but within our Dasein here and now, in this moment and within the perspectives that this moment has, this moment in which we get ready to deal with philosophy. Philosophy is to become free within us, within us in this situation. In which situation? In the situation that now primarily and essentially determines the existence of our Dasein, that is, our choosing, wanting, and everything we do.

§3. The preunderstanding of philosophy

By what is our entire existence now decisively determined? By our claiming our civil right to university. With this claim, however, we have given our Dasein a commitment; with this commitment, we have struck out in a certain direction in our Dasein, something has been decided in our Dasein. That can either happen with clarity about our existence or not—we may have entered the sphere of university existence through convention, even out of embarrassment.

If we are not simply hanging out here, partly to learn all sorts of useful things, partly to find some new form of entertainment, then something must have been decided in us. Every decision of existence is a breaking into the future of Dasein.

What has decided itself? Our vocation. By vocation, however, we do not understand our outward position in life, nor even how it is ranked in a specific, even elevated class of society. By vocation we understand the inner task that Dasein gives itself within the whole and essential aspect of its existence. The historical and factical repercussions of one's vocation always entail an outward position in life, yet in the first and last instance, this remains of lesser significance.

Yet to what extent have we given our Dasein a particular vocation with our claim to our academic civil right? With this claim—to the extent that we understand it at all—we have planted in our Dasein the obligation to assume something like a leadership within the respective whole of our historical being with one another. By this we understand not the outward assumption of a so-called leading position in the field of public life, not that here or there we perhaps play the role of superior or director, rather leadership is being obligated to an existence that in a certain way understands the possibilities of human Dasein as a whole and in the last resort in a more originary manner, and is to be exemplary in this understanding. To be this, it is by no means required for someone to belong to those figures who are prominent. Still less, however, does such leadership already entail without further ado some moral superiority over others—to the contrary, the responsibility that such leadership carries with it, a responsibility that precisely cannot be regulated and is altogether nonpublic, is a constant and intensified opportunity for moral failure on the part of the individual.

Yet why does a specific claim to such leadership lie precisely in our actual belonging to the university? It arises from the fact that the university, through the fostering of scientific research and in imparting a scientific education, provides Dasein with the possibility of assuming a new position within the world as a whole, one in which all of Dasein's relations toward beings experience a transformation and Dasein can, but not must, become more conversant with all things in a new way, because a specific transparency and enlightenment enters our Dasein.

The fact that we know more than others and know many things better, that we come to possess authorizations and exam certificates, is completely irrelevant. But that an inner privilege comes to prevail throughout our entire Dasein, one that in itself none of us have earned; thus the fact that, in a more originary ground, science cultivates within us the possibility of a leadership within human community as a whole, a leadership that is inconspicuous, yet all the more effective on that account—this determines the moment of our current Dasein.

Science and leadership, together in this unity, are accordingly those powers under which our Dasein—if it has any lucidity at all—is now placed, not in the sense of some fleeting episode, but as a unique stage that essentially determines the singularity of our Dasein. If we want to let philosophy become free in our Dasein here and now, and if the task of an introduction is to get philosophizing underway, then from this situation we shall also gain a certain understanding of what philosophy means. We must draw this preunderstanding that we initially need from an elucidation of the essence of philosophy in its relationship to science and leadership.

Leadership determines the vocation of your Dasein already from the very fact that you now exist at the university. Leadership here means, however, disposing over higher and richer possibilities of human existence that are not imposed on others but are presumably lived and modeled unobtrusively and in this way alone effectively. This concealed exemplarity of genuine leadership, however, requires its own clarity and assuredness, that is, Dasein itself requires a reflecting upon the fundamental positions taken by Dasein toward the whole of beings, a reflecting that continually renews itself, however, and that is determined directly from out of the respective historical situation of Dasein and has an effect on it. What thus lies within leadership—not only in it, of course—we call *Weltanschauung* [world-view].

The task of gaining a preunderstanding of philosophy in terms of those powers now determining our Dasein thus means nothing other than posing the question: How does philosophy relate to leadership, Weltanschauung, and science?

§4. *How does philosophy relate to science, Weltanschauung, and history?*

In particular, we shall have to ask: Is philosophy a science among other sciences, or is it the "universal" science as distinct from the individual sciences, or is it the "foundational science" by contrast with the derivative sciences, or is it not a science at all, that is, not to be determined in its essence at all if it is housed and classified under the general concept of science?

Correspondingly, regarding philosophy and Weltanschauung we shall have to ask: Is it the task of philosophy to cultivate a Weltanschauung, is philosophy the doctrine of a Weltanschauung, or does it primarily have nothing to do with world-formation? Does philosophy rest on a Weltanschauung, or is this connection not at all decisive?

Finally, we shall take the two groups of questions together: Is philosophy *either* science *or* Weltanschauung, or is philosophy *both* science *and* Weltanschauung, or is philosophy *neither* science *nor* Weltanschauung?

Yet we do not want to discuss all these questions concerning the relationship of philosophy and science, philosophy and Weltanschauung, and science and Weltanschauung as though we were comparing fixed quantities to one another, as it were—for we do not yet know at all what philosophy is. Rather, proceeding from the powers of science and Weltanschauung that determine us, we shall ask what they themselves mean, why philosophy is brought into relation to them precisely, and with what legitimacy. Thus we shall gain an initial preunderstanding of philosophy from the powers that determine us, that is, by recourse to our Dasein itself.

In these discussions, which at the same time are meant to make the situation of our current Dasein transparent in several of its fundamental traits, we shall come across a connection throughout that is of essential significance: philosophy and philosophizing, precisely in reflecting upon themselves, are repeatedly thrown back upon what we call history, especially because philosophy initially presents itself to us in and through the tradition that is transmitted to us historiographically. By history, I am referring here not to historical science but rather to the happening of Dasein itself. It will become manifest that it is not only philosophy that stands in a peculiar inner confrontation with history.

We heard already that philosophy presents itself to us as always already known in a certain way, in and through its history, or better: in the tradition that is transmitted to us historiographically. The same also holds true, however, for science and Weltanschauung, and they both are historical from the ground up, each in their own way. This means, however: Our consideration of philosophy and science, philosophy and Weltanschauung, entails at the same time the underlying question: How does philosophy in general relate to history, that is, to the essential determination of human Dasein itself, which is in itself historical?

We are thereby faced with three groups of questions:

   I. How does philosophy relate to science?
  II. How does philosophy relate to Weltanschauung?
 III. How does philosophy relate to history?

The discussion of these three groups of questions marks the first stage that we shall cover, so as to get philosophy underway in doing so.

We do not want to learn philosophy here; we do not want to increase our study of subjects by one subject further, if only because philosophy is not a "subject" at all. Philosophizing is not some matter of skillfulness and technique, and certainly just as little a game of sudden, undisciplined inspiration. Philosophy is philosophizing, and nothing more. It is a matter of grasping this simple point.

We said: Dasein never ever stands outside of philosophy; rather, philosophy belongs to the essence of the existence of Dasein. Therefore, we must get it underway within Dasein itself; what is required is, therefore, an investigation of the Dasein that we ourselves each are. It thus seems as though we would be getting into a psychological self-observing, as though philosophizing would amount to an egoistic preoccupation with oneself, a dissecting of one's own psychic life.

Negatively, we may at first just say this: freeing the philosophizing within Dasein has nothing to do with any psychological, let alone egoistic, gaping at oneself. Yet letting philosophizing become free within us is just as little some morally edifying fussing over one's own ego.

Our deliberations here have nothing to do with all of that. At issue is neither psychology nor morality. Presumably Dasein will come into a center of its own in the course of these deliberations, but this so-called anthropocentric standpoint has something strange about it. In this anthropocentric consideration we shall arrive at the insight that this being, the human being, which supposedly stands in the center here in love with itself, is in its innermost core ex-centric, which means that precisely in keeping with the essence of its existence it can never stand objectively at the center of beings. For precisely philosophizing will make it manifest that herein the human being is thrown out of himself and over beyond himself, and is altogether not the property of himself. In order for this insight that Dasein does not have itself as center to be really attained, Dasein must precisely come into the center in a certain way.

Subjectivism is overcome not by becoming morally indignant about it but by posing the problem of the subject, that is, the question concerning the subjectivity of the subject, in an actual and radical way. There thus lies a great truth in the demand that ancient philosophy already expressed: Γνῶθι σεαυτόν, know yourself, that is, know what you are, and be what you have come to know yourself as. This self-knowledge, as knowledge of the humanity in the human being, that is, of the essence of the human being, is philosophy, and it is as far from psychology, psychoanalysis, and morality as possible. In the course of such a reflection upon one's own Dasein, it may, however, emerge that we are grasping the entire nihilative character of the human essence from the ground up.

The first stage of our introduction is therefore determined by three questions: the relationship of philosophy to science, to Weltanschauung, to history. We begin with the first question.

Division 1: Philosophy and Science

1 What Is Philosophy?

§5. Is philosophy a science?[1]

Science is one of those powers that determine what, to a certain extent, we may call the atmosphere of the university. However, sciences are not an accumulation of knowledge that is taught and learned in the manner of technical subjects. Rather, to the concept of science there belongs primarily the fact that it is research. Science exists only in the passion of questioning, in the enthusiasm of discovery, in the relentlessness of rendering critical account, of demonstrating and grounding.

It is not just an extrinsic peculiarity of the German university, but its intrinsic merit and the source of power of its historical existence that it is not a technical college, but that the necessary technical knowledge is also acquired in the course of the labor of research in the more or less serious and penetrating pursuit of the very problems that science faces.

Because science determines the university in this manner and philosophy is taught like one subject among others, we are asking about the relationship of philosophy to the sciences. Is it one subject among others, or is it distinguished by being the universal science? Or is it indeed not only the science that embraces the others but the one that even grounds them, the foundational science?

All these questions move on the basis of the general presupposition that philosophy is in any case a science. It is indeed a characteristic of modern philosophy since Descartes that it attempts, in ever new approaches, to elevate itself to the rank of a science, indeed to the absolute science. We must disregard the particular questions concerning how philosophy relates to the other sciences and initially decide the question: Is philosophy a science at all? Is there any sense in speaking of scientific philosophy, in wanting to ground philosophy "as rigorous science"?

To the question of whether philosophy is a science, we may say by way of anticipation: no, philosophy is not a science. Is philosophy therefore intrinsically unscientific, does it not belong in the university, are those people therefore right who, echoing Schopenhauer and Nietzsche, regard so-called "university

---

1. Cf. §30.

philosophy" as a highly questionable creation? Yes and no. Is, then, the endeavor on the part of modern philosophy from Descartes through Kant and Hegel and up to Husserl to elevate philosophy to the rank of a science not only futile but fundamentally mistaken in its intent? Yes and no. Is, then, the term "scientific philosophy" as nonsensical as the concept of "wooden iron"? Yes and no. Does not the thesis 'philosophy is not a science' precisely also deny and disown the effort that phenomenology has been making for decades, to ground "Philosophy as Rigorous Science"—the title of a well-known essay by Husserl in *Logos* I, from 1910? Yes and no.

Our thesis 'philosophy is not a science' therefore remains ambiguous at first and must remain so, so long as it is expressed only negatively and only says in general what philosophy is not. From the fact that philosophy is not science it perhaps by no means follows that it would have to be, or even ought to be, "un-scientific."

Yet what does this thesis mean, then, that philosophy is not science? Initially this: philosophy cannot be subordinated to the concept of science as a higher genus. In the manner that we rightly say: red is a color, green is a color, or: physics is a science, philology is a science, so we may not say: philosophy is a science.

Yet if we so boldly declare: 'philosophy is not a science,' then no less decisively the question arises in response: What is it, then? We answer: philosophy is philosophizing. But surely this is a piece of information that tells us nothing, that seems to tell us just as much as: a table is a table. Yet we are not simply saying: philosophy is philosophy, but: philosophy is philosophizing. Thus an answer ultimately indeed lies hidden in this positive thesis: philosophy cannot be determined in terms of something else—in terms of the idea of science, for instance, but just as little in terms of the idea of "poetry" or of art—rather, if philosophy equals philosophizing, then that means: philosophy must determine itself from out of itself.

Far too little attention is paid to the peculiar problematic that lies within the fact that philosophy has to determine itself from out of itself. Even if—in a certain way—it were to be impossible, only philosophy itself could show that. Whether and how philosophy is possible, only it itself can decide. That philosophy is related back to itself is only a consequence of the fact that it is something originary.

If, therefore, we say that philosophy is not a science, and if science is not the idea or the ideal by which philosophy can or may be measured, then the thesis that denies philosophy the character of a science is not also without further ado claiming that philosophy is tainted with the shortcoming of being unscientific. If something cannot and should not be science, then being unscientific cannot be attributed to it as a weakness. Yet we heard already: 'Philosophy is not science' does not mean that it is unscientific, if unscientific means: contravening the norms and methods of science. Not unscientific, because not "scientific" either—these are not possible predicates in a primary sense. Only one thing is provisionally clear. The thesis says: philosophy does not belong under the "genus" science, if we may be permitted to use this term of formal logic for now.

Yet unequivocal as this information is, it remains unsatisfying in view of the historical fact that thinkers like Kant and Hegel endeavored to raise philosophy to the rank of a science. Perhaps the relationship of philosophy to science, precisely if philosophy is something that cannot be traced back to anything else, is an altogether peculiar one, one that we have not by a long way grasped if we declare: "philosophy does not fall under the genus science."

Indeed, it is not because it would not attain the ideal of a science and have to remain inferior to it, not because it would lack that which determines science as such, that philosophy is not a science but rather because there pertains to it in a more originary way that which science has only in a derivative sense. Philosophy is not a science—not on account of a shortcoming; rather, it is on account of an excess that it cannot be science, an excess, moreover, that is a fundamental one, not merely quantitative.

We said already that the expression "scientific philosophy," just like the expression "wooden iron," is ambiguous. The designation "roundish circle" corresponds much better to the expression "scientific philosophy." Here something is attributed to the circle that does not pertain to it; for the circle is indeed not roundish, that is, approximately round, but rather is absolutely round. Yet something is also attributed to the circle that precisely pertains to it in an exceptional sense, insofar as it perfectly represents the idea of round. Correspondingly, in the expression "scientific philosophy," something is attributed to philosophy that does not pertain to it—it is never merely a science; at the same time, however, something is attributed to it that it already has in an originary sense: it is more originary than every science because all science is rooted in philosophy and first arises from it.

To state of the circle that it is roundish is at once superfluous and inappropriate. That fact that the circle is not roundish, this not being able to be roundish, is not an inability but an excess of ability: it is essentially able to be more. To say of philosophy that it is science is at once inappropriate and superfluous. Correspondingly, it holds that it is not because of an inability, but because of an essential excess of ability that philosophy is not a science.

Yet because philosophy is science in a way that science never can be and because philosophy is more originary than science, and science has its origin in philosophy, it was possible to reach the point where the origin of science, namely, philosophy, was itself designated as science and determined as such, indeed even as the primordial science and as absolute science.

Scientific philosophy is not to be understood like "wooden iron," two things that are mutually exclusive, but rather like "roundish circle." Yet illuminating though this comparison may be, it too falls short and gives rise to a dangerous misunderstanding that we must eliminate right at the beginning. We cannot and may not designate the circle as "roundish," because it is absolutely round, that is, because "roundish" would merely be a deficient approximation to "round." The circle cannot be defined by something that to a certain extent presents only a shortfall, a privation of its essence.

Correspondingly, science is a deficient approximation to philosophy, which is therefore the purest and first science. Here is the place where the most fateful errors arise, errors that could also be supported by the said comparison. For philosophy is indeed not science, nor is it the purest and strictest; but nor is it, for instance, the strictest science and something else in addition and beyond. We can only say: what science is, for its part, already lies within philosophy in an original sense. Philosophy is indeed the *origin* of science yet precisely on this account *not* science—not primordial science, either.

The task is to hold on to this thought because without it, the tendency to determine philosophy as science imposes itself repeatedly, that is, inadvertently indeed to approximate it to a particular science, for instance to mathematics, as the supreme and most rigorous science. Whenever the step in the direction of the idea of science is taken, there is a failure to recognize philosophy's essence. No matter how rigorously one takes science and subsequently sticks on a Weltanschauung, the two added together and fused fail to attain the essence of philosophy.

As we have already emphasized a number of times, it is a characteristic tendency of modernity to determine philosophy with respect to the idea of science and, indeed, to the science of mathematics—mathematical taken in a very broad sense, certainly. However, we notice precisely the opposite intent within ancient philosophy, that is, in the decisive commencements of our Western philosophy in general, and this is no accident. In antiquity, philosophy does not fall under the sciences but the reverse: the sciences are particular kinds of "philosophies."

§6. Ancient and modern conceptions of philosophy

For φιλοσοφία, the Greeks characteristically have a plural: φιλοσοφίαι. Mathematics and medicine, which already in antiquity attained a prominent flourishing and independence, were accordingly called "philosophies." By contrast, what we simply call philosophy is, according to Aristotle's designation, πρώτη φιλοσοφία, "first philosophy," that is, not first within the philosophical disciplines, but rather philosophy in the original sense pure and simple. One usually interprets this expression *prima philosophia* as meaning that within the entirety of the philosophical disciplines, this would designate the first discipline, before ethics, aesthetics, and so forth. This is an erroneous conception, and it becomes still more erroneous if one reinterprets this concept of first philosophy in a modern way, as the first science, the primordial science. The originator of this fundamental error is Descartes, who appeals to the ancient concept of πρώτη φιλοσοφία for his laying the foundation for philosophy as science—according to the ideal of mathematics as the authentic science—and who designates his major work explicitly as *Meditationes de prima philosophia.*[2]

With this conception of first philosophy, Descartes in his second major work, the *Principia philosophiae*, endeavors to systematize the entire content of traditional philosophy, thus of Scholasticism, in a new form.[3] Thus, it comes about that ever since, the peculiar idea of first philosophy as a foundational science has been brought together with traditional metaphysics.

Kant's last and admittedly concealed endeavor is concerned with annulling this entire connection. His intent is not so much to ground a new metaphysics as opposed to traditional metaphysics but rather to rupture Descartes's combining of the mathematical ideal of knowledge with traditional metaphysics. This innermost intent of Kant's was no longer understood by his successors.

In modern philosophy, we therefore find the tendency to determine philosophy as science, but in ancient philosophy, by contrast, the tendency is to determine sciences as philosophies. In favor of which view should we decide? Or should we mediate the two tendencies in a compromise? While there may be compromises somewhere or other, surely not in philosophy.

We are faced with the task of posing anew the problem of philosophy and science. Anew does not here mean discarding the old and inventing something new but means, rather, retrieving the old problems under the protection of genuine tradition. If we therefore want to determine how philosophy relates to science, then it is time to first figure out for once what science means. Before we answer what is indeed this most urgent question, we shall briefly elucidate the expression 'philosophy.'

§7. The expression "philosophy"

The more precise elucidation of what the word φιλοσοφία signifies is not yet a determination of the essence of philosophy. On the other hand, however, elucidating the significance of precisely such fundamental words is not a matter of indifference. From doing so we can already glean hints concerning the essence of philosophy, albeit hints that are as yet indefinite and unsecured.

The Greek designation φιλοσοφία is a compound constructed from σοφία and φιλεῖν (φίλος), that is, from wisdom and to love; in a somewhat sentimental and grandfatherly way, one usually translates it as love of wisdom. This fundamentally tells us nothing, and we must attempt to bring out the sense that the Greeks understood in their living usage of this word.

---

2. René Descartes, *Meditationes de prima philosophia* (Paris: M. Soly, 1641; 2nd ed., Amsterdam: Elzevir, 1642).

3. René Descartes, *Principia philosophiae* (Amsterdam: Elzevir, 1644).

To σοφία there belongs the adjective σοφός, meaning the one who has the right taste for something, "a nose," an instinct for the essential, and who therefore immediately knows his way around something, who understands something from the ground up, that is, who can stand before a matter in an exemplary and therefore outstanding manner. Σοφία is therefore originally spoken of with regard to craftsmanship. In Homer's *Illiad* it is thus said of the carpenter (XV, 410–12): ἀλλ' ὥς τε στάθμη δόρυ νήιον ἐξιθύνει τέκτονος ἐν παλάμῃσι δαήμονος, ὅς ῥά τε πάσης εὖ εἰδῇ σοφίης ὑποθημοσύνῃσιν Ἀθήνης.[4] And Hesiod designates the one who is knowledgeable in sea voyaging and with ships as οὔτέ τι ναυτιλίης σεσοφισμένος οὔτέ τι νηῶν (*Works and Days*, 649).[5]

This expression σοφία is then also carried over to poetic art and music and in general to everything that can be understood in some sense and implemented accordingly. In the early period, the same meaning as σοφός was also attributed to the expression σοφιστής, as the seven sages were called. Originally, the term "sophist" did not have a pejorative, negative meaning. The German words *Verstehen* [to understand], *Verständnis* [understanding], still correspond best to these Greek expressions σοφός, σοφία, σοφιστής, but not the term *Verstand* [intellect].

Three things make themselves known in the expression σοφία: first, understanding from the ground up; second, understanding immediately and instinctively; and third, understanding as being familiar with something and capable of something in an exemplary and therefore authoritative manner. Understanding was thus initially restricted to the sphere of artisanship, though it must be noted that in the early period, craftsmanship had a quite different central position and function within existence [*Dasein*], that is, with regard to its fundamental relationship to things, than what one of our contemporary big-city literati could even have a clue about. Only because the understanding that pertains to artisanship was already latently a direct and authoritative understanding of the whole of the world was the expression σοφία then able to extend itself to signify every understanding, in particular an understanding of the fundamental possibilities of existence [*Dasein*] as a whole, the whole of those things manifest to human beings. This is to be understood as παιδεία. This is why, for a long time in antiquity, philosophy was synonymous with παιδεία κοινῶς, which we may roughly translate as "education," although not as our present-day "general education." Cicero thus ascertains the following with respect to the early development of the concept of "philosophy": *Omnis rerum optimarum cognitio atque in iis exercitatio philosophia nominata est.*[6] "All that is an understanding of things in their

---

4 *Homeri Opera*, Scriptorum Classicorum Bibliotheca Oxoniensis (Oxonii e typographeo clarendoniano Londini et novi eboraci apud Humphredum Milford).

5 Hesiod, *Opera et dies*, line 649, *Die Hesiodischen Gedichte*, ed. Dr. Hans Flach (Berlin: Weidmann, 1874), 27.

6 Cf. *M. Tullii Ciceronis de oratore, libri tres*, with introduction and notes by Augustus S. Wilkins (Oxford: Clarendon, 1892), III, 60 (16), 439.

proper essence, and a knowing one's way around in this very essence, was called philosophy."

This widening of the sphere of what can be understood and the extending of the concept of σοφία not only to music and poetic art but also to science and every kind of possibility of education is, however, characteristically accompanied by a restriction: This understanding experiences that it has limits. The more the human being learns to understand the world as a whole, the more he experiences that this understanding is not there to be taken possession of without further ado. Understanding requires a special and constant effort, one that must be sustained in advance by an original fondness for things. This fondness, this inner friendship with things themselves, is what is designated by φιλία—a friendship that, like every genuine friendship, in accordance with its essence struggles for that which it loves.

The more the σοφός becomes one who understands, one who, in an originarily free, trusting relationship toward things, struggles unceasingly to understand them, he discovers himself as φιλόσοφος. This understanding is therefore not something that would be realized without engagement but rather something that must be taken up into the freedom of existence and only in this way comes to exist.

The first demonstrable occurrence of the expression φιλόσοφος is in Heraclitus (Diels: Fragment 35).[7] In the fifth and sixth centuries AD we find in the *Introductions to Philosophy* of the exegetical school in Alexandria six different definitions:[8]

1. γνῶσις τῶν ὄντων ᾗ ὄντα ἐστί

2. γνῶσις θείων τε καὶ ἀνθρωπίνων πραγμάτων

    } ἀπὸ τοῦ ὑποκειμένου

3. μελέτη θανάτου

4. ὁμοίωσις θεῷ κατὰ τὸ δυνατὸν ἀνθρώπῳ

    } ἐκ τοῦ τέλους

5. τέχνη τεχνῶν καὶ ἐπιστήμη ἐπιστημῶν – ἐκ τῆς ὑπεροχῆς

6. φιλία σοφίας

Because philosophy has this free fondness and is thus a free, fundamental possibility of existence, it stands in danger of being misused and perverted. Philosophy

---

7. Hermann Diels, *Die Fragmente der Vorsokratiker*, vol. 1, 4th ed. (Berlin: Weidmann, 1922), 85.
8. Ammon. in Porph. Isag. (*Comm. in Arist. Graeca* IV, 3), 1ff; David Prol. (*Comm. in Arist. Gr.* XVIII, 2), 20, 25ff; Elias (*Comm. in Arist. Gr.* XVIII, 1), 7, 26ff.

can act as though it is philosophy, even when it is not. It becomes a semblance and precisely as semblance attains the greatest power and seduction. That means: with the awakening of the understanding that this understanding of the world as a whole demands φιλία—voluntary, struggling, genuine fondness—its contrary, semblance, also becomes manifest, and now σοφιστής, by contrast with φιλόσοφος, comes to signify the apparent philosopher, the opponent who looks like a philosopher and yet is not one but who conducts his business with this semblance. Where there is philosophy, there is also necessarily sophistry, not only in Plato's time, but at all times, and perhaps today more than ever. Indeed, if it looks like there is no sophistry there, then things are in a bad way with philosophy. This is why it is perhaps not the worst sign if today journalism is beginning to commandeer philosophy. Yet it is not the case that the philosopher would be standing on one side and, on the other, the sophist; rather, because philosophy is essentially a human, that is, finite, possibility, a sophist lies hidden within every philosopher.

The Greek expression is at the same time an indication of the innermost essence of philosophy, one that has for a long time not been grasped in its central function: its finitude. Finitude has not been comprehended by one ultimately conceding, with apparent modesty and a certain emotion, that our knowledge is incomplete. It is not because philosophy never reaches an end that it is finite. Its finitude lies not at the end but at the commencement of philosophy, that is, finitude must in its essence be taken up into the concept of philosophy. What is decisive is not wanting to get to the end of those paths once attained in their endlessness but rather striking out ever again on a new path.

We can clarify for ourselves one last distinguishing feature with regard to the concept and word philosophy by comparing it with corresponding titles that we use to designate sciences such as zoo-logy, theo-logy, anthropo-logy or philo-logy. The expression -logy corresponds to the Greek λόγος, that is, the making manifest, grasping, determining of something. Zoology, therefore, signifies the making manifest, grasping, and coming to know of animals, anthropology that of humans, theology that of God. Here, λόγος (-logy) is the expression for the manner of grasping particular fields of objects. In the expression philology, by contrast, λόγος is itself the object of the science, language, discourse; here, to be sure, there lies a certain φιλία. By analogy with philology, the object in philosophy would be σοφία. Philosophy, however, is not the knowledge of wisdom.

Philosophy names not what is to be dealt with and known there but, rather, the how, the fundamental manner of comportment. This is why we say: philosophy is philosophizing. Yet important though this elucidation of the word is, we should not allow ourselves to cling to this and to think that we have now already attained an understanding of philosophy.

2 The Question Concerning the Essence of Science

§8. Provisional question concerning the essence of science in terms of the crisis of science

In order now to clarify, however, how science as such lies within philosophy, and in such a way, indeed, that philosophy may never be called science, we must determine the essence of science in a provisional manner.

The question of what science is was posed often by the Greeks; it is ancient, that is, ever new. It is one of those questions that are not settled by one having a handy definition at the ready. The question concerning the essence of science forces us, rather, into a fundamental reflection. If, as we asserted, science is one of the powers of our Dasein, then it not only determines this Dasein, but, like everything essential, brings a specific un-ease into Dasein.

It is no accident, even if occasioned by many kinds of external circumstances, that one speaks frequently in our time of the crisis of science, not only of the crisis of this or that science, for instance, the crisis of physics or the crisis of the humanities in their present unsettling by Oswald Spengler. One detects a crisis of science in general. Today, admittedly—compared to the situation a few years ago—we can already recognize more clearly again that an effort is being made to avoid this dawning crisis and to keep all unease at bay. Widespread conservatism has the upper hand once again. Certainly this is no grounds for us now also to close our eyes in the face of this crisis, if only for the reason that this crisis is not some contingent postwar phenomenon like most think but rather lies latent within science. If the crisis belongs to the essence of science, reflecting on it can bring us closer to the essence of science. By giving a characterization of the present-day crisis of science, we not only want to experience something about the contemporary intellectual situation, but in doing so, we are attempting to grasp something of the essence of science.

We may speak of a threefold crisis of science, one that is factically situated differently in the individual sciences and that is explicit and acute in varying degrees.

1. The crisis within the inner essential structure of science itself.
2. The crisis of science with regard to its position in the whole of our historical and social existence [*Dasein*].
3. The crisis in the relationship of the individual to science itself.

Certainly, it would far exceed the limits of this lecture course and demand a thinking through of the innermost forces of our time that both inhibit and drive us, were we to attempt to depict the crisis in greater detail in these three respects. Individual hints with regard to the required characterization of the essence of science must suffice. At the same time, however, a reflection emerges that is important for us also with regard to later deliberations concerning philosophy as such.

a) The crisis in the relationship of the individual to science

We begin with the crisis just named: the position of the individual in relation to science. After the war, the call for a revolution in science was circulating. A romantic youth wanted to eradicate the old, academic science overnight and replace it with a new one. Certainly, what made itself felt here in a somewhat strident form was not simply a postwar phenomenon, for in the years immediately preceding 1914, when our generation was studying and we seemed to lack nothing at all, an unease had already awakened. We sensed an ossification in the activity of academic science, and together with this ossification, a specialization that did not enhance our powers of assimilation—such demands on our powers can be beneficial even today—but rather a specialization that concealed an impotence behind it, the inability still to convey the primary and original ontological content of the science in a straightforward manner that spoke directly to existence.

This ossification and this obsession with specialization in the activity of academic science was linked to something further, something that we merely intimated and were only able to express unclearly: it could no longer remain hidden that for all the progress made by the individual sciences, the connection was severed between the sciences and their content, on the one hand, and the ideal of a vital and vibrant education, on the other, and this disconnect was merely artificially covered over.

There thus arose an increasing uncertainty regarding the status of science as such, both during the period of its occurring at the university as well as in the subsequent impact of science within existence [*Dasein*]. This uncertainty regarding the existentiell status of science in existence, however, had for us before the war an additional special acuteness through the fact that we were convinced of the positive possibilities intrinsic to science and of its central function within existence and therefore did not let the intensity of our work diminish, including our collaboration within what was ossified and specialized. Finally, this uncertainty was in no way removed by the failure of philosophy, because its interpretation of science, which we shall hear about, seemed to us to forget and to conceal something that we merely sensed but were not in a position to grasp.

Here I would nevertheless like to note the positive function of Heinrich Rickert's theory of science, which authoritatively dominated German philosophy in the period before the war; compared to all positivism that was widely circulating, it was fundamentally superior. This is the situation that was interrupted by the war, a situation that I have characterized here from my own experience and only in quite general terms, and that of course can be surveyed much more clearly today in retrospect than was evident to us at the time.

This critical situation did not become intensified after the war, but rather merely popularized, as it were. This inner exigency with regard to science, one that we did not deploy against it, now became the topic of pamphlets, and now with the spread of this contagion everyone was unhappy with science. Everyone also believed they had the means to remedy the situation and to reform the university. The general antipathy toward science had intensified, as had the call for a revolution in science, not because specialization and ossification had increased, but because of an obsession with reform and the fantastical belief that one could transform science with the aid of programs. One forgot to first forge an entry into science so as to reform it from within, if necessary. The crisis had not become more acute or serious, but only louder. Yet what we already lacked before, the possibility of an understanding of science as such in the entirety of its essence— this shortcoming is manifest in its widespread consequences, without it being recognized fundamentally up to the present day.

That the position of individual existence in relation to science can enter a crisis surely has its grounds ultimately in the fact that it remains undetermined and unclarified in general how such a thing as science essentially stands within human existence [*Dasein*] as such. It is the problem of the existential essence of science.

If, on the other hand, we should succeed in making this question concerning the essence of science visible and tangible as an actual problem, and even in attaining an essential explanation of the existential essence of science, then this by no means removes the factical crisis for the individual. To the contrary, it becomes more acute in a way, in that it now becomes evident how impossible the romantic efforts to try to reform science from the outside, and indeed by way of artificially overpowering it or overcoming it with Weltanschauung and the like, must be from the start.

Not even a decade has gone by since the crisis was publicly disseminated in pamphlets—and everything has gone quiet and is back on the old rails—and yet not on the old ones; for, without wanting to pass judgment on you today or wanting to depict our generation as better: the intensity and seriousness of scientific work was different, different in kind, despite the fact that today perhaps equally fine examinations are passed as before. Yet whether the crisis is discussed publicly in pamphlets or not is inessential. The crisis is there, even if it seems that everything is in order.

The crisis named in third place points us to the fact that the essence of science must manifestly be comprehended in the context of human Dasein as such and in terms of its fundamental constitution, and that accordingly all definitions of science that are not drawn from this orientation fall short in an essential respect. From this it follows that science is not some construct to which there is then of course added a personal relationship, one that, however, is best left to the individual.

Certainly it is the individual in each case who must decide their factical, concrete relationship to a particular science, but this can be accomplished only within the sphere of possibilities that dictate how the playing field in general looks, within which the individual can decide in one way or another in a genuine manner.

b) The crisis of science with regard to its position in the whole of our historical and social existence

The second crisis we have named concerns the position of science in the whole of our historical and social existence. We already indicated that people have sensed more clearly for some time how the connection between science and the ideal of an effective education has been severed. It is no longer clear without further ado in what way not only the results of science, but scientific education itself, should be guided over and into the unimpeded growth of a genuine education of human communities. The cluelessness with regard to science and its function within "culture" as a whole is all the more pressing given that the powers of education and of existence that still determined existence in the nineteenth century to a large extent, if often now only as a good convention—the classical ideal of education marked by names such as Goethe and Schiller, as well as Christian religiosity of whatever denomination—that these two historical forces have to a large degree lost their ability to be effective.

Now, since science has become questionable to itself with regard to its own significance and an original goal and ideal of education no longer exists, science comes up empty, as it were. Admittedly, we are afraid to candidly concede this predicament. In all essential predicaments that can become critical, the human being tries to save himself by a flight into convention or some substitute. Why now the unceasing and indiscriminate effort to popularize the sciences? Efforts to educate the people, which may be required for social reasons, are only ever occasions or convenient opportunities to do so. If this tendency toward popularization proceeds from the sciences themselves and is industriously pursued by them—many scholars now only work on reference books and compilations that are often of third or fourth order (symptomatic)—then it must also have its ground in the sciences themselves. This ground is a twofold one: 1. the inner exigency, the loss of significance of science; 2. a shortcoming.

This tendency toward popularization is meant to remedy an exigency that is clearly sensed and understood, to create a substitute in response to a shortcoming, and to procure significance for science once more, and indeed to do so on a path that is almost self-evident, documenting more explicitly the practical effect of science. However, are these not the same thing: to make science practical, and to popularize science? Why, then, should the popularization of science be such a bad thing?

The popularization of science is indeed a bad thing, not on account of its negative consequences, but in its essence, as a fundamental misunderstanding, that is, as an intrinsic destruction of the essence of science itself, as an increasing annihilation and burying of the possibilities of restoring to science an original position within the history of Dasein.

All popularization of science, however much guided by serious motives, is a violation of its essence, because it fails to understand that science should never be equated with its results, results that are then passed from hand to hand in some concoction or other. It is not because science, in its so-called progress, continually outgrows its results, however, that this equation is to be rejected, but rather because science never makes itself known as science in its results. Popularization not only necessarily makes science superficial but intrinsically devalues it. Popularization goes against the essence of science because what is essential in science does not lie in what can merely be handed down, passed along from hand to hand, but rather in that which is appropriated ever anew. This original appropriation of the essential, however, is possible only in method, which is inseparably interwoven with substantive content and results. Certainly, method means something more than what is commonly designated by this term; method itself is more than technique.

Amid the general cluelessness regarding the meaning of science, popularization is not only an escape route, however, upon which a significance is now procured for science after all, and indeed a significance that can count on a general, and thus distinctly dubious, appreciation within so-called broad circles. Rather, it is the attempt to remedy a supposedly genuine shortcoming in order to realize what indeed belongs to the essence of science, namely, that science is in itself practical. One wants to make science, which is reproached for being "remote from life," to use a contemporary catchword, close to life once again. Something genuine lies within this tendency, insofar as one senses that the sciences indeed possess a purely theoretical character, that is, that they have the task of primarily investigating truth for the sake of truth, apart from all utility. Yet the results must in the end also serve something—an argument that everyone understands.

The question remains, however, as to whether the authentic practical character of science consists in its possible beneficial effects. This has become something self-evident for us through the so-called triumphs of technology on the grounds of natural science. This way of conceiving the practical character of science in turn presupposes that its truth consists in its results, which can then also be applied and utilized. However, science does not first become practical through the application of its results, rather it is practical in itself and as such has direct effects, if only we comprehend wherein its truth consists. The crisis regarding the position of science within culture as a whole thus also springs from a peculiar failure to recognize the essence of science, the essence of the truth that is peculiar to it.

The practical character of the individual sciences is varied but not easy to determine. From the example of medicine and/or of medical anthropology it is possible to elucidate how the practical character of medicine has become a problem, even though it is eo ipso a practical science. Its results are indeed indisputable, but questions have arisen as to whether the entirety of medical knowledge is located within that horizon, such that within the entirety of this knowledge a form of existence like that of the doctor can emerge directly. There exists the noteworthy fact that young people have medical knowledge, yet never experience what a doctor is, that medical knowledge and existence as a doctor are intrinsically connected, and that therefore, if one may put it this way, there is a fishy element somewhere within medicine, so long as this relationship has not been clarified. The same problem—with corresponding variations—arises and is latent within all sciences, even in those that seemingly have no relationship whatsoever to praxis.

If our assertion that science is in itself practical is a legitimate one, then the theoretical character of science must have its own story. What 'theoretical' means must then be determined from out of the essence of the truth of science.

Thus, it already becomes manifest that in the end this second crisis shares the same common root with the one named in third place that we have previously discussed and that there must be original grounds somewhere as to why both the position of the individual in relation to science, and the position of science within culture as a whole, are in each case grasped as indeed necessary, yet belated and extrinsic, supplements to science. To science, therefore, there belongs "in addition," stuck on from the outside, as it were, a personal relationship, and science has "in addition" a practical relation to the remaining possibilities of Dasein. This "in addition," however, is an indication that what is being discussed has not been comprehended from out of the essence of science, and this indeed because it cannot be comprehended given the prevailing conception of science.

The common root of the two crises cannot be grasped because the essence of science has not been adequately determined in advance, that is, it is underdetermined. The horizon for a possible determination of the essence of science is both too narrow and too obscure. Accordingly, it appears that we shall identify the root of the crisis directly if we reflect on the crisis listed first, which according to our formulation concerns the inner structure of the essence of science itself. Yet we already saw, in our deliberations thus far, that the crises only ever provide a pointer to where their root is to be sought but not where the root itself is to be found.

c) The crisis within the inner structure of the essence of science itself

The crisis within the structure of the essence of science makes itself known in what one today likes to designate by the slogan of a crisis of foundations. Thus one speaks of a crisis of foundations in mathematics. Although it is still completely obscure for mathematicians and philosophers today, precisely this crisis has gained a certain popularity, because the crisis concerns a science that for thousands of years was regarded as altogether unshakeable, one in which—according to the idea of ahistorical science—one proceeded from one discovery to the next. Yet this crisis of foundations exists not only in mathematics, and it is not only today that it exists, rather this crisis dwells within every science ever since there has been science. This means: What is indicated in the slogan of a crisis of foundations belongs to the essence of science.

Seen from the outside, it is at first noteworthy that the sciences that are subject to the crisis of foundations do not implode, but to the contrary often stand in a process of great development—just think of contemporary physics and biology too. One speaks of a crisis in the grounds that have been laid, a shaking of the foundations—and yet the structure does not start to totter. Because the image of grounds, foundations, and structure does not tell us very much, the task is to ascertain more precisely what the foundation of a science means here.

The sciences move within particular assertions, principles, and concepts, and these are, in their entirety, determined by foundational principles and foundational concepts. There is thus talk of how the latest physics has made the previous concept of causality, of cause and effect, unusable and, likewise, the concept of matter. In biology, there is a growing insight into the necessity of a new or pioneering delimitation of what is meant by a living creature, an organism. One is beginning to see that chemistry is an extraordinarily renowned and rich science but that it is out of the question to want to grasp the organism and its essence through mere chemism. In philology, a new reflection on the essence of language, on shaping anew the idea and structure of grammar, as well as on the concept and essence of "literature" and "literary genres," is awakening on all sides. In the study of history, the insight is growing that an understanding of the historical is not arbitrary and is indeed subject to essential transformations of a kind unknown to the natural sciences, though the latter, too, have their own laws of development. In Christian theology, only in Protestant theology, of course, there is the search for a new understanding of the concepts of faith and revelation.

These are arbitrary and trivial examples attesting to the fact that such guiding concepts for the individual sciences have become unstable and that a new delimitation of such concepts is being sought, with greater or lesser success, with greater or lesser sound insight into the possible paths for doing so.

However, the state of affairs is not that researchers would now, for instance, be unanimously endeavoring to clarify and secure the foundational concepts anew, or even be of one mind in conceding the necessity of such a task. To the contrary, the majority balk at this and see in such attempts an incursion of mysticism and metaphysics into their science. One wants to know nothing of this vague and general stuff, especially not when this supposed revision of the foundations of science is undertaken along with some effusive Weltanschauung and preached more with a bad pathos than with sound reasons. In the face of these questionable experiments, one appeals to the thoroughness and continuity of specialized research and rejects all such reforms. Where such a reflection is conceded as being necessary, however, one believes that the existing means of one's own so highly developed science would suffice for one to undertake this work oneself—thus, for example, for one to be able to comprehend mathematically the essence and foundations of mathematics.

Thus it comes about that the sciences and their representatives on the one hand appeal to secured facts and methods—a stubbornness that takes cover behind the mass of results—and on the other hand operate all too hastily with philosophical concepts and ideas borrowed from somewhere and superficially imported into science. In the crisis of science, they are tossed back and forth between that stubbornness and an effusiveness of mood addicted to reform and fail to make headway. One must thus concede that these crises of foundations are not seriously taken up or understood, that they show only how extraordinarily far the sciences today are—despite all their successes and all their results—from even understanding a crisis as such, that is, from insight into the essence of science.

Yet perhaps such a self-understanding of science is not at all necessary, if only the so-called progress of science proceeds uninhibited in its effects every day. Of what use is a definition of, say, physics for its advances, if the definition is indeed as incomprehensible to the physicist as all philosophical theories? "What should we do with that?" is the usual and almost spontaneous question in the individual sciences in the face of such concerns with fundamental principles. The mathematician does not at all need to know what the essence of mathematics consists in, so long as he finds correct and useful results. Yet in the end, material progress in the realm of facts, which is taken to be so important, is the very reason for this not being able to do anything with a reflection on fundamentals and, at the same time, also the reason for the inner exigency of science, which one seldom concedes quite openly to oneself yet which drives people down all the escape routes that we indicated.

Thus one avoids this inner crisis of science oneself because one lacks any understanding of how serious and fruitful questions may be posed here. Perhaps it is indeed the case that neither the individual science of its own accord, with its customary self-knowledge, nor a philosophy imported from the outside, can even awaken the very crisis. The root of the crisis is not at all attained with this alternative. The question certainly remains as to whether it is simply the failure of philosophy on the one hand and the reluctance of science on the other that do not allow the genuine crisis to be awakened—or whether the issue is that both philosophy and the sciences are operating with an idea of science that is inadequate for understanding the problem. The latter is indeed the case.

We do not stand so primordially within science as to grasp its crisis from the ground up, that is, to be critically seized by science itself in a serious sense. We do not have science as our own in such an elementary and transparent way as to be able, within science itself, to run up against its limits, so as to understand at these limits of science why, as science, it is delimited not by chance but necessarily. Until we arrive at the point where researchers in the individual sciences come to see that they can in principle never comprehend their science using its own means, or bring it onto its ground, all research into foundations is in vain. Mathematics cannot be comprehended mathematically, and no philologists will shed light on the essence of philology using philological methods.

We must first learn to understand what is meant by the foundation of a science, and to what extent foundational crisis precisely manifests the essential limits of the science as such. Whether and how the crisis of the sciences is further discussed publicly today or not is not essential; what is decisive, however, is whether we are willing and strong enough to prepare ourselves to pass through, or better, to enter into the crisis. For the crisis is not to be overcome, but to become vital, and not so that sciences would simply become better and less inhibited and faster in their advances, but rather so that the sciences in general may come to exist in the way that they want to in accordance with their essence.

Yet this transformation in the position taken by existence toward science is not a matter of organization and industriousness, and it will not come about overnight. It is characteristic of today's era that even if we have comprehended certain genuine possibilities and tasks, we have not yet learned what is entailed in realizing them. We are no longer able to wait, and that means, we have forgotten that the first task of every generation that wants something consists in it sacrificing itself for the coming generation, without resignation, but with the inner strength and assuredness of one who has understood that in all genuine human achievements, each individual can "only" be a precursor for every other.

What is essential is not a program or industriousness but rather the inner growth of history within an individual generation. The task is not to talk but to act. How, we are attempting to understand. Whether you understand it and really act is not something I control. Just one more thing may be added before we stop speaking about the crisis: it would be blind zealotry if, for example, in seminar meetings for your academic discipline you were now suddenly to start talking about how the sciences really stand in crisis and if you were to try to reform your science with the aid of some Heideggerian terminology.

§9. *A new reflection on the essence of science*

Our discussion of the threefold crisis gave rise to the following questions:

1. How does such a thing as science in general stand within human Dasein?
2. In what sense is science "practical"?
3. What is meant by the foundation of science, and to what extent does it manifest an inner limit within the essence of science?

Our characterization of the crisis in relation to the position of the individual toward science showed that not only is there a lack of clarity concerning how the individual should comport themselves toward science, but fundamentally it has not been asked at all in what sense science as such stands within the Dasein of the human being.

Correspondingly, the crisis of science with regard to its position within the whole of historical reality entails that it can be formulated as the question concerning the essentially practical character of science. One senses that science, precisely if it is theoretical in the authentic and genuine sense, can nevertheless not be detached and free-floating in relation to the concrete Dasein of history, and one seeks an escape from this lack of clarity and indeterminacy of the goal of science by way of the tendency toward popularizing, which is especially strong today. We saw, however, that this is not a contingent shortcoming of science but rather a violation of its inner essence. In its very meaning, science does not let itself be popularized. What is fundamentally being sought in doing so is to make science practical, without properly understanding wherein the practical character of science consists; yet only if one has clarified the latter can it also be established to what extent a certain technical character belongs to every science, and what position and role it itself has within the vital Dasein of science.

Finally, the crisis within the inner essential structure of science—or, as one says today, the "crisis of foundations in science"—made it clear to us that the issue here is really that of developing the self-understanding of the individual sciences in such a clear and original manner that the sciences recognize their own limit in this, so as at the same time to see light shed on what determines this limit, that is, on that other thing that sustains science itself yet cannot be comprehended, nor indeed even questioned, by science itself as science. This crisis of foundations is the one that, if correctly understood, clarifies the finitude of science in an original sense, that is, it makes manifest that science is one essential possibility of human existence.

At the same time, the result of our discussion was that these questions can be answered neither by the sciences themselves nor, however, by some philosophy or other brought to science from the outside.

The task, rather, is to run up against the limit of science in the process of elucidating its essence, so as to encounter something else in delimiting it.

These questions, however, are not to be answered sequentially right now; rather, while holding on to these questions, we shall begin with a new reflection concerning the essence of science.

If we simply pull out the question "What is science?" then we find ourselves completely at a loss. All sorts of answers indeed offer themselves immediately; this is an indication of the fact that that whose essence we are seeking is not entirely unfamiliar to us.

Thus, we can answer the question of what science is in the following way, for example: we find science wherever there are institutes in which investigations are conducted with the aid of apparatus. This statement may be valid for all natural sciences and for medicine but not for the human sciences. Yet what about the science of music, which we count among the historical human sciences? It too has institutes and even "instruments," such as the cembalo or the piano, but that manifestly have a quite different function than, say, an electron microscope or a thermometer. Fundamentally, however, all sciences have need of technical instruments—even if only books. Science is something printed in books. Still, the book has a different function in philology than the civil legal code in jurisprudence, or the Bible in theology. It is questionable whether the essence of science has been characterized using this instrument, namely, books—and not all books are instruments. It may follow from the essence of science that it relies on such technology, on institutes, books, apparatus; yet what follows from the essence is not the essence itself, and so the hint regarding technical concretion within science can be very essential and yet only superficial. We, however, by contrast are demanding an inner determination of the essence, and perhaps we may find it if we ask what all the apparatus is meant to serve.

Apparatus has meaning and purpose only in the service of research. Researching is a wanting to know that is not arbitrary in nature and is not directed toward arbitrary objects but is an investigative knowing that proceeds methodologically and systematically within the sphere of a range of questions delimited in a determinate way, and that above all aims at a kind of knowledge that can be proven in as exact a manner as possible and elaborated as having universal validity.

a) Science as methodological, systematic, exact, and universally valid knowledge

The predicates ἀκριβής and καθόλου have from ancient times been ascribed to scientific knowledge. Thus we can say that science is methodological, systematic, exact, and universally valid knowledge. Precisely the last two predicates have always counted as distinctive determinations of science. One often appeals to Kant, who once said: "I assert, however, that in every particular doctrine of nature there can be found only as much authentic science as there is mathematics in it."[1] A science is scientific only insofar as it is mathematizable. Thus the human science are not sciences at all, since they resist mathematization in principle. Mathematics, on the other hand, is then the authentic science, since it is, after all, indeed the most exact and its results are altogether universally valid. Thus runs the common interpretation of Kant's proposition. Yet whether all of this follows from that proposition, whether indeed, when correctly considered, it has at all the meaning that one thereby attributes to it, will become apparent later.

Exactness counts as a hallmark of science, and exact proofs are the goal and pride of providing scientific grounds. Exactness, however, rests on the mathematical character of the science in question. Yet this mathematical character cannot be forcibly imposed on a science just because one aims to cultivate it as an exact science. That which is to become an object of the science in question must of its own accord permit or resist being mathematically determined in the first instance.

If, however, the possibility of the mathematization of a science thus lies within the substantive content and kind of being belonging to its field of objects, then what is also required in addition is the motivation for the necessity of such mathematization. Thus living beings, as extended bodies, grant a certain possibility of being mathematically determined, but actualizing this possibility in a limitless manner would miss the goal of grasping and determining the organism as such. Exactness of knowledge, therefore, with respect to the object to be known, can indeed be inadequate. This in-adequateness, this lack of agreement with what the object demands, is a fundamental form of untruth.

Exactness in a science can bring untruth with it; it does not, therefore, belong essentially and necessarily to truth. If by the rigor of science we understand

---

1. Immanuel Kant, *Metaphysische Anfangsgründe der Naturwissenschaft*, preface, A IX, in *Immanuel Kants Werke*, ed. Ernst Cassirer, vol. 4 (Berlin: B. Cassirer, 1922), 372.

the manner and way in which knowledge that is adequate to the object can be attained and determined, then exactness does not necessarily ground the rigor of a science. Thus, the attempt undertaken in the nineteenth century to bring historiographical knowledge into line with the mathematical knowledge of the natural sciences signified an essential violation of the rigor specific to historiographical knowledge. A science need not be exact in order to count as rigorous. Presumably, however, the ideal of every science is nevertheless the rigor of the knowledge it acquires. Perhaps rigor as exactness in the natural sciences is much easier to attain than the rigor specific to the inexact sciences, which are no less rigorous on that account. Even when we say that to science there belongs the rigor of its knowledge, we have not found the determination of the essence of science we are seeking. The feature of rigor may perhaps be a necessary one for science, yet the question remains as to whether it is also already an original determination of science. This feature of rigor can also only follow necessarily from the inner constitution of the essence of science.

b) Science and truth—*Adaequatio intellectus ad rem*

That this is so, we can readily surmise from the way in which we have characterized rigor: the manner and way in which knowledge adequate to the object can be attained and determined. Rigor is accordingly a determinate feature of how the adequacy of knowledge to its object is appropriated. This adequacy of knowledge is articulated in the Scholastic definition of truth: *adaequatio intellectus ad rem.*

Rigor is the mode in which truth is attained, and it therefore has meaning and a function within science only insofar as science aims at grasping the truth. Scientific research and teaching is investigative knowing, a determinate kind of seeking, finding, appropriating, retaining, and communicating of truth.

Characterizing science as a determinate kind of knowledge, of aiming at truth, is ultimately incontestable, yet at the same time tells us nothing at this level of generality. Everything will depend on how knowledge and truth are conceived in general, and on where what is peculiar and specific to scientific knowledge and scientific truth is sought.

With the solution to these tasks, we stand at a fork in the road where it will be decided whether the essence of science is identified or irretrievably missed, missed in such a way, indeed, that such missing still carries the semblance of truth with it. For when science in general is posited as knowledge and truth, then what is essential seems to be secured, especially since extensive agreement indeed seems to prevail in one respect concerning what truth is, namely, in the view that truth is something that, as a property, primarily pertains to the proposition, to judgment.

§10. *Truth as propositional truth*

Truth is intrinsically the truth of judgment, of assertion. Judgments and assertions are expressed linguistically in propositions. Truth is propositional truth. "This lamp is lit," "This chalk is white," are simple examples of a propositional truth. Individual words and combinations of words such as "this lamp" or "this" or "lit" can neither be true nor false, but only the proposition as a whole, that is, the linking of the predicate "lit" with the subject "the lamp." This consideration is illuminating. Truth lies in the combining of representations, not in isolated representations. That truth has its locus in the assertion, in the proposition, is so little tinged by doubts that even Plato and Aristotle may be called as crown witnesses for this view. This conception of truth has remained unshakeable ever since, and belongs to the very few things that have been established with unanimity in the history of philosophy.

Our later deliberations will be centrally oriented toward this problem. For this reason, we shall briefly provide some evidence for this important conception of truth as propositional truth: Aristotle, *De interpretatione*, 4, 17a 1ff.: ἔστι δὲ λόγος ἅπας μὲν σημαντικός, . . . ἀποφαντικὸς δὲ οὐ πᾶς, ἀλλ' ἐν ᾧ τὸ ἀληθεύειν ἢ ψεύδεσθαι ὑπάρχει; ibid., 1, 16a 12: περὶ γὰρ σύνθεσιν καὶ διαίρεσίν ἐστι τὸ ψεῦδός τε καὶ τὸ ἀληθές. (συμπλοκή). *De anima*, 430a 27ff.: ἐν οἷς δὲ καὶ τὸ ψεῦδος καὶ τὸ ἀληθές, σύνθεσίς τις ἤδη νοημάτων ὥσπερ ἓν ὄντων. All discourse, all discursiveness has meaning, that is, all speaking oneself out that is a wishing, requesting, asking, commanding, or asserting means something. But not all of these modes of discourse are λόγος, that is, not all discourse is discourse that exhibits. A request to someone does not have the sense or the intrinsic semantic function of making something clear to him, of communicating something to him, but just of requesting something from him. Correspondingly, the command does not, in its proper sense, convey some piece of knowledge but rather is a demand to act. Not all discursiveness, therefore, is an exhibiting in such a way that the exhibiting of something would be the proper tendency of the discourse. Only that λόγος is exhibitive in which something like being true or being false occurs. In the discourse that is true or false, that is, in the assertion, in the proposition, there lies something like a synthesis, a combining. Thus, Aristotle subsequently says: there is truth or falsity only within the sphere of synthesis, that is, of the linking, the combining, of subject and predicate. This synthesis he also calls συμπλοκή, that is, the interweaving, the weaving together of two representations or two concepts.

So that the influence of this conception of truth as propositional truth and of the proposition as the connecting of representations becomes clear, we may refer to a definition of truth given by Leibniz: *Semper igitur praedicatum seu consequens inest subjecto seu antecedenti,* thus the predicate or the word that follows is always in the subject, that is, contained in (*inest*) the preceding, first-spoken word; *et in hoc ipso consistit natura veritatis in universum,* and therein consists the nature of truth in general, universally, the *natura veritatis in universum seu connexio inter terminos enuntiationis, ut etiam Aristoteles observavit.*[2] Leibniz, therefore, here names the truth of the proposition *connectio*, which is simply the Latin translation of σύνθεσις. Truth is *connectio* of two concepts or expressions. Truth belongs to *enuntiatio*, to the assertion.

Finally, we may document the following in §17 of Kant's lectures on logic: "A judgment is the representation of the unity of consciousness of different representations, or the representation of the relation between them, insofar as they form a concept."[3] Kant also says very concisely: I think = I judge = I connect, namely, predicate and subject. According to the general conception, therefore, the locus of truth lies in the act of connecting.

What, then, is the result of this characterization of truth as propositional truth for determining the essence of science? If science as knowledge aims at truth, yet truth lies in the proposition, then science as a coherent body of knowledge is a coherent set of true propositions; this coherence is determined by the propositions not simply being lined up alongside one another, but reciprocally grounding one another. The coherence of the propositions is a coherence of grounding. To the essence of science belongs, therefore, as Husserl has also said, the unity of the coherent grounding of a set of true propositions.[4] This is the definition of science that is customary today in the theory of science and epistemology.

We can take two things from this: 1. a determinate conception of truth as propositional truth; 2. at the same time, however, the conception of science in terms of that which, to a certain extent, it produces as its result. Science results to a certain extent in propositions, and this result of research becomes concrete in printed treatises and books. Thus Hermann Cohen, founder of the Marburg School, which is distinguished by a certain conception of Kantian philosophy, of Kantian critique in particular as a theory of science and of knowledge, has indeed said: "the fact of science lies before us in printed books."[5] This is implicitly the dominant horizon for the question concerning the essence of science. Yet the question is whether indeed this looking to the result of science hits on its primary essence.

---

2. *Opuscules et fragments inédits de Leibniz*, ed. Louis Couturat (Paris: Baillière, 1903), 518–19, *Primae veritates*, Phil. VIII, 6.

3. *Immanuel Kants gesammelte Schriften*, ed. Königlich Preußische Akademie der Wissenschaften, vol. 9 (Berlin: De Gruyter, 1923), 101.

4. Cf. Edmund Husserl, *Logische Untersuchungen*, vol. 1, 3rd ed., unaltered (Halle: Niemeyer, 1922), §6, 15.

5. Editor's note: Presumably an exaggerated formulation on Heidegger's part. Cf. Hermann Cohen, *Ethik des reinen Willens (System der Philosophie, Zweiter Teil)* (Berlin: B. Cassirer, 1904), 62f. Cf. also Cohen, *Kommentar zu Immanuel Kants Kritik der reinen Vernunft* (Leipzig: Meiner, 1907), 53.

The result is always that which detaches itself to a certain degree from the process of producing and finishing; it is the work, which frees itself from the process of the work's production. That process cannot be known without further ado or in its entirety from the work. The result is, as it were, the corpse, which, as Hegel said, has left its tendency [life] behind it.[6] We, however, are seeking not the corpse, not that which is passed from hand to hand and is already petrified, but rather the very immediacy of effecting, yet in such a way that we come to understand in terms of the essence of scientific effecting and its creating of works the sense and way in which the result belongs to science. We want to understand the essence of science as the finding and determining of truth, indeed in such a way that ultimately this understanding first gives us information about the way in which the results and propositions relate to science. That is, we want to comprehend science in its essence, not as a result, not as a work, but in the accomplishing of its effecting.

Yet if science is supposed to be the finding and determining of truth, it thereby becomes questionable whether the foundational concept of truth as propositional truth is sufficient to provide information about the essence of scientific truth. Perhaps characterizing truth as propositional truth and determining science in terms of its result entail one and the same fundamental error. Through a more radical grasping of the essence of truth, we must put ourselves in a position to see the essence of science too in a more original way from the outset. We must arrive at the point where, from the outset, we avoid conceiving science as a nexus of propositions.

a) The traditional concept of truth

We shall therefore now ask in a quite general way: How do matters stand with the concept of truth that guides, in an authoritative manner, how the essence of truth has been determined, both today and previously? The answer will be: the traditional concept of truth does not hit on the original essence of truth. The question thus arises, however: How, then, is truth to be determined more originally, such that from this it indeed becomes understandable why truth usually comes to be conceived as propositional truth? We shall not simply push aside this dominant conception, with its venerable age and its far-reaching significance, but we must, rather, from the positive clarification of the essence of truth, at the same time find the grounds for this dominant conception and thereby attain insight into the relative legitimacy of this conception.

---

6. G. W. F. Hegel, *Phänomenologie des Geistes*, Jubiläum ed., edited with revised text and with an introduction by Georg Lasson (Leipzig: Meiner, 1911), 5 (preface).

We have therefore to show two things: first, that truth, which is traditionally conceived as a property of judgment, as *adaequatio intellectus et rei*, is grounded in something else. That is, what one conceives as truth within judgment is indeed determined in a genuine manner, but the inner possibility of truth lies in something more originary, and this more originary phenomenon is what, secondly, we must characterize more precisely.

These are seemingly simple considerations, in which, nonetheless, something quite essential comes to language. In view of such seemingly trivial considerations, especially when one has already discussed them a number of times, it appears as though one could simply know once and for all such a connection between derivative and originary truth. It is characteristic that one can never know all these essential connections in the way that one has some piece of knowledge, but that I have to appropriate them for myself ever anew, and with each new appropriation, a new abyss shows itself to me. The essence of the simple and self-evident is that it is the authentic locus of the abyssal nature of the world. And this abyss opens itself only when we philosophize but not when we believe that we already know such matters.

b) Truth as feature of a proposition: The connecting of subject and predicate

The thesis of traditional logic and epistemology in the broadest sense is as follows: Truth is a property of the assertion. Initially we want to elucidate this thesis for ourselves by way of an example that we shall then use as a basis for all subsequent considerations. Truth as feature of a proposition is, in its most simple form, a connecting of subject and predicate, S—P. In this connecting we are supposed to find the locus of what we call the truth of a proposition. Let us take a simple example: "This chalk is white." In this statement, the determination "white," the predicate, is attributed to the subject, "chalk." The Greeks, especially Aristotle (*De interpretatione*, 5, 17 a8; 6, 17 a25), designate such attribution as κατάφασις. This expression means: "down from above to something," and therefore signifies, to a certain degree, saying down from above to the chalk that it is white, attributing to it this determination, this predicate. If I say of the same object: This chalk is not blue, then "blue" is denied it. This form of the statement the Greeks call ἀπόφασις, which means, I deny something to a given matter, speak it away from it. This distinction then later, at the end of antiquity and the beginning of the Middle Ages, passed over into Latin terminology, and since then κατάφασις has been called *affirmatio*, or as Boethius also says: *adfirmatio*;[7] and ἀπόφασις

---

7. Cf. Boethius, *De interpretatione: Patrologia Latina*, ed. J.-P. Migne, vol. 64 (Paris: Migne, 1891), 364 A.

is called *negatio*. In traditional logic, these expressions therefore signify a judgment that affirms or denies (*verum—falsum*). The two forms, κατάφασις as well as ἀπόφασις, however, can each be either true or false, that is, there are affirmative judgments that are true or false, and likewise negative judgments that are true or false. The affirmative judgment as true is: "The chalk is white." The affirmative as false is: The chalk is blue. The negative judgment as true is: The chalk is not blue. The negative as false: The chalk is not white. The peculiar determinations of negative and positive thus cross one another, whereby in the formula for the negative judgment there lies a peculiar doubling, one that we cannot express in German, since we posit negation only once, whereas in the positive statement "the chalk is white" we have no corresponding word that corresponds to the negation; we would really have to say that the chalk is indeed white.

Yet another connection is of interest, namely, the character of truth in the assertion, and its locus. If, for the sake of simplicity, we stick with the positive, that is, affirmative and true judgment "This chalk is white," then the truth of this proposition consists in the predicate's pertaining to the subject or in the belonging together of these two representations, "white" and "chalk," so that truth is a matter of this relationship of the predicate to the subject.

The judgment that we are taking as our basis by way of example may be illustrated as follows:

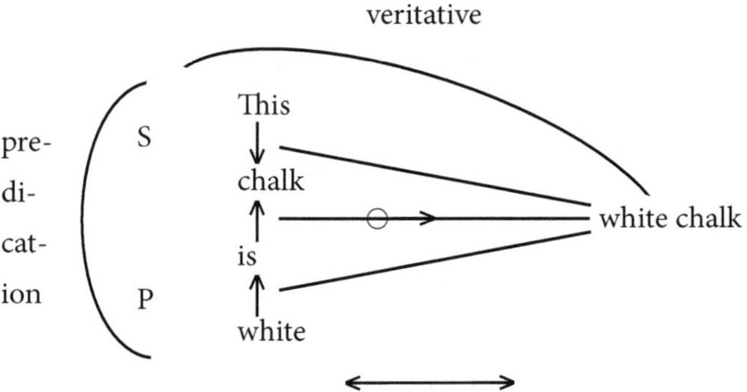

The vertical and horizontal directions of relations are meant to indicate that they are quite different in kind and that their connection is not such that they are linked to one another in an undifferentiated chain of relations ("proposition"—object).

Yet what, then, decides whether this P "white" pertains to the S "chalk"? From where does the vertical direction of the arrows in the figure derive its legitimacy? Where lie the grounds for the fact that "white" and "chalk" belong together, that this conjoining is a proper, legitimate one? After all, it does not necessarily lie in the idea of a piece of chalk that it is white; it could also be red or blue. The belonging together of S and P persists only because it, as such, already "belongs," is subject to, something other, as it were, namely, to the white chalk about which our assertion is made. The result is thus that the proposition "This chalk is white" initially presents a relation of S to P. This entire relation in the proposition, however, stands in turn within a relation to that which already lies before us, namely, to the white chalk, and only in view of this as lying before us can we make the assertion.

We thus see that a fateful ambiguity lies within the proposition: on the one hand, the formal relation of the P to the S, and on the other, the relation of this entire S-P-conjunction to that which the statement is about. The relation of the predicate to the subject we call the predicative relation in the proposition; it receives its legitimacy from a relation to that which the statement is about. We thus have two things: first, our predicating the predicate of the subject, and then our asserting this entire predication of that which lies before us, the white chalk. We must therefore distinguish the subject of the predication from the object of the assertion. The object of the assertion and the subject of the predication are two essentially different things. Each predicate has a subject, and this predicate is asserted of the subject. But every predication, that is, the entirety of the subject-predicate relation—not every predicate—has an object, about which an assertion is made. Here it is to be noted that this relation of the entire predication to the chalk is not the only one, for I can also make another assertion about that which is the object of the assertion here, for example: "This material body is light."

One can in no way interpret propositions such as, for example, "it is raining," or "there is lightning," so-called impersonal propositions, therefore, or "this human being exists," that is, existential statements, by means of the usual theory of the proposition and of the assertion. If one surveys the problems of the proposition and of truth in their entirety, this simple definition of the proposition is questionable. In the course of the development of modern logic, above all in Leibniz, this relation of the predicate to the subject, this *connexio*, is conceived more precisely as *determinatio*, so that the predicate has the fundamental function of determining. It determines the subject, and, corresponding to the distinction between positive and negative judgment, the distinction is also made between a positive and negative *determinatio*. This distinction is essential insofar as it contains within it two concepts that are of special significance for modern metaphysics, especially that of Kant and following, namely, the concepts of reality and of negation. Baumgarten defines what he understands by *determinatio* and *determinare*: *Quae determinando ponuntur in aliquo, (notae et praedicata) sunt determinationes, altera positiva, et affirmativa, quae si vere sit, est realitas, altera determinatio negativa, quae si vere sit, est negatio.*[8] "That which is posited

---

8. Alexander Gottlieb Baumgarten, *Metaphysica*, 2nd ed. (Halle: Hemmerde, 1743), §36, 11.

in something in the manner of determining it, namely its features and predicates, are determinations. One kind of determination is positive, and this positive, affirmative determination of the subject by the predicate, if it is a true positive determination, is called reality."

One must from the outset hold fast to this concept of reality as a positive true predicate to be able to understand the mode of questioning of the *Critique of Pure Reason* at all. The opposite concept to reality is negation, whereas today in epistemology we use reality in an altogether different sense than Kant and the old metaphysics. Moreover, this concept of *realitas* already goes back to Scholasticism, above all to late Scholasticism, to Suarez; *realitas* signifies nothing other than *essentia*, essence, something substantive, positive, an essence attributed to something. With a view to later, important considerations, I shall mention that this concept of reality is connected to the proposition, to *determinatio*, and specifically to the positive proposition.

If, therefore, one says that truth has its locus in the assertion or proposition, then this thesis is initially ambiguous. One does not know where truth is indeed situated, whether in the predicative relation or in the relation of predication to that which the assertion is about. Now, we already heard that manifestly the belonging of P to S as a predicative relation finds the standard of its appropriateness by way of this relation to that which the assertion is about. This predicative relation is an appropriate one when it corresponds to, takes its measure from, the thing, the *res*, the matter that lies before us that it is predicated of, and that the assertion is about. Correspondence is termed *adaequatio* in Latin, and *adaequatio intellectus ad rem* is the old Scholastic definition of *veritas*. We therefore name the relation of predication to that which the assertion is about the veritative relation, without yet thereby saying that this derivative relation constitutes the essence of truth.

Truth does not therefore lie in the relation of the predicate to the subject but rather in the relation of the entire predicative relation to that which the assertion is about, to the object of the assertion. We can separate the predicative relation in the proposition from the relation that concerns *adaequatio*, and thereby *veritas*, and that we therefore call the veritative relation of the proposition.

What is peculiar is that the predicative relation in a certain way is independent of the substantive content of *what* I assert. This relation persists whether I say "the chalk is white" or "this material thing is light." The predicative relation therefore has a certain independence from that which is asserted about an object in any given case, and what is asserted about an object and is free from the substantive content, not determined by the material aspect of the object of assertion, is termed the formal aspect. And because this relation provides information about the substantive content of what the object is, it is also called material truth, as distinct from formal truth. Yet one can call the predicative relation formal truth only under the presupposition that truth, as in traditional logic, primarily pertains to predication in general, to the assertion, to judgment. This "formal truth" we can better designate as "correctness," in order to ward off the mistaken view that truth is indeed housed primarily within predication. Insofar as the predicate is directed toward the subject, this directing itself toward the subject on the part of the predicate, quite independent of possible truth or untruth, is subject to certain rules, namely, the rules of so-called formal logic. Just as we separate the predicative and veritative relation in the proposition, so one must separate the rules of correctness in a proposition that say what must be the case in order for a P to be able to relate itself to an S in general from the demands and norms of the truth of the assertion.

The one initial result of these considerations is that assertion already hides within it a multiplicity of relations, and that the attribution of truth as a character of assertion is accordingly fluctuating and uncertain. Now, how does it come about that truth is primarily ascribed to the proposition, and why is this attribution of truth as a character of the proposition so self-evident? To what degree does precisely this attribution of truth to the proposition give rise to the confusion within which all epistemology and logic still move today, a confusion that cannot be undone by any newly invented theory, but only by going back to the origin and source of the misinterpretation?

Why is it natural to proceed from the proposition when one poses the question concerning the essence of truth? That truth is in some sense connected to cognition, to thinking, became clear early on already. In order to grasp the essence of truth, one will attempt to find within cognitive knowledge, whose concept already entails truth—for false knowledge is no knowledge at all—the element of truth and thereby the structure of truth.

c) The approach to the problem of truth in antiquity

The early period of philosophizing, in its original and fresh sensuousness, strives to make the question concerning the truth that belongs to knowledge its object in a form that is immediately accessible for everyone in a sensuous manner—and that is the enunciated word. It is the audible and written word, therefore, that presents truth and knowledge in a direct manner. Here we must also heed the fact that the Greeks, like all southern peoples, live much more intensely in public speech and discourse than we are used to. For them, to think really means to discuss publicly. Neither the book nor especially the newspaper played any role. Thinking as debating, as deciding with regard to truth or falsity, is public dialogue. This is why spoken discourse, the enunciated statement, is to a certain extent the actuality of truth, the tangible aspect in which truth presents itself; it is actual in λόγος.

This approach to the problem of truth is found quite clearly in pre-Platonic philosophy, in Plato, and still in Aristotle. Because the question concerning the essence of truth and knowledge takes its approach within the spoken word, that is, within λόγος, knowledge of the essence of truth is knowledge of the *logos*, that is, logic. One can understand the specific approach and limit of ancient, and thus of Western logic in general, therefore, only if one starts from this state of affairs, namely, that truth and knowledge present themselves primarily in the spoken word. This is why ancient logic in Plato and in Aristotle stands in a quite narrow inner connection, still barely illuminated today, admittedly, with that science and knowledge that concerns itself in particular with public discourse, namely, rhetoric. All the fundamental problems of Platonic logic are thus at the same time problems of rhetoric.

Truth therefore presents itself in the spoken proposition. The spoken proposition, however, initially takes the form of a sequence of individual words. This is why Plato takes the sequence of spoken words—τὰ ἐφεξῆς λεγόμενα (Plato, *The Sophist*, 261d)—as the basis for determining the essence of truth. In the investigation of this sequence of spoken words, that is, in the word-sequence of the proposition, the truth must therefore come to light. Now, Plato sees—this is one of his most exciting discoveries, one that for us has seemingly become self-evident—that the words spoken after one another are not simply mere isolated words in which we hop sequentially from one to the next but that here a peculiar unity is found, although we seek in vain for a link that connects the word-sounds with one another.

There thus arises for Plato the problem of how the individual words, these φωνή, in themselves stand in this remarkable and still obscure inner communion and unity, that is, the problem of the inner communion and unity (κοινωνία) of the manifold of words in the proposition. For Plato, the peculiar unity of this sequence of words consists in the fact that the words are not mere sounds, not the mere enunciation of sound, but signs that signify something; not just φωνή, therefore, but λόγος δηλοῦν. The propositional statement is a semantic unity, for Plato and Aristotle it is a sign of something, σημεῖον. The statement, the λόγος, not only signifies something, but in its signifying also refers to something that the statement is about, the white chalk, the thing itself, therefore, πρᾶγμα, or, as we may also say, the object. On the basis of its semantic unity that signifies something, the statement therefore stands at the same time in relation to the thing it refers to, or as Plato expresses this connection as a fundamental insight for the first time, this λόγος is λόγος τινὸς δηλώμα, discourse, assertion. This assertion is assertion *about* something, and indeed essentially so, not merely on occasion. What is asserted, and about what, by contrast, can change. In discoursing there thus lies a rich relational context that we have not yet exhausted at all. For this unity of signifying, the unity of what is thought, is determined by the thinking that enables it. Thinking itself, in turn, as an activity, a state (πάθημα), points back to the active soul.

The result is thus an increasing adding on of relation upon relation, and indeed proceeding from the sound of the word in judgment as the point of departure. We have already heard that, and to what extent, it is a "natural" one. Fundamentally, this sequence of relations will present itself even today for an initial determination. When all the relational structures are completely and thoroughly lined up to one another, then in a mediated manner, mediated by the structures that lie in between, a relation is thereby also produced between the two extreme ends: the subject-object relation. This also corresponds to the general state of affairs that we, the subjects, in a certain way stand in relation to objects, ἀντικείμενα (Aristotle), opposites, neighbors. It is just that, when we want to contemplate and determine this connection more closely, a series of mediating relations intervene. We therefore have before us a plurality of relations joined to one another, all running between relational structures that are present at hand in some way or other.

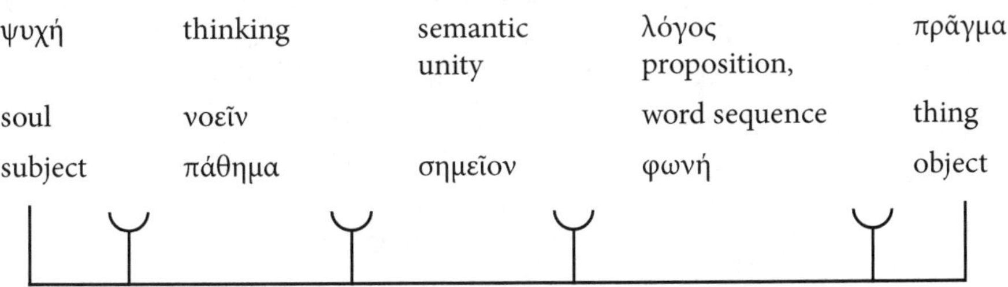

Subject-Object Relation

Yet something odd shows itself immediately. Are the relations that we added onto the two sides, proceeding from our starting point, incidental and arbitrary? Is it the case that we can also cut off the relations that we added, as it were, and prune everything down to our starting point once again? If the latter is the case, do we then really still have the statement that we basically started from? Or do we have, strictly speaking, a bunch of sounds? Did we in fact proceed from mere word-sounds, from the mere word-images, from the printed forms "ei," e i, and the like, or did we not, rather, proceed from the statement as we understood it? Indeed. When we proceed from the enunciated statement, then we are not in the first instance proceeding solely from the word-sounds; indeed, when we hear a statement enunciated, such as the one mentioned, our hearing is spontaneously directed toward apprehending what the speaker is saying and only incidentally, as it were, toward word-sounds. Indeed, a special process of abstraction and reorientation is required in order to hear the concatenation of word-sounds in a merely acoustical manner, and it even remains very difficult to hear it purely as such. Factically, therefore, we do not even proceed from the word-sounds; an enunciated statement is more; only because the unity of the statement was already understood could the question become pressing for Plato of where the sequence of words acquires this unity from.

In other words: the plurality of relations does not at all let itself be pruned down to the word-sounds of the statement, so that the latter would then still be the statement that we fundamentally have before us. To put it another way: the propositional statement = the starting point stands already within the nexus of these relations; the relations are not stuck onto it but rather are part and parcel of what the living, spoken statement is. The latter signifies something, and in its signifying it is related to an object, and in its being enunciated and being understood it belongs to a subject; all of this belongs together and lies at the foundation of the statement's word-sounds. The relational manifold is a whole that does not first arise by sticking together the parts but rather something on whose ground alone the parts have a meaning and function. The word-*sound* is such only as *word*-sound, and a word is not some noise but rather something significant, understandable. A word-sound, the linguistic and phonetic propositional form, has a foothold and meaning only within this relational whole in which it stands and by which the statement is embraced. This whole is what is primary and more original and only on its background can the parts be grasped as such and in their relations.

Is it not guaranteed from the outset that through this comprehensive horizon of the problem we shall hit on the essence of truth? And yet for all its entire wealth, it is afflicted with a fundamental shortcoming that entails that the question concerning the essence of truth can no longer get underway.

For what now becomes apparent is that all the parts and the nexus of these relations have indeed been familiar and discussed multiple times in their main traits since antiquity, but that precisely the comprehensive, or better, pervasive and organizing whole that prevails throughout has remained indeterminate with regard to its wholeness. Indeed, not even the question concerning the original whole, from which all the parts draw their essence, has been posed fundamentally and unequivocally as a problem. This whole, however, in which the true propositional statement is found, must manifestly also play a role in determining its truth.

Because one only ever moves within the said nexus of relations belonging to the statement, without asking about the original whole that first enables it as such, we shall not be able to grasp the essence of the truth belonging to the statement in an original manner. The question concerning the essence of truth, however, must here occupy us with respect to clarifying the essence of science.

§11. On the problem of the subject-object relation.
Predicative and veritative relation

By what right are we able to claim that the whole of these said relations has not been determined in its wholeness, indeed has not even been made a problem? Surely we have attained the whole of these relations if we look at the containment of all relations that lie between the two ends, when one links the two ends of this relational whole, thus soul and thing, or, as one says today, subject and object. The specific wholeness of this whole lies, then, in the subject-object relation.

What has been more frequently discussed and treated as a problem since the beginning of modernity, and especially today, than the subject-object relation? It is this relation, after all, that gives rise to the two main standpoints of philosophy, Realism and Idealism, along with their variations and mutations.

Certainly, all of this is indisputable. The question is only whether taking these two ends together really embraces the whole, whether its wholeness can be grasped in terms of the two ends and linking them together. That is impossible, however—if only because precisely these two ends, in the way they are linked together as ends, arise on the basis of an approach that has hitherto forgotten to first get a view of the whole that grounds them. The two ends subject and object, themselves the result of an unclarified and inappropriate approach, are unable to retrieve and determine the wholeness that was left undetermined to begin with by now coupling them together, in whatever manner.

Conversely, we must rather say: precisely the much-discussed problem of the subject-object relation in all its variations is indicative of the fact that one has not advanced beyond the ancient approach belonging to antiquity and has not yet grasped the central problem. This problem can be posed only when one has comprehended that the question of the subject-object relation, and especially all "epistemology," rests on the problem of truth, and not—as the usual opinion goes—the reverse.

One can indeed always invent new theories to solve the subject-object problem. Yet these inventions merely have the dubious merit of increasing the confusion and of providing ever new documentation of the fact that the decisive problem is manifestly not self-evident. The decisive problem consists, however, in nothing other than unfurling the question concerning the essence of truth, yet that means at the same time, in the question concerning the presuppositions and the original problem with regard to determining the essence of truth. The allegedly "new state of the problem in epistemology" may be distinctly interesting, and one can entertain one's readers with all sorts of things about it, but one is telling the reader nothing whatsoever about the state of the problem if one remains silent concerning what has been ascertained in this problematic with regard to the essence of truth.

The task now is to see positively that this problem of truth cannot be posed by being oriented exclusively and primarily toward the propositional statement.

It has become clear: The propositional statement has meaning and purchase only within an embracing whole. The wholeness of this whole must be determined first. If such a thing as truth appears within the propositional statement, then such truth, too, must also be determined in terms of this whole. More than that: Perhaps it is precisely the essence of truth that essentially co-determines this wholeness we are seeking.

We now see: 1. It is obvious, and almost compulsory in the question concerning the truth of knowledge, to seek this truth in the form in which it is most proximately accessible, the expressed statement, and to develop all further questions on the basis of this approach. We also saw: 2. that the λόγος stands in multiple relations. At the same time, however, we saw: 3. that despite the entire self-evidence of this point of departure, or precisely because of it, a preliminary and grounding question remains unposed, the question concerning the whole in which the nexus of relations characterized necessarily stands, the question concerning that whereby that entirety of relations becomes intrinsically possible in the first instance.

Yet how are we now to determine this whole, or bring it into view at all? We shall initially try to do so by recourse to the example "This chalk is white." With our analysis of the statement as predication and assertion we have basically already taken a first step in this direction. We saw straightaway that the concept of the statement as a predicative relation of the predicate to the subject, and as a relation of assertion relating the entire predicative relation to that about which the assertion is made, is ambiguous. This ambiguity tells us: The structure of the statement is a richer one, and points back into a structural whole that first grounds that which we initially contemplated. Because the structure of the statement is richer, the approach that starts from this structure is ambiguous.

Initially we became aware of something notable: the diverse forms of predicative and veritative relation. The statement as predication is at the same time an assertion about . . ., or better: The statement is an assertion about objects in such a way that this making an assertion about . . . has itself a predicative structure. The assertion is, as such, an assertion about the object, a relation to the object lies within the assertion itself. We called it a veritative relation, simply to indicate that within this relation to the object, truth comes to the fore. The essence of truth can be determined only if we investigate more incisively this relation to the object and ask: 1. In what does this relation of the assertion to the object consist? 2. Does this relation to the object pertain to the assertion as assertion? Is this relation to the object constituted within the assertion as such, or does the assertion merely make use of this relation to the object? These two questions belong most intimately together, and with the first, the second already answers itself.

Regarding the first question: If we want to determine the essence of a relation then our initial task is to first establish in general what the relation is between. A relation has its relational components (relata); one relational component of the assertion is the object, the other is the subject making the assertion. Each of us is a subject that relates him- or herself to this chalk in making the assertion, in repeating and executing it.

Yet with this trivial finding that the relation is the subject-object relation we have gained little toward ascertaining the relation of the assertion to the object—to the contrary, it is the title for a chain of problems and questionable theses.

Yet by explicating the manifold relations that are found between subject and object, have we not put ourselves in a position to now determine this relation more precisely? Does not this relational whole show the details of how the general subject-object relation is accomplished? It is one accomplished through thinking, semantic unity, word-sound, etc., such that we, as psychic subjects in each case, first relate ourselves to representations, from these to semantic meanings, from these to the object, and so by this path reach out from ourselves, from our consciousness, to the object. Certainly, it may still be a specific task to investigate and explain more precisely the accomplishment of these relations in detail, but in principle it is surely clear how we are to clarify the subject-object relation and thereby the veritative relation and thereby truth.

Yet on the other side, we know, after all, that the approach to determining the essence of truth from the expressed statement is indeed a natural one but also superficial and questionable so that everything else that results from this approach is also affected by the questionable character of this approach: the entire manifold of relations between subject and object. However, we cannot at this point appeal to the questionable character of this approach, since we must show in positive terms why it is questionable.

Yet this nexus of relations (the subject making the assertion, representation, meaning, object) is, after all, so obvious and has arisen so naturally, that one repeatedly has recourse to it.

And yet, whatever is so obvious is mere illusion! The relation to the object that lies in the assertion as actually accomplished in life does not at all have the character attributed to it by the theory of this relational nexus. In making the assertion "This chalk is white," we, the ones making the assertion, do not traverse that nexus of relations; we do not first direct ourselves toward one or two representations that we then connect, so as to eventually relate ourselves to the white chalk by way of these connected representations but rather the reverse and altogether differently: Prior to asserting the statement, we are already directly related to the thing itself, to the white chalk, and not in such a way that we would merely have a "representation" of it in our soul. Rather, in making the assertion, we already dwell in the presence of the chalk. We are already in the presence of the chalk, alongside it itself as this thing that is present at hand; in making the assertion, we are in advance referring to it itself directly. We, the subjects, relate ourselves directly to this being (chalk) itself; we are alongside it. Our, the subject's, relation to the object is an immediate "being alongside" the chalk. At first, and considered naturally, there is precisely nothing at all to be found of that complex and problematic nexus of relations.

We do not first arrive at the chalk by way of the assertion and the relational nexus in which it is allegedly suspended but rather the reverse: only insofar as we are already alongside the chalk, dwell alongside it, can it become the possible object of the assertion. It is only that which we are already alongside that we can make into the possible object of an assertion. The assertion is not at all our kind or mode of access to this chalk. Only because we are already alongside the chalk prior to making the assertion and do not first arrive at it by making the assertion as such—for this reason, and for this reason alone, can the assertion as predicative assimilate itself to what and how the thing is that the assertion is to be about.

We saw: The relation of the assertion, as assertion, to objects is, in keeping with the ancient definition of truth, that of *adaequatio intellectus ad rem*, the assimilation of thinking assertion to the matter. This assimilation of predication to the object, *adaequatio*, which one traditionally regards as truth, presupposes, however, for its inner possibility that we already in advance dwell alongside those beings about which an assertion is to be made that assimilates itself to them.

With this, our second question has also already been decided: Does the subject-object relation constitute itself in the assertion, or does the latter merely make use of the former? We see that the second is the case. Making an assertion about . . . already moves within, and as it were in the orbit of, our dwelling alongside the chalk.

3 Truth and Being

On the Original Essence of Truth as Unconcealment

§12. The original essence of truth

The result with regard to our first main question—to what extent is the traditional concept of truth not original, but points back to something?—is as follows: The traditional conception of truth identifies its locus as the statement. This identification of its locus, however, is ambiguous, insofar as the statement is at once predication and assertion. If it belongs to the statement in general, truth can only lie in the relation of assertion. This relation of assertion, the relation to its object, is itself grounded, however, in a dwelling alongside beings that necessarily underlies it and within which alone an object is accessible and can be determined by the predicative assertion.

Even if there is a certain legitimacy in attributing truth to the statement as assertion, truth is thus grounded in something more original that does not have the character of assertion. This other, more original dimension is what we must now pursue, in order thus to press forward to the more original essence of truth.

With this, we arrive at our second main question, that of how this original essence of truth is itself to be grasped. Our initial result was this: The assertion about the chalk arises within a dwelling alongside . . ., a being alongside. . . . This manner of being pertains to us, to those making the assertion. This direct, immediate being alongside the chalk itself is not something that we thought up by way of some theory or other about the assertion or about the relationship between subject and object. Rather, this relation showed itself precisely when we left all theory aside and merely pursued what is found in our natural making an assertion. We inquired concerning what it is that the assertion about the chalk aims at, according to its own intention that thrives within the assertion. Nothing to do with consciousness, the soul, or mere representations or pictures of things, rather just we ourselves, as familiar to ourselves, are relating toward the chalk itself, our being alongside . . . what is present at hand in the broadest sense. Admittedly, this is once more a distinctly trivial point. One has long since known of such things: ἀντικείμενα. Indeed, such things were always already seen. The difficulty does not lie in the fact that one would have overlooked this relating oneself to objects, that it would have been missing, but rather in the fact that one made it all too easy on account of its trivial character—for instance, in the usual form of argumentation that Realism also lets itself get cornered in and thereby finds itself on fundamentally erroneous paths—and in the fact that one proceeded all too quickly in search of explanations. That which one observed in a certain way—being alongside . . .—was not given its due at all and was covered over by theories.

Here, and in all corresponding trivial observations of this kind, the difficulty and what is decisive are to hold fast to what has been observed in such a way that the problems first result from that which initially shows itself and in the manner that it shows itself. One believes one is removing this trivial observation and raising it to the level of knowledge in responding to the question of how the soul can relate to things by rushing into a bunch of theories, just as—to use an analogy—one develops a thorough system of therapy, perhaps valuable in itself, without having made a diagnosis. The attempt is made to clarify this relation through a tremendous investment in astute theories and arguments, without first having secured the factual state of the matter that is to become a problem. One thus concerns oneself with problems that do not even exist and fails to see those that do result if one seeks to fathom the triviality rather than eliminating it.

That these theories and argumentation by formal logic always gain precedence over what we can directly perceive and grasp is due to the fact that all philosophical theories, at the moment they develop, enter into a broader connection to other theories, and a system, in the bad sense, is thereby established. To this is added the fact that, due to the disastrous influence and poor emulation of the sciences, philosophy oddly endeavors to admit as valid only those insights that can be rationally proven by way of some argument, with the result that one no longer sees the court of appeal of a direct intuition in its immediacy.

The task is to focus our effort on actually retaining and maintaining that which shows itself, the phenomenon, and the more straightforwardly, the more persistently; only in this way will the phenomenon unfold the entire incisiveness of those problems concealed within it. For, just as essential as the effort of initially securing the phenomenon is the insight that with this, we have not already achieved the solution to a problem, indeed not even the posing and working out of the problem. Overestimation of a mere description is just as fateful as the underestimation of such initial observation and securing. Precisely this disastrous view is gaining validity within phenomenology, where one presses for a direct exhibiting of things in the belief that if only one has described everything about how things are, then all is well. Yet with this, nothing is gained, the stage is merely set for the erroneous view that philosophy is botany.

a) Going back behind the subject-object relation: Being alongside . . .

When we emphasize that a being alongside . . . already underlies the making of an assertion, then the question arises of how this being alongside . . . is to be clarified with regard to its inner possibility. Being alongside . . ., dwelling alongside . . . in the first place characterizes a manner and way in accordance with which we human beings are. The being that each of us ourselves is, as human, we call human Dasein, or in short, Dasein. One fundamental feature of the manner and way in which Dasein is we call existence.[1] Dasein exists, and it alone. Only the human being has existence. Here too, existence is still ambiguous: 1. a way of being in general for Dasein, 2. and this because the way of being that is the leading one in various respects is not the only one but goes together with others at the same time.

That does not mean that other beings would not be actual but only that in the case of other beings, their way of being is a different one from the ground up. Animals and plants live; material things, "nature" in a quite determinate sense, are present at hand, things of use are ready to hand. Terminologically, the paradox results that the human being does not live but exists, although certainly it becomes apparent from a more precise interpretation of existence that the human being does not just "also" live "as well" but that that which constitutes the kind of being of the animal and of plants—namely, life—acquires a quite different sense of its own within the existence of the human being, insofar as he has a body. As distinct from the manner of being of things such as stones or pebbles, for instance, things like chalk, sponge, board, door, and window have yet another completely different manner of being that we designate as their being ready to hand. In addition, there are such things as space and number, which are also not nothing, and insofar as they are something, they are; we say of them that they subsist, they have subsistence. With respect to these different manners of being pertaining to beings, we can thus distinguish that which exists: human beings; that which lives: plants, animals; that which is present at hand: material things; that which is ready to hand: things of use in the broadest sense; that which subsists: number and space. In keeping with these fundamental manners of being, we can characterize realms, although the aspect of realms is not essential or primary. That which exists, that which lives, the present at hand, the ready to hand are not realms arrayed alongside one another but merely methodological concepts by which things are apprehended. "Nature" in the sense of cosmos, or as a counterconcept to art, is completely different from this way of apprehending nature; this problem has a quite different place.

---

1. *Deus—essentia—existentia.* To the essence of God belongs *existentia* (actuality); in accordance with his essence, he is that which cannot not be. His essence: *ens realissimum.* Were God not to be actual, he would be lacking something; since he can lack nothing, he must exist. Ontological proof of God, that is, the proof of his actuality on the basis of his ontological constitution, his essence. Critique in Aquinas, Kant, Schelling.

b) Being alongside . . . as a determination of Dasein's existence

Answering the question of what the essence of truth is depends on the extent to which we succeed in clarifying Dasein itself, that is, us ourselves in our existence, in such an original manner that we see from the essence of our own existence the extent to which something like truth belongs to it essentially.

Being alongside . . . is a manner of being pertaining to that which exists, which has this very specific fundamental manner of being, a fundamental manner of being that is documented, albeit in only one respect, in this being alongside. . . . If the latter is one mode of Dasein's existence, then the inner possibility of this mode of existence must let itself be clarified only through our adequately comprehending the existence of Dasein, that is, Dasein as such. Dasein, however, is nothing other than what we have hitherto called "subject," the subject that stands in the said relation to objects.

Have we now merely substituted a different word for the same being, Dasein instead of subject, or what have we gained? We see that we cannot simply operate with the subject-object relation, so long as it is not clear what 'subject' means here. Yet we shall experience the latter only if we let the subjectivity of the subject become a problem, that is, only if we ask what determines Dasein as a being in its original constitution, ask what this being is as such, this being that we have already ascertained exists in such a way that, in its existence, it dwells alongside other beings. We must retain this being alongside . . . as a determination of existence and ask: How must the existence of Dasein in general be determined, such that in the original constitution of this being, the inner possibility of such a being alongside . . . comes to light? We cannot and may not presuppose some concept of a subject and from there explain the assertion and the subject-object relation, but the reverse: we must retain as a determination of Dasein what we initially identified as a phenomenon and, commensurate with this determination, with this being alongside . . ., now determine Dasein itself, the subjectivity of the subject.

This elucidation of being alongside . . ., that is, this return to Dasein, occurs however with the guiding intent of finding the original essence of truth, and in order to understand from there the essence of science as one kind of truth. In our discussion of the crisis of science, we saw that it remains to be clarified what place science has within human existence, that is, within Dasein itself. The question concerning science and/or truth leads us back to the peculiar question concerning us ourselves. However, this is initially just an anticipatory and general characterization of the horizon that we now inquire into and that will become increasingly clear as our questioning becomes more definite.

Yet in order for us to see this horizon concretely in certain of its chief structures for the purpose of clarifying being alongside . . . in greater detail, we must determine still more concretely the point of departure for our questioning concerning the inner possibility of being alongside . . . as a mode of existence. Yet what more is there to be said about it?

Let us return to our assertion, "This chalk is white." Making this assertion about . . . is accomplished, and can only be accomplished, on the basis of our already dwelling alongside the chalk. When we make this assertion about the chalk and in so doing have it in view to a certain extent, we dwell not only alongside it in this process but also alongside other things. Before we execute the assertion, we are not preoccupied with the chalk at all. We direct our attention to the chalk only at the moment in which we follow the assertion that is expressed.

We thus see that our dwelling alongside things has notable modifications, that it does not necessarily mean being preoccupied with them. We dwell here in the lecture theater, that is, also alongside the door, alongside the lamps, the coat hooks, without being preoccupied with these things. Being preoccupied with things is therefore only one quite determinate mode within our dwelling alongside them. When we direct our attention to things, toward the thing itself, therefore, in the case of our assertion about the chalk, we are then able to apprehend the particular property of this thing's being white; in this paying attention to the thing, we experience at the same time that this thing that we are only now apprehending explicitly was already present at hand prior to this. It is intrinsic to the character of this paying attention to the thing that the thing itself to a certain extent says: I was there already, before you apprehended me. In this paying attention to things, we add nothing to them, we talk nothing into them in a certain sense; rather they, the things themselves, encounter us in such a way. Paying attention to things, seemingly an activity on our part, an apparent action, or as Kant says, an apparent spontaneity of ourselves, is, however, in accordance with its proper essence, precisely a letting be encountered, a peculiar passivity, a peculiar receptivity. In this letting be encountered, there is neither the "impression" of an outside nor a going out on our part, thus no inside either; there is neither a causal relationship nor a reverse transcendence. This letting be encountered is in a certain sense spontaneity, yet one that, in accordance with its intentional character, indeed has the nature of a taking in, of receptivity.

Kant was led astray by the spontaneity of thinking, and in general by the entire activity of consciousness in the broadest sense, into saying that there is thinking only where there is spontaneity—thus a determining with respect to things, ascribing them particular logical characteristics. This is a fundamental error. It is not necessarily precluded that where there is spontaneity, there is also precisely a peculiar receptivity. Precisely in our paying attention to something, as it awakens within us, there is a freeing of ourselves for things so that they can show themselves as they are.

c) Beings as they make themselves known in contexts of involvement

In our dwelling alongside things—even when inattentive—we always already have a manifold before us: not only chalk but sponge, board, lectern, coat hooks, caps, benches, doors.

Yet does this enumeration help us in the slightest to shed light on being alongside . . ., and as a consequence on our comportment toward things? Certainly, the details of our appropriate preoccupation with the chalk, writing on the board, may differ somewhat from the way in which I deal with a cap that I now put on or take off. From this, we can glean a definite manner of using and dealing with these items of use. Yet we have not yet exhausted everything that is entailed in the fact that not only this piece of chalk that we are making an explicit assertion about is present at hand but a number of other things. They are present at hand for us, however, not as in a junk store, in a scattered array unrelated to one another. The chalk may indeed lie next to the sponge, and both are next to the board. But this lying next to one another is a quite specific one in proximity to one another. It is codetermined by their material content, by what and how the things are. The chalk serves to write on the board, the sponge to erase what has been written on the board. These things are not simply just a number of things lying spatially next to one another but rather stand in a context, that of being serviceable for. . . . Within the medium of this context, they have specific relations among themselves. This context, however, is something earlier with respect to the things, that which already underlies them. The fact that chalk, sponge, board have this involvement is determined as a whole by the fact that here in the lecture theater, we make use of the opportunity to write up things, a writing up that serves to communicate more precisely what is being presented in connection with the lecture.

The lecture theater as a whole, however, is determined in advance by this task: a whole set of relations of involvement thoroughly governs the manifold of things present at hand here, together with the seemingly self-evident way in which all the things here are present at hand, to which we pay no explicit attention at all. The manifold of these beings, as they make themselves known to us directly, can be apprehended by us only because, and insofar as, we already understand such a thing as a lecture room in advance and are enlightened about it. In light of a specific context of involvement that is, as it were, dictated by the task—a public lecture—the beings that are present at hand manifest themselves in themselves, in what they are right here.

A context of involvement does not consist in the sequential determining of one thing by another, but in the fact that everything is in each case directed toward the whole, displays a reference toward this whole, and has such referral toward this whole to thank for "itself." Each individual thing has taken the whole up into itself. The whole of involvement, however, in turn becomes apparent only in this way; it is not something that would stand independently alongside or behind things, as it were, as something also present at hand among them.

Assuming for a moment that we did not understand such a thing as a lecture room, then we would certainly see things that are present at hand, indeed, but things that we would be unable to apprehend as such, in what they themselves are. What would then show itself to us would make itself known to us as no less real, no less imposing and present at hand. To the contrary, precisely insofar as we are not familiar with this context, what is present at hand is enigmatic for us and is all the more imposing and immediately actual in its enigmatic character. Yet because we factically know our way around, we have no inkling of the fact that we really always first apprehend this individual thing on the background of this understanding of a whole of involvement: writing up, lecture, lecture room, and the like. Each thing that we preoccupy ourselves with here, and that serves some kind of use, as such lets radiate this whole of relations of involvement that are determined by the lecture room.

Unexpectedly, we have thus gleaned some information about our being alongside things, namely, that it does not necessarily need to be an explicit preoccupying ourselves with them. Yet even if the chalk, unused by us, is just lying around, it lies there as chalk within the whole of involvement as characterized. Beings are manifest for us only through a context of involvement already being unveiled for us. We thus speak of a manifestness of beings in their contexts. Our being alongside . . . is, therefore, in the first instance a being alongside a manifold of beings that is thoroughly governed by a definite whole of involvement.

In this, our being alongside a manifold of things, beings as a whole are manifest, and indeed at a stroke. The sphere of these beings is therefore able to show itself in itself. The individual object that we set our sights on is this individual object precisely only within the context of a whole. This manifestness of beings within such a whole is so self-evident to us that we do not even take note of it; it is not by chance that we do not become explicitly aware of this whole, and thus stubbornly overlook it when reflecting upon objects in this domain.

d) Truth as unconcealment. Various ways in which beings are manifest

The manifestness of beings in themselves impresses itself upon us, however, when we rearticulate this fact negatively and say: these beings, just as they are present at hand here in themselves within this context of involvement, are not concealed from us, which they surely could be; they are unconcealed in themselves. Because they are unconcealed, we can make assertions about them and also check these assertions. The manifestness of beings is an unconcealment.

In Greek, unconcealment is really called ἀλήθεια, which we are accustomed to translate quite vacuously as truth. True, that is, unconcealed, are beings themselves; whereby and in what way is a further question. Thus, it is not the statement and not the assertion about beings, but beings themselves that are "true." Only because beings themselves are true can statements about beings be true in a derivative sense.

In the metaphysical tradition of the Middle Ages, however, there is also a conception of truth—*veritas*—according to which it pertains to beings themselves, to the *ens*. One thesis reads: *omne ens est verum*, each being is true. This statement, however, has a quite different meaning, namely, that each being, insofar as it is, is created by God; insofar as it is created by God, however, *ens creatum*, it must be thought by God. Insofar as it is thought by God as the one who does not err, by the absolute truth, it is true as something thought by God. Because each being is created, as a being it is something true, *verum qua cogitatum a Deo*. This concept of the truth of beings therefore rests on quite different presuppositions than in our exposition of truth.

Truth therefore means unconcealment; the Greeks, who philosophized with passion, have in their concept of what ranks as supremely positive and also as a supreme Good, in their concept of truth, a negative determination, an α-*privativum*. If this robbery belongs to the concept of truth, then this says that beings must first of all be torn from concealment or that their concealment must be removed from them, from beings. If beings thus lie in concealment, however, then they must have entered into such a concealment, especially since it is not at all clear why something that is must indeed be concealed. Yet what kind of occurrence is that, whereby beings enter into a concealment? In what way "is" this concealment of beings, with which all knowing struggles, as a finding of truth, as a discovering of unconcealment?

With this, we are posing questions that did not yet emerge for the Greeks, and certainly did not do so after them. The Greeks and the periods that followed are not acquainted with these questions because, in spite of the word ἀλήθεια, the ancients did not yet see explicitly that something negative lies within the essence of truth, and because they were therefore not able to be unsettled by this negativity. It was only in the first creating of the word in which the Greeks expressed themselves regarding truth that there was, as it were, this flash of lucidity concerning the essence of truth as pervaded by a negation. The word remained, but that lucidity from which it emerged turned back into obscurity and was held in that obscurity henceforth. Insofar as truth expresses itself, it becomes publicly accessible in the spoken statement as an interweaving of words and meanings and representations. The primary and sole form of truth is thus the predicative synthesis. Because this characterization of truth is still today the most self-evident one, yet at the same time sanctioned by the venerable tradition of philosophy, there is initially not the slightest inkling at all that at certain moments, something elementary became lucid in this word ἀλήθεια.

We must therefore first restore once more to this primal word its original content that has been lost, or better, we must first place it properly into the light. Concerning truth as the un-concealment of beings, as privation and robbery, as well as the overcoming of the concealment of beings and the freeing of beings from their concealment, the fundamentals can be studied in *Being and Time*, Part One, 212–30. There, the attempt is made for the first time to discuss this sense of truth in its fundamental significance and in the entire breadth that this concept has. What is still entirely missing is a thorough investigation into the history of the concept of truth in this radical and original sense, both with regard to the history of the concept of truth in philosophy and in the sciences and in general in the sense of the concept of truth that concerns practical truth, action. Nevertheless, we recently have an investigation of this kind that also proceeds from the fundamental manner of my questioning: Rudolf Bultmann, *Untersuchungen zum Johannesevangelium* [*Investigations into the Gospel of St. John*], in *Zeitschrift für die neutestamentliche Wissenschaft und die Kunde der älteren Kirche*, 1928, vol. 27, 113–63. Here, Bultmann publishes preliminary research for the major commentary that he is preparing, and he attempts to discuss particular fundamental concepts, among others and above all the concept of ἀλήθεια. The treatise is structured in two main parts. First, the concept of truth in the Old Testament is discussed, and the way it has been translated in the Septuagint. Here, related concepts of truth, stability, faithfulness, reliability, justice, and the like are elaborated. All these concepts that hitherto left one standing clueless when armed with the traditional concept of truth now find their first appropriate interpretation. Following this, the concept of truth in the Jewish and Judeo-Christian literature is examined. The second part of the treatise, ἀλήθεια in the Christian and Hellenistic literature, is important not only because the attempt is made for the first time to discern this history of the concept of truth in a concrete investigation but because Bultmann, with his typical thoroughness and acumen, presents new material with unprecedented incisiveness so that this treatise is of essential significance with respect to the history of science and of philosophy.

We shall hold on to this elementary character of the essence of truth and from here on try to understand by truth something like un-concealment, while knowing that we have not yet grasped it correctly, let alone being able to understand it. Subsequent considerations must aid us in this. For now, we shall attempt to pursue further the path we have set out on, that is, extending our elucidation of being alongside . . . (dwelling) far enough to gain a first sufficient insight into the essence of truth, sufficient for answering the question concerning the essence of science in light of the essence of truth.[2]

We saw that in our being alongside things, the latter are manifest to us; they themselves are encountered as unconcealed, and indeed in such a way that they make themselves known within a whole nexus of involvement.[3] The sphere of those nexuses of involvement that factically shine through on each occasion, the perspective on whatever is precisely manifest to us, can change, however, and is constantly changing: When we say chalk, sponge, board, and lecture room, then we are forcibly directing ourselves to a certain degree toward the vicinity of this particular space. The lecture room itself, however, is directly within the university building; this building is in this square of the city; the city of Freiburg is in a particular surrounding region; this region beneath the heavens, during day, during night, during a particular weather. This entire context is directly present for us in an unconcealed manner whenever we say that this chalk here is lying on the lectern. None of these contextual spheres of beings have fixed limits; they are not situated next to one another. Rather, the more expansive ones in each case shine as a whole through the more restricted ones, and shine into these.

This is to say, however, that manifold beings of a variety of different kinds are always manifest to us. We all move within certain circles of those beings that are manifest to us in an everyday manner, circles that are on average the same, indeed even identical in part. It is not our present task to pursue this point, since we are inquiring merely concerning the manifestness as such, the unconcealment of beings. It indeed seems to be sufficient that in so doing, we stick to a random example, the manifestness of the chalk, which makes it possible for this chalk to become the object of an assertion. Yet we heard already that not all beings have the manner of being of things of use. Those beings are also actual that are present at hand (stones), that live (plant, animal), that exist (humans). We are therefore now asking concerning the manifestness of all these beings, which admittedly may differ according to their manner of being.

Yet is this manifestness of beings a thoroughly uniform one, irrespective of the particular manner of being of those beings that are manifest? It appears so. For we can readily establish in the same sequential way that there are stones, trees, dogs, automobiles, "passers-by" (humans). Because these are all manifest

---

2. Not simply sufficient universally; for the idea of propositional truth, and precisely it, is also universal, but it is a bewitching universality of the indeterminate. The original essence, such that all essential variations and the kind of variation even of contortions and artificial constructs with regard to "practical truth" keep to propositional truth and then carry it over! The truth of hoping, wishing, questioning, and the like cannot be grasped in this manner.

3. Essence of truth: hitherto, the manifestness of what is present at hand. The same manifestness through and through? Is the character of truth untouched by the kind of being pertaining to beings? How are the two connected?

in the same way, we can also directly converse about all of these, make true assertions about them. This uniform possibility of assertion regarding all those beings before us is also proof of a uniform kind of manifestness, unconcealment, truth of beings.

However, we have already become suspicious on several occasions concerning what the assertion provides with respect to the essence of truth. Perhaps it is precisely the uniformity, the undifferentiated character of assertion and of talking about . . . that here once again gives rise to the illusion that the truth concerning beings is likewise of the same undifferentiated character, that the unconcealment of beings in its various ways is not determined by the particular manner of being pertaining to beings in each case.

It is indeed an illusion that all those beings that are precisely accessible to us are unconcealed in the same kind of manifestness, albeit an illusion for which there are reasons. Because this illusion is a very stubborn one, indeed even belongs to the essence of our everyday Dasein, shedding light on the reasons for, and possibility of, this illusion demands extensive considerations. We see repeatedly, however, that the assertion not only suggests to us a particular idea of truth but also implies that to a certain extent all those beings that we can make assertions about are of the same kind.

However, the manifestness (truth) of those beings accessible to us in an everyday manner in their manifold character is not a uniform, undifferentiated one, but differs in each case according to the kind of being pertaining to the beings that make themselves known. It is precisely because we initially do not heed the diverse character of beings, and for the most part never do, that we must examine this. For we are not to determine the essence of truth by orienting ourselves toward the assertion and its undifferentiated, leveled down, and leveling character.

§13. Manner of being and manifestness.

Diverse manners of being pertaining to beings

We can clarify the diversity of the truth of those beings that are manifest therein only by characterizing in greater detail the diverse manners of being pertaining to beings, and by demonstrating how such diversity demands a specific mode of truth in each case. Yet this would necessitate not only an interpretation of the diverse manners of being (presence at hand, life, existence, subsistence) but at the same time a sufficiently developed understanding of the essence of truth, in order to see how truth becomes modified through those manners of being.

We still lack almost everything necessary in order to carry out such reflections. We shall therefore have to make do. A rough characterization, one that does not include all manners of being, must suffice in order to gain a better understanding of the differences in an approximate manner to begin with. Our initial theme is now manners of being and their diversity as illustrated by two extreme modes: presence at hand and existence. Initially, therefore, we shall place on hold the problem of truth (cf. p.76ff.).

Beings, as we saw, always stand within a context, and this context precisely makes known something of the manner of being of the beings concerned: involvement, serviceability for . . ., items of use, things that are ready to hand. This is to say that the manifold of those beings manifest to us is not the merely uniform appearing next to one another of stones, plants, animals, and humans. Though all these beings, insofar as they are in space, indeed appear next to one another, or before, behind, or over one another, this seemingly uniform appearing next to one another is nevertheless different with respect to individual beings, and this not merely in a spatial sense.

We shall attempt to see somewhat more incisively this appearing next to one another of the manifold beings that are manifest to us in an everyday manner, among which we move, and to which we thus belong. To this end, we choose two extreme ways of being next to one another: presence at hand and existence. Among the manifold beings among which we ourselves appear, there are found those that have the same manner of being as we ourselves, Dasein, and those whose manner of being is different. From this results the dichotomy that all those beings that we find before us and to which we ourselves belong are either Dasein-like or non-Dasein-like beings.

Now, beings that have our manner of being, yet that we ourselves are not, but that are in each case the other, another Dasein, the Dasein of others, are not simply present at hand next to us with perhaps other things between. Rather, the other Dasein is there with us, Dasein-with; we ourselves are determined by a being-with with the other. Dasein and Dasein are a with-one-another.

Yet are not the board or chalk at the same time just as real as us, are they then set apart, not also with us, with us there at the same time, and are they not there with us all together with one another, and we together with those things? Strictly speaking, one cannot say of them that they are with one another, even though we must concede that at the same time as our Dasein, the sponge and the chalk are present at hand. Yet a being that has the manner of being of being present at hand can never be there [*da-sein*] with us, because it does not have the manner of being of Dasein belonging to it. Only that which is itself Dasein can be there-with. Being-there-with does not simply mean: also in being, but precisely qua Dasein; rather, the manner of being that is Dasein first imparts to the "with" its authentic sense. "With" is to be conceived as taking part [*Teilnahme*], while being alien, as an absence of taking part, is only a variation of taking part.[4] The "with" therefore

---

4. On taking part (*Teilnahme*), see note 5 in §13d).—Trans.

has a very determinate sense and does not simply mean "together," not even the being together of beings that have the same manner of being. "With" is a specific way of being.

Simultaneous actuality, that is, beings being actual at the same time, does not necessarily entail being with one another. The chalk and the sponge, or even the human being and the chalk, can be actual at the same time. Yet we cannot say in either case that they are with one another, for only human being and human being are with one another. We therefore distinguish quite generally the simultaneous actuality of beings that does not yet imply anything whatsoever about their manner and way of being together, and the simultaneous actuality of beings that have the same manner of being. If they have the manner of being of what is present at hand, then we speak of a being present at hand together; if the simultaneous actuality has the manner of being of Dasein, then we speak of a being with one another.

We shall now ask concerning the difference between being next to one another in the sense of the being present at hand together of things, and being next to one another as the being with one another of human beings.

a) Being present at hand together—Being with one another

Let us take as a simple example two boulders lying on a slope covered with gravel. We can say that they are together, but not present at hand with one another. Two hikers, however, who pass by on their way up the slope, are with one another. The difference is easy to grasp: the two rocks are material bodies, the two hikers are living beings, and moreover rational ones, who reciprocally apprehend each other with the aid of their reason. The human beings are indeed also present at hand next to one another but, in addition, have a consciousness of this being next to one another; one apprehends the other. Accordingly, their being with one another would be nothing other than a conscious being present at hand together.

This characterization of the difference between being present at hand together and being with one another is, at first sight, illuminating and appears to be accurate. It hits on something because it puts its finger on a difference: The boulders are not merely unconscious, as though they had lost their consciousness and were therefore unable to make use of consciousness; rather by their essence, they have no such thing. It is altogether refused these entities, between which a reciprocal interaction may subsist, to make their being next to one another into a relation of mutual apprehension. The two human beings, as rational living beings, are capable of this. Yet does being next to one another become a being with one another through such mutual apprehending? Suppose the two hikers, through a turn in their path, abruptly arrive at an unexpected view of the mountain range, so that they are suddenly enraptured and stand in silence next to one another. There is now no trace of a mutual apprehending of one another; rather, each stands captivated by the view. Are the two of them now merely next to one another like the two boulders, or are they in this moment precisely with one another in a way that they cannot be if they tirelessly chatter away together or even mutually apprehend one another and size up each other's complexes?

If, therefore, in this being enraptured by the view, in which there is certainly no talk of a mutual apprehending, there nevertheless lies precisely an original being with one another, then such being with one another cannot be constituted by a mutual apprehending. So little is this the case, indeed, that all mutual apprehending of one another between Dasein and Dasein already presupposes, conversely, the two being with one another. Mutual apprehending is founded in being with one another.

Being with one another therefore means more, indeed means something other, than two human beings appearing somewhere at the same time. Thus far, we have seen negatively that: 1. Being with one another does not mean also being at the same time, just with the qualification that such being would be Dasein. 2. Being with one another is also not a being present at hand together in such a way that the beings present at hand here have a mutual knowledge of one another; it is not also being at the same time but merely accompanied by consciousness.

Yet wherein is the essence of being with one another to be found in positive terms? We heard just now that mutual apprehending already presupposes being with one another, that is, mutual apprehending is first of all possible on the basis of being with one another. That seems to be an empty triviality, for if two beings are to mutually apprehend one another, then obviously each of them must actually be there to do so. Yet is this what we mean when we say that being with one another is the presupposition for mutual apprehending? Not at all. This presupposition that two human beings must factically be actual in order to actually mutually apprehend one another as actual requires no discussion. We are inquiring not about what must be actual in order for something else to become actual but about what must be possible in order for something else to become possible. For mutual apprehending in general to be possible as such, a being with one another must first be possible. Only on the grounds of this possibility of being with one another is there the subordinate possibility of a mutual apprehending between Dasein and Dasein.

Now, we saw already in another context how all apprehending presupposes manifestness. Back then, the issue was the apprehending of what is present at hand; now, it is that of apprehending Dasein. Dasein must already be manifest for Dasein in advance in order for mutual apprehending to be possible. Does this being manifest for one another of Dasein and Dasein hit on the essence of being with one another, or does it not belong essentially to being with one another at all? In any case, we must attempt to discuss being with one another by orienting ourselves toward this being manifest for one another.

If being manifest for one another is not identical to a mutual apprehending, then all modes of apprehending are precluded from the outset as insufficient for clarifying being with one another. Being manifest for one another does not, therefore, consist in the fact that I am familiar with the other—and conversely, the other with me—in his so-called inner life, that I know what is going on in him, what dispositions, peculiarities, or odd ideas he has; and just as little does it consist in apprehending his outer attire or behavior. If being manifest for one another should contain a pointer toward the essence of being with one another, then we shall ultimately find it where we ascertained a being with one another, for instance, in the two hikers being enthralled by the view. Here, there reigns precisely a mutual not apprehending one another, and yet a peculiar being with the other. The "with" points to commonality. What is communal lies in the fact that the one is just as enraptured as the other, that the same holds for both in common. The one comports himself just like the other. Does their being with one another therefore consist in the fact that both comport themselves in an identical manner and are able to do so? Yet surely, this is also true of the two boulders. What is possible for one can also transpire in the other. These things, indeed, are identical in their manner of being, much more than human beings. Even though both are in an identical way, they are surely not with one another at all.

b) Being with one another: Several comporting themselves toward the same

In the case of human beings, however, what is at stake is an identical comportment toward things, as, for instance, with the view of the mountain range. Being with one another means being in an identical manner, where being means: comportment toward. Being with one another means comporting oneself in an identical manner toward. . . . Is there such a thing at all, such that human beings comport themselves in an identical manner toward something?

Let us take our constant example: With a view to this chalk, we all now—with one another—make the assertion: this chalk is white. Making this assertion is grounded on our being alongside this item present at hand. Yet even just between two of us all, this being alongside the chalk of ours is never identical. Aside from everything else, the spatial orientation alone in which we are alongside the chalk in a different way in each case already shows that each being alongside . . . on the part of each individual is different. More than that, indeed, not only is no being alongside . . . on the part of any of us factically identical now, but it never can be identical without differences, not factically and not by our very essence. Still, the difference in spatial orientation can be remedied; surely, any Dasein can, for example, stand in my place and have the chalk before it from this perspective. Certainly, any of us can take the place of another, yet never at the identical time.

The point in time is necessarily a different one, and when it is identical, then the place is necessarily a different one.

Therefore, there is no being alongside . . . and correspondingly no comportment toward . . . that would be identical. If being with one another meant the same as comporting ourselves toward a thing in an identical manner, then there would be no being with one another. And yet surely, we say quite understandably that we all comport ourselves "with one another" toward the chalk. It is not, therefore, our comportment toward . . . that is identical; rather, what is identical is that toward which we are comporting ourselves. Yet do we, then, indeed see the identical piece of chalk? Does someone in the row farthest back see a piece of chalk that is identical to the one I am seeing? I claim, no! You will agree and say: of course not; what the viewer in the row farthest back sees as the face of the chalk is for me the reverse, the back side. What we see there, that toward which we comport ourselves, is thus also something different. Yet I say even more: In being alongside the chalk that lies before us, someone at the back of the room does not just factically not see the identical chalk that I am seeing, and not only because what we are seeing there factically shows differences, but rather because such a thing is essentially precluded in the present case. For someone at the back to be able to see an identical piece of chalk, identical to the one that I am seeing, there would have to be at least two pieces of chalk present at hand. Being identical essentially presupposes multiplicity. Each of us, therefore, does not see the identical piece of chalk, but with one another, we all see the same chalk. Sameness and being identical are two different things.

The question facing us concerns the essence of truth. Truth has initially shown itself to be determined generally as the unconcealment of beings. It therefore pertains to beings in some way or other that has yet to be determined. From this, we take it that truth is presumably determined by beings themselves in some way or another. Now we know, however, that beings are diverse with respect to their manner of being. From this, the question arises of whether, then, truth does not in the end essentially vary also in each case, in accordance with the manner of being of that whose unconcealment, or unveiledness, it is. The task thus arises of first of all making intelligible how beings are diverse with respect to their manner of being, so as from this to discern how, on the basis of these diverse manners of being, the truth of beings also changes.

To demonstrate the diversity in kind pertaining to beings, we are choosing two extreme cases: the being present at hand of things, and the existence of human beings. If we conceive of this in the traditional sense, we thus have on the one side—formulating it with reference to Descartes—the *res extensa*, extended corporeal things, and on the other side, the *res cogitans*, the thinking thing, or as Husserl says, reality, that is, the actuality of all objects on the one side, and consciousness on the other, a separation that according to him is the most fundamental categorial separation of all, a separation that is also central for Kant and for the whole of German Idealism. We shall not go into further detail about the historical background of this distinction between what is present at hand and that which exists, between things and human beings, but rather shall initially seek to make visible from an analysis of the phenomena themselves certain distinctions in the manner of being of what is present at hand, things, and that which exists, human beings.

We asked about the being next to one another of that which is present at hand and the being next to one another of human beings. We called the latter being with one another. If we now take up once again our previous attempt to determine being with one another, then we may say: it lies neither in the fact that we comport ourselves toward something in an identical manner nor in the fact that that toward which we comport ourselves in each case is something identical. Rather, being with one another can now mean at most that several people comport themselves in diverse ways toward what is the same. Comporting oneself toward the same does not preclude but rather even entails that the comportment is different. Yet are we, then, not with one another whenever one of us comports himself toward the piece of chalk, another toward the board or toward his notebook, and yet another perhaps toward his skis at home? In the latter case, admittedly, we would say that he is absent, even though he is sitting here on the bench.

We can thus comport ourselves toward diverse things and yet still be with one another in doing so. Of course, we immediately notice something striking: Assuming that each of us is now preoccupied with something different, with a different object in this room in each instance, then we are indeed together in this room, and yet not authentically with one another; we are all existing, as it were, away from one another in each case—this would give rise to a privative not-with-one-another. Yet is this ultimately due to the diversity of the objects that we are dealing with? Take the case of the two aforementioned hikers returning to their cabin in the evening; one chops wood, the other peels potatoes. Here, we will say without hesitation that the two are with one another—and not just because they are in proximity to one another. They are with one another despite the fact that they are preoccupied with different things, yet with a view to the same end, to preparing a meal, and beyond that, to taking care of their stay in the cabin; with a view to the same, this belongs to the essence of Dasein.

If we correspondingly imagine that each of us in this room is directed toward a random object that is different in each case, then in a certain manner, we are existing away from one another. Yet if we suppose that each person's being directed toward a different object consists in the single task of describing the room, then our being with one another would, by virtue of the sameness of the task, be more authentic than before. Such comportment toward the same on the part of several is one way in which being with one another makes itself known; perhaps it is one that necessarily belongs to human being with one another.

A view to the same is thus indeed essential to being with one another.

c) Sameness

We have seen the following: the sameness of that toward which we comport ourselves in being with one another plays a certain role for such being with one another. Which role? This remains obscure; indeed, it is not at all clear what sameness means here. Evidently, it needs to be defined more precisely if we are to understand the extent to which we may legitimately ask: In what sense do we comport ourselves toward the same, and what does the same mean here? For sameness, we have the term identity. This seems to be the simplest thing in the world. Something is identical with itself—we can say this of every object. Nevertheless, our presumed insight into what identity means is altogether insufficient to provide us with information about what we mean when we say that several people comport themselves toward the same, so that this, their comportment, is a being with one another. We must therefore seek to convince ourselves, concretely and step by step, of the fact that this commonplace concept of identity is utterly insufficient here, that is, we must put our individual concepts of identity to the test in relation to the phenomenon that we are dealing with here, being with one another as comporting ourselves toward the same, and do so with respect to their conceptual capacity.

That toward which we are comporting ourselves, that which we are alongside, is the same for us. This can mean: as the being that it is, it undergoes no change. Yet must something exclude all change in order to be the same? Not at all. Everything that is changeable and that changes is such in each case only insofar as it, the same thing, becomes changed. Were it not to remain itself then we could never say it has changed, but would have to say that something else has taken its place. We would not be dealing with a change in this being, but merely the exchange of this being for another one. Yet even in such a process of exchange, each being, the one and the other, is identical with itself. Sameness, therefore, does not simply mean lack of change. Indeed, we also comport ourselves toward something that is the same whenever we see a car drive past, something present at hand, therefore, that changes its place at each moment. Change—for example, a car driving past—does not exclude identity, but includes it. Change always presupposes that something that remains, something identical, maintains itself.

Yet what, then, does it mean that we comport ourselves toward the same, and in such a way that in this comportment, being with one another supposedly makes itself known? It does not mean that we comport ourselves toward something that does not change. Something that is the same, and toward which we comport ourselves so that this is a being with one another alongside . . ., can be in motion or rest; indeed, it can even stand altogether outside of these possibilities, such as, for instance, the number 5, which does not move, and this not because it is at rest. It cannot be at rest; only that which moves can be at rest. Rest is only a mode of movement. Our being alongside the chalk is alongside something that is at rest, that is, put fundamentally, something that is in motion. This being at rest of things is not as insignificant as it might appear.

We have already seen in passing that we comport ourselves toward the same, even though in so doing, each of us sees this very same thing differently. Sameness does not exclude change, and above all does not exclude difference. The difference in the views that this piece of chalk offers to each of us does not disturb us. And how should it disturb us, when ultimately precisely the difference in views assists in our actually seeing the chalk itself with one another?

Let us suppose for a moment that we would all constantly see, hear, and experience the things around us in an absolutely identical view. This would result in a fantastical "world"—or ultimately in no world at all. This fiction that all things would present themselves to everyone in the same way is found in the Kantian thought of the thing in itself. The thing in itself is only thought as the object of an absolute knowledge, namely God's, which does not see things through some relativity or other, through some perspective or other. On the basis of this assumption of a thing in itself, one would logically have to say that for God, there is no such thing as a world at all. This thought, which is not thought through to the end in Kant, is one we shall consider in more detail later when analyzing the concept of world. For now, we simply note that the manifold and diversity of views that the same things present to us do not disturb us but that this diversity, rather, perhaps has an essential function.

If we do not take into account this diversity in our apprehending things, but all comport ourselves in common toward the same thing through the very diversity of our views, what is it, then, that we are ultimately comporting ourselves toward? After all, we do not strip away the diversity of our views; first, we know nothing of such a stripping away, and second, we do not compare the views presenting themselves to us with those of others. And what would be left remaining after stripping away all the diverse views? One could say: precisely the chalk in itself. It may be that in a certain way of viewing nature—for example, in the theoretical view of physics and chemistry—we can regard the chalk in this way as an example of a material thing. Yet this is then certainly not the chalk that we refer to with one another; the chalk presents itself to us, rather, as the same useful thing for writing. What it is as a material thing is not important for us—quite apart from the fact that this remnant of the thing's material substance that supposedly remains the same is perhaps, indeed very probably, something different at each moment in time, that it is caught up in a constant displacement of its elemental particles. The same, therefore, is not this material substance in the physical sense. It thus appears as though we enter an abyss with all these questions concerning the sameness of this same thing toward which we comport ourselves in being with one another.

What, then, is left that sameness and comportment toward the same could mean? Do we, for instance, apprehend the same as the same in this common being alongside the chalk? We are indeed alongside the same chalk, but we do not apprehend it as the same; we are not directed toward the chalk in its sameness, let alone toward sameness itself. Do we perhaps apprehend as what is meant the state of affairs of the chalk being identical with itself? This sameness, then, does not refer to the identity of the thing, either.

Thus far we have already heard so many different things about this enigmatic sameness that everything is becoming confused, without our gaining the slightest information about being with one another. This confusion, however, is intentional initially, in order to show that these seemingly self-evident concepts like sameness are insufficient. We seemingly attained only purely negative results:

1. The same does not mean something unchanged and unchangeable, not a lack of change, therefore.
2. The same does not mean something that maintains itself as remaining identical amid a diversity of views; it does not mean permanence of substance, therefore.
3. The same does not mean the formal identity of a being with itself.

With this, we have exhausted the major concepts of sameness. In this lies a pointer to the fact that we shall not make progress in this way; indeed more, that sameness here is something original.

The more diverse our ways of inquiring into what sameness could mean there in our being with one another alongside the same, the further removed we seem to get from what we are supposed to clarify. And yet we have one result: summarizing all our negative results, we can see that with sameness, we are not dealing with a sameness that pertains to beings solely or primarily with respect to themselves.

We set out from the observation that we do not see different pieces of chalk, but one and the same. This being of all of us alongside one and the same piece of chalk is supposed to make known a being with one another. We are alongside the same; it is the same through and through for all, and not just identical in each instance, it is the same for each one of us. From this, we can see that we are speaking of a sameness that is relative to us. In the end, this relation to us belongs to the essence of this sameness. Whether, to what extent, or why a relational character belongs to sameness and identity, we shall not discuss now. That such a thing is also found in the formal, empty sameness of something with itself can readily be shown; this identity is a feature of the relation of something to itself.

The sameness of something expresses the relation of something to itself. Yet this is just an initial conception of identity. With this idea of sameness, we shall not get any further, indeed will not even arrive at the phenomenon that unsettles us. Sameness is a relation that in keeping with its very sense turns back toward that which is the same here, a relation that does not lead away from whatever is in question but indeed only ever leads back to it itself.

We now see, however: here is something the same that is named such, not because it is identical with itself—though it may be that too—but because it is the same for several people. Now the knot seems to be loosening. This relation to several is indeed just the relation of apprehending. This relation of apprehending does not belong to the essence of this sameness, rather, something identical is apprehended by several. We can, therefore, make do with the usual concept of sameness after all, but we should just not reflect on it exclusively, but would have to also heed the fact that several are apprehending something identical. We can now say that sameness may very well be a determination of the object itself, but this being that is identical with itself stands in addition in a relation of being apprehended. This relation then indeed makes the being that is present at hand relative to several other beings of the character of Dasein. The state of affairs is thus that of a being that is identical with itself and then in addition, as this identical being, is something that can possibly be apprehended by several.

d) The same as common

Yet—if several people apprehend something identical, this is not at all what we have before us as the phenomenon to be clarified. The first phenomenon happens constantly: someone in Berlin sees an automobile, and a peasant in the Black Forest sees his cow; there is more than one person, and each apprehends something identical, and yet not something the same in being with one another, and yet, even here, there is still a being with one another. So the point must remain that in being with one another alongside the same, this sameness expresses an essential relation, and indeed one that does not simply revert to the being itself, but precisely leads away in the direction of several people.

Yet how so? That which is present at hand, which we are alongside, is thus common to us; it is the same for several so that these several become a "we" on the grounds of this "the same for them." Whether the "we" is indeed the result of a coming together of several, we shall leave open initially. Yet what does it mean that that which is present at hand, alongside which we dwell, is something common for us in this being with one another? What does commonality mean here?

We spoke of the fact that individual colors, such as red, green, and blue, have the character of 'color' in common; color is the genus, just as the species oak, beech, and fir have the character of 'tree.' Manifestly, the chalk is not something in common in relation to us in this way, to us as several people. For one thing, this piece of chalk is not at all a genus, but a particular individual useful thing, present at hand here and now. If, on the other hand, we were to think of chalk as a genus in relation to different examples and kinds of pieces of chalk, then the genus chalk is not something that would contain us human beings as species under it; for after all, we are not pieces of chalk, in the way that fir and beech are trees. This is all too self-evident, yet it still remains enigmatic what it means that this chalk is something common for us.

If we meditate for a moment on what we really want to clarify, namely, a preliminary concept of philosophy, then we seem to have set out on curious paths. On the path toward solving the question of what philosophy means, we have arrived at the problem of how a piece of chalk could be present at hand as something common for us in our being with one another. That indeed seems initially to be a major wrong path. It is therefore necessary that we now remain aware of the intrinsic context of our considerations or keep this context in mind. This is required not so that you are merely able to recount the individual steps of the lecture course, for instance—there is nothing to cram here. Keeping the context of our considerations present to us, which is necessary at all times, is not like with mathematics, for example, where we deduce particular propositions from particular axioms. The context of our considerations is important, rather, on account of our commitment to the matter that we are constantly dealing with. We shall thus see that we shall not at all have to retrace this long path in order to arrive back at philosophy but that we can give the answer at any moment if we are adequately prepared. This is why we are clarifying the context as an external aid precisely at the moment when we have arrived at a question that seemingly lies far removed from our proper theme.

We set out from the question concerning the essence of philosophy and are seeking to characterize it in a threefold respect: in its relationship to science, to Weltanschauung, and to history. We set out on the first path, its relationship to science, so as to experience what philosophy is by clarifying the essence of science. This question concerning the essence of science has led us back to the question concerning the essence of truth. Truth presented itself to us initially as propositional truth; we soon saw that the assertion presupposes a being alongside that which we are making the assertion about, and that in this being alongside what is present at hand, that which is present at hand is itself unconcealed for us. The unconcealment of beings is, in a provisional concept, called truth. We then attempted to become acquainted with the essence of truth by showing the way in which it is manifold in its structure, in keeping with those beings in relation to which it is unconcealment.

Our current theme is the analysis of the diversity of ways and manners in which beings are, oriented toward two domains of beings, that which is present at hand and Dasein. In the course of this analysis, we saw how the truth concerning beings must change by virtue of the diversity in the kind of being of those beings. We thus set aside for a while, to a certain extent, the question concerning the essence of truth, and are now occupying ourselves with the differences in the being of beings. By way of example, we have taken as our basis the being next to one another of that which is present at hand, and the being with one another of Dasein.

We are now already taking various paths in trying to comprehend the simple, and at first trivial state of affairs that we dwell together with one another alongside the same thing. We saw initially that the attempt to clarify what the sameness of those beings toward which we comport ourselves means fails, so long as we make use of the usual concepts of sameness and identity. We are with one another alongside the same, and here sameness means neither lack of change, nor thing-like substantiality or permanence as substance, nor the formal identity of an object with itself.

The question is, what does the sameness of a being that is present at hand mean for us in positive terms? We finally came to determine sameness here as initially meaning the equivalent of commonality. The piece of chalk, in a sense yet to be determined, is something common for us. We have thus arrived at this specific question concerning the commonality of a thing for us.

To what extent—we must now therefore ask anew—can the chalk be something common in our being alongside it? Well, perhaps by our sharing [*teilen*] the chalk to a certain extent, and that can mean that we distribute [*verteilen*] it among ourselves, that we break it into pieces [*zerteilen*].[5] Yet for one thing, we are not permitted to do that at all; it does not belong to us, but to the state. It is therefore not something common for us and ours in the sense that it would be our freely disposable property. We are not allowed to break it into pieces and distribute it, nor do we do that; we leave it undivided, and yet we ourselves share it. Sharing something without breaking it into pieces means reciprocally leaving something for one another to be used and be in use. This chalk is something common for us in the use that we make of it or are able to make of it. We have thus determined the way in which it is something common for us, but what this commonality itself means, what its essence consists in, and to what extent being with one another may be clarified by this is not yet clear.

---

5. Here and in the following sections, Heidegger deploys a complex discourse built around the German *Teil*. A *Teil* is a part; *teilen* means to share but also conveys the sense of dividing into parts. Yet the latter, in the context of Dasein's being-in-the-world, does not mean distributing or breaking into pieces (*verteilen, zerteilen*), as Heidegger indicates here, but is to be understood as having a part in, or partaking in something. Partaking is having a share in (*Teilhaben*), a taking part in (*Teilnehmen, Teilnahme*), and what Dasein ultimately partakes and shares in is the unconcealment of beings. This sharing in the unconcealment of beings for its part first enables *Mitteilung*, communication, which has the literal sense of sharing (*Teilung*) with (*mit*).—Trans.

e) Is partaking something common?

Our question is whether the commonality of the chalk in use is the commonality that is primarily constitutive of being with one another alongside. . . .

The fact that we share the chalk in using it is surely possible only if this chalk stands at the disposal of us all, that is, ready for possible and legitimate use, left for us in lying before us. Making use of it entails that it is manifest to us for this end, that we are already alongside it with one another, that it is something common in and for our being alongside . . ., even if the latter is not an explicit preoccupation with it. In order for us to be able to share the chalk in our use of it, it must first already be something common in a more original sense; we must already share it in advance in such a way that it is left freely up to us whether to make use of it or not. Already before such use, and for such use, we must all already partake in the chalk, so as to leave it for ourselves reciprocally in using it or to refrain in common from using it.

What kind of partaking [*Teilhabe*] is this, and in what respect is the chalk something common for us in this partaking? The initial task is to clarify what it is that we share whenever we all have the same chalk, this particular useful thing, lying before us, and do so even and precisely when we are not making use of it, when we are not expressly preoccupied with it, but let it lie there just as it is in itself. It is precisely in this, in our letting the chalk lie there, in what and how it *is* as this thing to be used, that we must find what we are seeking: namely, our partaking in the chalk, this original sharing of the chalk in accordance with which it is something common and our being alongside it is a being with one another.

Our being alongside the chalk is, we say, a letting the chalk lie there as it is, a letting lie, just because it is something and is in such a way that it lies before us. Lying before, being present at hand before us, is the way in which this chalk is in itself as this useful thing, its manner of being; we let it lie there, we let it be, just as it is in what it is. Our being alongside the chalk is something like a letting be of the chalk.

We let this being be; we take nothing from it and give it nothing; we do not push it away and do not pull it close; we leave this being to itself, and precisely in this leaving, we encounter the chalk in what and how it is, as this chalk.

f) Of the letting be of things

We let things be as they are, leave them to themselves, even and precisely when we are preoccupied with them, no matter how intensively. Indeed, precisely in and for its use, I must let the thing be what it is. If I were not to let the chalk be chalk, if I were to crush it in a mortar, for instance, then I would not be using it.

This letting be of things lies in our using them and in our not using them, and indeed, it underlies all our useful dealings with things. Yet not only in useful comportment, in quite different kinds of comportment toward quite different kinds of beings too, in aesthetic comportment, for instance, there lies a quite determinate letting be of a painting, for example, or of a sculpture, and this quite apart from whether the artwork in question makes a special impression on me or not.

This letting be of things in the broadest sense lies in principle before any special interestedness or any particular indifference. This, our letting be, our leaving things to themselves and to their being, is a specific indifference on our part, an indifference on the part of Dasein that belongs to its metaphysical essence. This 'indifference' is possible only within care. The casualness in this leaving is not some utter neglect. Letting beings be is not nothing, as it were; certainly, we do not contribute, for instance, to the fact that nature is what and how it is, we cannot do anything about that, and yet this letting be is a "doing" of the highest and original kind and is possible only on the grounds of the innermost essence of our existence, freedom. This metaphysical indifference toward things will very much claim our attention as we follow our path.

Initially, we have come to see one thing: our being alongside things—if we remain in the realm of what is present at hand—is, in the grounds of its essence, a letting be of things in the sense characterized. This is why an interested being preoccupied does not necessarily also belong to being alongside . . ., and why conversely even a disinterested or unwilling comportment toward things, indeed even every turning away from them, is a being alongside. . . .

We have seen: we must already in advance have a part in things, in order to be able to leave them for ourselves to use; a letting be of things, however, already underlies all usage, for instance.

Does, then, that partaking in things consist in the letting be of beings that we have characterized? Surely, the letting be of something in how and what it is does not intrinsically entail a reciprocal sharing of the being? Must we then in each case let the being be in advance in what and how it is in order to be able to share the being? Or is it the other way around: must we share the being in advance in order to be able to let it be in itself? Does letting be presuppose partaking, or does, conversely, partaking presuppose letting be? What does presuppose mean here? Initially, it remains to be clarified what partaking means. In what do we share? What is it that is common in this, and in what way is that which we share something common?

That we share in what is present at hand means:

1. We do not carve it into pieces and distribute it among ourselves, but instead leave it undivided.
2. We reciprocally leave it for ourselves to use, and even in merely letting it lie there unused, we already share it.

In positive terms: we share the being without anything happening to it in the process, without it being altered. We share the being without in the process reciprocally passing along, giving up, or giving away anything that pertains to the being, anything that belongs to the being and that yet at the same time is ours, after all; we share such a being as something common, in such a way that what it is that is common here plays a role in enabling our being with one another.

What is it, then, about beings that—if we can put it this way—pertains to them in a certain way and that we can share, without the beings being altered in the least by this? Something that pertains to beings and yet that surely must also be at our disposal, if we are indeed supposed to be able to share it. There are particular properties that pertain to the being—to the chalk—as a thing of use and as a material body, it has a particular manner of being. Yet it is precisely this, what and how it is, that we let be. Our being alongside what is present at hand is a letting be. We take nothing away from it and do not lay claim to anything about it as our work. Yet this is not at our disposal, after all; rather—if we may put it this way—the chalk, this is just what and how it is.

Yet we heard already, namely, in interpreting our being alongside this present at hand thing, that this being, it, is unconcealed in all this, that is, is true in the original sense. Unconcealment (truth) pertains to the being; the being is what is primarily true; the statement about it is only subsequently true. This unconcealment is something that does not disturb the chalk in what and how it is; it remains what it is and how it is, even if no one is dwelling in the room and is alongside this present at hand thing. Nor is it altered by being unconcealed for us. Our being alongside the chalk does not wear it out, for instance. The chalk is true in our being alongside . . .; it is unconcealed. Truth is therefore something that pertains to the chalk and yet does not belong to its present at hand inventory of properties as chalk.

This unconcealment of the chalk is that in which the chalk shows itself in itself as this thing of use, that in which it makes itself known as the being that it is. Unconcealment (truth) is therefore that through which we let precisely this being be as itself, in what and how it is.

Yet now we see, however, that this letting be of things stands in a conditional relationship with partaking in beings. Letting be happens, and can only happen, in such a way that in this process, that which we let be there is manifest, that is, true. Letting be stands in a conditional relationship with truth. Furthermore, this truth (unconcealment) is something "about" beings, something that pertains to them, yet nevertheless does not alter them. When the chalk becomes unconcealed, becomes manifest as the being that it is, nothing happens to it, there is not some natural process that takes place within it, and yet something happens with it: it enters into a history.

We are inquiring with regard to a partaking in beings in which we share in something that pertains to beings, without anything about beings being lost or altered in the process. What do we share in this remarkable partaking in beings? We share in their unconcealment, their truth. Only insofar as we share in the unconcealment of beings are we able to let them—beings—be, just as they make themselves known. And whenever we share in unconcealment, something is common for us that does not constitute a fragment of the chalk that could therefore only ever be the possession of one person, as it were. Nor is unconcealment a present at hand property of the chalk, such as its white color, for instance, a property that could be separated from the chalk.

§14. We share in the unconcealment of beings

We share in the unconcealment of beings. What is common is the truth of beings. The same that we were seeking is truth, and it is this same too, as unconcealment, that makes it possible for that which is manifest within unconcealment to show itself as this being that is manifest and, indeed, to show itself to all those who have this unconcealment in common.

Our initial point was that being with one another makes itself known in the comportment of several toward the same. Sameness for several is commonality, having something in common, sharing in unconcealment. Being with one another alongside beings is our sharing in the unconcealment (truth) of the beings in question.

Have we now solved the puzzles? Not at all! For now, we have only discovered, perhaps without seeing it entirely clearly, that unconcealment is that which we share in common. We see roughly that there is something in which we share, and indeed in such a way that on the one hand, beings themselves remain untouched in this, and on the other hand, that they can make themselves known to us precisely as themselves within what is common.

Truth is that in which we share. With this, however, the essence of truth as unconcealment has only become more problematic—and so it should! We share in beings, that is, in their unconcealment, which is precisely that of the beings in question and thus pertains to them—how, is obscure and remains so initially. That in which we share on the one hand pertains to beings, and on the other hand is something that we, as human beings, dispose over among ourselves, as our possession.

The question is: How do we stand in relation to such a thing as the unconcealment of something present at hand? How do we partake in such a thing? Partaking in the unconcealment of beings is—by way of unconcealment—partaking in beings. Yet this, our having a share in unconcealment—from where is this having taken? Is this having a share in truth (unconcealment) grounded in a taking part? And is it in more carefully characterizing this taking part in truth that we shall first gain insight into how and why we share in such a thing as truth?

Being with one another alongside . . . is a sharing in the unconcealment (truth) of what is present at hand. Truth belongs to what is present at hand, and yet it is not a property present at hand in it. It is not something present at hand. At the same time, however, truth is something that Dasein shares with Dasein, something that therefore belongs in turn to Dasein.

The unconcealment of what is present at hand occupies a strange dual position: it belongs in a certain way to what is present at hand and, at the same time, to Dasein. What is the truth of that which is present at hand, such that it has, and can have, this dual position? Solving this problem will depend on whether we can adequately clarify our sharing in truth, so as to attain the insight we are seeking into being with one another, a specific manner of being of Dasein.

Before we pursue this problem, that is, the question concerning the essence of truth that propels us further, we want to pause our investigation for a moment and to recall once more the path and context of our considerations. From the problem of the essence of science, there arose the question concerning the essence of truth, which presented itself initially as the unconcealment of beings. Since there are beings with different manners of being, there are correlatively different kinds of truth too. Initially, therefore, we must make visible the diversity in the ways of being of beings and in the meantime defer the problem of truth. The manner of being of what is present at hand and that of Dasein must be clarified with regard to their being next to one another, being present at hand together, and being with one another. The question concerning the essence of being with one another must be posed, thus the question concerning the structure of one manner of being, that of existing Dasein. The answer emerged: being with one another is a sharing in truth.

a) Being with one another is a sharing in truth

What kind of odd result is that? While analyzing being with one another, we characterized it provisionally as a being alongside something that is the same, something common, which we interpreted more precisely as a sharing in something. This sharing in something presented itself to us initially in the form of a reciprocal leaving ourselves something in use. It emerged, however, that even without our making use of something, we already have beings—what is present at hand, lying before us—in common before us in a certain way, so that this sharing in something in being with one another alongside something present at hand cannot therefore lie in the accomplishing of use itself, but rather in a way of being of Dasein that already lies prior to all use and that first makes possible our common making use of something.

The question now becomes: What is this something common in which we share? We are now compelled to exhibit this something common in a direction of investigation that is focused not on a particular use, but on a comportment prior to this, one that we characterize as a letting lie of beings in their essence, a letting be of things. In this letting be of things, there lies an original indifference on the part of Dasein, one that lies prior to all being interested or being disinterested. Yet even if we assume this letting be of things as the characteristic feature of our sharing in something common, the question repeatedly arises: What is it really that we share in? This sharing in beings is accomplished in our being alongside . . ., and we characterized this being alongside . . . by the fact that what is present at hand is unconcealed. That in which we share, our thesis ultimately was, is the truth concerning beings, their unconcealment, so that the problem now arises of ascertaining more precisely the extent to which, in being with one another, we share in the truth concerning things, and how a sharing in truth, in the unconcealment of what is present at hand, is possible.

In pursuing the task of characterizing a particular manner of being, and doing so while disregarding the problem of truth, we came upon truth. To being with one another, to the structure of such being, to the structure of the way in which Dasein is in relation to Dasein, there belongs truth, if being with one another indeed means: sharing in truth.

What does that mean? To the "being" [*Sein*] of this being [*Seienden*] that we call Dasein, and that we ourselves are, there belongs truth. What is its essence? Only if this becomes clear will the "being" [*Sein*] of Dasein also. Unexpectedly, the question concerning the manner of being of a being has become the question concerning the essence of truth. For only if what the essence of truth is becomes clear will our sharing in truth, and that means, being with one another as a manner of being of Dasein, become graspable. We are discussing the essence of truth with a view to characterizing the manner of being of Dasein as distinct from that of what is present at hand. It is now necessary to discuss truth with a view to clarifying a specific manner of being: that we must indeed characterize truth in this way as belonging to the being of Dasein itself. This is not some arbitrary fact, but already points ahead to a determination of the essence of truth in general: that its locus is not the propositional statement but rather Dasein (or indeed the reverse).[6] From this, we may already take a quite fundamental insight and an answer to the leading question of how truth as unconcealment of beings relates to beings, whether and how truth becomes modified in keeping with the manner of being of beings.

---

6. Editor's note: In the typescript, there is a handwritten addition by Hildegard Feick that is neither found in the manuscript nor in the transcripts. It concerns the more precise sense of the phrase "or indeed the reverse" [*oder gar umgekehrt*] and answers the question this phrase raises in terms of the fundamental position of Martin Heidegger's later thinking. With this addition, which presumably stems from the period when the typescript was produced, the text reads: "a determination of the essence of truth in general: that its locus is not the propositional statement but rather Dasein, the clearing (or indeed the reverse: that the essential locus of Dasein is truth as unconcealment)."

We are seeking to determine the manner of being of Dasein, as distinct from that of what is present at hand, by orienting ourselves toward the being with one another of Dasein and Dasein. Being with one another proved to be a sharing in the unconcealment (truth) of what is present at hand (one possible way of being with one another and/or necessarily belonging to it), as a manner of being. Truth is accordingly constitutive for the structure of being with one another as an essential manner of being of Dasein.

b) The unconcealment of what is present at hand

Truth (unconcealment) accordingly belongs to Dasein itself, to *what* this being is and to *how* it is, *how* it exists. How does truth (unconcealment) belong to the Dasein that we ourselves are? If we now seek to answer this question, then let us recall that we previously already attributed truth qua unconcealment to that which is present at hand, for we said, after all: the being itself is primarily true and not the statement about it. Unconcealment accordingly "belongs" to what is present at hand, and now it is supposed to belong to Dasein, as constitutive for the being with one another of Dasein. Does it accordingly "belong" both to what is present at hand and to Dasein, or does it indeed lie as it were "between" what is present at hand and Dasein? How does unconcealment belong to the thing that is present at hand—does it belong to it at all? And what does "belong" mean here?

We saw, after all, that the unconcealment of the chalk is not something that would be present at hand in it; we cannot ascertain unconcealment as something present at hand in the chalk, move it back and forth with the chalk, for instance, or wear it down by writing. Indeed, on the basis of the chalk's unconcealment, we apprehend precisely the fact that this being does not first become what and how it is by its being unconcealed for us, and correlatively, neither does it cease being what it is and in the way that it is by its being concealed from us.

If we are to state what a piece of chalk is in general, then it is quite certain that unconcealment will not appear in this definition. Chalk is not necessarily unconcealed; its essence also admits of its being concealed; unconcealment is not an essential determination of chalk as chalk nor of the sponge as sponge. Yet perhaps unconcealment is an essential determination of what is present at hand insofar as it is present at hand?

However, if we consider a rock somewhere in a ravine that no human has ever set foot in, then surely this being can be present at hand as what and how it is without ever having to be torn from concealment, without ever being unconcealed, indeed while being altogether unaffected by concealment and unconcealment. Perhaps it is necessary within certain limits that what is present at hand be unconcealed in order to apprehend its manner of being, but it surely does not follow from this that what is factically present at hand necessarily be manifest in its what and how. Unconcealment is not an essential determination of what is present at hand. For this reason, we are not allowed to say that unconcealment (truth) "belongs" to what is present at hand, but only that unconcealment (truth) accrues to what is present at hand and/or may accrue to it. What is present at hand does not have it of its own accord qua something present at hand.

Here, though, lies a further problem, one that we have hitherto passed over for the sake of simplicity but that I shall briefly mention in an interim remark and that will occupy us later. Perhaps it has come to your attention that the nonbelonging of unconcealment to what is present at hand was suddenly demonstrated by reference to a random rock somewhere in a ravine and not by reference to the chalk. This was necessary because the chalk, as it lies before us as a thing of use, is strictly speaking not something present at hand; that does not mean that it would only apparently be real, but rather that as a thing of use, it has its own manner of being of something ready to hand. We deliberately did not take into account this distinction between the present at hand and the ready to hand but took the present at hand in the broader sense of things as distinct from Dasein. This indeterminacy now takes its revenge—as it always does—insofar as presence at hand in the strict sense (rock) and readiness to hand (chalk) are indeed different manners of being that also relate differently to their truth. Ultimately, truth necessarily accrues to what is ready to hand; it can accrue to what is strictly present at hand, but need not. This necessary accruing of unconcealment in the case of the ready to hand and this possible accruing of unconcealment in the case of the present at hand must nevertheless be rigorously distinguished from the belonging of truth to Dasein.

Truth of what is present at hand: as possible accrual of unconcealment.

Truth of what is ready to hand: necessary accrual of unconcealment, (a) necessarily having passed through truth, (b) not necessarily factically in use as ready to hand (historical truth!).

Truth of Dasein: belonging of truth to the being of Dasein.

The unconcealment of what is present at hand does not therefore belong both to what is present at hand and to Dasein but rather merely accrues to what is present at hand, and indeed not of necessity, "and" admittedly belongs to Dasein. Indeed, unconcealment accrues to what is present at hand and can accrue to it only because and insofar as it belongs to Dasein. Yet how does the unconcealment of what is present at hand belong to Dasein? We saw initially that the unconcealment of what is present at hand is something in which we ourselves share. Yet is it, then, altogether necessary that we, insofar as we exist as human beings and are as Dasein, share in the unconcealment of this chalk? Manifestly not, for surely we can also exist without the unconcealment of this chalk being something common for us. The unconcealment of what is present at hand does not, therefore, belong essentially to Dasein. In the end, however, it is indeed not necessary that we dwell with one another alongside this chalk, yet we must surely dwell alongside what is present at hand, which is then the same for us. It is not the unconcealment of a piece of chalk that belongs to the essence of Dasein, but perhaps the unconcealment of what is present at hand is something in which we necessarily share in our factical being together? But just in this factical being together, then! To being with one another, thus to the Dasein of human beings, there perhaps necessarily belongs a sharing in the unconcealment of what is present at hand, precisely insofar as human beings are indeed factically together with human beings; to the being with one another of Dasein and Dasein, there belongs unconcealment but not to Dasein "in and for itself." For a Dasein, after all, need not necessarily and constantly be factically together with others; it can also be alone, *solus!*

When Dasein exists alone somewhere, then it is indeed not factically together with others. That is clear as day. Dasein thus need not necessarily and constantly share with others in the unconcealment of what is present at hand. Yet does it follow from this that the unconcealment of what is present at hand does not belong essentially to Dasein? Even when a human being exists alone somewhere, he dwells alongside what is present at hand. This entails that what is present at hand is manifest to him. Even solitary existing is a being alongside things in such a way that here things are in each case manifest, that is, unconcealed within certain limits, yet always in some way or other in any case. Unconcealment accordingly belongs essentially to Dasein, that is, to each Dasein as such, whereas what is present at hand is not necessarily unconcealed as such. Unconcealment merely accrues to what is present at hand; it can do so yet need not. To Dasein, by contrast, there necessarily belongs the unconcealment of what is present at hand.

c) The belonging of truth to Dasein does not declare truth to be something "subjectivistic"

Yet if truth in the sense of the unconcealment of what is present at hand belongs to Dasein and not to what is present at hand, if truth accordingly lies neither in what is present at hand nor "between" the latter and Dasein, but solely in Dasein, even when Dasein is entirely isolated by itself, does not the truth regarding what is present at hand then become something "subjective," a pure affair of the subject? And if truth is something subjective, does not the thesis of the essential belonging of truth to Dasein become from the outset a denial of all objective truth, of all truth in itself? If we deny that there is a truth in itself and say that it belongs essentially to Dasein, to the subject, then truth is only ever relative to the particular factical Dasein in each instance, and from this denial of the objectivity of truth, there then arises so-called relativism. Every relativism, however, is skepticism, and all skepticism is the death of all knowing and, as one also says, of human existence in general. This is a popular form of argumentation that almost never misses its target. Seemingly altogether perceptive, it nevertheless relies less on the strength of actual substantive arguments than on a kind of intimidation by pointing out and anticipating the consequences.

If truth belongs to the subject as subject and to it alone, if truth in accordance with its very essence thus lies in the subject, then it is necessarily something "subjective." It is hard to raise any objection against this thought, and the attempt to show, for instance, that truth does not belong to the subject would indeed be misplaced. But the question is and remains: What does "subject" mean here, and correlatively, what is meant by "subjective"? There must be clarity concerning this, especially if one draws such far-reaching consequences from the subjective character of truth. No matter how convincing it pretends to be, the argumentation concerning the subjective and relative character of truth cannot conceal the fact that its foundation is an entirely defective one. It can be shown that the relationship between truth and the subject that this argumentation is based on is not at all adequately clarified because the concept of subject remains undetermined.

For it could be the case that precisely because truth belongs to Dasein, truth cannot be "subjective"—"subjective" in the sense of subjective and subject that is presupposed in the usual argumentation. In its traditional sense, the subject is an I that is initially encapsulated within itself and cut off from all other beings, an I that behaves in a distinctly self-absorbed manner within its capsule. This conception of the mere subject we call bad subjectivity, bad because it completely misses the essence of the subject. We designate the subject terminologically as Dasein. Ultimately, the essence of subjectivity is precisely not something "subjective" in the bad sense. The essence of truth and its essential belonging to Dasein can show us this. For if truth belongs to the subject, but truth means the unconcealment of what is present at hand, then the unconcealment of what is present at hand belongs essentially to the subject, that is, it belongs essentially to the subject not to be encapsulated within itself but to be always already alongside what is present at hand.

If, to begin with, we remove from the subject, as it were, its being alongside what is present at hand, then we no longer have a concept of the subject at all. This approach does not at all depict a concept of the I, of the subject and subjectivity, but merely a phantom and the gratuitous construction of an I. Because truth—here taken initially only as the unconcealment of what is present at hand—belongs to Dasein, that is, to the subject, Dasein is for this reason by its very essence in each case already alongside what is present at hand. This being alongside what is present at hand belongs to the concept of the subject. We thus see that the thesis concerning the belonging of truth to the subject does not proclaim truth to be something "subjectivistic," but rather precisely determines subjectivity in its being alongside what is present at hand and unconcealed. The essence of truth qua ἀλήθεια therefore provides the pointer for clarifying the concept of subjectivity, whereas one otherwise proceeds in the opposite direction. One has some concept or other of the subject in the background, mostly oriented toward Descartes, and seeks to gain clarity about what truth means, how its relation to this subject, which is not further defined, is to be thought. We can now see that the essence of truth itself compels us to fundamentally revise the concept of the subject hitherto. The belonging of truth to the subject in the correctly understood sense does not make truth into something subjective in the bad sense but the reverse. This belonging of truth to the subject can precisely become the impetus to determine the concept of the subject in the correct manner for the very first time.

Yet even if we have thus dismissed this obvious objection that might easily bother us at the beginning, and according to which the belonging of truth to Dasein entails a subjectivity of truth in the bad sense, it still remains for us to clarify what we are really asking after: How, then, does truth as the unconcealment of what is present at hand belong to Dasein? We seek clarity about this in order to understand how Dasein can share with Dasein in such a thing as truth. This sharing in truth, however, is a feature of the being with one another that is precisely our theme.

We have already gained an essential insight, namely, that the belonging of truth to Dasein is not necessarily a sharing, that a Dasein can also comport itself alone toward what is present at hand. The unconcealment of what is present at hand can therefore belong to Dasein as alone. The belonging of truth to Dasein is possible without a being with one another, without a sharing in truth. Sharing in truth is not constitutive for the manner and way in which truth is found within Dasein. This can also be formulated fundamentally as follows: Being with one another is not constitutive for being alongside what is present at hand. Dasein can also dwell alone alongside what is present at hand. A depiction of being with one another does not therefore lead us to any insight into the primary mode of being of Dasein.

Yet our way of proceeding may still be justified by our saying: being with one another may first arise from two or more Daseins being together; but this is still after all a being together of Dasein and Dasein and not of things that are present at hand. Even in being with one another, therefore, the specific manner of being of Dasein must come to the fore. This will indeed suffice for the provisional contrasting of one manner of being against another.

However, even if it is only being with one another that now especially preoccupies us, and if we hold on to the fact that it is a sharing in truth, then we should not take too lightly the result just attained, namely, that being with one another is not constitutive for being alongside what is present at hand. From this, we saw that the belonging of truth to Dasein is not necessarily determined by a sharing in truth, because Dasein can also factically exist alone. And in this, there indeed lies an essential determination concerning the essence of truth in general, whose clarification we are seeking.

d) Being alongside what is present at hand and being with one another belong equiprimordially to the essence of Dasein

In our critique of the commonplace concept of the subject, we saw that to Dasein, there belongs a being alongside what is present at hand. This being alongside . . ., however, is not necessarily a being with one another. A Dasein can also be alone, as we have already said repeatedly and is indisputable. Yet perhaps we were done too soon with this convincing observation.

If someone is alone, then others are not there, and then there is no being with one another. Yet what does being alone mean here? Does it mean there is only one there instead of several? Does "alone" signify the same as singular? Manifestly not. For then a Dasein could only be alone if it existed as singular. But I can be alone even if others and more than one are there too; indeed, precisely in a mass of human beings I can even be alone and am alone in a way I could not otherwise be at all if no others were there.

Being alone is therefore by no means synonymous with others not factically being there. Being alone always means: being without others. In this without-others, whoever exists alone is necessarily and essentially related to others, in a specific sense, to be sure. Alone can mean: 1. abandoned by others; 2. undisturbed by others; 3. not needing others. This means that in being alone there is a being without one another; without one another, however, is a specific being with one another. Accordingly, every being alone is also a being with one another, and being with one another is then not synonymous with others also factically being there.

In that case, however, our entire prior reflection collapses and its result is void. We formulated the result as follows: Being with one another is not constitutive for being alongside what is present at hand, that is, the manner and way in which the unconcealment of what is present at hand belongs to Dasein is not necessarily a sharing in truth. Now, however, we see that if being alone as being without one another is essentially a being with one another, then a being with one another also lies even within a being alone alongside what is present at hand. Yet this then means: the manner and way in which the unconcealment of what is present at hand (truth) belongs to Dasein is necessarily and essentially a sharing in truth.

Every being alongside what is present at hand, even when alone, is a being with one another. Being alongside what is present at hand is accordingly not one isolated possibility in which Dasein exists, and being with one another another possibility, rather every being alongside . . . is being with one another. Conversely, every being with one another is by its very essence a being alongside what is present at hand. The latter is no less essential than the former. Neither being alongside what is present at hand nor being with one another has priority over the other within the essence of Dasein. Both belong necessarily to the essence of Dasein; they are equiprimordial.

From the thesis that being alongside . . . just like being with one another belongs essentially to Dasein whether Dasein is alone or factically with others, we see that the concept of subjectivity or the concept of Dasein encompasses a peculiar fullness and that one must guard against leaving the concept of Dasein or of the subject too indeterminate or too underdetermined. That is the fundamental shortcoming in the development of the concept of the subject since Descartes. The disaster of modern philosophy really begins with Descartes, because with him, the ego, the I, becomes so impoverished that it is not a subject at all anymore. In Descartes, *ego sum* is without being alongside . . ., without being with one another. Descartes did not even fundamentally inquire about such things, nor about how this ego is, what this *sum* in the *ego sum* signifies by contrast with the being of the *res extensa*, for instance. This concept of the I is to a certain degree truncated from the outset. Nevertheless, Descartes has the merit of having inquired concerning the subject, whereas the era prior indeed discovered all kinds of features regarding the subject, the human being, but these concentrated more on discerning certain fundamental modes of comportment of the subject, the so-called faculties of the soul.

Being alongside what is present at hand, as factical in each instance, is not necessarily a factical being with others who are factically present; nevertheless, being alongside what is present at hand is by its very essence a being with one another. From this, it becomes clear that being with one another does not mean factical existing together with others who are factically present. Being with one another does not first accrue to a Dasein through others factically arriving on the scene. Rather, every Dasein qua Dasein is determined in its being as being with one another, and for this reason, and solely for this reason, it can also be alone. That is, if others are indeed not factically there, Dasein is essentially not just one, but alone. If being with one another is an essential way of being of Dasein and does not just accrue to it conditionally, then every individual and individuated Dasein is always still in this way of being, also namely in the mode of being alone.

The fundamental error of solipsism is that it forgets to actually take the *solus ipse* seriously, that every "I alone" is, as alone, already essentially with one another. Only because the I is already with others can it understand another. But it is not the case that the I would at first be singular, without others, and then arrive at being with one another by some enigmatic route.

If, however, Dasein as such is essentially determined in its being as being with one another, and if every being alongside what is present at hand is a being with one another, then the manner and way in which the unconcealment of what is present at hand belongs to Dasein as a specific kind of truth is also always and necessarily a sharing in truth. Yet what, then, is truth, and how is it, if its belonging to Dasein is determined by a sharing in truth?

Truth merely accrues to what is present at hand, it does not belong to its essence; however, truth belongs to the essence of Dasein. We asked, "How?" and initially have got no further, it seems. Being with one another indeed belongs necessarily to this how, yet even with this, we remain stuck in place, so long as truth itself has not been grasped more originally. Unconcealment, in which Dasein shares, is essentially something common, something that belongs to Dasein and yet in this belonging to Dasein is precisely not and never its own, the property of the individual.

Yet to what extent must truth be grasped still more originally? We spoke of the unconcealment of what is present at hand. Unconcealment does not belong to what is present at hand as such, but merely accrues to it. Who lets unconcealment accrue to what is present at hand? Well, the being to whose being truth belongs, Dasein. Yet from the fact that truth belongs to the essence of Dasein does it also indeed follow that Dasein lets truth accrue to what is present at hand? How is that supposed to happen? After all, Dasein does not decide what is meant to accrue to beings, but the reverse: Dasein directs itself precisely toward them.

We have already pointed to the fact that Dasein, so far as it exists qua Dasein, always already dwells alongside what is present at hand in the broader sense. Dasein is not only factically not, but by its very essence never merely something encapsulated in itself, confined within closed walls, but rather is essentially open toward what is present at hand. We can also express this as follows: Dasein is by its very essence un-covering.

e) The being uncovering of Dasein. The truth of what is present at hand and ready to hand as uncoveredness

Dasein as such un-covers what is present at hand, which means, not that it on occasion makes the discovery that there are also things present at hand but rather that as Dasein, it has always already un-covered what is present at hand, that is, removed it from being covered over. So far as Dasein exists, something like the un-covering of what is present at hand occurs. Even the Dasein that never makes a so-called discovery throughout the entire duration of its existence is un-covering insofar as it dwells alongside what is present at hand. Human Dasein can also make discoveries in the narrower sense, for example, that of a hitherto unknown island, only because qua Dasein it already dwells alongside beings and thus, for instance, travels the ocean. Whether it makes "discoveries" in the narrower sense or not, Dasein is by its very essence un-covering; it always already encounters what is present at hand in uncoveredness. We therefore give the unconcealment of what is present at hand, that is, the truth of such beings having the manner of being of the present at hand, a specific designation: the truth of what is present at hand is uncoveredness. With this, we indicate that not every unconcealment of beings is uncoveredness but only the unconcealment of those beings that have the manner of being of what is present at hand or ready to hand. The uncoveredness (unconcealment) of what is present at hand occurs through Dasein's existing, and uncoveredness of what is present at hand only is if and so long as Dasein exists, Dasein that, in its existence, is uncovering.

Insofar as Dasein exists, therefore, what is present at hand is manifest. We return repeatedly to this fundamental aspect of the essence of Dasein because it is of central significance. What is present at hand is manifest with the existence of Dasein, yet this does not necessarily mean that it is grasped or even that it would have to be comprehended as present at hand but means only this: insofar as Dasein exists, it is alongside unconcealed beings that it itself is not, in whatever way it may make use of this unconcealment. That is: Dasein does not, in the course of its existence, first emerge out of some immanence over to other beings. Dasein is never such that it would to a certain degree live by itself in a capsule; it is never simply a subject in the bad sense.

4   Truth—Dasein—Being-With

§15. Being uncovering in early human and early childhood Dasein

If this thesis is of central significance, then its fundamental content must also be secured and, above all, must be accurate in fact.

Yet how do matters stand regarding the essence of Dasein in the case of a child and in the early times of peoples? The following methodological remarks concerning the role of early childhood Dasein and early human Dasein are to be understood in principle in terms of the interpretation of Dasein for fundamental ontology and not as anthropology, for instance. There is also a distinction to be made here: early human and primitive are not the same. It would be entirely mistaken to put the heroic period of the Greeks on the same level as the Dasein of contemporary savages.

What has to be said in principle concerning the question of prehistorical, early human Dasein or early childhood Dasein is this: these are not altogether different in essence, if they are indeed also to be understood as human, and this is also precisely what the objection that they are other forms of human Dasein says. Here, too, we are dealing with human Dasein. If the term *Dasein* is to be used meaningfully, then it must be based on a concept of essence. Yet if the levels and periods of the early stages of the human are different, whether those of the child or of prehistorical times—the fact that they lack a specific luminosity is not a shortcoming—then there arises the fundamental methodological question of how such different Dasein is to be grasped. This can only occur in a privative manner, that is, proceeding from an underlying positive conception of Dasein and not without a guiding thread provided by the idea of the human being in general. That by which I measure must be determined in advance, and this standard is accordingly—like every foundation of a privation—not inessential but codetermines whatever it is that is to be determined in a privative manner.

On the basis of psychological, psychoanalytic, anthropological, and ethnological research, we have richer possibilities today for gaining insight into particular contexts of Dasein. Yet the facts and phenomena that such research produces require a fundamental, critical revision as soon as they are employed with regard to essential kinds of Dasein. This revision must be guided by the fundamental thesis that if, in the case of childhood Dasein as well as that of the Dasein of primitive peoples, we are dealing with a human Dasein, then an essentially historical character underlies it, even if this is not recognizable without further ado. Nevertheless, problems of a quite unique kind are to be found here whose problematic character we shall become acquainted with.

I have often enough been asked, mostly in the sense of an objection, why in the investigation of Dasein I only include death in the inquiry and not birth as well. I proceed in this manner because I am in fact not of the opinion that birth is merely the other end of Dasein, an end that could and should be treated by posing the problem in the same way as that of death. In the investigation of Dasein, one cannot without further ado simply take birth into consideration as well instead of death, in the way that a botanist investigating a plant, instead of starting from the blossom, can also start from the other end, from the root. Precisely with regard to the fact of birth, which in a certain way does not lie entirely behind us, it is true that that which seems to us to come first, what we were at first, is what comes latest for our knowledge. We must necessarily proceed backward to our birth, yet this is not simply an inversion of being toward death. For this going back, we require a quite different elaboration of our place of departure than for approaching every other limit of Dasein. The same holds correspondingly for the interpretation of childhood, if it is not merely to be conducted with a view to some psychological or pedagogical aim or other.

If we attend in a quite elementary way to the manner of Dasein belonging to a child in the first moment of its earthly Dasein, we see a crying, wriggling movement into the world, into space, without any goal, and yet directed toward. . . . The lack of a goal does not mean undirectedness, and directedness is not being directed toward a goal; rather, directedness in general means: toward . . ., over to . . ., away from. . . .

What initially determines this Dasein are restfulness, warmth, nutrition, a state of sleep and of latency [*Dämmerzustand*]. From this, it has been concluded that this Dasein is initially to a certain degree still curled up and enclosed within itself, that the subject is still entirely wrapped up in itself. This very approach is fundamentally wrong, insofar as the child's reaction—if we may use this expression to orient ourselves—has the character of a shock, of fright. Perhaps its first cry is already a quite determinate shock. Fright is a susceptibility [*Empfindlichkeit*] to being disturbed, a primal form of holding back, a comportment of letting something be, yet also a form of consternation, a being struck by . . ., in which whatever it is that the child is struck by is still concealed. This being struck, however, is already a way of finding oneself [*Befindlichkeit*]. The essence of shock can be clarified only in connection with the phenomenon of fright and of anxiety. Shock signifies that we find ourselves disturbed, that a discomfort sets in that is to be staved off.

It is not the case that the child first emerges from an enclosed subject in the course of its first weeks and arrives at objects; rather it is already—and not just when it has been torn from its state of latency—directed out toward . . .;

it is already outside alongside. . . . A being of some kind is already manifest to the child, although there is as yet no comportment toward this being, no turning toward it ensues. Turning away and warding off and this self-centered need for restfulness, warmth, and sleep have a quite peculiar negative character. Until these phenomena such as warding off, turning away, and resistance have been clarified in their ontological structure, we cannot begin to interpret a state such as that of the child in its essence. The state of latency that such an early Dasein is in does not mean that no relationship to beings would be there as yet but only that this comportment toward . . . has no definite goal as yet. Being alongside beings is to a certain degree still clouded, not yet illuminated, so that this Dasein is as yet unable to make any definite use of those beings that it is always already alongside in accordance with its essence.

Being torn from a state of latency does not mean emerging from the sphere of the subject; rather the clouds clear from being outside alongside . . ., it becomes bright, and the first seeing of things occurs in this brightness. That which it is alongside dawns on Dasein. This is a dawning of a having that is already there before this.

The primary interpretation here must initially begin to show how the child's merely turning away differs from a warding off. Turning away is a mere avoidance of . . ., yet in avoidance there is already a definite warding off, a repelling of. . . . In fleeing in the face of something, there is already an over against, but not yet an active one; from turning away and warding off, we must distinguish the resistance with which the real countermovement begins, the setting oneself against. All these phenomena of intentionality are at the same time such that their full unfolding articulates the initial situation in which such a Dasein finds itself in its initial helpless exposure to the world.

§16. The uncoveredness of what is present at hand and the manifestness of Dasein

We have seen that the uncoveredness, the unconcealment (truth), of what is present at hand stands or falls with Dasein's being uncovering, that is, with its existence. Truth accordingly belongs to Dasein as a Dasein that is essentially uncovering. Insofar as Dasein dwells alongside what is present at hand, it maintains itself in the uncoveredness of what is present at hand. Now, we saw earlier that the manner and way in which truth (the unconcealment of what is present at hand) belongs to Dasein is necessarily a sharing in truth. Is maintaining oneself in the uncoveredness of what is present at hand in being alongside the latter indeed a sharing in truth? Every being alongside what is present at hand, even when alone, is supposed to include within it a being with one another. All uncoveredness of what is present at hand, in accordance with its essence, is supposed to be one that Dasein shares with others, and uncoveredness accordingly an uncoveredness that Dasein never keeps for itself, as it were, closed off, as a possession enclosed within itself. All uncoveredness of what is present at hand is already essentially supposed to be shared with. . . .

Are these not distinctly odd and unfounded theses that are simply contradicted by the bare facts? The fact that someone has ascertained something, has uncovered something previously unknown, surely does not mean that others already know it. That person can quietly keep the truth to himself. How, then, in light of this undeniable possibility, can we assert that the truth concerning what is present at hand is necessarily something in which Dasein shares with others?

Suppose that someone makes a particular discovery, of a rare plant and its location; it could be that the lucky finder keeps his find to himself for his entire life and no one else ever learns of it. In that case, surely this rare plant and its otherwise unknown location have become manifest for this individual Dasein, and this unconcealment belongs solely to this Dasein; in that case, the unconcealment of what is present at hand can surely indeed belong to a Dasein as individual.

If the lucky finder keeps the truth to himself for his entire life, then that means, after all, that he carefully protects it from others and guards against communicating it to others.[1] What this already reveals is that he shares this truth with others, but just in the mode of withholding it; he shares it with others in this way only because the unconcealment of what is present at hand is by its very essence something common. The finder cannot do otherwise than to keep it to himself or communicate it; in either case, this truth is something that is not his property, even if he can make the claim to have found it first. Keeping something to oneself is a protecting from. . . . Yet what does it mean that he cannot do otherwise, that he moves within this either/or? It means that this truth is something in which he necessarily shares with others. But how is it such a thing and why? To what extent is the unconcealment of what is present at hand essentially something that Dasein shares with Dasein? One thing that is clear is that this sharing in such truth does not mean that others necessarily explicitly appropriate it for themselves. On the other hand, the fact that someone keeps it to himself does not already mean that the truth would at first indeed be his possession alone. It cannot be this, because by its very essence, it is available for others and can never belong to the individual in any way other than by his protecting it. Yet what does that mean? This Dasein must close himself off from others. What does he close off? This unconcealment of the thing that is present at hand, that is, the fact that this Dasein maintains itself in the uncoveredness of what is present at hand; the Dasein closes off its uncovering being alongside this present at hand entity. The

---

1. As noted earlier, the German *mitteilen*, to communicate, literally means to share *(teilen)* with *(mit)*.—Trans.

ways and means by which this factically occurs are not important for now. What is essential is something else. The Dasein must close off from others this, its being alongside the plant in question, if it wants to remain alone with this truth. It must close off, because this being alongside what is present at hand is otherwise disclosed, that is, is unconcealed, in common.

Dasein as such is unconcealed in its being alongside what is present at hand. What does that mean? We have already indicated the extent to which Dasein, precisely through its being alongside what is present at hand, has always already exited from itself. In other words, Dasein is not at all, and is never, something that would at first and on occasion dwell within a so-called sphere of interiority. Strictly speaking, therefore, we cannot even say that it has exited from itself. (Nor is this "from itself" meant in relation to such interiority or immanence.) In short, Dasein as being alongside what is present at hand is manifest to itself, that is, it already brings with it its own being open toward what is present at hand such that it, the Dasein that is open in this way, is openly manifest to itself. Dasein is of its own accord disclosed, not only on occasion but essentially; qua Dasein, it is unconcealed, even if another Dasein does not factically apprehend it.

Elementary though these connections are within the essential constitution of Dasein, it is nevertheless difficult to make them clearly visible at the beginning— and this in turn for reasons that are not accidental. Since we are only at the beginning of our reflections, that is, since we still have a relatively restricted horizon for our problematic, an appropriate understanding of the structures in question is made especially difficult. Later, certainly, you will be surprised as to why such straightforward relationships cannot be grasped immediately at a stroke.

We shall try to help out by discussing an example. First, let us establish the problem and our thesis once again: the unconcealment of what is present at hand, we are saying, is by its very essence something in which Dasein shares with Dasein, whether another Dasein is factically present and factically appropriates the truth for itself or not. The unconcealment of what is present at hand is essentially something common, something that belongs to Dasein, and in such a way that it does not belong to it as its fenced-in, individual possession; rather, it belongs to it in such a way that by its very essence, it is precisely given away, that is, it is never first Dasein's own possession and then given away.

How is that possible, that is, what is this unconcealment of what is present at hand? Uncoveredness; in being alongside . . ., what is present at hand gives itself as unconcealed, insofar as Dasein is intrinsically uncovering. As being alongside . . ., Dasein is being uncovering. As something that is in this way, Dasein itself is in itself manifest. Yet how so? Da-sein means: bringing with itself for the first time the sphere of possible manifestness, the "There" [*Da*] in which, standing into it, what is present at hand can also first become manifest. Such manifesting itself, however, occurs essentially, not occasionally or subsequently. Dasein is disclosive, uncovering, and thus bringing with itself partaking in sharing-with, in communicating.

Unconcealment never belongs to an individual as such. As something common, it stands publicly at the disposal of everyone, as it were; it must therefore essentially be set free by every Dasein. The unconcealment of what is present at hand is for its part necessarily itself unconcealed. Yet since the unconcealment of what is present at hand is not itself something present at hand, and the unconcealment of what is present at hand is called uncoveredness, the unconcealment of what is present at hand, insofar as it itself is unconcealed, can never be something uncovered. If, however, the unconcealment of what is present at hand belongs to Dasein, and in such a way that it itself is unconcealed, then this means: Dasein, insofar as it exists as Dasein, is unconcealed as such. The unconcealment of Dasein, however, as distinct from the unconcealment of what is present at hand, from uncoveredness, we name disclosedness.

Dasein as such is disclosed of its own accord. It does not first become unconcealed by another Dasein tearing it from concealment. Insofar as Dasein exists, it has torn itself from concealment, or brings its unconcealment along with it, so to speak.

Hitherto with respect to Dasein, we have mainly discussed only being alongside what is present at hand. Simply with a view to our being alongside things, we must also initially attempt to see the extent to which being alongside what is present at hand is necessarily unconcealed as that which it is. We shall now compare the being present at hand together of things and the manner and way in which Dasein and these things are next to one another. A bench stands next to a house; they may even be spatially right up against one another. The bench, as we say, can be touching the house; nevertheless, in this being "next to" it, the house is not in any way manifest to the bench as a house, and vice-versa. We may not even say that the house is concealed for the bench; rather, in relation to one another, these things lie altogether outside the possibility of reciprocal concealment and unconcealment. To put it very cautiously, we do not have the least criterion to assume anything else even as a possibility. The farmer, by contrast, who stands on the meadow in front of his house, is also next to his house and to the bench as well; but in this being next, the house and the bench are manifest, which does not mean that the farmer would now have to be explicitly apprehending his house and the bench in front of it. The farmer's standing next to them is a being alongside what is uncovered. And conversely, in what way does the house stand next to the farmer? It does so in the same way as it stands next to the bench; for it does not have the farmer before it as something unconcealed. On the other hand, however, the farmer is also not something present at hand. We can provisionally say that the house is present at hand within the sphere of what is present at hand in relation to the farmer and is something uncovered for the farmer. This sphere of what is uncovered can change in its details, yet Dasein always takes with it, as it were, such a sphere of what is uncovered; wherever it dwells, it moves within such a sphere, and this moving is always a being alongside . . .; whatever it is alongside can be near to a greater or lesser extent.

This is all very straightforward. Let us now suppose that we are approaching the house from a great distance, and we see something standing in front of it, something that looks like a thick post or like something that is set into the meadow in front of the house. Suddenly, this post starts to move; it moves in the direction of the door of the house and disappears inside. And as we experience the movement of this self-moving thing that is present at hand, it proves to be a human being. How do we come to take a moving, present at hand thing that disappears into a hole as a human being, when from our great distance we see neither a face nor hands, nor hear him speak? Yet he started moving of his own accord. Yet suppose that, at the moment it started to move, we were not focused on what we presumed to be a post—we just see it move toward the hole and disappear inside. And when we follow something moving, then we pay attention to its direction; factically, we also already see its direction at the same time, therefore, we see what this thing is moving toward, the hole, therefore—no, the door of the house; from this door of the house that we also see in advance as that toward which the thing is moving, we apprehend as well what and how this being is, that is, we apprehend that it is using the entrance to the house, and in this making use of it, it is not simply undertaking a change of place but is behaving, as we say. It is precisely this behavior that we apprehend in relation to the item of use.

What we apprehend, therefore, is neither something present at hand that is moving, nor a mere space between it and something else, nor this something else as a hole, nor simply all of these things together, however; what we apprehend fundamentally is a being alongside what is present at hand, that is, what is thus unconcealed for us in its specific unconcealment for such being alongside . . ., the fact, as it were, that the door is a door for whatever it is that is moving—the door in its unconcealment, in its uncoveredness for whatever it is that is self-moving, the latter as an uncovering being alongside. . . . In this uncovering being alongside the house, the being makes itself known as Dasein. This being alongside the house, however, is itself already disclosed for that Dasein (the farmer).

§17. *The manifestness of Dasein qua Da-sein*

We have undertaken a series of attempts to shed light on being with one another as a being alongside the same. In doing so, we have not directly attained our goal. And yet these attempts are not without results, but each time, we have arrived at insights that are essential for coming to terms with our task in the right way, such as the fact that truth belongs to the manner of being in question, that Dasein is not identical to a subject, that subjectivity has hitherto always been underdetermined, so that one was able to think they could first arrive at such essential components of subjectivity as being alongside . . . and being with one another as belated supplements, on the grounds of an inadequate concept of the subject. Overall, accordingly, we have attained a multiple loosening up of the contexts of problems that from here on we need not so much to extend as to radicalize. With a view to our next goal, what we have accomplished hitherto has also given us the preparation with whose aid we can venture to exhibit positively the way in which truth as the unconcealment of what is present at hand belongs to Dasein.

Our thesis whereby being with one another is to be characterized as a peculiar manner of being of Dasein was this: the unconcealment of what is present at hand (uncoveredness) is by its very essence something in which Dasein shares with Dasein, whether another Dasein is factically present or not, whether the other Dasein explicitly appropriates the truth for itself or not. The unconcealment of what is present at hand is essentially something common; it never belongs to an individual Dasein as individual. Unconcealment stands at everyone's disposal in a peculiar way. Accordingly, every Dasein must, as uncovering, also always already have set free and given away the uncoveredness of what is uncovered. The unconcealment of what is present at hand does not belong to what is present at hand but to Dasein; but it belongs to Dasein in such a way that it is nevertheless not found within it as a possession contained within the individual. Unconcealment is also not something individually possessed at first, for instance, and then given away; rather, its belonging to Dasein is a giving away. How is such a thing possible, and why is it necessarily thus?

We have seen that what is present at hand gives itself as unconcealed in our being alongside . . ., insofar as the latter is intrinsically uncovering. Dasein cannot at all be next to and alongside something present at hand in the way that something present at hand is "alongside" something present at hand; every and all being there next to is an uncovering being alongside . . . in which whatever we are alongside is maintained in uncoveredness. The "alongside" in being alongside . . . is an open for . . . that essentially opens itself. We have already contemplated this state of affairs on a number of occasions, without it losing any of the wonder it entails. Thus far, however, we have always paid attention only to whatever it is that we are alongside and to the fact that the latter is openly manifest in and for our being alongside. . . . Yet we have deliberately overlooked something no less essential: this, our very being alongside . . ., we as being alongside . . . in this way, are "also" openly manifest together with the manifestness of what is present at hand. Even when a Dasein dwells alone alongside something present at hand, its being alongside . . . is manifest, and it is so even if the Dasein in question does not apprehend or reflect upon itself at all, even if it is not turned back and turned around, even if it does not think of itself in being alongside what is present at hand. Being alongside . . ., therefore, is openly manifest *prior to* all objectification by others and is openly manifest *for itself.*

We shall make this visible by exhibiting an elementary state of affairs in which we, as being there, constantly move, one that is everyday and self-evident to such a degree that it seems not to be there at all. Let us take our example: A stone is present at hand next to a stone, and so too Dasein is alongside Dasein, being alongside . . . next to being alongside. . . . Not at all. Rather, when one Dasein steps next to another Dasein, the one steps into the sphere of manifestness of the other, or more precisely, their being alongside . . . moves within the same sphere of manifestness. What is meant by this?

Being alongside what is present at hand is not, for instance, something like a feeler that Dasein extends toward things and then withdraws again. Rather, Dasein means being alongside . . .; but this essential being alongside things is again not something like a constantly deployed tube, in whose interior, that is, encapsuled, the subject steals out to things, and so with every Dasein by itself, each inside its tube. Rather, this being alongside . . . is as such openly manifest; it is never enclosed, not even when Dasein is alone alongside something. Rather, being alongside . . . is essentially of such a kind that another Dasein can enter into it—as openly manifest—at any time. If that is to be prevented, then Dasein must first close itself off, that is, it is already open in advance and essentially open, because being closed off is only ever privation.

Being alongside what is present at hand and uncovered is, as such, never enclosed, but something disclosed; together with being alongside . . . being open toward what is present at hand, this being alongside . . . is itself unconcealed and, conversely: only being that is itself manifest as such is being alongside. . . . It is what it is, namely, being alongside . . ., as self-disclosive; self-disclosing belongs to the essence of such being. Being alongside . . . is disclosed disclosively, and insofar as being alongside what is present at hand belongs essentially to Dasein, this means: Dasein is, as such, disclosed.

Yet what does that mean? Dasein is not first disclosed on the grounds of being apprehended by another (already for the reason that the apprehending of Dasein means the apprehending of a being that is intrinsically disclosed). Dasein discloses itself, therefore, one will say, if not for others, then for itself. Then we have the long-familiar fact that the human being has consciousness of objects and in this also has a consciousness of himself, self-consciousness. Every consciousness is also self-consciousness. A statement that was discussed ad nauseam in German Idealism, one that Kant too makes foundational and that Descartes already knows, runs as follows: *cogito aliquid = cogito me cogitare aliquid.* If precisely the concept of consciousness prevented the attainment of the correct concept of subjectivity, then supreme critical caution is called for even and precisely when there is talk of self-consciousness. Yet we saw that in being alongside . . . there is not necessarily any knowing of oneself, any turning back to oneself; indeed, precisely our elementary and unadulterated being alongside . . . becomes absorbed in things and is not burdened by reflection. Nevertheless, we must say: it discloses itself precisely then. Self-disclosing, which we assert of being alongside . . . as determining its essence, does not necessarily mean making oneself into an object for oneself, not even making oneself manifest for oneself.

We are saying that uncovering being alongside what is present at hand discloses itself. This neither means: "Dasein becomes manifest through others and for others," nor does it mean: "In addition to what is present at hand and uncovered, Dasein also apprehends itself." The thesis, "Uncovering being alongside what is present at hand discloses itself" says something much more primordial. It means that in being alongside . . ., and as such, Dasein precisely brings with it first of all something like a sphere of manifestness. This being, which not without grounds we call Da-sein, lets such a thing as a "There" [*Da*] first be [*sein*] insofar as it exists, that is, first lets it be in and through its being. Dasein is that being that is such a thing as a "There." The "There": a sphere of manifestness in relation to which what is present at hand too can first of all be manifest, that is, uncovered.

The "There" [*Da*] is not a location, a place, as contrasted with an "over there" [*dort*]; Da-sein does not mean here instead of over there, nor does it mean here and over there, but rather is the possibility, the making possible, of an oriented being here or being over there. The "There" is, among other things, space that has irrupted in itself and yet is not ruptured in so doing. Da-sein is a breaking into space, not simply in the sense that an extended, material thing takes up a space, for instance, but rather in such a way that space is openly manifest in its space-like character; yet Da-sein is not only that. More precisely: the space that is broken open in this way is only one essential determination of the There, by which we can demonstrate primarily one essential component of the being that we are. Certainly, it is not by chance that many linguistic significations that do not intend anything spatial at all nevertheless have spatial signification. Here, it becomes visible that space plays a central role within metaphysics, one that admittedly can be made a problem only in an originary connection with time radically conceived. No physics and no geometry can reveal the essence of space; these disciplines remain eternally outside of this problematic and, metaphysically speaking, only grasp something that is a matter of indifference for space. Only an altogether vacuous offshoot of its problematic shows itself to natural science, to physics. By contrast, art as sculpture or painting is to a certain degree able to conquer space in a quite different way.

Da-sein is a being that essentially discloses itself; this means it is a being [*Seiendes*] in and with whose being [*Sein*] a sphere of manifestness first irrupts, not subsequently or occasionally, but insofar as it exists. It forms (double meaning) this sphere of manifestness: It, qua Da-sein, constitutes it and gives it form. With the existence of the human being, there occurs this irruptive breaking into beings, in such a way that beings stand into the sphere of manifestness as manifest, stand into the manifest There, as which Dasein can now also find itself.

§18. Dasein and being-with

Being alongside . . . is disclosed disclosively. It brings the sphere of the There with itself and moves within it. When another Dasein is factically present, then that Dasein is never merely also there, but rather, in accordance with its essence, is there with, and indeed it is not also in being, but rather in being with, because it is Da-sein, placing itself into the same sphere of manifestness. No matter how similar or identical one stone may be to another, they are never present at hand with one another, that is, what is present at hand cannot be with something else at all. In being present to another Dasein, Dasein is with it not because it too has the same qualities as the first, but because it is Dasein, that is, because, insofar as it is, it brings a There along with it, and as bringing a There with it, necessarily enters into the sphere of the other in such a way that they share this sphere with one another.

The "with" is to be found only where there is a "There." Each of the various instances of being alongside . . . is being with; it is not that the one and the other are alongside what is present-at-hand; rather, the one another is a with one another. Da-sein and Da-sein cannot be factically in any other way than by each being the There, and in this, the factical spatial remove of the places where they reside is completely inessential. Each being the There, however, already means precisely: giving away into the same sphere of manifestness.

With regard to the phenomenon of being alongside . . ., it has already been emphasized a number of times that Dasein does not maintain itself within an inner sphere and through some kind of maneuvering nevertheless come to experience something of the outside. Dasein, rather, is as such already outside alongside . . ., having stepped out of itself or better: stepping out of itself; qua Dasein, it never is in any other way and yet is so without abandoning itself in the process; this stepping out to . . . is Dasein itself, its essence. It does not need to abandon "itself," because it is itself as stepping out. The "out," however, surely seems to imply an "inner." Certainly, the question is only how that "inner" is determined and whether it has to be conceived in the way that the traditional doctrine of the immanence or interiority of consciousness conceives it. The manner and way in which Dasein is alongside itself is essentially codetermined by the manner in which, as being alongside itself, it is nonetheless essentially a stepping out.

Yet if Dasein and Dasein never exist next to one another, then this means that each, as essentially stepping out, has also already stepped into the manifestness of the other. Even if they are not concerned about one another, they maintain themselves necessarily, as the Da-sein that they are, within the same sphere of manifestness; to bring the latter, qua Dasein, with oneself means: to share it with beings of one's kind. In the essence of a being-there [*Da-sein*] lies being-with [*Mit-sein*], even if another being factically does not exist at all. Dasein already brings with it the sphere of possible neighborhood; it is intrinsically already neighbor to . . ., whereas two stones, for example, cannot be neighboring. In being-with, however, there lies a giving away and freeing of the There—as a manifest irruption in which beings can for their part make themselves known, each according to its kind.

Accordingly, the uncoveredness of that which is present at hand, an uncoveredness that arises in a being alongside . . . that uncovers, is something that belongs to the disclosedness of the There. Only a being that discloses itself in the said sense can, indeed must, be uncovering. Every uncoveredness of what is present at hand is therefore—as belonging to the disclosedness of a Dasein— necessarily also already given away and shared, because the disclosedness of the There, that is, Da-sein, is necessarily being-with [*Mit-sein*]. Being uncovering belongs to disclosedness and thereby to Da-sein. Precisely because disclosedness belongs in this way to Da-sein, and because that which is common, and thus an indication of being with, belongs to the disclosedness of being, such disclosedness is not, indeed never, a possession contained within the individual but rather something which each Dasein already shares with . . . in its self-disclosive being-with.

We have thus shed light on the inner possibility of being with one another as an essential manner of being of Dasein. In so doing, we have seen *how* truth qua unconcealment of what is present at hand is constitutive for a being with one another, and originarily belongs to Dasein in such a way that uncoveredness is for its part possible only in the disclosedness of Dasein, that is, of that unconcealment that the being that we call Dasein brings with it.

We have made visible being with one another as a structure belonging to the essence of Dasein and have done so on one particular, deliberately chosen path that necessarily entails a one-sidedness, but one that is inconsequential. We must now speak briefly about this apparent one-sidedness, because misunderstandings can easily become entrenched, and because determining being with one another as an essential determination of Dasein is partly underestimated and partly overestimated.

We have demonstrated being with one another in terms of a readily accessible being with one another alongside the chalk that is present at hand. Certainly, the following objection must already have occurred to you on a number of occasions: Being alongside one and the same present at hand entity may indeed present one "mode" of being with one another, but in our case, it is surely a distinctly superficial and indifferent being next to one another, and a vague being with one another. That is certainly the case, yet this takes nothing away from the fact that even in such a vague being with one another, its essence or a part of its essence becomes visible. For strictly speaking, being alongside one and the same thing is not a mode of being with one another—thus, one particular kind among many others—but rather an essential component of each and every being with one another; that is, our being alongside the chalk, the sponge, and whatever is present at hand here belongs essentially to our being with one another, which is constituted by other things too: my lecture, your listening to the lecture; yet to this, there belongs a being alongside what is present at hand, although not necessarily precisely this one; even somewhere out there in the mountains, the being with one another is a being alongside . . . something that is precisely manifest there in whatever is present at hand at any time.

We heard already that in the traditional concept of the subject, being alongside . . . is omitted. Nor, as we shall see, is it as yet grasped as an essential moment of subjectivity if one regards the subject as intentional consciousness. Intentionality fails to attain its true and central implications so long as "consciousness" is retained and so long as, precisely with the aid of intentionality, we fail to explode the interpretation of the human being in terms of consciousness. Yet because the subject is thought of as pruned, as it were, of this being alongside . . ., as a truncated subject, the question concerning being with one another and its essence also gets on the wrong track. Because both subjects are underdetermined, the mediation between them must, as it were, be given a more complicated setup than is essentially necessary. The underdetermination of subjectivity gives rise to an overdetermination of the relation of subject to subject. For now one has two subjects—yet initially in such a way that no communication is as yet possible—and one orients the problem around the issue of how these two truncated subjects come together.

In this scenario, the subject of which one is supposedly certain is one's own I, the I-subject, which indeed is not posited as being alone in its isolation; the other therefore becomes a You-subject, one that likewise lacks appropriate determination, that is, a second I. Now the question is raised of how a first I comes to a second I, and of how, through this coming together of two *Is*, a being with one another arises. When these two are together, one lets them discuss how they can comport themselves to a common thing outside. The problem of being with one another becomes in its approach the problem of the so-called I-You-relation, and the way this relation is constituted is designated as empathy; it is the window through which, as it were, a subject that in each case finds itself within a container makes the transition over to another.

Yet insofar as being with one another as a problem is in general reduced to the common denominator of "empathy"—however empathy may be conceived—the decisive insight has not been attained that being with one another already belongs to the essence of Dasein as such, indeed in such a way that this Dasein as such is also already being alongside. . . .

Dasein is being with one another alongside. . . . If being with one another is thus grasped as belonging to the essence of every Dasein, this does not mean that there is no problem: to the contrary, we shall indeed show how the task must now be to inquire precisely concerning the inner possibility of being with one another, and how this question finds its answer from an elucidation of Dasein as such.

Only because every Dasein as such is intrinsically—we have shown how in one respect—a being with, that is, with one another, only for this reason is human community and society possible in its diverse variations, levels, and degrees of genuineness and nongenuineness, endurance and fleetingness.

Yet might not being alongside . . . indeed have a priority? How can Dasein-with [*Mitdasein*] be extracted from this, namely, as the a priori of what is understood therein (in being with)? It can only ever be shown how an other as such is ontically recognized. Yet even for this, Husserl's path is unsuitable, first, because he still remains trapped within an egological sphere that is conceived idealistically and in an unclear manner and, second, because he is oriented toward the grasping of the pure thing and of data instead of toward concrete relations of existence.

If one conceives of being alongside . . . in a quite broad sense, as being alongside "other" things, undifferentiated beings that we are not, then this very undifferentiatedness is not a vacuous indeterminacy but rather plenitude; the projection that lies within being with is then already included. That being with . . . has priority is documented by the factical relationship whereby the "primitive" indeed personifies, regards as animate, the "other," including things.

§19. *Leibniz's* Monadology *and the interpretation of being with one another*

The problem of being with one another is not in the first instance a question of the relation of subject to subject, but prior to that, a problem belonging to the determination of the essence of a subject as such. Facts concerning being with one another have always been known. Aristotle already speaks of the human being as ζῷον πολιτικόν, a living being that can be in community. Only because the human being is such a being, can he also be a herd animal, as Nietzsche is used to saying. This problem of community was therefore always already discussed in philosophy, especially in ethics, yet was not posed as a problem of the metaphysics of Dasein.

In Leibniz, the reciprocal exchange between subjects becomes a question only indirectly and for the first time in his *Monadology*.[2] It occurs indirectly,

---

2. On Leibniz's *Monadology* and the interpretation of being with one another, cf. the Logic lecture course of summer semester 1928, manuscript pages 25–35 (Martin Heidegger, *Metaphysische Anfangsgründe der Logik im Ausgang von Leibniz*, Marburg lecture course of summer semester 1928, Gesamtausgabe, vol. 26, ed. Klaus Held [Frankfurt: Klostermann, 1978, 2nd rev. ed., 1990], 86–122, translated as *The Metaphysical Foundations of Logic* by Michael Heim [Bloomington: Indiana University Press, 1984]).

for here too the first task is that of determining the concept of the subject in the traditional sense as a truncated subject, though indeed in an essentially deeper and extended sense. As a consequence of this monadological interpretation of the subject, Leibniz arrives at a particular view concerning the possible commerce between subjects, the exchange between them. The being with one another of human and human is an instance of the exchange between substances in general.

We can consider Leibniz's *Monadology* only briefly, so as to contrast it with the above interpretation of Dasein and being with one another and thereby to provide a summary clarification of what was said there, by way of comparison. Certainly, it could also be shown how the *Monadology* first displays the richness and depth of its conception precisely if one does not simply attempt to grasp it starting from the traditional concept of the subject, a concept that Leibniz himself so little overcomes through the *Monadology* that he rather precisely presupposes it for this. Aside from that, however, the Leibnizian monad is one of the boldest ideas ever to emerge in philosophy since Plato.

Leibniz designates substances as monads—in Greek, *monas* = unity—as unities. Unity means: simplicity, that which is originary, determinative of the whole, individuality; τόδε τι, Aristotle's οὐσία. ἕν—ὄν—οὐσία, cf. *Metaphysics* Γ 2, 1003 b23/b32. In the ancient doctrine of Plato and Aristotle, every being, as a being, is in each case one; it is constituted by a quite specific unity. According to Leibniz, the being of each and every being is properly grounded in this specific unity. For Leibniz, *monas* is that which originarily gives unity, the simple that unifies and, as unifying, individuates. For this reason, he designates every independent being with regard to this primary determination of unity a monad: the unity that unifies simply and in advance and thereby individuates.

The problem of the monad is thus nothing other than the revisited problem of the substantiality of substance or, as we can also say, of the subjectivity of the subject; for in Leibniz, as fundamentally also still in Kant, subject means *subiectum*, that which underlies, ὑποκείμενον, that which is of its own accord. According to Leibniz, all monads, all substances—including corporeal substances—thus, the elementary particles of a body, have a soul.

That the monad has a soul means: *monas* has *vis*, urge, *nisus*; *appetitus*, *repraesentatio*. It is unifying from the ground up, taking into unity in advance and maintaining what it represents; every monad in each case mirrors the totality of beings, though each from a different point of view and differing in degrees of awakeness. There are dull, drowsy, slumbering monads that constitute the corporeal as such. From these, there is a scale leading up to God, the central monad, God conceived according to Christian theology. From here, one can understand why Leibniz designates every monad as a *speculum vitale*, a living mirror.

In urge itself, in what and how the monad itself is, it in each case procures for itself this view of the whole, seen from a particular point of view. Insofar as each monad of its own accord represents the whole from a particular point of view, it is in a certain way the universe. For this reason, Leibniz designates the monad *mundus concentratus*.

Every monad as such individuates itself; every monad is in each case independently "formative" of the whole. Dasein too, human beings, are conceived as monads. Being formative of their own accord, they essentially have no need to receive; in their essence, there lies no receptivity from the outside. Monads have no windows, because they do not need them; they do not need them, because they have everything within themselves, are entirely closed, not open. They need no commerce, no relation to others; rather, the whole is in each case within all, and all are as *entia creata* by way of the whole in the sense of the supreme monad. It is "empathy," however, that gives the monad windows; empathy indeed is, as it were, the window.

By contrast, our interpretation agrees with Leibniz in this: the monad, Dasein, has no windows, because it needs none. But the reason is different: human beings need no windows, not because they have no need to go out, but because they are essentially already outside. This reason, however, is indicative of a totally different determination of the essence of the subject. The task is not to supplement the monadological approach and improve it by way of empathy but to radicalize it.

§20. *Community on the grounds of the with-one-another*

On the grounds of the with-one-another, community becomes possible, but the with-one-another is not first constituted by a community of *Is*. "Constitution" of the with-one-another is ambiguous, as the concept of constitution readily becomes: (a) the concept means, as in Neo-Kantianism, construction in the sense of letting something arise out of simple, though indeed not psychological, elements; then, here at least, it becomes nonsensical; (b) the concept means the demonstration of an essential construction that is in itself always already whole and indivisible; then, it is legitimate, yet certainly must be grounded in its methodological character. The with-one-another as something elementary is not to be derived but must presumably be elucidated with respect to the constituents belonging to its essence, which are all equiprimordial. Within this constitution belonging to the essence of each individual Dasein, there is no place for "empathy." For if this word is meant to have any meaning left at all, then this can be only on the grounds of the presupposition that the "I" can indeed initially be within its own ego-sphere and must from there then enter into the other and its sphere. Because it is already outside, the "I" neither first breaks out of itself (out of its window) nor breaks into the other, because it already encounters itself outside together with this other and does so there precisely in a genuine sense, as can be shown.

The with-one-another cannot, therefore, be explained via the I-You relation or in terms of it but rather the reverse: This I-You relation presupposes for its inner possibility that Dasein already in each case—both the one that functions as the I and the one that functions as the You—is determined as being with one another, indeed even more: the very self-apprehension of an I and the concept of I-ness first arise on the grounds of the with-one-another, but not as an I-You relation.

It is equally erroneous to let the with-one-another first arise from a truncated I as it is to claim that the I-You relation is the basis, so as to determine Dasein as such starting from there; instead of an egoistic, solipsistic approach, an altruism—this only doubles the error, and there is a solipsism of two. It is likewise erroneous to regard the with-one-another as sole principle.

In its essence, the being that we in each case are, the human being, is a neuter. We name this being: Dasein. Yet it belongs to the essence of this neuter that, insofar as it exists factically in each case, it has necessarily fractured its neutrality; that is, Dasein, as factical, is in each case either male or female, it is a sexual being; this entails a quite determinate with-one-another and toward-one-another. The limit and extent of the effects of this characteristic are factically different in each case; it can only be shown which possibilities of human existence are not necessarily determined by the sexual relationship. Yet precisely this sexual relationship is possible only because Dasein in its metaphysical neutrality is already determined by the with-one-another. If each Dasein, which factically is in each case male or female, were not already with one another in accordance with its essence, then a human sexual relationship would remain altogether impossible.

It is therefore the crudest nonsense imaginable when one tries to explain the with-one-another as determination of the essence of Dasein the other way around, on the basis of the sexual relationship. Ludwig Feuerbach, in a blind and inadequate opposition to German Idealism, introduced this error, an error that people are attempting to replicate today, but that does not become truth by people trying to make Feuerbach's crude materialism more tasteful with the aid of contemporary phenomenology. The fundamental thesis of Feuerbach's anthropology, his doctrine of the human being, runs: the human being is what he eats.[3] This thesis contains something right—but when something half-true is declared as a universal principle, confusion always arises.

To the essence of the human being belongs this fractured neutrality of the human essence, which is to say, however, that this essence can be made a problem only primarily starting from neutrality, and only in relation to this neutrality is the fracture of neutrality itself possible. Sexuality is only one moment within this problem and, indeed, not the primary one (thrownness). Because Dasein exists

---

3. *Der Mensch ist, was er ißt.* The homophony of *ist* ("is") and *ißt* ("eats") gets lost in translation.—Trans.

as bodily, the factical apprehension of the other by the one and of the one by the other is subject to certain conditions; but the relations of apprehension between Dasein and Dasein, relations that are coconditioned in a bodily manner, do not constitute the with-one-another but rather presuppose it and are for their part determined by it.

In order to make it clear from the beginning that the with-one-another neither comes about primarily by way of an individuated I, nor can it be explained in terms of the I-You relationship, the analysis started from being alongside something present at hand. Yet if being alongside . . . is an essential moment of the with-one-another, then being alongside . . . must also remain determinative for the various factical possibilities of the with-one-another, of community, for example.

We know only too well, for example, that genuine and great friendship neither arises from nor consists in the fact that an I and a You in their I-You relationship touchingly gaze at one another and entertain themselves with their trivial emotional needs but that it grows and stands firm within a genuine passion for a common cause, something that does not exclude but perhaps demands that each has his own distinct work in each case and goes to work differently. We may just recall the friendship between Goethe and Schiller.

On the other hand, it is not decisive what one does but how he does it; yet he can only exist in a particular how if he has taken hold of a what that is to be thoroughly governed by the how. Being alongside something common, however, is always essential for the with-one-another.

Certainly, this does not exhaust the interpretation of the essence of being with one another; the direction in which it is to be elaborated and will later concern us has already become clear. The being qua human being is one that brings its "There" with it, the manifestness within which Dasein can first explicitly comport itself to itself and be itself in various ways. Self and I are not the same. This being a self of Dasein, however, does not in turn first come about through reflection upon itself; even reflection-free absorption in something is a being a self. From this, it already becomes clear that Dasein is equiprimordially always already being alongside . . ., being with, and being a self. There remains the question of the unity of these and of yet other essential determinations.

For our initial purposes it must suffice to have clarified, through the preliminary interpretation of the with-one-another—an interpretation always oriented toward the whole—the manner of being pertaining to the being together of Dasein and Dasein, by contrast with the being present at hand together of two things, which constitute two extreme ways of being.

Entirely excluded remains the question concerning the essence of "life," of "animality," of plant being. If we are altogether honest, we do not even know today how we should properly pose this question, quite apart from the answer.

5 The Realm of the Essence of Truth and the Essence of Science

§21. Summary of the interpretation of truth

The distinction between the manner of being of Dasein and of that which is present at hand was to become clear in order to show that, in keeping with the difference in their manners of being, the corresponding truth concerning the beings in question is different. We inquired into the essence of truth in order to answer the question: What is science? Strangely, what has now emerged is that this second question has also been answered along with the first. With respect to the correlation between truth and beings (represented by Dasein and what is present at hand), we discovered a series of essential insights, which at the same time afford us a first look into the essence of truth in general.

We shall summarize what we have said so far in eight theses[1]:

1. Truth is correlated with what is present at hand in such a way that it can accrue to such beings, yet need not do so, but in no case does it belong to the essential content of what is present at hand. The unconcealment of beings that have the manner of being of presence at hand, however, we call uncoveredness.

2. When that which is present at hand is unconcealed, that is, when uncoveredness factically exists, then this happens only in such a way that an uncovering Dasein exists, that is, a being to the constitution of whose being it belongs to be disclosed, that is, to be a There. Dasein is a being that is unconcealed of its own accord. This unconcealment of Dasein we call disclosedness.

3. We thus have two fundamental ways in which beings are unconcealed: truth as disclosedness and as uncoveredness. These are also correlated in quite different ways with the beings manifest therein.

4. This difference in the correlation of truth with respect to Dasein and what is present at hand goes back to the fact that even the truth of what is present at hand, uncoveredness, is grounded in disclosedness, which for its part

---

1. First recall once again: Truth is *unconcealment, the manifestness of beings,* whatever their manner of being may be.

belongs to the constitution of Dasein's being. The uncoveredness of what is present at hand is possible only together with, that is, as belonging to, the disclosedness of a Dasein.

5. Yet because Da-sein is essentially disclosed, the togetherness of Dasein and Dasein must in each case be a being with one another. Dasein is, qua Dasein, essentially being with. . . . . Only on the grounds of this "with" pertaining to each individual Dasein are the different ways of being toward one another, for one another, against one another, and without one another possible.

6. Yet because uncoveredness is by its essence disclosed in each case (and can only thus be what it is), the unconcealment of what is present at hand is something that Dasein has necessarily always already given away. In the manifestness of Dasein, uncoveredness is shared with . . ., even without someone sharing being factically present.

Through the interpretation of truth that we have summarized in these six theses, we are already in a position to determine the essence of truth in a more fundamental manner, although still not in a way that is sufficiently radical and universal. We shall offer this formulation in two further theses:

7. Dasein is essentially in the truth. (Cf. p.142f.)
8. Truth exists, that is, its manner of being is existence, and that is the way in which such a thing as Dasein is.

The two theses belong most intimately together, but do not say the same thing. At first we shall elucidate them only to the extent demanded by our initial goal so as then to attempt directly to determine the essence of science.

Regarding 7: The statement can at first mean: Dasein is in possession of the truth, in possession of the first and ultimate decisive forms of knowledge. Yet this is not what is meant. The thesis is not meant to say anything about whatever truths Dasein factically possesses but rather says that the constitution of Dasein's being is the locus of the essence of truth. Truth here does not signify what is decisively true, nor everything true taken together, but signifies, rather, the essence of truth qua unconcealment. The statement means that Dasein as such maintains itself in the unconcealment of beings, to which beings there belong at least what is present at hand, the ready to hand, other Daseins, and this particular Dasein as one's own in each case. The irruption of the There, the unconcealment of beings, belongs to the essence of the being of this being.

This does not yet say in what way these beings that are in principle manifest with the existence of Dasein are specifically apprehended or even explicitly differentiated and set apart in their manners of being. For this reason, the statement, as an assertion of essence, decides nothing concerning which particular truths are attained, in what way, or with what justification or insight.

We can take this opportunity to briefly make note of the ambiguities that lie within the concept of "truth" and that often lead discussions astray. Truth can mean, first, the truth about something, that is, a truth, something true about it. Truth can also mean, second, everything true that there is, the entirety of what is true. The word is understood as having this signification when one says that God is the source of all truth. Third, truth can mean the essence of what is true as true. We are using the word truth in this third sense when we say that Dasein by its very essence is in the truth.

However, the statement could also mean: Dasein is in the truth and accordingly excluded from error. This interpretation of the statement also is not what is intended. The statement says neither that Dasein is factically excluded from error, nor indeed that Dasein by its very essence would not be capable of erring. Rather, the statement precisely first expresses the condition of possibility of error and of un-truth. For only the kind of being that from the very start maintains itself in unconcealment can have something remain concealed from it.

Yet concealment as counterphenomenon to unconcealment qua truth is for its part not yet necessarily un-truth qua error; nonetheless, we must hold fast to an essential concept of un-truth, whereby un-truth as concealment means the equivalent of non-unconcealment. Over against this general concept of un-truth, the task is now to determine the specific concept having the sense of falsity, error, lie, and mendacity. For in its usual significance, un-truth means not only the absence of unconcealment, that is, concealment, rather un-truth is a defective unconcealment, that is, one that pretends to be unconcealment of something and is taken to be such yet is not. Un-truth in this narrower sense always arises with a claim to be truth as unconcealment, and therein lies its semblance. Yet this un-truth too is in turn not necessarily a lie, that is, untruth does not necessarily need to be conveyed as such or with the intent to deceive and against one's knowing better. The lie in turn is not synonymous with mendacity. Yet this very possibility of being-un-true makes clear how mendacity, as a specific concealing, necessarily presupposes manifestness, unconcealment. For one who is being mendacious does not simply conceal, he does not simply withhold the truth from others; nor does he, for instance, factically lead them to something untrue; rather, he sets out to present himself as one who brings truth, he makes himself manifest as such a one.

All of these phenomena of un-truth like falsity, error, deception, lie, and mendacity that differ among themselves are possible only because Dasein in general brings manifestness with it in the being of the There, and that means: is in the truth. Yet if different possibilities of existence accrue to human Dasein, then the manner and way in which Dasein is in the truth must also be determined in terms of its existence in each instance. If Dasein exists, it is, as such, in the truth, in unconcealment, and at the same time also necessarily in untruth. Factically, it always moves within a free either/or. Beings have always already become manifest, and have done so as a whole in each instance, in however restricted a compass, and however rough and unarticulated the manner in which they are manifestly determined may be.

Regarding 8: Truth exists. Truth itself therefore has the manner of being of Dasein; insofar as this manner of being is determined as existence, we must say: unconcealment can only be what it is as existing. Yet is truth not in statements, in statements having validity? True statements, it has been said since Lotze, are valid independently of the one who acknowledges them. Truths are something in themselves. There are beings in themselves and truths in themselves, or where beings in themselves are denied, the latter (truths in themselves) count as substitutes, although where they get their validity from remains obscure. True statements are valid, but this does not say that truth is valid. The converse is rather the case: because statements are not originarily true, "validity" is also not the original manner of being of truth; truth, rather, is not merely and not primarily valid, but exists. Only because truth qua manifestness (disclosedness) of Dasein exists in the manner of being of this being, indeed co-constitutes existence, can assertions about beings be true, and for this reason alone, in turn, can true statements be valid. To talk about true statements and validities in themselves is meaningless and superficial. If no Dasein exists, there is also no truth, yet just as little is there untruth. Then there is absolute night, in which, as Hegel says, all cows are black; indeed, more closely considered, even that is not possible.

Yet if truth thus stands or falls with the existence of human Dasein in general, and if, moreover—according to our seventh thesis—the manner and way in which truth becomes existent is determined in terms of Dasein in each case, does not truth then become a merely human affair, whether one conceives the being of the human being as subject or as Dasein? Does not the human being then become the measure of all things? Is not the thesis that "truth exists, it has the manner of being of the human being" synonymous with the statement that Protagoras the sophist already declared and that Plato relates to us in his dialogue *Theaetetus*, when he has Socrates say (152a): φησὶ γάρ που πάντων χρημάτων μέτρον ἄνθρωπον εἶναι, τῶν μὲν ὄντων ὡς ἔστι, τῶν δὲ μὴ ὄντων ὡς οὐκ ἔστιν.[2] "This Protagoras says: Of all things the human being is the measure, of beings, that they are, of nonbeings, that they are not."

The human being as the measure of what and how things are—is truth not thereby surrendered to human arbitrariness and to human taste? Must not this consequence drawn by the Greeks affect precisely our interpretation of truth, an interpretation, after all, that we orient around the original signification of the

---

2. *Platonis Opera*, recognovit brevique adnotatione critica instruxit Ioannes Burnet (Oxonii e typographeo Clarendoniano, 1899ff.), Tomus I.

ancient word? However, precisely the correctly understood sense of truth qua unconcealment shatters this objection. For that Dasein "is" essentially in unconcealment means: it can be precisely only insofar as it comports itself toward beings that make themselves known within unconcealment. It is precisely solely because Dasein is in the truth, that is, alongside and relating to manifest beings, that its being bound to beings becomes possible and necessary.

We mentioned furthermore, at the point where we introduced this concept of truth, that the Greeks themselves were not able to hold fast to the fundamental insight revealed in the coining of the word ἀλήθεια and were unable to elaborate it in its essential content. Instead, the statement cited from Protagoras is a striking example of how an orientation toward the physiological and psychological faculties of the human being intervened in the interpretation of truth. This means in principle that the Greeks—despite the major insights of Plato and Aristotle—were unable to clarify the essence of truth to the point where this clarified essence of truth would have led them to determine the concept of the human being and his essence accordingly, precisely in terms of this essence of truth. Instead, the interpretation of the essence of truth, as we have shown, enters the path of a psychological explanation in the broadest sense.

The theses "Dasein is in the truth" and "Truth exists" do not imply a bad relativization of truth in relation to the human being but the reverse: They place the human being by his very essence before beings in such a way that—as an essentially disclosed being—he can first of all direct himself toward whatever has necessarily become manifest with the disclosedness of his There. Only if Dasein, as disclosed and uncovering, can direct itself toward beings can it make appropriate assertions about them. From this clarification of the originary essence of truth, we come to see something else originary: the disclosedness of the There— and that the truth of assertion is grounded in this, and in what way. The assertion about . . . is made possible through being alongside what is present at hand, uncovering what is present at hand, through disclosed Da-sein as assertive. The essential belonging of truth qua unconcealment to Dasein guarantees a possible objectivity of truth. Certainly, there is a relativity of truth, indeed a most essential one that does not endanger objectivity but, to the contrary, precisely makes possible the richness and manifoldness of objective truth.

Only because Dasein is essentially in the truth can it make assertions about beings. The locus of truth is not the propositional statement but rather the converse: the statement has its locus, its intrinsic possibility, in "truth" qua unconcealment of the There. The statement is not the locus of truth, rather, truth is the locus of the statement. The "locus" is that through which the intrinsic possibility is determined. We thus see how the traditional concept of truth, the truth of the statement, can be traced back to the originary unconcealment of Dasein, which we have called disclosedness for short.

That this is so must prove itself by whether and how we now succeed in delimiting the concept of science in terms of the determination of the essence of truth that we have reached. This interpretation of the essence of science must be such that it helps us achieve an actual understanding of the unclarified questions concealed within the crisis of science that we depicted at the beginning: The issue was precisely the possible relationship of science to human existence, to the existence of the individual and that of the historical community of culture.

§22. Determining the essence of science in terms of the originary concept of truth

Our starting point was the predominant definition of science: science is a coherent set of true, grounded statements that are valid, a set of truths, where truth is indeed synonymous with a true statement. Science is a kind of truth. We have kept to this characterization, but done so in then asking what truth itself means and whether truth is primarily the truth of statements. We have now seen that the essence of truth is the unconcealment of beings, and this unconcealment belongs to the existence of Dasein. It is only because truth in its originary sense is the unconcealment of Dasein that it can, in its derivative sense, also become a feature of assertion about beings, of assertion that Dasein undertakes in its being alongside and being with and toward beings.

We can thus initially see, purely by way of anticipation, that if science in general is in some way a kind of truth, but truth as unconcealment belongs to the essential constitution of existent Dasein, then science in its originary sense is necessarily something that belongs to Dasein's existence. This means that science is not related also to human Dasein only in passing or subsequently, nor is it simply produced by human Dasein, but rather, as a kind of truth, it is an essential determination of Dasein; it signifies nothing other than a particular manner and way of being-in-the-truth. This is not to say that every Dasein as such would necessarily have to pursue science. That science belongs to human existence means: the intrinsic possibility, and not just the factical emergence of science is grounded in the essence of truth as an essential component of the constitution of Dasein's being. It belongs to the essence of this intrinsic possibility that science is itself in turn a free possibility of Dasein, that is, not absolutely necessary; for we have seen that being in the truth is essential and that beings are thereby already manifest. Truth means unconcealment of Da-sein, and science is a kind of truth. Science is therefore one kind of unconcealment of Dasein, that is, a how of human existence. A horizon has thereby been attained in principle for an interpretation of science in terms of the constitution of Dasein's existence or, in short, for an existential concept of science. It is the tendency toward such a clarification of the idea of science, however, a tendency that has not been understood, that fundamentally gives rise to and prevails throughout the crisis of science.

Our task is now to work out this existential concept of science, so as by working out the concept of science to encounter a limit within science itself, in order to see concretely that to be what it can be in accordance with its essence, science must indeed already be something more, something else that is more originary. This something else proves to be philosophy. As we already emphasized, we are not therefore comparing science and philosophy as fixed quantities; rather, in and through our interpretation of the essence of science, we encounter philosophy.

The following interpretation of the essence of science is a principle one, in its intention indeed the most principle one possible in general; that does not mean, however, that it would be complete in every respect. Our goal is neither to project a general systematics of possible sciences—a systematics of the sciences is not an ordering of sciences that are present at hand but rather a free construction of possible sciences, that is, of those that are necessary in essence—nor can it be a matter of discussing all the concrete questions that impose themselves in the crisis of the sciences. Presumably, however, what is decisive must come to light with respect to these questions, and this because in demonstrating the essential character of existence pertaining to science, an entire series of questions that one is otherwise accustomed to pose concerning the relationship of the individual to science resolve themselves of their own accord.

a) Science as a kind of truth?

Science is a kind of truth. Truth, however, belongs essentially to Dasein. Dasein exists in the truth; truth is existent. Science, as a possibility of Dasein's existence, is one possibility of being-in-the-truth. The truth of Dasein is unconcealment, encompassing both disclosedness and uncoveredness; with the existence of Dasein, beings are manifest, not just any beings but what is present at hand in the broader sense, "nature," as well as what is ready to hand, Dasein, and Dasein-with, yet all these beings always in a certain way as a whole. Factically, this whole is determined differently in its wholeness, and often left indeterminate too, yet even in such indeterminacy it is precisely there in a characteristic way. The beings that are themselves manifest are not necessarily differentiated already according to different manners of being, and here too all manifest beings are indeterminate, undifferentiated among themselves. Yet all beings are in this way attuned through and through in terms of the whole that itself remains indeterminate. Indeterminacy is a specific determinacy (the mana idea).

Beings can, furthermore, be manifest in each case to quite different extents and to different degrees of clarity and distinctness in each instance, and all of this before any science. For insofar as Dasein exists, beings as a whole are already manifest. Because science is just one particular free possibility of Dasein, and indeed one whose accomplishment is subject to particular conditions, science only ever arises already on the grounds of a manifestness of beings that is already existent along with Dasein. If, therefore, we speak of pre-scientific truth, we do not mean by this some piecemeal, crude knowledge that is not rigorously grounded. The pre in prescientific also does not simply designate a lesser degree of truth, as though scientific truth would be superior without further ado; rather, the term "prescientific" means, in light of the concept of truth we have developed, that Dasein is already in the truth prior to science. Prescientific Dasein is necessarily prior in order to scientific Dasein, but not subordinate to it; to the contrary, it first provides the ground for scientific Dasein. Prescientific truth expresses precisely the fact that science is not an existentiell necessity and that human existence could neither primarily nor solely be determined by science.

Pre-scientific Dasein is one that has not yet passed through science; scientific Dasein is one that is determined by science, which does not mean that it itself is familiar with science at the individual level in every case or even explicitly pursues science. Our contemporary Western-European Dasein is a scientific one, insofar as the unconcealment of beings is in part stamped and determined by scientific knowledge. Even the Dasein of a contemporary human being who is not scientifically educated is in this sense a scientific one. The so-called radio amateur works, for example, with particular apparatus for particular ends without having a clue about what is really going on there. Or if a smart peasant farmer, for instance, desires to read the *Nibelungenlied* and someone procures for him a so-called decent edition, then the manner and way whereby he comes to this work is a scientific one, transmitted through philological labor. Even the contemporary understanding of Christian faith has passed through a theology influenced by science.

b) Prescientific and scientific Dasein

Scientific Dasein accordingly means: Dasein whose unconcealment of beings is in part determined by scientific knowledge, without the fact that this unconcealment is determined in this way being recognized or even merely familiar as such, let alone attained by the particular Dasein in question itself. Prescientific and scientific Dasein are therefore by no means equivalent to the distinction between primitive and nonprimitive Dasein, quite aside from the fact that this latter distinction itself remains equivocal. Primitive can denote simple, as distinct from complicated, but that is not synonymous with lower and higher culture, with barbarism and education. Primitive Dasein may very well have a higher status and its own genuineness and originality and need not be barbaric. Conversely, nonprimitive, complex Dasein may very well be barbaric and nongenuine as well.

These two nonequivalent distinctions between simple and complex, barbaric and educated, are also not equivalent to prescientific and scientific Dasein in this particular sense. Scientific Dasein is not necessarily already educated, and it also need not be complex. Scientific Dasein is accordingly not necessarily of higher rank, and does not preclude barbarism. Despite science, or precisely even perhaps with its help, a nameless barbarism has become widespread among us today, one that perhaps very few sense, because the majority feel good in it. One need not wish for the return of the mail coach to be able to see the inner coarsening and corruption of taste brought about today by the technicity that would be impossible without science.

Our contemporary, factical Dasein is a scientific one, and we can no longer erase this scientificity from our Dasein. Certainly this does not mean that we would be hopelessly abandoned to its evil consequences or would have to wish to restore a prescientific Dasein. For the latter too bears within itself the possibility of barbarism and of education, while scientific training indeed does not yet necessarily mean education. From these remarks, it already becomes clear that science as such does not necessarily already bring with it an elevation of human Dasein, and that science, because it is a possibility of Dasein, can necessarily be in one way or another, can have an effect in one way or another.

The fact that our contemporary Dasein is a scientific one, however, certainly conditions the manner and way in which we arrive at a knowledge and interpretation of prescientific Dasein. If scientific Dasein is possible only on the basis of prescientific Dasein, then the latter also necessarily still lies within scientific Dasein, insofar as science as a kind of truth transforms the unconcealment of Dasein into one of a different kind. It will become apparent where the fundamental limits of such a transformation lie. In coming to know prescientific Dasein, however, we must choose the path of reconstruction. We shall not discuss at this point what reconstruction and construction mean here in general. In any case, though, a reconstruction of prescientific Dasein is not attained simply by presenting reports about primitive Dasein in a universalizing form, not only because primitive is not equivalent to prescientific but also because even where there could be overlap, the reports, the very manner of questioning, and their linguistic rendition are already subject to contemporary interpretation, that is, are in part scientifically determined.

The interpretation of prescientific Dasein is in general not an empirical question of prehistory. Rather, ethnological reports and mythological tradition speak their language only if the essential kind of Dasein they are to provide information about has already been determined in advance. Still, they are indispensable pointers in this regard.

In the question concerning the essential constitution of prescientific Dasein we must furthermore distinguish between the conception that such a Dasein has of itself and the conception that emerges through a reconstructive interpretation. For the latter, the former belongs as part of its object, as the explicit self-interpretation proper to prescientific Dasein. For us here, the issue cannot, of course, be that of a detailed unfurling of this problem but merely one of characterizing a few main features of prescientific Dasein that will serve to set it into relief.

By prescientific Dasein, we understand Dasein whose truth (unconcealment) is not fundamentally determined in part by scientific knowledge. That is not to say that such Dasein would not have forms of awareness or knowledge at its disposal: to the contrary, it has knowledge of an altogether original kind. Uncovered—in the sense in which we are using the term—are the land in tilling the field, the sea in voyaging; cultivating the land and voyaging impart knowledge of the weather, the seasons, knowledge of the stars, reckoning with time. There likewise belongs to such Dasein the art of healing human beings; everything has emerged in the direct confrontation of Dasein with the beings to which, qua Dasein, it always already sees itself referred. What we have initially listed are neither the first or only things; before this, and prevailing throughout everything, the whole of beings is manifest in a mythology that provides orientation about the course of the world and the fates of human beings. Such orientation does not consist in certain bits of knowledge or statements but rather finds its primary concretion in cult and sacrifice. In the early period, all remaining modes of comportment and forms of uncovering beings such as tilling the field, voyaging, the art of healing, and knowledge of the stars are permeated by this fundamental mythical conception of Dasein as a whole. This specific prescientific disclosedness of Dasein has also always already come to word, has spoken itself out in the word, μῦθος, and as such also already creates for itself its own form of tradition, prior to all historiography as the science of history. That which we call art likewise stands entirely in service of this determination and interpretation of Dasein. Furthermore, being with one another in tribe and lineage is regulated by sacred custom; birth, death, and afterlife find their interpretation in terms of the whole of beings thus disclosed.

In this way, what is present at hand, ready to hand, the Dasein-with of others, and one's own Dasein are manifest in prescientific Dasein, and all of this pervaded by beings as a whole and their mythical powers, which are conceived in different ways each time (cf. the mana idea). Prescientific Dasein thus has its own specific truth. Now, if science is one kind of truth, and if it presupposes prescientific truth, then with and through it, a transformation of truth must occur. Accordingly, the essence of science will become visible if we focus on the changeover from prescientific to scientific Dasein. In asking after this changeover as a transformation of the truth of Dasein, we are asking about the emergence of science. We are not, however, investigating how individual sciences have emerged and developed in the course of history. Nor are we asking historiographically concerning the factical causes, motivations, or various stages in the factical development of a science, just as little as concerning the causes of the factical standstill or even decline of individual disciplines.

Asking about the emergence of science for us now means: What belongs to the inner possibility of what we call science? What must necessarily happen if science is to arise, quite apart from how it is factically in individual instances?

This changeover from prescientific to scientific Dasein can seemingly be readily determined; we need only compare with one another the starting point and end point of this occurrence, that is, what initially suggests itself to us, assessing prescientific Dasein from the perspective of our scientific Dasein. Even though we can arrive at prescientific Dasein only by way of reconstruction, we do, after all, have scientific Dasein at our disposal insofar as we ourselves in our factical Dasein are scientifically determined. Yet here, a deception can easily creep in. For the fact that our Dasein is factically determined by science does not yet guarantee that we would also know and comprehend what science is. What we today give that name may indeed be genuine science; yet it does not directly provide us with the concept of science. Perhaps a certain acquaintance with science is required in order to determine its essence; yet such acquaintance is by no means sufficient. We are thus fundamentally no better situated with regard to scientific Dasein than with respect to prescientific Dasein; indeed, the danger of a misinterpretation of the essence of scientific Dasein is perhaps even greater, precisely because we ourselves are scientifically determined. There is the danger that we take certain external and prominent features of science to be its essence. We must construct the essence of science and of scientific Dasein no less than that of prescientific Dasein.

This is an odd situation: what we want to compare, we do not even have; for the purpose of considering this changeover from prescientific to scientific Dasein, we have neither the starting point nor the end point. For now, I am drawing attention only in passing to this altogether peculiar aspect of our situation and of our manner of proceeding; we do not wish to reflect further about it, but to actually proceed and to venture something remarkable, namely, to arrive at what is to be compared precisely by comparing what we fundamentally do not yet have.

In comparing prescientific Dasein from the perspective of scientific Dasein, one thing is manifestly clear. With regard to its truth, that is, to the kind of unconcealment of beings, prescientific Dasein rests extensively on naive errors, superstition, arbitrariness, and lack of refinement. Only science brings the genuine truth about beings. A simple example can make this clear, for instance the manner and way in which the sun is uncovered. For the Greeks of the early period, the sun was the god Helios, the god who travels through the heavens in his fiery chariot and descends in Oceanus. Later this depiction loses force; the sun becomes a disc that traverses its orbit. Soon the disc shows itself to be a fiery globe, a ball that moves around the earth. After that, the earth in turn becomes a globe that moves around the sun as center, and finally, this solar system is only one among many others. Our sun then came to be extensively studied through the solar spectrum.

Where, then, is the truth? Is contemporary physics and astronomy precisely able to claim that it uncovers the cosmos just as it is? Where is the criterion for judging that the contemporary view of the solar system is the only true one, and thus truer than the earlier view and especially the mythical view? Yet do we not continue to speak of the setting of the sun? Is that just a way of talking? Do we not actually see the sun set, and does not this unconcealment of the sun govern our everyday Dasein?

c) Scientific truth

By what right do we simply decree that myth is superstition? Yet if we have no right to do so, are there then different truths with regard to beings, and how do they relate to one another? If we concede, or understand in principle, that even in myth there lies a specific truth, then manifestly there no longer exists any difference in essence between prescientific and scientific truth; rather the two are only different by degree, namely, insofar as in science there is more knowledge to be found, individual points are determined more precisely and better grounded in their interconnection. But at what level, then, does scientific truth begin, and where does prescientific truth cease? Does not precisely the truth of myth have the advantage of a uniform coherence, and does not its power rest in part on the fact that everything is coherently grounded, whereas in many of the sciences we can no longer see the actuality of beings for sheer facts?

Scientific truth is thus neither the sole truth nor the highest one. Nor can the essence of this truth lie in the fact that the greatest possible mass of facts becomes manifest in it or that the determination of those facts brings with it a high degree of precision. Through such comparisons, we shall not arrive at the essence of science or at a characterization of the essence of scientific Dasein; we see at most that it does not without further ado have that distinction that one would like to accord it on the basis of a certain Enlightenment mentality.

Yet how else are we to shed light on the essence of science and of scientific Dasein? Science is a kind of truth; truth belongs to Dasein. Insofar as Dasein exists, it is in the truth. If we hold fast to this idea of truth, and thus take science to be one kind of being-in-the-truth, we immediately hit on something familiar: science is simply a particular attitude. We have known since antiquity that science is a so-called theoretical attitude—theoretical as distinct from practical. Theory and praxis mean: mere thinking and speculating on the one side—the carrying out and applying of thought and knowledge on the other.

Yet science is not just one mere mode of comportment but a possible fundamental stance held by human existence, a βίος, θεωρητικὸς βίος. Because not only the idea of Western science but also that of philosophy is essentially determined starting from here, we must discuss more precisely what antiquity understood by this—admittedly here only the most essential points for our particular intent. A more encompassing discussion would have to answer a series of questions that are intrinsically connected.

§23. Science as a possible fundamental stance of human existence. Βίος θεωρητικός—Vita contemplativa

At the pinnacle of the culture of antiquity, the theoretical stance represents the highest ideal of life, one that then had an effect on the entire development of Western science; so long as Western science exists, this βίος is thus "alive." This ideal of life repeatedly pressed for a renewal—the only question is "how?" and whether it was adequately interpreted.

If our contemporary scientist has consciously become different, if he has distanced himself from the origin, and if we are no longer prepared at all for the interpretation of antiquity, then the attempt to renew this ideal of life once more in a so-called neo-humanism must meet with the gravest reservations. It remains a feeble affair on the part of scholars, who perhaps flock around a journal ("*Antiquity*"), but it fails to reach into the roots of contemporary existence; to the contrary, one wants to evade the abyssal character of contemporary existence instead of hearing the open calls or first preparing our hearing to do so.

The βίος θεωρητικός as a problem entails several questions: 1. How did this fundamental stance of Dasein arise? 2. How did the self-interpretation of this βίος transpire? 3. What conception of life, Dasein, existence underlies its emergence and interpretation? 4. How is this βίος set off from others, and what rank does it have in relation to the others? 5. What are the particular metaphysical presuppositions for the conception of this βίος as the supreme one?

In terms of these five questions, only the main issue can be clarified in what follows. First, the elucidation of several words is necessary and unavoidable, providing pointers for understanding the issue. Θεωρητικὸς βίος, *vita contemplativa*, is the fundamental contemplative stance of Dasein. Βίος means "life," whence the word "biology"; "zoology" is derived from ζωή. The human being is ζῷον λόγον ἔχον, the *animal rationale*. Βίος and ζωή both name life, but βίος often has a distinctive meaning: Biography, life story, "life" not in the biological or zoological sense but qua "Dasein," existence. Βίος Ἰησοῦ, the "life of Jesus," is a narrative, depicting the story of his life. In our case, the issue is not the narrative of a life story, nor such a life story itself as factical, with all its events and circumstances, but rather the fundamental orientation of a Dasein insofar as it is determined by an essential stance that it can assume for itself, a possible fundamental stance of human existence. Constitutive for this βίος is προαίρεσις, anticipation, the free anticipation of a particular possibility of Dasein. To Dasein, there belong several βίοι and the possibility of choosing between different fundamental orientations.

Θεωρητικός, θεωρός, θεωρία refer etymologically to θέα and Ϝόρ (ὁράω). Initially, θεωρός refers to the spectator who is present at something that offers a view, for example, one who visits the festivities of the Olympian Games; θεωρεῖν means to look at, to contemplate, to be absorbed in the look of something, to tarry in its overwhelming spectacle, thus in particular θεωρῆσαι τὸν οὐρανὸν καὶ τὴν περὶ τὸν ὅλον κόσμον τάξιν.[3]

In Herodotus (I, 29), *theoria* means contemplation of the world.

In Plato, θεωρεῖν is the contemplating and observing of the sensuous and suprasensuous world. The concept of the Platonic Idea grew out of this fundamental stance of *theoria*, of θεωρεῖν. Θεωρητικός is not yet used by Plato; it is first used by Aristotle as the ability to comport oneself in such a way, this contemplating as a possibility.

Βίος θεωρητικός is thus a new fundamental stance of human Dasein as a tarrying contemplating of the whole of the world. Aristotle gives θεωρία the sense of comportment that is "theoretical" (in the Greek sense). The word θεωρητικός is coined by him. He sees in θεωρία the authentic movedness of life, the purest sense of ἐνέργεια, that is, the "first" movement as such, τὸ θεῖον. The toward-which is the ἀεί.

It is characteristic of the etymology provided by ancient philologists following Aristotle[4] to relate θεός and θεωρία to the contemplating of divine things, to the overwhelming, to God, θεός. Soon after Aristotle, the Aristotelian concept of God itself comes to be reinterpreted in a religious-ethical sense or provides the categorial structure for this. The development of θεωρία in the Antiochian skeptical school then leads to "theoretical" now not only being distinguished from "practical" but from its association with faith, that is, it is understood in the sense of "from reason alone." The etymology that Alexander of Aphrodisias provides is thus understandable and is an important document for the history of the meaning of the Aristotelian concept of God and of the sense of θεωρία: τὸ γὰρ θεωρεῖν / καὶ ἀπ᾽αὐτοῦ τοῦ ὀνόματος δῆλον / ὡς ἔστι περὶ τὴν τῶν θείων ὄψιν τε καὶ γνῶσιν· / σημαίνει γὰρ τὸ ὁρᾶν τὰ θεῖα.[5] In the Antiochian exegetical school (which philosophically again itself stood under a purely Aristotelian influence), θεωρία is equivalent to ἱστορία; ἱστορία: witnessing of beings, not in the

---

3. Hermann Diels, *Die Fragmente der Vorsokratiker. Griechisch und deutsch*, vol. 1, 4th ed. (Berlin: Weidmann, 1922), 382. Cf. also the reports about Anaxagoras (Life and Teaching) (ibid., 375ff.).

4. Alexander of Aphrodisias, *In Aristotelis Analyticorum Priorum: Librum I Commentarium*, ed. M. Wallies (Berlin: Reimer, 1883), Prooemium, 3, lines 20–21.

5. Ibid.

special sense of the "historical" but also including events of nature, earthquakes, and the like.

θεωρία as equivalent to ἱστορία is scientific investigation of facts, in contrast to ἀλληγορία as mystical interpretation in terms of the history of salvation, Eriugena. Typology σκιὰ τῶν μελλόντων versus σῶμα (the actual).[6]

The Latin translation of θεῖα is *vita contemplativa*; *templum*, τέμνειν, τέμενος (*tempus*) is the demarcated precinct as the locality of the augur, and at the same time, the vault of the heavens in which he demarcated regions and determined the signs of the gods. *Contemplari* means: "to embrace with one's look the holy region on earth and in the heavens." Later, it is not the heavens that are ultimate but God; it therefore now means: contemplating and looking upon God, immersion in the light of the Godhead. *Contemplari* becomes a specifically religious and theological expression; *vita contemplativa* and *vita activa* designate religious forms of comportment.

Thomas Aquinas: *Contemplatio aliquando capitur stricte pro actu intellectus divina meditantis et sic contemplatio est sapientiae actus, alio modo communiter pro omni actu, quo quis a negotiis exterioribus sequestratus soli deo vacat, quod quidem contingit dupliciter, vel inquantum homo Deum loquentem in Scripturis audit, quod fit per lectionem, vel inquantum Deo loquitur, quod fit per orationem.*[7]

Contemplation is on the one hand conceived in the strict sense for that act of the intellect which, *divina meditantis*, meditates on the divine, so to speak. *Contemplatio* is thus the proper *actus* of wisdom, of *sapientia*. In a broader sense, however, *contemplatio* is taken to be that act in which, freed from external affairs, one frees oneself, one's time, for God alone. In both the narrower and the broader sense, *contemplari* means to contemplate, meditation on divine things. This latter meaning of *contemplari* can in turn be twofold, the reading of scripture and prayer.

In the Middle Ages already, there came to be distinguished from the concept of *contemplatio* that concept that is used in Modernity to designate the theoretical, namely, the concept of *speculatio, speculari*. When in German Idealism Fichte, Schelling, and Hegel speak of speculation, they mean nothing other than

---

6. Cf. H. Kihn, *Über θεωρία und ἀλληγορία nach den verlorenen hermeneutischen Schriften der Antiochier*, Theolog. Quartalsschrift 62 (1880), 531–58; cf. Kihn, *Theodorus Magnesia und Innitius Afr. als Exegeten* (Freiburg: Herder, 1880), Instituta regularia divinae legis (Bdtg.-f.M.A.).

    Literature: Paul Boesch, *"θεωρός": Untersuchungen zur Epangelie griechischer Feste*, Diss. (Berlin, 1908); Franz Boll, *Vita Contemplativa* (Sitzungsber. d. Heidelb. Akademie der Wissenschaften, Phil. hist. Klasse, Jg. 1920, Abh. 8, esp. 23ff.). Georg Curtius, in his *Grundzügen der griechischen Etymologie*, 4th ed. (Leipzig: Teubner, 1873), 253, connects θαϝ with the Doric θᾶμαι, θαέομαι, θεάομαι, "astonishment."

7. Thomas Aquinas, *Scriptum super libros sententiarum magistri Petri Lombardi episcopi Parisiensis (1253–1255)* (Paris: Lethielleux, 1929), 4 sent., dist. 15, quaest. 4, art. 1, solutio 2, ad primum.

theoretical knowing. The distinction between *contemplatio* and *speculatio* consists in the fact that in *contemplatio* as a religious stance God is directly contemplated, whereas *speculatio* is distinguished by the fact that it *divina in creaturis inspicit*, that is, contemplates the divine insofar as it makes itself known in what is created, *quasi in speculo*, as if in a mirror, as though the created were a mirror of God. Here *speculari*, which goes back to the Latin *species*, aspect—all concepts from the sphere of seeing—although still oriented toward divine things, acquires the tendency to mean that knowing which the human being accomplishes of his own accord, a knowing that is thus not primarily determined by faith. Speculation then means a free reflecting on things. Later, and also in Kant, speculative simply becomes a designation for the theoretical: speculative metaphysics as distinct from practical metaphysics.

One must keep in view these fundamental meanings of the word "theoretical" and the context in which the word arose in order to understand, on the one hand, the direction in which the interpretation of science moves with the aid of the so-called theoretical stance, yet on the other hand so as also to be able to clarify the extent to which a limit is found within this interpretation of science, which means so as to make clear that we must take decisive steps in order to attain a more original understanding of the essence of science by contrast with the interpretation of science that has become customary and altogether self-evident since antiquity.

The initial task is to clarify what βίος θεωρητικός means as distinct from other possible βίοι.

Aristotle speaks of the βίοι right at the beginning of *Nicomachean Ethics* A3, and does so in a characteristic context. The task is to delimit the whole that originally and authentically determines human existence as such. τὸ ἀγαθόν, εὐδαιμονία, ζωή as πρᾶξις, not ποίησις. πρᾶξις is that acting that attains its end in the one who is himself acting; the human being is an end in himself. Yet what in the human being and in being human is the ἀκρότατον ἀγαθόν, that for whose sake the fundamental possibility of human being may be taken hold of and actualized in accordance with his essence? Upon what path is this ἀγαθόν to be found?

The βίος θεωρητικός is analyzed not in connection with clarifying the essence of science, but rather in the context of the question concerning the ἀνθρώπινον ἀγαθόν; yet this is also enquired after in *Metaphysics* A1 and A2. τὸ γὰρ ἀγαθὸν καὶ τὴν εὐδαιμονίαν οὐκ ἀλόγως ἐοίκασιν, ἐκ τῶν βίων ὑπλαμβάνειν . . . (Nic. Eth. A3, 1095 b14f.).[8] That which underlies and determines the βίοι is to be grasped. For this purpose, those βίοι are suited that especially stand out from the

---

8. *Aristotelis Ethica Nicomachea*, recognovit Franciscus Susemihl (Lipsiae in aedibus B. G. Teubneri, 1882).

others. τρεῖς γάρ εἰσι μάλιστα οἱ προύχοντες, ὅ τε νῦν εἰρημένος [ἀπολαυστικός] καὶ ὁ πολιτικὸς καὶ τρίτος ὁ θεωρητικός (1095 b17–19). Of these τέλη, it holds true that δι' αὐτὰ γὰρ ἀγαπᾶται (1096 a8f.).

Τἀγαθὸν δὲ οἰκεῖόν τι καὶ δυσαφαίρετον εἶναι μαντευόμεθα (1095 b25f.). When we seek the supreme Good, we already intimate and presume that it is something that is at home in us ourselves qua human beings and can be wrested from us only with difficulty. Accordingly, it is a possession that lies within existence as such. Cf. *Nicomachean Ethics* A6: τὸ ἄριστον: 1. ζωή, 2. πρᾶξίς τις, 3. καὶ τὸ εὖ, the ἀγαθὸν that is determined through simple apprehending, in which the supreme possibility is actualized. τέλος is that wherein something is completed, yet in this very completion first becomes actual and does not cease, for instance. εὐπραξία, αὐταρκές is an acting and existing that attains its end within itself, that is, is completed precisely when it purely and simply acts. Therein lies the distinction between ποίησις as productive activity and πρᾶξις as existentiell action. In the producing of something, the work is separated off and present at hand in itself. For this reason, the ἀγαθόν cannot lie in the first-named βίος; in this βίος, human beings are—like cattle—given over to enjoyment; "merely enjoying" too is indeed also something for the sake of itself, but it is possible only in giving oneself over to the occasions and objects of possible enjoyment, inconstantly and without duration.

The second βίος seeks the ἀγαθόν in public esteem, τιμή, however δοκεῖ . . . ἐν τοῖς τιμῶσι μᾶλλον εἶναι ἢ ἐν τῷ τιμωμένῳ (1095 b24f.). What is sought there is more up to the one who confers esteem than to the one who attains it, that is, the latter is dependent on public opinion, is in a hidden manner a slave to such opinion. Since here too Dasein does not have full independence of itself, the ἀγαθόν cannot lie here, for there is no possibility for this. Both βίοι fail to take hold of the ἀγαθὸν ἀκρότατον. τρίτος δ'ἐστὶν ὁ θεωρητικός, ὑπὲρ οὗ τὴν ἐπίσκεψιν ἐν τοῖς ἐπομένοις ποιησόμεθα (1096 a4f.). Cf. *Nicomachean Ethics* Z13 and K7ff.

§24. The original belonging together of theory and praxis in θεωρεῖν as making beings manifest

The fundamental theoretical stance is supreme. Why? In the *Nicomachean Ethics* K6, we read (1176 b1ff.): [εὐδαιμονία] εἰς ἐνέργειάν τινα θετέον . . . [1. καθ'αὑτάς, 2. δι'ἕτερα.] καθ'αὑτὰς δ'εἰσὶν αἱρεταὶ ἀφ' ὧν μηδὲν ἐπιζητεῖται παρὰ τὴν ἐνέργειαν.

K7: εὐδαιμονία κατ' ἀρετὴν ἐνέργεια, εὔλογον κατὰ τὴν κρατίστην (1177 a12f.). κρατίστη τε γὰρ αὕτη ἐστὶν ἡ ἐνέργεια . . . [θεωρητική] . . . ὁ νοῦς τῶν ἐν ἡμῖν . . . περὶ ἃ ὁ νοῦς (1177 a19ff.). θεῖον ὁ νοῦς πρὸς τὸν ἄνθρωπον (1177 b30). The fundamental theoretical stance is that πρᾶξις in which the human being can be authentically human. It should be noted that θεωρία is not only a πρᾶξις in general but the most authentic one.

Aristotle may have sensed that at first sight there is something irreconcilable here, in θεωρία as ἄριστος βίος and the latter πρακτικός. In *Metaphysics* A1 and A2, Aristotle develops in detail how the theoretical stance is formed by increasingly disregarding "practical" utility and use and aiming solely at contemplating beings in themselves, μὴ πρὸς χρῆσιν. How should θεωρία still be practical, then? Surely it must be, if ἄριστος βίος ὁ πρακτικός? Aristotle responds quite unambiguously in *Politics* H (VII) 3, 1325 b16: ἀλλὰ τὸν πρακτικὸν οὐκ ἀναγκαῖον εἶναι πρὸς ἑτέρους, καθάπερ οἴονταί τινες, οὐδὲ τὰς διανοίας εἶναι μόνας ταύτας πρακτικάς, τὰς τῶν ἀποβαινόντων χάριν γινομένας ἐκ τοῦ πράττειν. ἀλλὰ πολὺ μᾶλλον τὰς αὐτοτελεῖς καὶ τὰς αὐτῶν ἕνεκεν θεωρίας καὶ διανοήσεις· ἡ γὰρ εὐπραξία τέλος, ὥστε καὶ πρᾶξίς τις.[9] "Nor is it necessary for the one acting to act in relation to others, as some think; nor is it the case that only those deliberations would be actions that occur with a view to what springs forth from an action, but it is much rather the case that that action is practical which presents its own completion within itself, and those contemplations that are undertaken for their own sake. For the τέλος of the human being is εὐπραξία."

From this passage, we may conclude that the essence of action does not consist in its being related to others; not only that thinking is "practical" which aims at and is undertaken with a view to some practical accomplishment that results from it, the producing of something. Rather, "practical," that is, acting, πολὺ μᾶλλον, to a much greater degree, is that contemplating and determining that is αὐτοτελής αὐτῶν ἕνεκεν, finding its completion within itself and undertaken for the sake of itself. The completion lies in the highest possible good action, that is, in the how, and for this reason, in order for this how to be possible, a corresponding what of possible action must be there.

From this it is clear that πρακτικός and πρᾶξις, practical and praxis, do not mean being active in applying and using something, but rather acting and action. The practical is not the work, the consequence of the action, but is the action itself. We precisely must not associate the "practical" in the contemporary sense with πρᾶξις. Authentic action is precisely that which does not first acquire its meaning through its possible use or so-called practical value but that which rather actualizes that movedness that lies within acting—accomplishing its work by the fact that qua ἐνέργεια, it is itself τέλος.

We thus come to see that thoughtful contemplation is in any case an action. Yet why should θεωρία, precisely, be the supreme βίος, the εὐπραξία pure and simple? To what extent is θεωρεῖν, the theoretical stance, the supreme πρᾶξις, authentic action? Initially one could say that all contemplating is surely the contemplating of something, of beings. Therefore, this action too is referred to

---

9. *Aristotelis Politica*, nova impressio, ed. Franciscus Susemihl (Lipsiae: Bibliotheca Teubneriana, 1894).

something to which it relates. Furthermore, we heard that the ἀγαθόν ἀκρότατον is supposed to be enduring; yet beings change, after all, arise and pass away, and offer no enduring possession without further ado. How would Aristotle have to respond here? Certainly, θεωρεῖν relates to τὰ ὄντα; yet only that which never is not, that is, which is always in being, ἀεὶ ὄν, is in being in the authentic sense. Only insofar as pure contemplation directs itself toward that which always is does it give itself, as this tarrying alongside what endures, the character of constancy.

Yet admittedly this has only shown more emphatically that θεωρία as πρᾶξις is referred to ἕτερον, to something else. To what extent can it then be αὐτοτελής, and only on the basis of this characteristic be a οἰκεῖον ἀγαθὸν ἀνθρώπου? To what extent is θεωρία a πρᾶξις αὐτοτελής, directed toward beings, and yet τέλος within Dasein, completion within itself, when surely it is precisely directed toward beings, away from itself, from the action? Precisely the essence of action, in order for it itself to be able to be as τέλος, indeed need not be grasped for this. But the objects are, after all, ἕτερον.

What character does θεωρεῖν then have? In *Nicomachean Ethics* Z, Aristotle shows quite clearly that it consists in ἀληθεύειν, in the making manifest of beings; in this πρᾶξις, beings are not worked upon; rather, the unconcealment of beings is brought about by acting, that is, the action is a bringing to happen of unconcealment, of truth. Truth, however, is a determination of the essence of Dasein—according to our interpretation, not the traditional one—as an existing, acting Dasein and being-in-the-truth. θεωρεῖν is indeed action of such a kind that, as making manifest, it simply lets manifestness happen, manifestness that, as itself belonging to Dasein, brings Dasein to what it can be insofar as, qua existing, it is in the truth, an essential possibility of Dasein. When this happening itself grasps itself as "end" and completion, then there happens precisely the manifestness of beings.

Certainly, θεωρεῖν is directed toward beings; certainly this action is thus directed toward something that it itself is not, but θεωρεῖν does not have as its goal to produce beings, as it were, or to shape them or work on them in some sense or other but, as the term says, merely to contemplate them. What is at stake is simply knowledge of beings as such, that is, the manifestness of beings that arises in purely contemplative knowledge. It now becomes clear how decisive the correct working out of the concept of truth is; only now does ἑώρακεν, ὁρᾶ become understandable: precisely to let the being be, just as it is; that means, however, to grant it unconcealment, to hold oneself in such manifestness as contemplative Dasein.

Beings in their unconcealment, τὸ ὂν ἀληθές, are that for the sake of which θεωρεῖν acts. This is why, when they speak of the fact that contemplative knowledge investigates beings, the Greeks frequently say that it investigates truth, but that means in the Greek sense: beings in their unconcealment. Truth in this sense is the τέλος, that wherein this action as being-in-the-truth completes itself. ἀγαθόν, οὗ ἕνεκα, that for the sake of which the action is done, is unconcealment, yet this as an essential determination of Dasein itself.

We cannot discuss in detail why the βίος θεωρητικός became the supreme life for the Greeks (Plato, Aristotle) and whether it is so without qualification and in what sense. For us, the essential result remains that θεωρεῖν stands in an essential connection to πρᾶξις (existence, Dasein) and truth, unconcealment, and specifically knowledge of the ὄν as ἀεὶ ὄν, of that which always is. An ambiguity still remains: (a) not simply a particular region of beings that have this manner of being—fundamental lack of clarity about ontology as universal ontics; but rather (b) the being of every being as "essence," that which always persists in each being, that which is always already encountered in it.

Yet we already analyzed this in connection with the traditional definition of science, in grasping more radically the traditional concept of truth and seeing that science is a kind of truth, one way of being-in-the-truth. But what we are seeking is precisely what is unique to this manner and way. Does depicting it as "theoretical" provide sufficient information?

Theoretical means: contemplative comportment—yet we do not call all contemplation or meditating on something science. (Meditative Dasein is not science.) Even if we regard contemplation in a distinctive sense as immersion and rapture, as the comportment of the mystic, this latter term already indicates that such *contemplatio* is very far removed from science, and indeed is separate from it in principle, if science is indeed the arch-enemy of all mysticism.

Yet even if one grasps theoretical comportment in a nonmystical sense and interprets "theoretical" as the mere contemplation of things, this does not capture scientific comportment. For in the sciences there is also "practical," technical work—as all experimental research documents but also, for instance, philological and historiographical work with manuscript editions or archeological excavations. Such activities belong to the said sciences; they are not extrinsic measures, but are demanded, rather, by the objects of the science in question.

We thus see once more that science, which one calls the theoretical attitude, is, first, practical as action, and second, practical in the sense of technical work and accomplishments. The term "theoretical" covers over precisely this dual nature of action pertaining to science. Still, the term cannot be accidental. It indicates one essential moment of science, without grasping it at its core. For this core is not grasped even if we interpret "theoretical" as "merely contemplative" while including its practical character or even if we interpret the "merely contemplative" as "for the sake of knowledge," "for the sake of truth." Ultimately, we shall come close to "theoretical" comportment and its essence only by asking concerning πρᾶξις, concerning the specific nature of action pertaining to knowledge for the sake of truth.

§25. Construction of the essence of science

a) Being-in-the-truth for the sake of truth

All comportment of Dasein—as we already know—is as such a being-in-the-truth. Yet not all being-in-the-truth is as yet expressly such for the sake of truth. Holding oneself in the manifestness of beings and comporting oneself toward those beings does not necessarily entail expressly being aware of this manifestness as such or indeed being concerned with it as such. Knowing for the sake of truth is accordingly a quite specific holding oneself in unconcealment—for the sake of an unconcealment of beings themselves.

With this, we arrive at the central problem of an interpretation of the essence of science. The question must be posed: Where do we find what is distinctive about that manner of existence of Dasein in which such a thing as being-in-the-truth for the sake of truth occurs? What does this entail? We can also formulate this problem in a manner that makes it evident that an orientation toward the "theoretical" and the meaning of this word fails to attain the problem. The question to be asked is then: What is the originary action, the primordial action on the part of Dasein, in which such a thing as the seemingly praxis-free, merely contemplative attitude of science becomes possible? In this first formulation the question concerning an existential concept of science is also clearly expressed. We shall now attempt the construction of the essence of science.

Science means: Being in the unconcealment of beings for the sake of unconcealment. We shall start from this last aspect: for the sake of truth means for the sake of the unconcealment of beings. Existing Dasein is concerned with beings being unconcealed and with comporting itself toward beings in their unconcealment. What is at stake is truth, that is, not primarily a valid statement but rather the unconcealment of beings themselves. The task is to let beings be what and how they are.

Yet have we not also already encountered this letting be of beings when characterizing our dwelling alongside the things around us? Yet this comportment toward things cannot be called scientific. Certainly, in all comportment toward beings there lies a certain letting be of beings; yet now the concern is expressly with the unconcealment of beings, that is, that beings come to manifest themselves in themselves and that this becoming manifest should occur. The letting be of beings now does not simply lie within the comportment of Dasein, rather, Dasein as existing transposes itself precisely into this letting be of beings. Dasein accomplishes a particular fundamental existentiell movement in which it expressly gives itself in advance the task of letting beings in themselves attain their legitimacy and come to word. Beings are indeed also manifest already without and prior to science; indeed, that letting be of beings that is supposed to characterize science, as a quite unique one, must even always already make use of the manifestness of beings. For only by doing so can it let these, namely, beings themselves, be in themselves. Beings must already be manifest prior to, and for, the specifically scientific letting be. Science must be able to find beings before it. It is part of science that it always already has beings lying before it, and indeed as manifest in some way. We name these beings that lie before it, and that science can therefore always already find before it, the *positum*.

However, if beings already lie before us, after all, and indeed as manifest, what, then, is the purpose of science? Yet if science is possible, then despite all manifestness of beings in which Dasein always already holds itself, there must still exist a specific concealment of beings that only science as such overcomes.

Let us take an elementary example: In land cultivation, one of the many things that manifests itself is that the soil offers resistance when plowing, and so the plowshare must accordingly have a certain hardness and durability. This connection between the soil and the plowshare, however, is not further considered as such or even contemplated at all; it is simply familiar within a certain usufruct and working of the soil, of the earth. The same relationship of pressure and counterpressure can be encountered when building a house, where a corresponding solidity of the foundation is demanded, and so too with the piers in bridge building and similarly in many other contexts of dealing with things in using or making them.

In our dealings with things a certain knowing our way around with them thus develops: As a rule, matters stand in such and such a way with these things. This regularity, however, appears less as a feature of things themselves than as a guide for how to comport ourselves toward them. Things are indeed manifest in a certain way, and yet in this they need not fully present what they are in themselves. For the possibility exists of focusing on the said relations of pressure and counterpressure without regard to the fact that they are taken into account in a process of use. These relations can emerge as ones that pertain to every material thing, to every mass, and indeed in such a way that they are subject to a universal law of gravity.

What has then happened when beings, material things, emerge in such a way? What must have happened for things to be able to manifest themselves in such a way? Is it sufficient to say that practical, technical experience has been extended beyond its narrower perspective of land cultivation, house building, and bridge construction? Yet what does extend mean here? Does it mean, for instance, that corresponding plowshares and foundations must be produced in other places and in relation to other objects too, that all human beings must take this rule into account? Here, however, only the field of application of the rule is extended, and there is no talk of mass, density, or gravity. A mere extending of practical-technical experience is thus of no help.

Here there is indeed no talk at all anymore of a rule for comportment in the technical negotiation of matters. Accordingly, what is at issue is not an extension of the rule's field of application. If an extension plays a primary role here in general, then it is manifestly surely in the sense in which we can say that these relations are present at hand not only where we have to deal with soil and stone in our practical labors but also in places we do not reach in our activities and do not even need to reach. At issue now is no longer merely an extension in the field of application of rules for comportment—for we are also speaking now of things that cannot even be affected by such comportment nor need to be—rather, the entire field that is now being spoken of shows itself in another light; the region of our most proximate practical-technical labor is now only a small section of a more comprehensive region. The insight now dawns that these practical measures are taken because ultimately all material things have such properties.

In the extension now being considered, it is so little a matter of extending practical measures of comportment that practical-technical comportment is precisely disregarded and we look only to how things are in themselves. In other words, the presumed extension of technical experience is fundamentally a complete transformation of our fundamental orientation toward beings. Yet what is the significance of this simply looking at material things and taking distance from any practical-technical labor?

b) The originary action. The letting be of beings

Does this "simply" mean that we are no longer involved with things and refrain from practical dealings? However, the beings with which we are dealing do not already manifest themselves in themselves in the way we have characterized merely through our ceasing to handle them. To the contrary, doing nothing, as the interruption of an activity, may manifest things all the more insistently with respect to their wanting to be dealt with, that is, as objects that demand to be worked upon.

"Simply looking at" things in themselves is by no means identical to merely doing nothing. The "simply" does not at all mean something lesser or a restriction, something negative, but rather something eminently positive. Simply looking at means becoming singularly focused on things presenting themselves in themselves. This expresses the fact that things do not at all do this of their own accord, no matter how tangibly they may be present at hand in themselves. The opportunity must, as it were, be created for them to manifest themselves as the beings that they are. This is the originary action. Contemplative tarrying alongside things is not some idleness; yet presumably it requires leisure to develop an activity in the supreme sense.

Yet what is that supposed to mean, that we must help things to manifestness? If beings are to show themselves in themselves, then we are not to undertake anything with them; we are not allowed to alter anything about the beings but are precisely to step back so that they, beings, can manifest themselves of their own accord. Precisely now the task is solely for us to leave beings just as they are and to take them as they present themselves.

An activity is therefore found within the action of science that has the character of a stepping back in the face of beings. This strange activity of stepping back is starting to become alien to us today, because we are increasingly of the opinion that "action" and "activity" are found solely or predominantly where there is bustle, where business gets conducted or force gets enacted, and because we are forgetting that reverence in the face of things demands a much greater effort of devotion than all overrunning and leveling out.

Precisely this letting be of beings in which the issue is solely the unconcealment of beings thus ultimately entails a particular "effort," if indeed a mere "interruption" (doing nothing) does not yet let beings become manifest in themselves. Mere contemplative tarrying is therefore not some quietistic comportment. Yet what does it mean that we are to let beings be in a distinctive sense, as that which they are? We cannot annihilate them, after all, and if that is not possible, then letting-be also has no sense. That beings are what and how they are is not, after all, something they have through our grace. They lie already before us, they are a *positum*, and we are only able to find them before us. What more, then, can letting be mean?

This is the same question that we already posed earlier, when we asked: What must happen in order for things to become manifest in the new way we have depicted? Things no longer showed themselves as soil, foundation, or bridge piers but as material bodies, centers of mass that stand in definite relations. Beings show themselves in another light; that means, what beings are is now determined differently; they are no longer soil, foundation, piers, but "simply" material things. What they now are, however, contains in itself a series of determinations: material thing in motion, moved in the sense of change of place in time. Accompanying this different way of determining what they are is a different conception of how they are: they are no longer ready to hand for practical-technical involvement, but—outside of this—simply material bodies merely present at hand, beings qua nature. What and how things are has been determined differently; the belonging together of these determinations we designate in short as the being of the respective beings.

§26. The change in the understanding of being in the scientific projection. The new determination of beings as nature

Yet how is this different way of determining beings accomplished? We have already seen that it is accompanied by a notable extension of its field, which is no longer restricted to the things of utility closest to us; rather, resistance, pressure, weight, gravity are said of all material things.

Does, then, the new determination of beings as nature arise through an extension of the field, or is, conversely, the extension of the field a necessary consequence of the new way of determining beings? Manifestly, the latter is the case. Merely extending our field of experience always leads only to things of utility; but in this particular way of determining beings as nature something else is surely happening. No matter how many things of utility we compare, we would never arrive at "nature" except by already regarding things in this way in advance. Yet how does this new way of determining beings occur, then, if it does not first arise from an extending but even precedes it? After all, it cannot precede it by first comparing all beings qua natural things; for such comparing already presupposes the new determination of beings. Such comparison would be possible only in this light, if it were to be possible at all.

When we are trying to clarify how this new way of determining beings precedes, we must first of all look more closely at what is happening here. There is a determination of beings qua nature. We are not adding new beings, we are not turning to other things; rather those that are themselves already manifest come to be newly determined and do so with regard to what and how they are, with regard to their being. The beings lying before us are no longer regarded as ready to hand things of use (chalk), no longer as objects of technical manipulation or maintenance but rather as present at hand material bodies. What and how beings are—the what-being and how-being of beings, the constitution of their being—being is determined differently, and indeed in such a way that it now first becomes possible to interrogate beings as that which is present at hand in itself and to do so with regard to what and how they are in particular and individually and under particular factual conditions.

Once again: it is not that another being is added and discovered, rather, the being of those beings already manifest is seen differently in advance, regarded and determined differently, and in such a way that this determination of being precedes the experience of beings. We can illustrate this by way of an instructive example, namely, the emergence of mathematical physics in modernity, as grounded by Galileo. We are not taking this example as authoritative grounding for our interpretation of the essence of science, however, but only as evidence of such factical emergence.

One calls modern physics mathematical physics and sees a characteristic feature of it, compared to medieval physics, in the fact that it proceeds inductively. It observes the facts just as they are, whereas medieval speculation sought to procure a knowledge of nature merely from general concepts. Yet already in antiquity there was a science of nature that observed the facts and likewise in the Middle Ages. Its inductive character does not, therefore, hit on the essence of modern physics. Furthermore, it is said that modern natural science, as distinct from previous science, works with the experiment. Whereas the old science of nature was dependent on contingent observations, in the experiment nature is to a certain degree forced to answer particular questions. Yet we know that the natural science of antiquity also worked with the experiment already, and yet did not have the character that physics attained through Galileo. Third, the distinction consists in the fact that modern physics is mathematical, whereas the medieval knowledge of nature was unable to make any use of mathematics in this sense and was unable to do so because the development of modern mathematics goes together with the rise of mathematical physics.

"Mathematical" here does not in the first instance mean that mathematics calculates and attains precise results in terms of numbers; this is merely a consequence. Mathematics is a way and means of grasping nature as posited in this manner, of bringing the being of nature to expression. Nature is posited as determined and determinable by quantities. *Quantum—extensio*, space, time, movement, force. Modern physics is mathematical because the a priori is determined in a certain way. Each experiment (together with the instruments of measure used in it) is posited and interpreted in light of a prior determination of the being of beings.

Galileo's epochal insight was to recognize that if I want to interrogate nature in what and how it is by way of the experiment, I must first already have a concept of what I understand by "nature," and that all investigation of facts, all experimentation, must be preceded by a delimitation of what is understood as nature. However, Galileo did not pose this question in a purely Platonic way, but rather established a concept of nature whereby nature is conceived as a nexus of bodies in motion, of beings whose fundamental character lies in their spatial and temporal extension, where motion is nothing else than change of place in time. By fundamentally determining nature in this way, the manifold of beings is made directly homogenous, that is, identical in kind, in the sense that nature is determined uniformly in a quantitative-mathematical way with respect to both its spatial and its temporal character.

Yet even with this we do not yet hit on the proper essence of how the ground is laid for mathematical physics. This achievement of Galileo's laid the ground for physics because the mathematical, the ability to determine quantitatively, is nothing other than a determination of the essence of a body as an extended being that is in motion. Mathematical physics became a genuine science because through the nature of the mathematical it determines in advance the constitution of the being of what belongs to a thing of nature. The mathematical character of physics posits a clarified concept of the constitution of the being of those beings that are to be treated here, namely, nature, as the ground of all its experimental investigations. From here we can understand Kant's statement: Any particular doctrine of nature is a science only to the extent that it contains mathematics. This means that a science is a science only insofar as it succeeds in delimiting in advance the essential constitution of those beings that it has as its theme. This is the properly mathematical character of physics.

If one understands Kant's statement in a radical way—not as though all sciences would have to adopt the mathematical method—then it is saying that each science must see to it that the beings that it takes as its object are already adequately determined in advance in their essence, so that every concrete question has a guideline as to what constitutes an object for this science. In terms of the example of mathematical physics, the result is therefore that it is only on the grounds of the mathematical thus understood that something like an experiment is possible. For an experiment is not the arbitrary observation of some process or other but rather the setting forth of a process of nature under such conditions that can be measured with the aid of suitable instruments. What is essential in the experiment is not observation but rather the interpretation of what is observed, of the process occurring here. Such an interpretation presupposes that the process I am observing has already been comprehended in advance as a natural process. This holds not only for physical experiments but indeed for every instrument that I employ in physics. Measuring means taking note of coincidences. Take the clock, for example. Every day we look at the clock and ascertain the time. Is the coinciding, the coincidence of the position of a pointer with a particular mark on the dial supposed to signify a measuring of time? This measuring of time has become so self-evident for us that we do not even notice what a world of presuppositions lies in our looking at the clock. This use of the clock is a measuring of time only if I regard this thing as a clock, that is, oriented toward the measuring of time, toward the sun. Thus, an instrument that serves to measure can be used only if an understanding of nature already underlies such use.

What this discussion is meant to make clear is this: that the way in which beings are determined as nature precedes all concrete observation. I can compare things as things of nature only if I already know in advance what pertains to a thing of nature. It thus becomes manifest that this change in how beings are determined is evidently accomplished as a change in how the constitution of being of those beings is determined, a change in our determining what beings are and how they are. We designate these together as the being of beings. In contrast to things of use, a universal realm of material things called physical nature suddenly shows itself. This changeover therefore rests on a change in how the being of beings is determined and indeed on a change in how being is determined, a change that precedes every concrete experiencing of this being, nature.

Hitherto we have always spoken of the unconcealment of beings, of the fact that we comport ourselves toward beings, and that beings can ultimately also become the object of a science. Now we are suddenly speaking not of beings, but of their being, and of the fact that grasping and determining the constitution of being pertaining to beings makes the latter accessible for scientific knowledge. In addition, we have noted that this new way of determining how the being of beings is constituted precedes the concrete, scientific investigation of beings.

a) How the understanding of being precedes every conceptual comprehending

What does it mean here to apprehend such a thing as being? And indeed, to apprehend being in advance? How is this supposed to make possible precisely the apprehending, that is, the making manifest of beings?

To apprehend the being of beings initially appears to be a strange and unreasonable demand. Beings—certainly, we are familiar with them; after all, we comport ourselves at all times toward manifold kinds of beings. We can thus also easily and assuredly point to beings and thus substantiate what we mean by beings. Houses, humans, trees, the sun, the earth: these are beings that we can appeal to, but being—what are we to think here? Being is manifestly distinct from beings and is not itself something that is; for otherwise we would have to designate it too as a being. "Being"—if we are completely honest and are not deceiving ourselves, then we must concede that there is nothing for us to think here. Being— it indeed looks like nothing, if, after all, it is not supposed to be something that is. That which is not, is nothing. Being would then be the nothing. No lesser a philosopher than Hegel states in his *Science of Logic*, his metaphysics: being and nothing are the same.[10]

In any case, it is indisputable that if we are completely free of illusion, we must concede that with our attempt to grasp something like being we come up empty. So, there is no such thing. This would be a premature conclusion. Perhaps it is only the case that *we* are not now in a position to grasp something like being. However—do we not understand something like being? If I ask: What is that? then everyone will immediately answer: That is a piece of chalk. From this, it becomes clear that you have understood the question. The question was raised of what this thing is, of its what-being. We understand when I say: Today is Friday. The book "is" delivered. We understand this "is" and likewise its variations: was, will be, has been.

A strange state of affairs: on the one hand, we are not in a position to apprehend being, yet, on the other hand, we understand it nevertheless. We understand it not only when we happen to say or hear "is" but rather in all talking, calling, requesting, questioning. When we hear the call "Fire!" this means that fire has broken out, but not simply in the sense of a taking note of something, such as "here it is warm," for instance; rather, the call is at the same time an expression of alarm, of being in a state of alarm, and a plea: Bring yourselves to

---

10. Cf. G. W. F. Hegel, *Wissenschaft der Logik. Erster Teil: Die objektive Logik* (Nürnberg: Schrag, 1812), 75 (First Book, Chapter 1, C. Becoming, note 2).

safety or come and help, and this means: conduct yourselves in such and such a manner, that is, be in such and such a way in your present being. Accordingly, in hearing this call we understand the being of fire and how we ourselves should be, and we understand being present at hand and being-there [*Da-sein*]. Yet we understand it even if we do not express ourselves, and comport ourselves in silence toward beings. We must make this strange situation quite clear to ourselves: in one breath we declare it to be a hopeless demand to apprehend something like being as distinct from beings, and yet we understand it. Understanding the being of beings accordingly does not already mean apprehending such being and above all does not mean the conceptual grasping of being as thus apprehended.

Yet in our initial characterizing of the different manner of determining beings as nature—as distinct from things of use—we pointed not only to the fact that the constitution of the being of beings was determined differently but also to the fact that such determining of being preceded the concrete experience of beings. Not only do we therefore understand something like being, but such understanding being (our understanding of being) is of such a kind as to precede our experience of beings. We say that our understanding of being is pre-cedent, goes ahead compared to our experience of beings. It goes ahead in such a way that we are first able to encounter beings, as it were, in the brightness that emerges from our antecedent understanding of being holding a light before us. We understand being and understand it in advance.

Yet if that is the case, then an understanding of being is not first there when we pursue natural science or any other science but at all times and everywhere that we comport ourselves toward beings, wherever beings are manifest, and accordingly also already in prescientific Dasein as well as in scientific Dasein and even if Dasein does not explicitly pursue science. An antecedent understanding of being already lies, and must lie, within our everyday and most insignificant and trivial dealing with things. If, for instance, we perform an action that we pay no further attention to at all, such as opening a door, something we do a number of times each day, this entails our taking hold of the handle. If we did not understand in advance what is meant by a thing of use—equipment for working, driving, writing, measuring, lighting cigarettes, that is, equipment in general—then we would not be in a position to make use of the handle as such.

Yet a skillful ape or dog is likewise capable of opening the door and going in and out. Certainly, the question is only whether, when it touches and presses something here, it is taking hold of a handle, and whether it is opening such a thing as a door. We thus speak as though the dog were doing the same thing as us; yet there is not the least evidence available to indicate that the dog is indeed using a handle. Indeed even more: There is not the least evidence for saying that it is comporting itself toward a being here, even though it is relating to something that is familiar to us as a being.

A thing that we rightly call a knife is something that we would never be able to recognize, and could never use, as a knife, as a thing for cutting, unless we understood something like: a thing for . . ., a piece of equipment for cutting. We do not learn what a piece of equipment is by using a knife, equipment for writing, equipment for sewing, but the reverse: we can find such beings before us only because, and insofar as, we understand such a thing as equipment. This is something that we understand in advance, we already bring such understanding with us, and only for this reason can we learn how to handle such equipment. We understand in advance such a thing as equipment and being ready to hand, and yet are far removed from being able to say what equipment signifies as such, what it is to be conceptually grasped as. An understanding of being is not yet a conceptual grasping of being. In our comportment toward beings, of whatever kind, we always move within an antecedent and indeed preconceptual understanding of being.

Because even in our nonscientific comportment toward beings we already move within an antecedent understanding of the being of these beings, we altogether fail to notice, even initially to a certain extent and for a long time, what is fundamentally happening when instead of using things of use we investigate material bodies with respect to their relations of movement and laws. We do not notice that a change in our antecedent understanding of being has occurred. Rather, it looks as though beings have just become different. Indeed, even those researchers who for the first time ground a science and get it going, and who thus for the first time accomplish this change in our antecedent understanding of being, as it were—while others merely reenact and follow this change—even they have no knowledge of what is fundamentally transpiring here; in any case, they do not necessarily need to have such a knowledge.

b) The change in our understanding of being: An example from physics

The change in our understanding of being presents itself to them, rather, in the form that all scientific representations have, as a delimiting of concepts; only it is now the most general fundamental concepts and representations that are determined: mass, force, velocity, movement, place, time; these provide adequate characteristics with respect to the field of a given science. Yet what these concepts fundamentally refer to, remains obscure; they indeed appear as the most general concepts in relation to beings (nature, for example). What is referred to in these concepts is not further inquired into; these fundamental concepts appear in definitions, yet the definition itself provides only the framework and rule for investigating the beings in question.

If we take a general definition from physics: $d = v \cdot t$ (distance equals velocity times time), then this provides a determinate delimitation of what is understood in physics as distance. In response to the question: What is a distance? no reflection is undertaken concerning the possibility of traversing a space; rather, distance is defined with respect to its spatio-quantitative stretch, because the body that passes through a distance is grasped from the outset as a quantitatively determinable thing that changes place. Conversely, we can determine v by the quotient d/t. If we posit t = 1, we have the concept of velocity. The very fact that we express the definition of time by a quotient or a product shows that natural process is conceived from the outset as a homogenous unity of material things in motion. If the physicist goes beyond his definition that is necessary for questioning in his physics, then even the more incisive determining of what he defines is determined by the perspective provided here by mathematical physics. This can be seen in Newton's *Principia* (1714): *Tempora et spatia sunt sui ipsorum et rerum omnium quasi loca. In tempore quoad ordinem successionis, in spatio quod ordinem situs locantur universa. De illorum essentia est, ut sint loca, et loca primaria moveri absurdum est . . . Tempus, spatium, locus et motus sunt omnibus notissima. Tempus absolutum, verum et mathematicum, in se et natura sua sine relatione ad externum quodvis, aequabiliter fluit, alioque nomine dicitur duratio.*[11] "Times and spaces are so to speak the placeholders of themselves and of all things, all things are accommodated in time with respect to the order of succession, in space, by contrast, with regard to the order of their objective position."

We see from this that space and time are regarded as that within which objects are ordered as in motion and, indeed, in such a way that they can be determined mathematically. This is still operative in the Kantian thesis that time and space are that within which things are ordered.

Newton also adds, however, that it belongs to the essence of space and time that they are *loca*, locations, placeholders to a certain extent, but such places or media that are themselves no longer within something else but are rather the medium for themselves. Because they are the *loca primaria*, the final and ultimate media, they themselves can no longer be moved, even though precisely time is characterized by the uniform flow of succession. Newton says: *tempus aequabiliter fluit*, time flows uniformly. He introduces the determining of these fundamental concepts such as *tempus, spatium, locus* by saying that these are the objects that are most familiar to everyone; they are defined by him only to the extent that they come into question within the framework of the foundational approach to a nature posited as a nexus of motion of select things.

This is discussed only to the extent that what is understood here by nature and natural process has been ascertained in advance for every concrete question of natural science, and it is discussed only in this form. The essence of nature is

---

11. Issac Newton, *Philosophiae naturalis principia mathematica* (Amsterdam: sumptibus Societatis, 1714), 7, 5.

delimited in a certain provisional manner; yet this constitution of being of the being (nature) is not itself the proper object of a questioning. Yet how is use made, then, of time and of space? In the change in our understanding of being, in the transition from apprehending things of use to apprehending nature, what occurs is an antecedent projection of its constitution of being, yet in such a way that the constitution of being does not become an object; what occurs is a projection of the constitution of being, therefore, that is nonobjective.

c) The positivity of science. The antecedent, nonobjective projection of the constitution of being that demarcates a field

Now, it is important to see, however, that not only is the being of beings determined differently in advance in this projection but that in and with this projection of being, a field of beings is delimited, demarcated. For it is thereby decided in advance what belongs to the field of nature, even without this entire field being factically surveyed beforehand or even simply familiar. The antecedent, nonobjective projection of the constitution of being is a projection that demarcates a field.

Yet this projection is not an extrinsic drawing of a borderline but rather the projection of the constitution of being pertaining to beings. This means: those determinations that this projection establishes in advance concerning the being that is "nature" will come to the fore in all concrete knowledge of a particular natural process and will do so in such a way that all concepts and propositions of physics implicitly have recourse to these determinations. That is to say: the pieces of knowledge attained in physics find their ultimate and/or first grounding there, and every special proof in physics is grounded in the constitution of being that has been established. The antecedent, nonobjective projection of the constitution of being that demarcates a field is, therefore, one that provides the ground, a grounding projection. Foundational concepts are those representations that, in their constitutive interconnection, provide the ground for all knowledge of beings.

We thus see overall that the antecedent, nonobjective projection of the constitution of being that nevertheless grounds and demarcates a field lets those beings whose being it determines come to the fore and appear for the first time by virtue of this determining that has been characterized. Against the background of being as projected in this projection, beings thus determined first get set in relief. In and with this projection of being, the beings in question first become manifest as available, that is, as lying before us for concrete observation. The projection first thrusts beings into the light, without altering anything about the beings. Beings become manifest as lying before us, as *positum*. Only if beings become manifest in this manner as lying before us can they be known in themselves. Knowledge of beings in themselves—this is how we characterized scientific knowledge. Such knowledge is accordingly knowledge of beings as *positum*, or positive knowledge. The essence of scientific knowledge as positive knowledge consists, then, in whatever constitutes the inner possibility of this "positive" character, of this manifest lying before us in themselves. The inner possibility of this positive character of science we call positivity. The essence of science lies in positivity. The latter, however, for its part consists in whatever makes possible the actual lying before us of beings in themselves. That is the characterized projection of the constitution of being pertaining to beings.

In our first contrasting of scientific comportment with prescientific comportment we said the following: science does not first uncover beings in general in the sense that nothing would be manifest prior to this and Dasein would comport itself toward beings only on the grounds of science. Rather, all scientific comportment installs itself on the grounds of an already existent comportment toward beings. Beings must already lie somehow manifest before us in such a way that science can make those beings manifest precisely as lying before us, as the *positum* that they are in themselves.

How is it possible that beings lie before us in themselves as manifest? In what is the possibility of the positivity of the *positum* grounded? The projection of the constitution of being not only is an antecedent, nonobjective one that demarcates a field but is at the same time a grounding projection. It constitutes the inner possibility—possibility = essence—of a knowledge of beings as lying before us. Science, however, is positive knowledge. The said projection is, therefore, the essence of the positivity of science.

6 On the Difference between Science and Philosophy

§27. The projection of the constitution of being pertaining to beings as the inner enabling of positivity, that is, of the essence of science. Preontological and ontological understanding of being

We have now indeed succeeded in shedding light on the essence of science: it is positive knowledge and has the character of positivity. Yet with this elucidation of the essence of science as positive knowledge have we not completely deviated from the questioning that was guiding us? The guiding question, after all, was (cf. p.125f.): Wherein lies the distinctiveness of that manner of Dasein's existence in which such a thing as being-in-the-truth for the sake of truth occurs? The question was pursuing an existential concept of science. To this end, we engaged in a discussion of what this means: for the sake of truth, that is, for the sake of the unconcealment of beings, for the sake of beings being manifest in themselves. We saw earlier in general that this occurs in a letting be of beings. In the case of scientific comportment as being-in-the-truth for the sake of truth we must be dealing here with a quite specific letting be of beings. We also formulated the question as follows: What is the originary action of Dasein (πρᾶξις) in which such a thing as the theoretical attitude becomes possible? What is the original essence of the theoretical?

Instead of now providing the answer to what this specific letting be of beings is as scientific knowledge, we have arrived at a characterization of scientific knowledge as positive knowledge. Are we supposed to have found with this what we are seeking, the originary action of Dasein that enables the theoretical attitude? Is the essence of the theoretical supposed to be clarified by our now saying: The theoretical attitude is positive knowledge, that is, knowledge of beings in themselves, making manifest for the sake of manifestness?

Indeed. For we are not simply saying that scientific knowledge, as theoretical, is positive; rather we have uncovered what belongs to positivity, that is, we have found that which enables positivity as such. It is the antecedent, nonobjective, grounding projection of the constitution of being pertaining to beings that demarcates a field. This projection that we have characterized is, as a projecting of the being of beings, nothing other than the letting be of beings that we were inquiring after. This projecting as *letting* be of beings is the sought-after originary action of Dasein in which the theoretical attitude, that is, the making manifest of beings for the sake of their unconcealment, alone becomes possible. In the projection that enables positivity lies the originary πρᾶξις, the originarily practical character of the theoretical. More than that: the projection of the constitution of being pertaining to beings as the inner enabling of positivity, that is, of the essence of science, is nothing other than the essence of the theoretical, originally grasped. The distinctiveness of that manner of existence in which being-in-the-truth for the sake of truth occurs, that is, of science, lies in this primordial action that we have characterized as the projection of a constitution of being.

Yet it will be said: certainly, this projection enables positivity, the essence of science; but what is this projection itself? By what right do we call it a primordial action of Dasein, the distinctiveness of a manner of existing? What is this projection of the constitution of being itself, such that it enables such a thing as being-in-the-truth for the sake of truth? It must then surely stand in an inner relation to the essence of truth. In what relation does this projection of a constitution of being stand to what we came to know as the essence of truth?

We are thus faced with a new, central question. We have only just attained our answer to the question concerning the existential essence of science, and this answer has itself become a question.

How do matters stand with this projection that enables the positivity of science, that is, its essence, and its relationship to truth? We saw that in all our Dasein we understand such things as "is," "was," "will be," "being" in general, but do not comprehend it conceptually, so little indeed that we are not even in a position to grasp being itself that is understood in a certain way. Yet this understanding of being surely enables us, after all, to apprehend beings in general *as* beings. The understanding of being understands the being of beings, that is, it has always already and in advance "addressed" beings *as* beings, with respect to their being.

To address something as something, the Greeks call λέγειν, λόγος; here, they are not necessarily thinking of utterance, of "external dialogue," of ἔξω versus ἔσω λόγος; rather, λόγος is also regarded as λεγόμενον. This expression λόγος has the same ambiguity as our corresponding concepts. By a "saying" we understand on the one hand what is spoken but, second, the speaking itself. The "addressing" of beings as beings, the address of beings, of the ὄν, with respect to their being may be designated as λόγος of the ὄν, λόγος τοῦ ὄντος—onto-logos, *ontologia* in its modern coining. Understanding of being is ontological understanding. Knowledge of beings, of the ὄν, in themselves is ontic knowledge.

"Addressing something as something" does not yet mean conceptually comprehending in its essence that which is thus addressed; understanding something as a being with respect to its being does not yet mean apprehending the essence of being. We are indeed using the expression "ontological"—"ontology" for the thematic apprehending and conceptual comprehending of being itself. Yet up to the present day, and precisely today, the use of this language is fundamentally indeterminate and ambiguous; ontological is often used for ontic—and this again in the sense that one lets beings be valid in themselves and does not volatilize them idealistically. The ontological tendency in contemporary philosophy then means the tendency toward Realism. Yet this ontological tendency is marked by the fact that it precisely fails to pose the problem of ontology, does not even understand it. Moreover: onto-logy, bio-logy; the former like the latter counts as a positive science, only the former deals with all beings in general. Seen in this perspective, the understanding of being that illuminates and guides all our comportment toward beings is not yet ontological, not a conceptual comprehending of being. We therefore name the understanding of being that is not yet a conceptual comprehending or brought to the concept a preontological understanding.

We want to set straight in summary form this apparently purely terminological discussion: Knowledge of beings, the ὄv, is ontic knowledge. Scientific knowledge, positive knowledge of that which lies before us, is a particular kind of ontic knowledge. For even in our technical handling of things, in our dealings with them, there lies a knowing that we designate as circumspection and knowing one's way around; in general, every comportment toward beings, the ὄv, is ontic comportment. Underlying this, however, guiding and illuminating it, is an understanding of being that is not yet a "conceptual comprehending" of being— a pre-ontological understanding of being. The latter can develop into an explicit apprehending and conceptual comprehension of being itself: into ontological understanding. We must hold fast to these major distinctions.

Ultimately, there are also intermediate stages here, one of which is precisely *that* projection of the constitution of being that is undertaken, for example, by the researcher of nature, delimiting nature as a field. For what speaks in this projection is neither merely a preontological understanding of being nor as yet an explicit apprehending and conceptual grasping of being itself; it is a peculiar in-between with respect to preontological and ontological understanding, a kind of explicit understanding of being, which does not entail that it would already have to be recognized and understood as such. Yet with these definitions we have gained more than a terminology; we have sharpened a problem in such a way that it can no longer be overlooked anymore.

Our most recent question was: In what relation does the projection of the constitution of being stand to that which we identified as the essence of truth? This relation must be a very close one, if precisely this projection enables being-in-the-truth for the sake of truth. The projection of a constitution of being is in general a preontological understanding of being. Being is understood, although not explicitly apprehended. Now we know that beings too can be manifest for us without our being explicitly directed toward them or apprehending them;

indeed, beings are to a large extent manifest in this way. The unconcealment of beings does not consist in beings being apprehended; such apprehending is possible only on the grounds of the former; the former can persist without the latter. Now we say: the understanding of being, not knowledge of beings, has the character of projection. What is distinctive about projecting is that Dasein thereby gives itself to understand something such as being, movement, location, time. What it thereby gives itself to understand in the projection is not the explicit object of an apprehending focused on it; the physicist, for example, does not speculate concerning time as such and its essence, yet at the same time he does work with time, because it is contained in every one of his propositions; he works with it, it is given in a certain way, and necessarily so, and yet not an object.

If, therefore, such a thing as being is understood and given, although not also conceptually comprehended, in the projection of a constitution of being, then within this being understood and being given of being there lies a certain unconcealment of being itself. In our understanding of being, being itself is unconcealed, that is, the understanding of being is true and has its truth. Now, we designated the unconcealment of beings as manifestness, and we distinguished between the manifestness of beings qua Dasein, disclosedness, and the manifestness of what is present at hand, uncoveredness. The unconcealment of beings, the truth of the ὄv, we can therefore call ontic truth in general. The unconcealment of being is then accordingly called ontological or preontological truth.

§28. Ontic and ontological truth. Truth and transcendence of Dasein

We have thus arrived at the following distinction:

1. Truth of being: unconcealment qua unveiledness; preontological or ontological truth.
2. Truth of beings: unconcealment as manifestness; ontic truth.
   a) Manifestness qua disclosedness: unconcealment of Dasein.
   b) Manifestness qua uncoveredness: unconcealment of what is present at hand or ready to hand.

Now, if being-in-the-truth for the sake of truth, that is, the ontic, positive truth of science, is possible only in and through the projection of a constitution of being, yet this antecedent projection is a kind of understanding of being and the latter, as understanding of being, unveils such a thing as being and thus is true, then the specific being-in-the-truth as science, this ontic truth, is grounded in ontological truth.

Yet scientific truth is only *one* kind and *one* possibility of making beings manifest, and Dasein comports itself toward beings extensively without undertaking science as such. All and every comportment toward beings, every ontic truth of whatever kind, is possible only on the grounds of ontological truth. Furthermore, we saw that it belongs to the essence of human Dasein to be in the truth, that is, to comport itself as a disclosed being toward manifest beings; indeed, with recourse to this characterization of truth, we attempted a first delimitation of the distinctive essence of Dasein itself—as distinct from what is present at hand. Truth can accrue to the latter, but it must belong to Dasein, that is, it belongs to the essence of Dasein's constitution of being. In what way, we did not say. This truth in which Dasein essentially maintains itself now proves to be ontic truth, but that means, one that for its part demands an originary truth for its own possibility: the unconcealment of being in the understanding of being.

Accordingly, there lies within the essence of Dasein a still more original being-in-the-truth, or to put it another way: the essence of Dasein itself must be grasped still more radically with respect to this original truth of our understanding of being, so radically that we may say: the human being is that being to whose essence, that is, to whose constitution of being, it originally belongs to understand such a thing as being. Existence is fundamentally only possible in and through the understanding of being. For only such understanding enables Dasein to comport itself toward beings and in comporting itself toward beings that it itself is not, to comport itself toward itself as a being.

In view of the insights now attained, we require a brief recollection of what was discussed earlier. We started out from a characterization of science according to which it comprises a "foundational nexus of true propositions." This required an analysis of the truth of propositional statements and assertions. The analysis showed that the propositional statement is not the original locus of truth but that truth, rather, belongs essentially to Dasein and is, conversely, the locus (inner possibility) for statements.

The insights gained were summarized in eight theses. The eighth thesis was: Truth exists. Yet now we have seen: Not only is truth not primarily the truth of assertion, but even the interpretation of truth as the unconcealment of beings does not yet identify its original essence. We thus arrive at a ninth thesis (cf. p.105f. for theses 1–8):

> 9. Truth, however, regarded as the unconcealment of beings, exists only if existing Dasein understands such a thing as being, that is, only if the unveiling of being, ontological truth, belongs to the essence of Dasein's existence. (Cf. p.146, thesis 10.)

More original than ontic truth is ontological truth; the latter enables the former. Yet we have only roughly characterized this ontological truth—the projection of being—in contrasting it with ontic truth. What ontological truth itself is has not been clarified. Our answer to the question concerning the original essence of truth, that it is ontological truth, itself becomes a question in turn, if indeed a more penetrating illumination of that essence is possible.

We thus see that the question concerning the essence of truth pushes us to ever more original interpretations and in such a way that, because truth indeed belongs to the constitution of Dasein's being, this goes together each time with a more radical interpretation of Dasein. What is meant by understanding being, giving oneself to understand such a thing as the being of beings in projection? What does such projecting mean, and how is it possible?

With this we recall anew the fundamental fact of human Dasein that we have characterized several times: We understand such a thing as being and do not conceptually comprehend it. Being is unveiled and yet concealed. The attempt to illuminate what being means, how it is to be conceptually comprehended, and how the projection of being gives us to understand such a thing as being, what is meant by understanding of being—illuminating all of what thus determines the essence of human existence leads us anew into abysses.

We must attempt to grasp the primordial action of the letting be of beings for its part in its essence, that is, we must inquire into its ownmost inner possibility and thus procure an insight into what occurs here in such projecting of being. To this end, we want to provisionally shine light into this abyss merely from afar, so as to understand one thing: that there are still problems here and that these problems are the most central ones.

The understanding of being is a giving oneself to understand being and this as projection. This entails, first, an aspect of action, and second, at the same time an action that gives itself something, gives itself to understand something, receives it, and that means holds on to it. However, action, activity, does not here mean producing ontically but rather showing in overstepping. We brought this projecting of being closer to us by characterizing the change from prescientific-ontic truth to scientific ontic truth, that is, positive truth. We said that the positivity of science is enabled by this specific letting be; such a letting be, however, is found within every comportment toward beings. A projection is the presupposition not only in the development of science but at all times and everywhere, wherever and whenever Dasein comports itself toward beings. Yet this does not occur occasionally or from time to time in Dasein but essentially and constantly so long as Dasein factically exists. This entails: Dasein is, as such, projective. This projection—we saw further—is antecedent. Dasein must already have given itself to understand something like being, in order to be able to comport itself toward beings.

The projection is in a certain way earlier, it precedes, and beings manifest themselves to us in such a way that—in a veiled manner—it is in coming from being as already understood that we first come upon what we only now, precisely in light of our understanding of being, let be encountered as beings. From being that has been understood in advance we first of all come back to beings, or more precisely: insofar as we constantly already comport ourselves toward beings, we have always already come back to beings in and from out of an antecedent projection of being.

In this antecedent projection of being, we always already overstep beings in advance. Only on the basis of this elevation, of such an overstepping, do beings become manifest as beings. Yet insofar as the projection of being belongs to the essence of Dasein, this overstepping of beings must also always already have occurred and occur within the ground of Dasein.

We designate this antecedent overstepping of beings by the foreign word *transcendere*, and name the overstepping *transcendence*. Dasein as such is transcending—transcendent. The fundamental essence of the constitution of being of the being that we ourselves in each case are is the overstepping of beings. With this overstepping, transcendence, there lies within Dasein as such a primordial and unique elevation of itself. Only because this elevation lies essentially within the existence of Dasein can existing Dasein fall, and that means, be determined in its way of being by what (in *Being and Time*) we call falling.

Now, if ontological truth in the authentic sense, as the antecedent projection of being, is for its part possible only on the basis of overstepping, that is, of the transcendence of Dasein, then ontological truth is grounded in transcendence, that is, it is transcendental. By this we understand, first, everything that belongs to transcendence as such; and second, we name transcendental everything that according to its inner possibility points back to transcendence. What transcendental means can be discussed only when the essence of transcendence has been determined.

In Kant this occurs incidentally in a certain sense, and without clarity regarding the presuppositions and demands of an adequate illumination of the essence of transcendence. For Kant, "transcendent" means "exceeding." The term is used for concepts (representations) that exceed the possibility of experience, of ontic knowledge, illegitimately overstepping it, concepts that ascertain something about beings in themselves without their being given in a corresponding intuition (where "in themselves" here means: relative to God). "Transcendental," by contrast, is a kind of knowledge in which there are "concepts" that relate not to objects—in themselves—but to the possibility of ontic knowledge, to the possibility of synthetic knowledge a priori, of a knowledge that essentially belongs to the ontic kind of knowledge; here, therefore, what is at issue is knowledge of beings that is shown its limits and/or what enables it, which in positive terms means: restriction.

Transcendental knowledge is ontological knowledge. This is admittedly still ambiguous; it can mean: 1. Preontological understanding of being as constitutive for ontic knowledge, 2. Explicit interpretation of this preontological understanding of being as such ontological knowledge in the strict sense.

Yet why is ontological the same as transcendental? Because ontology goes together with transcendence. To what extent? In Kant, "transcendental" is often employed in a more restrictive sense; it also refers to an illegitimate exceeding. In Kant, it is more a critical-negative concept vis-à-vis theological-dogmatic metaphysics. We are understanding it in a positive sense, in terms of the essence of transcendence itself, which Kant did not explicitly make into a problem.

Transcendence is the enabling of that knowledge that does not illegitimately exceed experience, that is not "transcendent," but rather is experience itself. The transcendental provides the indeed restrictive, yet thereby at the same time positive definition of the essence of nontranscendent knowledge, that is, of the ontic knowledge that is possible as such.

With respect to the traditional concept of transcendence we must note the following: 1. It is not original, but rests on presupposed determinations that have not been clarified, such as "subject" (cf. §14 and on the entire problematic, summer semester 1927); 2. Moreover, it remains narrowly confined to knowing, and knowing is in turn conceived as theoretical, and the latter once again as investigative. Transcendence here means: climbing out of the subject and over to an object. The transcendent is the object, that toward which we go out, that to which we relate.

For us, transcendence does not mean going out to an object; the subject is already outside, and it is only outside alongside beings insofar as it itself is disclosed. The being that it itself is and other beings have in advance already been overstepped. What is transcendent in the proper sense of transcending is Dasein, and only because it transcends in the ground of its essence is it possible that beings qua present at hand and beings qua Dasein may not be distinguished initially. Mythic identification precisely presupposes transcendence.

As an aside we may note the following: here we are developing a more fundamental, more originary, and more explicit concept of the transcendental than in Kant. Kant indeed saw the transcendental for the first time, although in a distinctly narrow perspective and not in a sufficiently originary manner. Yet precisely because he failed to determine transcendence itself explicitly or to make it a central problem his concept of the transcendental cannot be sufficient.

From the outset, we must say in principle that the problem of transcendence and of the transcendental has nothing whatsoever to do with Idealism or Realism but is much more originary than the dimension in which this distinction arises, so much so that the distinction can be decided only on the basis of transcendence understood correctly. Just as little does transcendence have anything to do with knowledge or theory of knowledge primarily. We thus arrive at a tenth thesis with respect to the essence of truth, having presented in theses 1–8 the transition from the truth of assertion to original, genuine ontic truth (pp.105-10), and in thesis 9 traced ontic truth back to ontological truth (p.142).

> 10. Ontological truth (unconcealment of being) is for its part possible only if Dasein, in accordance with its essence, is able to overstep beings, that is, only if as factically existing it has always already overstepped beings. Ontological truth is grounded in the transcendence of Dasein; it is transcendental. Conversely, however, the transcendence of Dasein is not exhausted by ontological truth (cf. thesis 11 below).

Transcendence as constituting Dasein's essence in turn underlies ontological truth. It is on the grounds of transcendence alone that what we earlier called Dasein's irruption, as existing, into beings becomes possible. Only because Dasein is transcendent in the ground of its essence are ontological truth "and" ontic truth possible. We deliberately say ontological *and* ontic. For it is not the case that we are merely unfurling a series of conditions next to one another here, ontic conditioned by ontological and ontological truth by transcendence. Rather preontological truth, that is, projective understanding of being, is as such an understanding of the being of beings, whether such beings indeed factically exist or are present at hand or not. Conversely, experience of beings, ontic truth, is such only in an understanding of being.

Ontological truth and ontic truth stand in a primordial connection—corresponding to the distinction between being and beings. These are not two realms that are simply posited next to one another by "and"; rather, the problem is the specific unity and distinction between the two in their belonging together. They themselves, as distinguished in this distinction, can be conceptually comprehended in their essence only in terms of what enables this distinguishing as such. In other words: transcendence is not only the inner possibility for ontological truth and then indirectly for ontic truth as well but is precisely the condition of possibility for this "and as well," for their connection, indeed for the possibility of distinguishing between being and beings, on the basis of which distinguishing we can speak of ontology at all. This distinction we designate as "ontological difference," "ontological" in the sense explained (cf. p.139ff.). We thus have a further fundamental thesis:

> 11. The transcendence of Dasein is the condition of the possibility of the ontological difference, the condition for the distinction between being and beings being able to irrupt at all, for there to be able to be this distinction. Yet even with this the essence of transcendence is not exhausted.

Despite how indeterminate this may still be for us at present, the one and only issue that we have been directed toward initially must have become clear: We asked: What is the essence of science, and to what extent does science have a limit? It has now become clear that science is not something simply given among many other things that one can be occupied with, but that in order to be what it is, it must have sunk its roots in the original essence of Dasein itself, in transcendence. We can now already understand more concretely what was earlier indicated as an anticipatory definition of science: It is a possibility of Dasein's existence. If it is a genuine possibility, however, science must also necessarily limit itself, if indeed every possibility carries its limit within itself, in fact bringing with it a limiting of itself. The question concerning the essence of science indeed became a burning issue for us only so that we could see from its essence in what way science limits itself.

Manifestly what is at issue is not the kind of limiting in which science would, as it were, merely run up against something else that it is separated from by a fence, not a fencing off that can be a matter of indiffference for it, but a limiting that as such precisely lends it its proper essence. Science must necessarily take a limit for itself and provide a limiting. The limit lies within it itself, as the other that it is and that, precisely as science, it no longer has power over. This other, however, gives science the force of its essence and in such a way that this other is richer and capable of still more, other than just sustaining the possibility of science.

The specifically scientific turning toward beings in themselves in wanting their truth occurs in the projection characterized; only in this projection do beings become manifest as lying before us. Only if they lie before us as thus manifest can they be made the object of an interrogation. Only if they have become the object of a questioning can they become a theme for possible investigation. Investigation demands the fixing of a theme, thematization, this demands prior objectification, this demands something lying manifest before us already, and this is possible only in projection. This projecting, however, which thus sustains the entire passion of the scientific turn to the matter, is grounded in transcendence as the fundamental constitution of Dasein.

Science makes beings into its object and can do so only through the ontological projection, the transcending, in which Dasein "comports" itself to "being" (world, inter alia). Transcending is the other that science as such does not have power over and that it precisely needs in order to be what it can be. Transcending accomplishes the limiting of science and thereby brings it precisely to itself. Science directs itself only toward beings as its object, and it can do so on the basis of the ontological projection. We heard, however, that this projection also always already demarcates a field and thereby eo ipso establishes each science on one particular region in each case, restricting it to that. On the basis of what gives it its essence (projection), each science must confine itself to a region. Science is essentially individual science, that is, within the essence of science as positive ontological knowledge there lies the fact that there cannot be any so-called general science. The expression "individual science" is therefore already a tautology and misleading, because it suggests the thought of a general science.

The ontological projection thus accomplishes a double limiting that is intrinsically unitary: 1. Science is knowledge of beings and not of being; 2. As science of beings, it is in each case the science of a determinate region, and never of beings as a whole. This limiting occurs in transcending, and it occurs necessarily if science is to become actual, existent. Precisely through the fact that science sets itself the task of making beings manifest in themselves, it must accomplish the ontological projection, that is, in its essence comport itself to something no longer accessible to science itself with its means, something that is thus fundamentally concealed. Science must thus necessarily venture into a vicinity of what is concealed that constantly surrounds it. The being-in-the-truth pertaining to science is precisely a being surrounded by concealment. Even this concealment of being is in each case only a restricted one for each science. Science is necessarily limited, and in such a way that it does not even have the limiting concealment around it that indeed installs itself with the actuality of science.

We thus see at the same time what was only provisionally indicated earlier, namely, that concealment necessarily accompanies unconcealment in each case. What gives science its lucidity in the sense of the manifestness of beings places it in the dark at the same time—in the sense of the concealment of being. The relative lucidity of scientific knowledge of beings is surrounded by the imposing darkness of the understanding of being. For even in the ontological projection that occurs with the grounding and development, and generally in the history of science, being is indeed understood and de-limited in a certain way but not apprehended, that is, not expressly comprehended conceptually as being. The understanding of being, however, occurs in transcending. If this understanding of being can develop into a determining and even conceptual comprehending of being as such, then different possibilities must lie within transcending itself in accordance with which it can occur inexplicitly or explicitly. If transcending is explicitly and expressly accomplished, then this means initially and among other things: the question is raised as to what this being that is projected in the projection of being itself means and how such understanding becomes possible. Now, if transcendence constitutes the fundamental essence of human Dasein in general, then what occurs in explicit transcending is nothing less than essentially transcending Dasein becoming essential in the explicit letting happen of transcendence. This becoming essential of Dasein in explicit transcending, the explicit questioning concerning being as such, is nothing other than philosophizing.

§29. Philosophizing as transcending belongs to the essence of human Dasein

> 12. Transcending is philosophizing, whether it happens inexplicitly in a concealed manner, or is explicitly engaged.

We showed that the essence of the theoretical lies in the letting be of beings in themselves and we called this letting be a primordial action of Dasein. The richness with which letting be occurs in the ontological projection, in transcending, now becomes clear; this transcending, however, is the fundamental occurrence of existence itself. Earlier, we called this letting be of beings a metaphysical indifference, a peculiar releasement in which beings in themselves come to word. This releasement, however, must spring from an originary acting, it is nothing other. Yet to act is to be free. In order for the properly binding character to be possible that proceeds from those beings that are manifest in themselves and demands a specific substantive content, an ontological projection (transcending) must occur, that is, a free action. Binding and necessity become possible only where there is freedom. Explicit transcending is thus a primordial action of Dasein's freedom, indeed the occurrence of Dasein's very space of freedom, which means, however, existing in the ground and out of the ground of Dasein.

Explicit transcending, however, as questioning concerning being as such, is philosophizing. What we merely asserted in the first hour of the course thus becomes clear: Human Dasein as such philosophizes; to exist means to philosophize. Dasein philosophizes because it transcends. In transcending lies understanding of being. Understanding of being, however, as we heard, belongs to Dasein and does so at first and for the most part in such a way that Dasein indeed understands being but does not conceptually comprehend it. Dasein could not exist as what and how it is without having unveiled and understanding such a thing as being in the ground of its essence.

The essence and core of the human being, however, have long been regarded as lying in what we call the "soul." Plato therefore says (*Phaedrus*, 249 e4–6): πᾶσα μὲν ἀνθρώπου ψυχὴ φύσει τεθέαται τὰ ὄντα, ἢ οὐκ ἂν ἦλθεν εἰς τόδε τὸ ζῷον.[1] "Every Dasein has, in the ground of its essence, already caught sight of beings, that is, of what in beings constitutes being, or else it would not have been able to enter into this factical Dasein" (without such looking toward being).

It is nothing other than this primordial fact of Dasein, however, that becomes a problem in explicit transcending, that is, in philosophizing. We thus see that philosophy does not first need to think up some object or other for itself or search far and wide; Dasein itself in its essence—as transcending—carries within

---

1. *Platonis Opera* (ed. Burnet), Tomus I.

itself the possible question concerning being and its meaning. In this regard too, Plato saw what is essential: Ὁ δέ γε φιλόσοφος, τῇ τοῦ ὄντος ἀεὶ διὰ λογισμῶν προσκείμενος ἰδέᾳ, διὰ τὸ λαμπρὸν αὖ τῆς χώρας οὐδαμῶς εὐπετὴς ὀφθῆναι, τὰ γὰρ τῆς τῶν πολλῶν ψυχῆς ὄμματα καρτερεῖν πρὸς τὸ θεῖον ἀφορῶντα ἀδύνατα (*Sophist*, 254 a8–b1).[2] "The philosopher has devoted himself entirely to bringing constantly into view beings (as beings—being), by bringing them to the concept in discussing them. He maintains himself in the brightness of the understanding of being, and because he resides in such a bright locale, it is difficult to see him. For in the case of the many, the eye of the soul, their understanding, is not in a position to endure looking toward the divine that lies out beyond beings."

We may take it from this that philosophizing belongs to the essence of human Dasein, but that the many are nevertheless unable to free themselves from the fetters of what happens to be in currency, of what one speaks about and of what one must have seen. Philosophizing is the prerogative only of those who are ready to understand that what is essential resides metaphysically in the simplicity and originality of one's own Dasein and awaits liberation.

The same thought of Plato's that the philosopher ἀεὶ προσκείμενος τῇ τοῦ ὄντος ἰδέᾳ was expressed by Aristotle in his own sober, yet no less radical manner (*Metaphysics* Z 1, 1028 b2f.): καὶ δὴ καὶ τὸ πάλαι τε καὶ νῦν καὶ ἀεὶ ζητούμενον καὶ ἀεὶ ἀπορούμενον, τί τὸ ὄν, τοῦτό ἐστι, τίς ἡ οὐσία.[3] "And so that which always has been, and is now, and will in all future times be sought after, that against which our seeking and questioning repeatedly shatters, is nothing other than the question: What is being?"

Here the important insight comes to light that this questioning concerning what being is repeatedly leads to predicaments from which there appears to be no way out. In other words: the fundamental question of philosophizing, "What is being itself?" is the question that seeks to and must become a question time and again. We generally have an erroneous view of Greek philosophy, and of Plato and Aristotle in particular, as though they created well-rounded and closed systems that can be passed down to future eras as dogmatic doctrinal content. Yet we find nothing to indicate that they were of the opinion of having now solved what is essential for all future generations. What gives Plato and Aristotle their inner greatness is this self-superior, free transmission of the same fundamental task to their successors.

(Today, where pseudo-philosophy and metaphysics are proclaimed in every alley, the task more than ever is to let the fundamental question of philosophizing become a question, that is, to first develop once again as such the question

---

2. Ibid.

3. *Aristotelis Metaphysica*, recognovit W. Christ (Lipsiae: In aedibus B. G. Teubneri, 1886).

concerning being. For now, we must comprehend that precisely this developing of this question is already philosophizing itself.)

Explicitly transcending, as philosophizing, is renewed questioning concerning the being of beings; to interrogate being as such means to seek to conceptually comprehend it. Philosophizing asks concerning the concept of that which we always already understand. From here it becomes visible that precisely philosophizing is besieged by the seductions of its most stubborn adversary, the assumed self-evidence of things.

Philosophizing means seeking to conceptually comprehend being as such, developing the understanding of being in its inner possibility and bringing it onto its ground, developing understanding, understanding as projecting, explicitly accomplishing the projection, and that means: determining this projection itself in its inner possibility so that it can be accomplished as a projecting that conceptually comprehends, as the development of our preontological understanding of being into an ontological one, in such a way that the former is first illuminated by the latter.

Philosophizing means seeking to conceptually comprehend being as such and fundamentally grounding ontology as a problem. Yet we are not simply saying that philosophy is ontology, and are especially not saying it in the sense of taking over some traditional concept of ontology and imposing it on the essence of philosophy. That philosophy is ontology means at most: In its essence it is a problem that flows from that which constitutes the fundamental essence of Dasein's existence; that philosophy is ontology then means: if we succeed in conceptually comprehending this, then the full inner orientation of the essence of philosophizing must let itself be unveiled from there and primarily and solely from there.

§30. The different realms of questioning in philosophy and science

This is to say: with our current characterization of philosophizing as questioning concerning the concept of being, we have by no means exhausted the essence of philosophizing or grasped it in its core; this particular path toward the provisional characterization of philosophizing is indeed not to be circumvented as methodologically the first, but we deliberately proposed three paths. Only traversing the remaining two, together with the path we have now traveled, can first bring us to our goal.

Something essential has come to light, however: As the development of our understanding of being, philosophizing is transcending, that is, the letting-happen of that which enables existence in its ground. Philosophizing is an existing from out of the ground of the essence of Dasein. Philosophizing means: becoming essential within transcendence. For only transcendence enables the projection of being, among other things. This projection therefore essentially needs transcendence as the horizon of projecting. The question concerning being needs the transcendental horizon.

(This, however, demands unveiling transcendence in its essence. Transcendence is the fundamental essence of Dasein itself, of the being that we ourselves are. What is required, accordingly, is an unveiling of the constitution of Dasein's being and of the essence of existence. Now, it can be shown that the original constitution of Dasein's being, and that means at the same time the ground of the inner possibility of transcendence, is temporality. Time, therefore, must determine the transcendental horizon for the fundamental question of philosophizing, the question concerning being. The fundamental question of philosophy is the question concerning being and time. This is why Part One of the investigation that bears that name is titled: "The Interpretation of Dasein in Terms of Temporality, and the Explication of Time as the Transcendental Horizon for the Question of Being.")[4]

It must now have become clear, at least roughly, to what extent the decisive thesis that we proposed in the first hour of this lecture course is indeed legitimate: We never occupy a position outside of philosophy but always already exist within it, and do so essentially, insofar as we, as human beings, indeed transcend. An introduction to philosophy is therefore not leading us into one field outside of others but rather the introducing, the setting in motion, of philosophizing. This now means: the explicit letting happen of transcendence, making ready and binding what sustains our knowing, participating in questioning concerning the essence of being. Yet this introducing is thus far just an initial run-up—by way of illuminating the essence of science.

The extent to which the concept of a scientific philosophy is a nonconcept, just like the thought of a "roundish circle," must now have become clear as well. Science is positive knowledge, that is: 1. directed toward beings; 2. together with this, necessarily directed toward one domain of beings in each case. Philosophy, however, is precisely neither of these: 1. directed not toward beings but toward being; 2. directed not toward one domain, nor toward all domains taken together, but rather if directed toward beings, then in terms of the question concerning being, directed toward beings as a whole. A science of beings as a whole, however, is essentially impossible. Why? This will become clear later, on our second path.

Yet philosophizing is not simply distinct from science but something more: that which enables the essence of science, namely, positivity, lies in a transcending, and the latter as such is philosophizing. In transcending, philosophy has

---

4. Editor's note: There is no corresponding record of this paragraph in the transcripts. The square brackets in the manuscript also indicate that Heidegger did not present this paragraph in his lecture.

originally and explicitly something that pertains to science only in one respect, and indeed in such a way that science itself does not have power over that which sustains its essence.

If indeed the essence of science as positivity lies in transcending, then philosophizing as transcending is more scientific than any science can ever be. The epithet "scientific" is therefore not only superfluous to philosophy—we could still let that pass—but a misunderstanding, and indeed one that springs from a fundamental lack of clarity regarding the essence of science and especially the essence of philosophy.

Philosophy is transcending, that is, philosophizing. The extent to which you have understood this may confirm itself in your attempting to recognize, from the interpretation of the essence of science that we have undertaken, the extent to which the threefold crisis of science is a necessary one and that precisely in philosophizing this crisis becomes more acute in a genuine sense, that is, becomes an essential one, one that should also therefore not be allowed to be made the object of journalistic discussions.

Admittedly—the more seriously we strive to philosophize, the clearer it becomes that philosophizing, although it occurs within the essence of Dasein, indeed, precisely because it occurs there and only there, requires a liberation and guidance of its own, a liberation in which Dasein must use violence against itself. All violence, however, shelters pain within it. And what is understood [?] and comprehended conceptually in philosophizing is not something that can be talked about just like everything else, namely, all the things to be learned and acquired from beings. Plato knew about everything that philosophy carries within it as the turning of our gaze toward being itself, and he depicted it often in various ways, above all in the *Phaedo, Phaedrus,* and *Symposium*; in the *Republic*; and in the *Seventh Letter.*

Phaedrus (247b): The ascent of the soul to catching sight of being brings πόνος τε καὶ ἀγών, hardship and struggle for the soul[5]; *Phaedo* (79d, 81a): πλάνος, the errant wandering of the soul.[6] In the *Seventh Letter,* composed in his old age, we read (341c): ῥετὸν γὰρ οὐδαμῶς ἐστιν ὡς ἄλλα μαθήματα, ἀλλ᾽ ἐκ πολλῆς συνουσίας γιγνομένης περὶ τὸ πρᾶγμα αὐτὸ καὶ τοῦ συζῆν ἐξαίφνης, οἷον ἀπὸ πυρὸς πηδήσαντος ἐξαφθὲν φῶς, ἐν τῇ ψυχῇ γενόμενον αὐτὸ ἑαυτὸ ἤδη τρέφει.[7] "What philosophy enquires about is not sayable, that is, discussable like other things we may learn, but is something that happens and has happened in the soul, namely, on the basis of and through a genuine being together, being with one another alongside the matter itself, something that grows from this communal

---

5. *Platonis Opera* (ed. Burnet), Tomus II.
6. Ibid., Tomus I.
7. Ibid., Tomus V.

effort concerning the matter." If this communal effort concerning the matter happens, then philosophizing too happens, "suddenly, just like the spark from a fire leaps over from one to the other, so that this spark leaping over brings brightness and light within which being becomes visible."

§31. A summary of what has been presented. The understanding of being as the primordial fact of Dasein: The possibility of the ontological difference. The ontological difference and the distinction between philosophy and science

In the previous hours of this lecture course, we initially attempted a general characterization of what is meant by an introduction to philosophy; it means introducing, setting in motion philosophizing. In this context we determined philosophizing itself provisionally as a free action from out of the grounds of Dasein.

Insofar as our Dasein here and now, as we undertake such an introducing of philosophizing, is determined by science among other things, our task was to clarify philosophy via a discussion of the relationship between science and philosophy. This question became all the more pressing given the many attempts to ground philosophy "as science," to posit a scientific philosophy as the ideal.

In the face of this, we initially asserted: The idea of a scientific philosophy is as nonsensical as the thought of a roundish circle. This was meant to express the following: philosophy is by its very essence, not only in degree, more scientific than any possible science and is so by virtue of the fact that it first enables such a thing as science in general. What gives science the possibility of itself, however—and not only it—is something higher and more originary. Philosophy cannot, therefore, be determined in accordance with its essence by that which owes its very origin to philosophy.

The goal of our discussion of the relationship between science and philosophy was therefore to indicate, in terms of the inner essence of science itself, that a necessary limit is found within science, but a limit whereby science is precisely delimited in its essence, that is, enabled; a delimiting, moreover, that is accomplished in what we then addressed as philosophy.

In order to see the necessary limit within the essence of science, our initial task was thus to determine this essence itself, setting out from the traditional concept of science: the coherent grounding of a set of true propositions. This led to a discussion of the essence of truth. Propositional truth is a derivative phenomenon vis-à-vis originary truth in the sense of the unconcealment of beings that belongs to the essence of Dasein itself. Beyond the idea of truth as the manifestness of beings in the dual sense of the being uncovered of what is present at hand and the disclosedness of Dasein, we were led further back to a more originary truth, the unconcealment of being. Dasein is always already, and necessarily, in this most originary truth; this was demonstrated in terms of our understanding of being. The understanding of being as the fundamental constitution of Dasein is as self-evident as it is enigmatic.

Yet from here the essence and genesis of the sciences as knowledge of beings shows itself, of beings as in each case already lying manifest before us and necessarily circumscribed in accordance with a region. Positivity is grounded in an antecedent, nonobjective projection of a constitution of being that demarcates a field.

A particular scientific investigation moves within a particular problem, a particular question posed to whatever has been made a theme. Thematization, setting a theme, presupposes givenness of an object. An object, however, is given to me as an object only in the act of objectification. I can objectify something only if this something already lies before me in advance as manifest; manifest beings lying before us, however, can lie before us as manifest beings only if these beings have already been understood, that is, have been projected in advance in their being, with respect to their being. We thus see a quite determinate sequence of levels within the structure of science. The central phenomenon is this projection of the constitution of being.

The decisive phenomenon that we have thereby hit on is the primordial fact within the essence of Dasein itself, the fact that we understand such a thing as being or, said more pointedly, that we accomplish the distinction between beings and the being of beings. The understanding of being is nothing other than the possibility of carrying out this distinguishing between beings and being or, in short, the possibility of the ontological difference.

We showed finally that the possibility of such a distinguishing between beings and being rests on what we designate as transcendence. If Dasein indeed maintains itself in the most originary truth, it must transcend as such; only as such can it comport itself toward beings at all, and only for this reason can it distinguish itself as a being from beings as others and be itself as a being, exist. Being a self qua existence is possible only on the grounds of transcendence. Here, a new and fundamental possibility of questioning opens up: transcending as understanding being and as conceptually comprehending being. This transcending as explicit is nothing other than philosophizing. The twelfth thesis thus runs: Transcending is philosophizing. Transcendence, however, is the essential constitution of Dasein; explicit transcending qua philosophizing is Dasein's becoming essential in its existence.

In everything essential, however—this is what distinguishes it—there is no progress and accordingly no devaluation either. Actual philosophizing can by its very essence never be surpassed, but must itself be recovered ever anew. Wherever and whenever actual philosophizing happens it enters of its own accord directly into dialogue with the historical past of philosophy and then sees that there can be no novelty in philosophy, but thus also nothing antiquated either; it stands on the other side of old and new. We therefore clarified briefly from the decisive inception of philosophy, Plato and Aristotle, that the question concerning the concept of being is the central question of philosophy—τί τὸ ὄν—and that it belongs to the essence of Dasein (soul) to understand being—ἡ ψυχὴ τεθέαται τὰ ὄντα—and that only for this reason is the factical existence of Dasein possible. Certainly, history can only be brought to speak if one does not simply repeat what has been said, that is, simply appeal dogmatically to an earlier philosophy, whether that of Aristotle or Kant; history will only return what is essential if it is brought to cophilosophize through living philosophizing itself.

Our discussion of the relationship between science and philosophy has not yet explicitly determined philosophy in its entirety but only to the extent that it was brought into relation to science. Science has a double limit: First, science is knowledge of beings and not of being; and second, knowledge of beings is always and necessarily of a demarcated region, and not of beings as a whole. Neither being as such, nor beings as a whole as such, nor the intrinsic connection between being and beings is ever accessible to a particular science or to all of them together, yet not simply inaccessible, but rather such that science is able to undertake its research solely on the basis of this inaccessibility and within the sphere thus delimited. A general science is an absurd concept. What becomes manifest from this delimitation of science is above all the absurdity of attributing the epithet "scientific" to philosophy in any sense.

With this interpretation of the essence of science, we may perhaps have touched its core, yet the interpretation is not thereby complete. Earlier, we showed already that the character of the "theoretical" not only is indeterminate but does not at all suffice for a full determination of the essence of science, especially not if we ask: What is essentially entailed in science factically actualizing itself?

On the one hand, the projection of the constitution of being is decisive; yet an understanding of being is always an understanding of the being of beings. A relationship to beings must also occur in and with this projection, and indeed a unique one that is marked by the tendency toward working on, mastering, and controlling beings. Τέχνη is not simply a preform of ἐπιστήμη but enters into it essentially; the mastering, controlling, and making use of knowledge is not simply the aim of technics in the narrow sense but of all vocational praxis. Science always aims at "achievement," philosophy at "education" in the fundamental sense of Platonic παιδεία. In science, which is always unfinished, there is therefore necessarily progress and development, results, that is, something that becomes dated, whereas in philosophy there are no results to be notched up, and it can therefore never become dated either, insofar as it is genuine.

Yet precisely through this rigorous delimiting of science from philosophy the necessary connection of science to philosophy becomes apparent. A fruitful, reciprocal determining is assured, however, only where the essential distinction extends into the existence of the scientific researcher and of the philosopher and is engaged there. Philosophy in the productive sense of philosophizing is rooted quite differently in the innermost and entire existence of the philosopher than is scientific investigation in the researcher. The scientific work of one individual can in principle always be represented by someone else; the scientific discoveries that one person makes could also have been made by someone else. Never so in philosophy; each is whole and unique in him- or herself. Philosophizing is therefore alive and effective only if it is in turn awakened by others in an originary and independent manner and is in this sense retrieved. This retrieval and renewal, however, if it is genuine, is never a mere duplicate.

The relationship of the student to the scientific researcher is therefore essentially different from that of the one cophilosophizing to the philosopher. Wanting to model the latter relationship on the former one signifies a thorough failure to recognize the essence of philosophizing. The tendency to do so, however, is constantly close at hand, especially for us, precisely because the philosopher and the researcher superficially move within the same sociological framework and identical situation at the university, and because the social and official status of philosophy professors does not yet guarantee that one who talks about philosophy is a philosopher. Yet with what we have said, we have already talked a little too much about philosophers, and yet a hint must be provided. Max Scheler especially has devoted his attention to this problem, in his work on "Problems of a Sociology of Knowledge."[8]

What is more important, however, is to get philosophizing itself going, just as it is to concretely grow into the particular science in each instance; for only then do these distinctions come to be experienced properly and become effective in a sustained manner.

At the beginning of this lecture course, in the first hour (cf. p.6), we said: for now, we know only, and indeed more in the sense of an assertion, that philosophizing belongs to human Dasein, it happens within human Dasein as such. Insofar as it exists, Dasein philosophizes, if only inexplicitly and mostly inauthentically. Yet Dasein never exists in general, rather, as concrete, it exists in a particular circumstance and creates essential or inessential situations for itself as the case may be. If in philosophizing we are developing the concept of philosophy, we must therefore enquire from the perspectives of our current situation, with a view to the powers that determine our current Dasein in its belonging to the university.

---

8. Max Scheler, "Probleme einer Soziologie des Wissens," in *Versuche zu einer Soziologie des Wissens,* ed. Max Scheler (Munich: Duncker & Humblot, 1924); revised version in Max Scheler, *Die Wissensformen und die Gesellschaft* (Leipzig: Neue-geist, 1926).

The introduction is meant to let philosophizing become free in us, in us now, insofar as our Dasein is determined by the two powers of science and leadership. We have taken the first path through science, and we have seen that philosophizing as transcending does not occur as one arbitrary comportment among others but occurs in the ground of Dasein as such.

What at the beginning was an assertion has now become an insight, admittedly an insight that has not yet uncovered the full essence of philosophizing—although not in the sense that we would have one piece of the concept to which other pieces could be added. This is why from the outset we proposed two further paths that are to help us bring the full concept of philosophy explicitly to our understanding: a discussion of the relationship between philosophy and Weltanschauung, and of the relationship between philosophy and history. If "Weltanschauung" is something totally different from science, then the second path will also have a different character. The insights that we gained on the first path can and must nevertheless illuminate and facilitate the second.

Division 2: Philosophy and Weltanschauung

1 Weltanschauung and the Concept of World

§32. What is Weltanschauung?

Our second path too corresponds to our first path in that we are again not holding philosophy and Weltanschauung next to one another as fixed quantities and comparing them. Rather, by working through the question "What is Weltanschauung?" we shall determine our relationship to it.

On our first path, that of characterizing philosophy by working through the question "What is science?," we saw that philosophy is the limit of the essence of science; science owes to philosophy its inner possibility. Philosophy essentially underlies every science, yet philosophy is not absorbed into science.

The relationship between Weltanschauung and philosophy is not of that kind. We cannot say without further ado that philosophy necessarily and explicitly belongs to the inner possibility of a Weltanschauung, but if anything, the reverse: A Weltanschauung already lies within the inner possibility of philosophy, and consequently by extension science too is only ever possible on the basis of a particular Weltanschauung.

Yet all such pointed antitheses and convenient formulae are pernicious, easily become errors and give rise to mistakes. For now, we wanted only to indicate that our second path emphatically does not run parallel to our first, neither in terms of content nor in terms of its way of treating the problem. On the surface, all they have in common is that here too we must initially ask: What is Weltanschauung? Even if we only pose the question casually, we notice that what is being asked about here, namely Weltanschauung, is a very much broader, more multifarious, more universal phenomenon, yet also in turn more blurred in its limits, than science.

a) The word *Weltanschauung*

The very designation "Weltanschauung" is obscure and easily leads one astray. Added to this is the fact that the word itself is a specifically German coinage from the late eighteenth century. It has no equivalent in other languages or in earlier periods, which of course does not mean that what is meant by the word would not also have been actual outside the realm of the German language or in earlier times, prior to it being coined. For the fact that the most immediate signification of the word does not in itself provide its properly intended meaning is shown by the first use of the word, which does not yet have the signification that it does today.

So far as we can see, the word crops up for the first time in Kant's *Critique of Judgment* and does so as an intuiting and contemplating of the sensuously given world, the *mundus sensibilis*, thus a straightforward apprehending of nature in the broadest sense. Goethe and Alexander von Humboldt use the word with this signification. This use of the word in the sense of a contemplating of nature soon dies out, and does so under the influence of a signification that the word receives from Romanticism. This can be seen from a use of the expression Weltanschauung in Schelling, in his *Plan of a System of the Philosophy of Nature* (1799): "Intelligence [i.e., spirit] is productive in two ways, either blind and unconscious, or free and conscious; unconsciously productive in a Weltanschauung, consciously in the creating of an ideal world."[1] Here, accordingly, Weltanschauung is not assigned to the sensuous contemplating of nature but is an act of the intelligence, albeit the unconscious intelligence, yet still a productive act, that is, a productive forming of a world picture. Schelling even speaks of a schematism of Weltanschauung, of a schematic form for diverse possible Weltanschauungen, that is, ways of productively apprehending and interpreting the whole of beings. Here this productive forming of a world picture is not merely a theoretical act, however. A few years later, Hegel in his *Phenomenology of Spirit* speaks of a moral Weltanschauung. We thus see that the term Weltanschauung no longer has anything in common with what the word signifies in Kant. Görres uses the phrase "political Weltanschauung." The historian Ranke speaks of a religious and Christian Weltanschauung. Soon there is also then talk of a democratic, a pessimistic, or a medieval Weltanschauung. Bismarck says: "There are, after all, peculiar Weltanschauungen in very clever people." In this way of speaking, we already see the present-day usage in the broad signification of the word Weltanschauung that is also obscure, however, and hard to grasp at first.

Our task initially will be to feel our way through this blurred and ambiguous concept toward what it is that we mean indeterminately, and yet with a certain assuredness, whenever we today speak of a Weltanschauung. We all know what we mean, after all, when for instance we recognize particular assertions by others as an expression of their Weltanschauung, as convictions that are no longer amenable to being objectively discussed or proven scientifically. We also notice with more or less assured adroitness when we are transitioning from scientific

---

1. F. W. J. Schelling, *Einleitung zu dem Entwurf eines Systems der Naturphilosophie* (1799). *Friedrich Wilhelm Joseph von Schellings sämmtliche Werke*, ed. Karl Friedrich August Schelling (1856–61), part 1, vol. 3 (Stuttgart and Augsburg: J. G. Cotta, 1858), 271.

discussions to theses of Weltanschauung and vice versa. Today, moreover, we are not only extremely tolerant of the diversity of Weltanschauungen but also open and receptive to their different versions in art, religion, philosophy, and politics. Indeed, we already take a particular intellectual enjoyment in detecting and observing such differences, and we are inclined to give ourselves particular credit if we are able to summon a corresponding tolerance and let anything and everything be valid. Letting everything be valid and understanding everything even count as a particular sign of a supposed superiority and freedom, whereas fundamentally they are merely a hidden cowardice and impotence, the lack of courage for truthfulness, which, as human willing, is always and necessarily "one-sided" and demands a struggle that today already is almost regarded as indecent. In this we see the ruinous effect of Nietzsche, or of his small-minded parroters who make what for him was a means of critique into an end in itself.

Also characteristic is the following: explicit attention to Weltanschauung, to its concept, discussions about it, and concern with it always emerge whenever and wherever an integrated, coherent, and exclusively dominant Weltanschauung—one that is then indeed not noticeable as such—is lost or has broken down. Whether an integrated and pervasively dominant Weltanschauung is really an ideal cannot be stated without further ado. The fact is that whenever an integrated Weltanschauung and culture breaks down, the problem of Weltanschauung always comes alive.

Yet despite this, or indeed precisely because everything impresses itself upon us with the tint of Weltanschauung and we move within such views, automatically asking what kind of Weltanschauung lies hidden behind things, our embarrassment becomes especially great when we are asked to say what a Weltanschauung is. The reason for this embarrassment, which one usually very quickly avoids, lies initially in the uncertainty concerning the horizon from which we are to delimit what a Weltanschauung is. That this horizon for being able to determine the essence of a Weltanschauung fluctuates has a number of reasons that we shall not pursue here in detail. The fact exists.

With the question concerning the essence of science, the horizon from which we can determine it is clearer from the outset: science is a kind of knowledge—but Weltanschauung? We indeed seem to understand what *Welt* [world] means and what is meant by *Anschauung* [view].[2] Yet we also see immediately that by Weltanschauung we do not mean an intuiting [*Anschauen*], contemplating as observing, neither a prescientific nor a scientific contemplating—θεωρία;

---

2. The German *Anschauung*, often rendered as "intuition" in philosophical contexts (as in the Kantian "forms of intuition," space and time), literally means a looking (*Schauen*) at (*an*) something, a viewing of something. *Weltanschauung* is thus sometimes translated as "worldview."—Trans.

looking [*Schauen*] also does not mean aesthetic, artistic contemplation, and this is so little the case that we indeed attribute a Weltanschauung to the artist himself in each case, one that speaks in and from out of his work. Nor is *Anschauung* some particularly mysterious act of intuition, a particular ability to see things that are hidden from others. A Weltanschauung is no mere contemplation of things and just as little an aggregate of knowledge about them; a Weltanschauung is always the taking of a position and indeed in such a way that we maintain ourselves in it on the basis of our own conviction, whether one of our own that we ourselves have formed or one that we merely emulate and copy, one we have fallen into.

More than this: This conviction is not something that we merely "have," that we occasionally make use of, that we accommodate like an insight we have gained or a statement that has been proven; rather, a Weltanschauung is the foundational, motivating force of our action and our entire Dasein, even and precisely when we do not explicitly appeal to it or make a decision by explicit and conscious recourse to it.

Anschauung here has rather the meaning of "view" [*Ansicht*], as when we say: I am of such and such a view, whereby we appeal to something that we are certainly convinced of, but that we cannot simply prove or impress on someone else by theoretical argumentation, a view that is concerned not with random individual things but with the whole of beings.

This comes to the fore in the expression "world." However, this word too means many things, and even today, it still predominantly means the whole of beings in the sense of the universe, of nature. However, we also speak of world history and mean by this history as a whole, universal history, yet while excluding the course of nature as such. That Weltanschauung very readily and frequently suggests the narrower signification of a natural scientific world picture makes itself known in the fact that we like to supplement it by saying: *Welt- und Lebensanschauung* [a view of the world and of life]. We thus see that the characterized view also, indeed even centrally, concerns "life," that is, Dasein.

Weltanschauung therefore concerns non-Dasein-like beings (nature in a practical respect, etc.) and Dasein, yet not just the two domains next to one another and taken together, but in their reciprocal relation. At the center of the view on beings as a whole stands a "view of life," in such a way that the view of life is at the same time the effective force giving direction to Dasein itself.

From this provisional characterization of what we mean by Weltanschauung we can discern that this phenomenon is not simple and that initially we are still far removed from a clear and sharp conceptual delimiting of its structure. Yet we shall be able to arrive at this only once we have established what we already asked about, the horizon from which something like Weltanschauung can be determined. Where does such a thing belong? As a "view" it is a comportment

[*Verhaltung*]—or better—a stance [*Haltung*] on the part of Dasein and, indeed, one that sustains and determines Dasein from the ground up in such a way that in this stance Dasein sees and knows itself as positioned in relation to the whole of beings. Illuminating and conceptually determining the essential structure and function of something like Weltanschauung will therefore only adequately succeed once we have a correspondingly original insight into the essential constitution of Dasein.

b) Interpretations of Weltanschauung: Dilthey—Jaspers—Scheler

We thus see here a state of affairs corresponding to our first path; the question concerning the essence of science led to the question concerning the essence of truth, but truth is a fundamental constitution of Dasein itself. That could only become visible, however, by our freeing ourselves from the traditional concept of the subject and of subjectivity, that is, through a more radical interpretation of the constitution of Dasein's being. We may accordingly assume that the much more opaque, and yet more central phenomenon that we call "Weltanschauung" and that points back into the constitution of Dasein's being will especially necessitate an ontological interpretation of Dasein. That the phenomenon of Weltanschauung remains so extensively undetermined, and that the question of the relationship between Weltanschauung and philosophy is still in such an altogether poor state, are also due to the lack of such an ontology of Dasein. Yet if it is a problem that belongs to the essence of philosophy, then it is as ancient as philosophy itself; this can easily be shown from Plato's *Republic*, for example, Books V–VII. The question is in a poor state despite important approaches to interpreting the essence of Weltanschauung that have been undertaken in recent times above all by Dilthey, then by Jaspers and by Scheler.

Dilthey says the following: "In each moment of our existence [*Dasein*] we find a relationship of our own life to the world [*Welt*] that surrounds us as a whole that we can survey [*als ein anschauliches*]. We feel ourselves, the value of life belonging to the individual moment and the values of the effects that things have on us, but this in relation to the objective world. As reflection progresses, the connection between our experience regarding life and the development of a world picture is maintained."[3] This interpretation of reality from the perspective of our inner life Dilthey calls Weltanschauung. "In the structure of Weltanschauung an inner relation of life experience to our picture of the world is always contained, a relation from which an ideal of life can always be derived."[4]

---

3. Wilhelm Dilthey, "Das Wesen der Philosophie," in *Die Kultur der Gegenwart* I, 6 (Berlin and Leipzig: B. G. Teubner, 1907), 37f. *Wilhelm Diltheys Gesammelte Schriften* (Leipzig: B. G. Teubner, 1924), vol. 5, 378f.
4. Ibid., 38 (380).

According to this characterization we thus have three components in the structure of Weltanschauung: life experience, world picture, and, arising from the relation between these two, an ideal of life. "The structure of Weltanschauung is accordingly a nexus in which components of different provenance and different character are united."[5] Dilthey here continues to take the meaning of the word Weltanschauung in the sense of the contemplation of what is present at hand in the broadest sense, "knowledge of the world," theoretical stance—for only then is it meaningful to explicitly justify the use of this term for the complex phenomenon depicted: "The application of the name Weltanschauung to a spiritual formation that includes knowledge of the world, ideals, the giving of rules, and the positing of supreme goals, is justified by the fact that the intention to undertake particular actions is never posited within it, and it thus never includes particular practical comportment."[6] Dilthey wants to say that Weltanschauung is never directly practical; for this reason, it can be designated as a kind of theoretical stance. Yet this is a thoroughly artificial reasoning and a failure to recognize the authentic and central significance of "world." Dilthey sticks to the most superficial signification of the word.

Dilthey distinguishes three fundamental forms of Weltanschauung: the religious, the artistic, and the philosophical. The latter he calls metaphysics,[7] and distinguishes three types of philosophical Weltanschauung: first, materialism and the positivism grounded on the knowledge of nature; second, objective idealism; third, the idealism of freedom. We cannot go into a more detailed analysis of Weltanschauung in Dilthey here.

In a more comprehensive manner with a different philosophical orientation Karl Jaspers has then dealt with the problem of Weltanschauung in his *Psychology of World Views* (1919; 3rd ed., 1925). Compared to Dilthey's efforts, this work is distinguished especially by the wealth and fullness of possible Weltanschauungen, and by the incisiveness of interpretation and breadth of what it presents. Yet in determining the essence of Weltanschauung, Jaspers is oriented by Dilthey. Three aspects are investigated: attitude, world picture, and the life of spirit; the work is structured accordingly. Once again, we shall not go any further into this.

Finally, above all on the sociological side, Max Scheler has made essential contributions toward illuminating the essence of Weltanschauung.

We shall enquire instead in the direction where the fundamental problems lie that especially need to be discussed. What is Weltanschauung—not this or

---

5. Ibid.

6. Ibid.

7. Only on the basis of this conception of the essence of metaphysics, a conception that is once again superficial, can Dilthey arrive at his skepticism regarding its possibility.

that particular Weltanschauung or the possibility of their variation, rather what is the essence and the inner possibility of such a thing as Weltanschauung in general? We are asking not simply to have a general guiding concept for the study of Weltanschauungen that are concretely and factically possible, rather with this question of essence we are pressing into a new, central dimension of the problem. Our concern is not with the "psychologization" of the world (Jaspers), just as little as with the structure of the "life of the soul" (Dilthey), also not with the question of psychology or anthropology concerning what the human being is but with the question of Dasein.

Already in the case of the relatively distinct phenomenon of "science," it seemed necessary to take as our basis for interpreting its essence, as our point of departure and guiding thread, an already given conception that we could then subsequently indeed recognize as superficial and derivative. We have a much greater need for a certain handle, however, in the case of a construction such as that of Weltanschauung, which easily becomes blurry and hard to grasp. Here we do not even have a somewhat ordinary definite opinion about it. What is called for is therefore to take as our basis a more distinct conception of Weltanschauung.

In the following attempt at a more radical determination of the essence of Weltanschauung as such we shall retain Dilthey's characterization as our guiding thread: "In the structure of Weltanschauung an inner relation of life experience to our picture of the world is always contained, a relation from which an ideal of life can always be derived."[8] Three basic components are named, of different provenance and different character, yet standing in a connection, in an "inner relation"; the ideal of life can be derived from the first two.

Here the following seven questions arise:

1. Are these basic components determined in a sufficiently original manner in themselves?
2. Are they of different provenance or not?
3. How is their connection possible?
4. Have they come together, or do they necessarily grow from a more originary structure that is one of Dasein itself?
5. What is this primordial structure of Dasein in which the inner possibility of Weltanschauung is grounded?
6. How must Dasein be brought into view in principle in order to make visible this primordial structure?
7. How is this original structure of Dasein related to philosophizing, which we now know occurs as explicit transcending within transcendence as the fundamental constitution of Dasein? (Cf. the answer on p.241f.)

---

8. Dilthey, "Das Wesen der Philosophie," 38 (380).

§33. *What is meant by world?*

To proceed securely in a methodological respect with regard to these questions we shall begin with a radical discussion of what the expression "world" means and shall pose the problem of an original interpretation of the essence of the phenomenon of world so as to gain an adequate concept of world. For the failure to clarify the essence of Weltanschauung in Dilthey, Jaspers, and Scheler has its grounds in the indeterminacy of the concept of world.[9]

What is meant by world? What was previously already understood by the term κόσμος, *mundus?*

The general result of the historiographical consideration in "On the Essence of Ground"[10] is as follows: the expressions κόσμος, *mundus*, world have a dual signification: an ordinary one, beings qua nature, and a philosophical one that admittedly is not explicitly grasped conceptually. World is not a regional term, it does not refer to this or that being but to the how of beings as a whole; yet in this signification "world" is often related to Dasein in such a way that Dasein itself is directly designated as world. World, therefore, is the how of beings as a whole and yet related to Dasein, which, after all, is only one being among others. How is world related to Dasein, and conversely: How does Dasein relate to world, and what does world then mean?

Thesis: We shall claim that Dasein does not relate occasionally to world, on this or that occasion; rather the relation to world belongs to the essence of Dasein as such, to existing as being qua Dasein; fundamentally, "Dasein" means nothing other than being-in-the-world; the latter is to be attributed to Dasein as its fundamental constitution.

Everything depends on how, and to what extent, we understand the essence of world correctly in this. A more precise discussion of being-in-the-world, which we attribute to Dasein as such, must sharpen the problem of the concept of world for us. Being-in-the-world is the structure of transcendence, of overstepping.

That which oversteps is Dasein; what is overstepped are beings as a whole; that toward which the overstepping ensues is world. The "toward which," however,

---

9. For continuation of the systematic discussion see p.241f.

10. Cf. Martin Heidegger, *Vom Wesen des Grundes. Beitrag zur Festschrift für Edmund Husserl zum 70. Geburtstag: Ergänzungsband zum Jahrbuch für Philosophie und phänomenologische Forschung* (Halle: Niemeyer, 1929), 71–100. Also published separately by Max Niemeyer, Halle (Saale). (Since the third edition of 1949 published by Vittorio Klostermann, Frankfurt a. M. Also included in Heidegger, *Wegmarken* [Frankfurt: Klostermann, 1967], translated as *Pathmarks*, edited by William McNeill [New York: Cambridge University Press, 1998].) Cf. also Heidegger, *Metaphysische Anfangsgründe der Logik im Ausgang von Leibniz.* Marburg lecture course, summer semester 1928. Gesamtausgabe vol. 26, ed. Klaus Held (Frankfurt: Klostermann, 1978), translated as *The Metaphysical Foundations of Logic* by Michael Heim (Bloomington: Indiana University Press, 1984). Cf. also on Kant's concept of world, p.174ff.

is not a being. Strictly speaking, it is not at all something to which Dasein could comport itself—and yet we speak of a relation to world. How and what is world here?

a) The concept of world in ancient philosophy and in early Christianity

In the decisive beginnings of ancient philosophy something essential already shows itself.[11] Κόσμος refers not so much to the beings themselves that press upon us and surround us, nor to all these beings taken together, but signifies, rather, the "state," that is, the how in which beings are, and indeed as a whole.

Κόσμος οὗτος thus designates not this region of beings as delimited from another but rather this "world" of beings as distinct from another "world" of the same beings.[12] The world already underlies every possible fragmenting of beings; such fragmenting does not destroy the world; that which is ἐν τῷ ἑνὶ κόσμῳ[13] was not first thrust together into a region but rather is pervasively determined in advance by world as a whole. Finally, a further essential feature of the κόσμος shows itself in Heraclitus: ὁ Ἡράκλειτός φησι τοῖς ἐγρηγορόσιν ἕνα καὶ κοινὸν κόσμον εἶναι, τῶν δὲ κοιμωμένων ἕκαστον εἰς ἴδιον ἀποστρέφεσθαι.[14] "To those who are awake there belongs a world that is one and common, each who is sleeping, however, is turned to his own world." Here world is placed in relation to fundamental ways in which Dasein exists. When we are awake, beings show themselves in a thoroughgoing uniformity that is accessible to everyone in an average way. In sleep, the world of beings is one that is exclusively individuated with respect to each Dasein at the time.

From these brief indications several things already become visible: 1. World means more a how of the being of beings rather than beings themselves. 2. This how determines beings as a whole in each instance. 3. This determining is in a certain way always antecedent. 4. That which antecedently determines beings as a whole in their how is relative to fundamental ways of existence of human Dasein. World belongs to Dasein in some way, even though it embraces all beings in their entirety.

Certain though it is that this understanding of what is referred to by κόσμος—an understanding that is not very explicit as yet and more dawning—can indeed be compressed into the said meanings, it is equally indisputable that the word at the same time always functions as a naming of the beings themselves that are experienced in such a how (in the way that "flow," for example, names the

---

11. Karl Reinhardt, *Parmenides und die Geschichte der griechischen Philosophie* (Bonn: Friedrich Cohen, 1916), 174f. and 216n.
12. Cf. Hermann Diels, *Die Fragmente der Vorsokratiker. Griechisch und Deutsch*, 4th ed. (Berlin: Weidmann, 1922), vol. 1, 151, Parmenides, fragment 2; 187ff., Melissus, fragment 7.
13. Ibid., 402f., Anaxagoras, fragment 8.
14. Ibid., 95, Heraclitus, fragment 89.

flowing water itself, yet can also signify the flowing as such), a distinction that, behind the possible change in meaning, in the existential signification coming to the fore or remaining in the background compared to the other signification, points back to a difference that is ontologically fundamental, that between being and beings in general.

It is no accident, however, that in connection with the new, ontic understanding of existence that broke through in Christianity the relation between κόσμος and human existence became sharpened and clarified, and thereby the concept of world in general. The relation is experienced in such an original way that κόσμος now comes to be used as the term for a particular fundamental manner of human existence. Κόσμος οὗτος in Paul (cf. I. Corinthians and Galatians) refers not only and not primarily to the state of the cosmic but to the state and predicament of the human being, the way in which he is positioned with regard to the cosmos, the way in which he values goods. Κόσμος is being human in a mentality turned away from God, that is, a particular fundamental way in which the human being is positioned in relation to all beings and thereby to himself (cf. ἡ σοφία τοῦ κόσμου). Κόσμος οὗτος refers to human Dasein in a particular historical existence, distinguished from another one that has already irrupted (αἰών ὁ μέλλων), the future state of the human being in bliss.

The Gospel of St. John uses the concept of κόσμος unusually frequently—above all in relation to the Synoptists—and at the same time in a quite central sense. World designates the fundamental shape of human Dasein removed from God, the character of being human pure and simple. Consequently, world is then also a regional term for all human beings together, without distinction between wise and foolish, righteous and sinners, Jews and Gentiles. The central signification of this completely anthropological concept of world finds expression in the fact that it functions as a counterconcept to Jesus being Son of God, which for its part is conceived as life (ζωή), truth (ἀλήθεια), light (φῶς). This concept of cosmos, as we know from recent research, is not specifically New Testament, St. John's, or Hellenistic but extends much farther into the Manichean-Mandaic cultural circle.

This inflection in the signification of κόσμος that begins in the New Testament then appears unmistakably, for instance, in Augustine and Thomas Aquinas. According to Augustine, *mundus* signifies on the one hand the totality of what is created, thus the equivalent of *ens creatum*; yet just as often *mundus* stands for *mundi habitatores*, and indeed in the specific existentiell sense of the *dilectores mundi, impii, carnales. Mundus* non *dicuntur iusti, quia licet carne in eo habitant, corde cum Deo sunt.*[15]

---

15. Augustinus, *Opera Omnia*, accurante J. P. Migne (Paris: Migne, 1845–1849), Tomus IV.

Augustine will have drawn this concept of world just as much from Paul as from the Gospel of St. John, a concept that then played a role in determining Western intellectual history. Evidence for this may be provided by the following excerpt from the *Tractates on the Gospel According to St. John*. For John 1, 10 (Prologue): ἐν τῷ κόσμῳ ἦν, καὶ ὁ κόσμος δι'αὐτοῦ ἐγένετο, καὶ ὁ κόσμος αὐτὸν οὐκ ἔγνω Augustine gives an interpretation of *mundus* in which he shows the dual use of *mundus*, in *mundus per ipsum factus est* and *mundus eum non cognovit*, to be twofold. In the first signification, *mundus* means as much as *ens creatum*. In the second, *mundus* means the *habitare corde in mundo* as *amare mundum*, which is equivalent to *non cognoscere Deum*. In context the excerpt reads: *Quid est, mundus factus est per ipsum? Coelum, terra, mare et omnia quae in eis sunt, mundus dicitur. Iterum alia significatione, dilectores mundi mundus dicitur. Mundus per ipsum factus est, et mundus eum non cognovit. Num enim coeli non cognoverunt Creatorem suum, aut angeli non cognoverunt Creatorem suum, aut non cognoverunt Creatorem suum sidera, quem confitentur daemonia? Omnia undique testimonia perhibuerunt. Sed qui non cognoverunt? Qui amando mundum dicti sunt mundus. Amando enim habitamus corde: amando autem, hoc appellari meruerunt quod ille, ubi habitabant. Quomodo dicimus, mala est illa domus, aut, bona est illa domus, non in illa quam dicimus malam, parietes accusamus, aut in illa, quam dicimus bonam, parietes laudamus, sed malam domum: inhabitantes malos, et bonam domum: inhabitantes bonos. Sic et mundum, qui inhabitant amando mundum. Qui sunt? Qui diligunt mundum, ipsi enim corde habitant in mundo. Nam qui non diligunt mundum, carne versantur in mundo, sed corde inhabitant coelum.*[16]

"World" accordingly signifies beings as a whole, and indeed as the decisive how according to which human Dasein positions and holds itself in relation to beings. Thomas Aquinas likewise on one occasion uses *mundus* as synonymous with *universum, universitas creaturarum*, yet then also with the meaning of *saeculum* (worldly mentality), *quod mundi nomine amatores mundi significantur. Mundanus (saecularis)* is the counterconcept to *spiritualis*.

b) The concept of world in Scholastic metaphysics

Without going into the concept of world in Leibniz, we shall mention how world is determined in Scholastic metaphysics, which came to have direct significance for Kant.

The two philosophical contemporaries of Kant who were of particular influence on the way he posed his philosophical problem were Baumgarten and Crusius. Both composed a metaphysics, works that Kant consulted throughout his entire life, using them as a basis for his lectures and giving several commentaries

---

16. Augustinus, *Tractatus in Ioannis Evangelium*. Ibid., Tomus III, Tract. II, cap. 1, n.11.

on them. It is characteristic that in Scholastic metaphysics the meaning of the concept of world again turns entirely in the direction of the ordinary concept in the sense of the whole of created beings. From here we can understand the titles of those disciplines that are definitive for the *Critique of Pure Reason*.

In the course of its Scholastic development in the sixteenth, seventeenth, and eighteenth centuries, metaphysics came to be divided into a *metaphysica generalis* and a *metaphysica specialis*. Metaphysics as such has beings as such and as a whole for its theme. *Metaphysica generalis* asks concerning what belongs to beings in general. It poses in general terms the question of the being of beings. It is ontology. In the Kantian development and in the more radical posing of the question concerning the possibility of metaphysics in the *Critique of Pure Reason*, ontology becomes transcendental philosophy. *Metaphysica specialis* deals not with beings in general, but with beings in particular, that is, with the main regions of beings themselves, and three such main regions are distinguished: nature, the human being, and God. Accordingly, there are three disciplines. Cosmology, which deals with nature, grasps the cosmos in the narrower meaning of nature, of those beings that indeed also include the human being as a created being, yet it does not thematize the human being in his humanity. The human being is the theme of psychology, or also of pneumatology, insofar as he is seen as fundamentally determined by the soul. The third discipline is theology, which deals with God, the human being, and nature—yet not in the sense of an empirical science. This philosophy of nature is not natural science, the psychology is not today's psychology, the theology is not theology of revelation; rather, these three fundamental regions of *metaphysica specialis* are defined with regard to their essence. The concept of "essence" is called *ratio* in this period. This cosmology is therefore a *cosmologia rationalis*, the psychology is accordingly a *psychologia rationalis*, the theology a *theologia rationalis*. It is not a theology of the scriptures that has revelation as the source of its knowledge, but is instead a knowledge of God in terms of reason alone.

We can see that this Scholastic metaphysics underlies the fundamental problem of the *Critique of Pure Reason*, and that without the outline of this metaphysics, we cannot understand the *Critique of Pure Reason*. Within special metaphysics, this outline intrinsically contains cosmology, or *Weltlehre* [doctrine of world], as Crusius says in German. From this we can take it that the concept of world has undergone a narrowing compared to its existentiell signification in Augustine and Aquinas. In his *Metaphysics*, Baumgarten thus defines the concept *mundus* as follows: *Mundus*—he also uses *universum* or πᾶν—*est series (multitudo, totum) actualium finitorum, quae non est pars alterius.*[17] Here, world is the totality, the

---

17. Alexander Gottlieb Baumgarten, *Metaphysica* (Halle: Hemmerde, 1739), 2nd ed. (Halle: Hemmerde, 1743), §354, 87.

whole or the sum of finite things, the entirety, which is no longer part of something else. From this definition we may take two things: 1. World is the term for finite, that is, created beings in the sense of *ens creatum*. 2. World is the kind of realm that is itself no longer part of another.

In a corresponding manner, only in greater detail and with more philosophical independence, Christian August Crusius develops the concept of world in his metaphysics: "A world means the kind of real association of finite things that is not itself part of another one in turn that it would belong to by means of a real association."[18] Insofar as world is concerned with finite things, this concept of world is also oriented toward the counterconcept God. World, however, is also distinguished from an "individual creature," and no less from "several simultaneously existing creatures" insofar as they "stand in no association whatsoever." Just as little is world a nexus of a number of simultaneously existing, finite things that do stand in association yet are nevertheless part of a higher association. World is a real association of finite things such that the unity of the association is no longer part of another.

In Crusius, what is characteristic for the conception of world is how he determines the problem of a world doctrine: The essence of world in this sense can only be clarified on the basis of principles from general metaphysics, that is, from ontology. Insofar as world is concerned with existing things, all that is attributed to every being must be attributed to this entirety of actually existing things as a fundamental determination. One can arrive deductively at essential aspects of what belongs to a world from particular principles of general metaphysics. Yet insofar as the world is an association of finite things, that is, created by God, further aspects can be discerned in looking to rational theology, insofar as one can elaborate deductively from the concept of God what belongs to a being insofar as it is created by God. Here we thus clearly have the type of rational theology that Kant subjects to a fundamental critique. The doctrine of world is possible only insofar as it is grounded on the general doctrine of the essence of beings, ontology, and then on natural theology. World is the regional term for the supreme unity of association of the totality of created beings.

In the next hour of the lecture course, we shall briefly clarify how Kant takes as a basis this traditional concept of world developed in cosmology by Scholastic metaphysics, but at the same time goes essentially farther, and how on the other hand in a strange manner and way the existentiell concept of world that Augustine laid out makes an appearance in Kant, though without the specifically Christian determination of the human being. At the same time, we shall

---

18. Christian August Crusius, *Entwurf der notwendigen Vernunftwahrheiten, inwiefern sie den zufälligen entgegengesetzet werden* [i.e., outline of all rational truths] (Leipzig: J. F. Gleditsch, 1745), §350, 657.

see how in Kant these two concepts of world stand next to one another without the question being raised of their original unity. Following the historiographical orientation we shall then attempt to develop positively the fundamental structure of world.

§34. *Kant's concept of world*

The sense of the concept of world and its content in Scholastic metaphysics can be gathered from the status of the "doctrine of world" (cosmology) within the framework of the disciplines of traditional metaphysics. In characterizing the problem of the doctrine of world, we can thus broaden it into a problem of metaphysics in general. Kant's philosophizing moves initially and for an extended period within such metaphysics, and does so in part with the intent of bringing assuredness and unanimous agreement to this metaphysical knowledge, especially its highest and most essential parts (cf. the letter to Johann Heinrich Lambert of September 2, 1770).[19] Compare the titles of his precritical writings:

> *Principiorum primorum cognitionis metaphysicae nova dilucidatio* (Habilitation thesis, 1755).
> *The Sole Possible Basis for a Demonstration of the Existence of God* (1763).
> *An Attempt to Introduce the Concept of Negative Magnitudes into Philosophy* (1763).
> *Inquiry Concerning the Distinctness of the Principles of Natural Theology and Morality* (1764).

In the course of these efforts regarding metaphysics, however, metaphysics becomes increasingly questionable for Kant. That is, he does not simply declare metaphysics to be impossible; he does not act skeptically toward it but asks, rather, concerning its essence. Posing the concrete question concerning the essence of metaphysics, however, means gaining initial clarity about the character of what presents itself as metaphysics and has dominance in his time.

We have already outlined the framework of traditional metaphysics and have seen how it proceeds, for example, in Crusius. Yet something more that is essential must be said at the outset regarding the character of this metaphysics. The idea of such metaphysics is determined by ancient philosophy, above all by Plato and Aristotle. We can say that metaphysics is knowledge of beings as such (ὄν ᾗ ὄν) as a whole (καθόλου). On the basis of the insights that we gained on our first path, we can further clarify this traditional idea of metaphysics. Knowledge of beings, and indeed theoretical knowledge of beings, is science. Aristotle therefore also calls it ἐπιστήμη. Yet it is science of beings as such as a whole, general science

---

19. *Immanuel Kants Werke*, ed. Ernst Cassirer, vol. 9. *Erster Teil: Briefe von und an Kant 1749–1789* (Berlin: B. Cassirer, 1918), 73ff.

of beings. Now, we have already seen—from the very essence of science—that such a general science is nonsensical, intrinsically impossible. However, it does not follow from this that metaphysics is impossible, but rather that its concept is a problem, that the question must indeed be posed as to what this knowledge of beings as such as a whole means, and what problematic we are faced with, how such knowledge is possible at all and necessary as such. Kant admittedly did not take the problem of metaphysics this far, yet he did accomplish decisive work in preparation for this.

Kant, rather, initially takes up the traditional idea of metaphysics affirmatively and merely asks explicitly about its essence, that is, its inner possibility. *Metaphysica specialis* is metaphysics proper, metaphysics in its final purpose; it is preceded by ontology as its forecourt, its propaedeutic. Kant must accordingly ask initially concerning the essence, the inner possibility of the foundational discipline of metaphysics, that is, the inner possibility of ontology, and from determining the essence of the latter there then arises a prefiguring of the possibility of *metaphysica specialis*. This dual question concerning the essence of metaphysics, of *metaphysica generalis* and *metaphysica specialis*, is posed and answered in the *Critique of Pure Reason*, specifically in the "Doctrine of Elements." The latter is divided into Transcendental Aesthetic and Transcendental Logic, and the Transcendental Logic into Analytic and Dialectic. The Transcendental Aesthetic and Transcendental Analytic are the new and first authentic determination of *metaphysica generalis* (ontology), the Transcendental Dialectic that of *metaphysica specialis*.

The *Critique of Pure Reason* is a laying of the ground for metaphysics. It is neither a demolition of metaphysics nor—as Neo-Kantianism says—a theory of knowledge for the mathematical natural sciences. Rather, as Kant himself says in a letter when sending his newly published work to his friend Marcus Herz in 1781, the *Critique of Pure Reason* is the metaphysics of metaphysics. It is the problem that has made no further progress since Aristotle composed the treatises that we know as Books Γ and E of his *Metaphysics*—indeed, more fatefully still, it was no longer alive as a problem at all that would have the pointedness of a real question. Individual metaphysical questions were indeed posed anew, such as the question concerning substance in Leibniz and indeed even the question concerning a new laying of the ground for *prima philosophia* in Descartes—and yet it is only with Kant that the question concerning metaphysics as such, concerning its essence, origin, and necessity, is to be found.

Every genuine renewal of such fundamental problems is a radicalizing transformation of that which is up for discussion; in and through the Kantian (and every) laying of the ground for metaphysics, its essence is transformed. For our particular question, however, this means that the problem of *metaphysica generalis* and at the same time that of *metaphysica specialis*, of cosmology, become transformed and, thereby, the problem of the concept of world. Given what we have indicated regarding the *Critique of Pure Reason*, this means that the problem of the concept of world is raised for the very first time.

Before we attempt briefly to develop the problem of the concept of world in terms of the questioning unfolded in the *Critique of Pure Reason*, we must draw attention to the treatise of Kant's that represents the transition between the pre-critical period of his thinking and the appearing of the *Critique of Pure Reason*. It is the treatise of 1770: *De mundi sensibilis atque intelligibilis forma et principiis*. With this work, Kant introduced himself as professor of logic and metaphysics at the University of Königsberg. As the title already indicates, the concept of *mundus* is discussed. In the first section, *sectio I*, Kant deals with the concept of world in general: *De notione mundi generatim*. See in particular §2: "*Momenta, in mundi definitione attendenda, haec sunt: 1. materia, 2. forma, 3. universitas.*"[20]

Ad. 1. In terms of *materia*, the question of what a world consists of is being asked. Kant responds: "*Materia (in sensu transcendentali) h.e. partes, quae hic sumuntur esse substantiae.*"[21] World consists of independently subsisting things that are. The plural is to be noted. "*Verum vis vocis mundi, quatenus usu vulgari celebratur, ultro nobis occurrit. Nemo enim accidentia, tanquam partes, accenset mundo, sed, tanquam determinationes, statui. Hinc mundus sic dictus egoisticus, qui absolvitur unica substantia simplici, cum suis accidentibus, parum apposite vocatur mundus, nisi forte imaginarius.*"[22] In a less than appropriate way it is called "world"; a single existing entity is not a world.

Ad. 2. What is the form of that which we call *mundus*, that is, how is the plurality of substances as such determined? *Forma mundi* "*consistit in substantiarum coordinatione, non subordinatione. Coordinata enim se invicem respiciunt ut complementa ad totum, subordinata ut causatum et causa, s. generatim ut principium et principiatum.*"[23] *Coordinatio* is a *nexus realis*, that is, determining itself in terms of the essential content of substances, not an *unum ideale*, a unity that is thought of, *in quod mens multitudinem cogit*, in which it is merely a thinking that forces things together. Thus: "*Nexus autem, formam mundi essentialem constituens, spectatur ut principium influxuum possibilium substantiarum mundum constituentium.*"[24] *Nexus* is *commercium*. The form of the world is the *nexus realis* as *commercium* of *substantiae*.

Ad 3. *Universitas:* Here the question concerns the unity of how world is determined (*forma + materia*). The question concerning the nature of this third essential moment in the concept of world is, as Kant emphasizes, the philosopher's

---

20. Ibid., vol. 2. *Vorkritische Schriften*, ed. Artur Buchenau (Berlin: B. Cassirer, 1912), 402ff.
21. Ibid., 405.
22. Ibid.
23. Ibid., 406.
24. Ibid.

cross, and here is also the place where the problematic of the concept of world starts in the *Critique of Pure Reason*. First Kant defines how the unity of multiple substances is determined: "*Universitas . . . est omnitudo compartium absoluta*," the absolute, unconditioned totality of entities that in each case have among themselves the reciprocal character of a part. The moment of *universitas* he names *totalitas absoluta* for short—c.f. the *Critique of Pure Reason*, A324, B380ff. This concept of absolute totality can presumably be thought but is not given. What kind of concept is the concept of world, that is, what is world in general according to its innermost essence? With this, the problem of the *Critique of Pure Reason* is already anticipated, and we shall see that Kant, by way of a critique of the concept of world, at least advances in the direction of a more radical understanding of the phenomenon of world.

a) Kant's concept of world in the *Critique of Pure Reason*

In the philosophy of the seventeenth and eighteenth centuries, the concept of world is treated in *cosmologia rationalis* as a discipline of *metaphysica specialis*. This concept of world, approached in this way, already becomes problematic in the dissertation of 1770 and does so with respect to the aspect of *universitas* together also with that of *forma*. Here, *mundus* is conceived as "*totum, quod non est pars*," and indeed "*qua terminus syntheseos*";[25] the counterconcept is *simplex* as the term for analysis.

What kind of definition is this? What kind of concept is the concept of world in general? In relation to these questions, the problem becomes transformed and deepened through the fact that in the *Critique of Pure Reason*, metaphysics as such becomes a problem—in the sense of a new laying of the ground. To achieve clarity, we must place five questions before us:

1. What is metaphysics in general?
2. In what direction must the essence of metaphysics be clarified?
3. To what extent is determining the essence of metaphysics a critique of pure reason?
4. What is the approach and outline for laying the ground of metaphysics?
5. What are the main theses and steps of this laying the ground?

It is a tall order to give an interpretation of the *Critique of Pure Reason* in a few hours. Much will of necessity remain rough and may therefore be easily misunderstood. On the other hand, we cannot circumvent gaining some perspective and insight into how we are thrust toward the center of the work, despite the gaps and indefiniteness with respect to the discussion of individual details.

––––––––––

25. Ibid., 403.

This is the task posed for us with the initial intention of clarifying the concept of world; yet together with this, we shall get a preview of a problem for our third path while at the same time looking back at our first path.

Ad. 1. What is metaphysics in general? We have already identified the general concept: Knowledge of beings as such as a whole, knowledge of beings in general, that is, in concepts, and this means at the same time: from concepts and merely from concepts. This aspect of metaphysics has become more acute in the philosophy of modernity since Descartes through this general, rational knowledge of beings as a whole becoming assimilated to mathematical knowledge, which develops the entirety of its knowledge deductively from a few fundamental principles, that is, axioms, completely independent of experience. The most significant effort with a view to such a rational metaphysics is undertaken by Leibniz, to the point where he attempts to trace even truths of fact, *veritates facti*, back to truths of reason, *veritates rationis*, and to ground them in the latter. Admittedly Leibniz provided only individual contributions, approaches, and pointers; he did not succeed in attaining an overall plan with a view to metaphysics as a whole. This task was taken over by his students—Wolff, Baumgarten, Crusius— as they integrated the results of Leibniz's philosophy into the framework of Scholastic philosophy. Kant points to the conflict of opinions and uncertainty of the results.

Ad. 2. What direction does clarifying it take? It aims at the possibility of knowledge of beings in general. Metaphysics proper is the goal, "metaphysics and final purpose." The question is: From where does this metaphysics take its authorization and certification, given that on the one hand, experience only ever gets to see an individual being, and that on the other hand, pure concepts do not relate to beings without further ado? In the question concerning the possibility of metaphysics as knowledge of beings as such as a whole the issue is therefore the question concerning the essence of a knowledge of beings, the possibility and essence of metaphysics, the problem of the possibility of knowledge of beings in general. What does that mean, and what does it entail? Is there such a thing?

Yes, says Kant. We have the example of the scientific knowledge of nature in the mathematical physics of Galileo and Newton. Kant's question is fundamentally directed toward knowledge of beings. What is characteristic regarding this knowledge of beings in the sense of mathematical physics lies in the fact that a light came on for all researchers into nature, that is, for all those who essentially got such knowledge going. It occurred to them that nature could only be known or, more precisely, that nature could only be interrogated in the experiment, if a plan of nature was itself first projected in advance. Knowledge of beings must therefore be preceded by a peculiar knowledge prior to all experience, in which it gets decided what belongs to a nature in general. Such a knowledge that, prior to all experience of beings, precisely determines the constitution of being pertaining to beings, Kant calls a knowledge a priori, one that is earlier in the sense that it precedes empirical experience in the order of grounding. This strange knowledge whose fundamental significance is familiar to the researcher into nature is an a priori knowledge; it determines what belongs to a nature. It determines the essence of nature, its substantiveness or reality. Reality for Kant does not mean the way in which we use the term today, as the actuality or existence of beings; Kant, rather, uses reality in the sense of Scholasticism, as that which determines a *res*, a matter, in its what-content. Reality is therefore synonymous with *essentia*. The whole of Neo-Kantianism has completely failed to understand this concept, and was therefore driven in part to pose nonsensical kinds of questions.

What is at stake in the knowledge of beings is an antecedent, a priori knowledge of the essence of the beings in question, of the matter, a substantive a priori knowledge, the kind of knowledge that gives me information about what belongs to a matter; a knowledge that extends our knowing Kant calls synthetic. A knowledge of beings must therefore be preceded by a substantive knowledge of the constitution of their being, a synthetic knowledge and, insofar as it is antecedent = a priori, a synthetic knowledge a priori.

Synthetic knowledge a priori is possible knowledge of beings. The question concerning the possibility of ontic knowledge thus becomes the question concerning the possibility of synthetic knowledge a priori, that is, of ontological knowledge. How is knowledge of being possible? The problem of the possibility of metaphysics becomes the problem of the possibility of ontology, that is, of *metaphysica generalis*. In his effort to lay the ground for metaphysics proper (*metaphysica specialis*), Kant is sent back by the problem itself to *metaphysica generalis*, and the latter becomes a problem for the first time since Aristotle. The fundamental problem of the *Critique of Pure Reason* is ontology as such; it is not in any way a theory of knowledge nor even a theory of natural science, as Neo-Kantianism wants to claim. If it is concerned with a theory of knowledge at all, then it is with a theory of ontological knowledge; but even this formulation is skewed and leads away from the central problem.

Ad. 3. To what extent is determining the essence of metaphysics a critique of pure reason? Reason is what is supreme in the human being, the ability to know a priori; yet the essence of such knowledge needs to be circumscribed; in such circumscribing there ensues a delimiting in relation to excessive demands and transgressions of the limit; traditional metaphysics is an example of the latter. Critique therefore means a circumscribing of essence, thus at the same time a delimiting, restricting; this is why it is also polemically directed and co-determined by this. It is a critique of finite, human, pure reason. The "business of this critique" is "to alter the procedure of metaphysics hitherto." Kant also names the *Critique of Pure Reason* a "treatise on method," which means, however, that it "specifies nevertheless the entire outline . . . as well as its entire internal structure."[26] Method here does not mean technique but rather the question concerning the possible complete determination of an object, the fundamental question concerning the latter itself.

Ad. 4. What is the approach and outline of the laying the ground for metaphysics? The question is raised concerning the possibility of pure knowledge, of knowledge in general, concerning intuition and concept and the unity of the two, and indeed of pure intuition and pure concepts. This is a transcendental question.

If we look at the table of contents of the *Critique of Pure Reason*, then we see a fundamental division into Doctrine of Elements and Doctrine of Method. The Doctrine of Elements develops the elements, the foundational aspects. We can confine ourselves to this part. The Doctrine of Elements, and indeed the Transcendental Doctrine of Elements—Transcendental is essential here—has two parts. The first part is the Transcendental Aesthetic, the second is the Transcendental Logic. How this division comes about, we shall see later. The Transcendental Logic is in turn articulated into two divisions, the first of which is the Transcendental Analytic. The second division is the Transcendental Dialectic.

If we take the schema of the *Critique of Pure Reason* in this way, it is not evident without further ado how this work is supposed to be connected with the problem of traditional metaphysics. If, however, from the outset we understand the work not according to its outer arrangement, but conversely understand the arrangement as it lies before us in terms of the fundamental problem of the work, then it immediately becomes clear what we are dealing with here. What Kant treats in the Transcendental Aesthetic, which in a certain way still points toward the traditional problems, and in the Transcendental Analytic—all of this is nothing other than laying the ground for *metaphysica generalis*; and what he treats in the Transcendental Dialectic is the laying the ground for, and critique of, *metaphysica specialis*. That the cut is made precisely through here is especially notable for the Kantian way of posing the question and is one aspect that will have to be subjected to an essential critique by us. This is connected with the influence of traditional logic on Kant's work. This division of traditional metaphysics is reflected in the outline of the Transcendental Doctrine of Elements.

b) Excursus: Kant's laying the ground for metaphysics

Ad. 5. What are the main theses and the steps of this laying the ground? We shall distinguish between the main theses and the execution.

---

26. Immanuel Kant, *Kritik der reinen Vernunft*, newly edited by Raymund Schmidt according to the first and second original editions (Leipzig: Felix Meiner, 1926), preface, B XXIIf.

α) *The main theses*

It is characteristic of all philosophical investigations that they start with seemingly simple and elementary principles but that behind these principles an entire world of presuppositions thrives; to the lay person and to the person of letters in philosophy it looks as though these would be unproven presuppositions. What we shall now discuss are the insights that Kant from the outset lays at the basis of the discussion of the problem of metaphysics, which he does not thematically elaborate at all, yet for which he has a sure insight. This is to say that what Kant does not express in detail, and what philosophy does not say, is always the essential.

We can reduce these fundamental theses to three:

1. A thesis concerning what knowledge in general is.
2. The problem is the finitude of human knowledge.
3. The object of such knowledge is what is knowable itself as an appearance, not as a thing in itself.

1. The first sentence of the *Critique* provides information about what belongs to knowledge in general: "In whatever manner and by whatever means a given knowledge may relate to objects, intuition is that through which it is in immediate relation to them, and to which all thought as a means is directed" (A 19, B 33). From this sentence we can take two things: First, that the essence of knowledge lies in intuition.

This first sentence of the *Critique* speaks radically against the view of Neo-Kantianism. One may say that the fundamental shortcoming of Neo-Kantianism consists in the fact that it has failed to read the first sentence of the *Critique*. In the Marburg school it has been overstated that for Kant, the essence of knowledge is thinking. He says explicitly: the essence of knowledge is intuition, and all thinking as a means is directed toward intuition. The entire *Critique* is built on this first sentence.

Intuition is called αἴσθησις in Greek. Aesthetic means the doctrine of αἴσθησις. According to the tradition, thought is the object of logic. If knowledge consists of intuition and thought, then the Aesthetic is the doctrine of intuition and the Logic the doctrine of thinking. This is the source of the conclusion of the Marburg school that seeks to interpret the Transcendental Aesthetic out of the *Critique of Pure Reason*. What is decisive not only for the outline of the work but for the entire problem is to hold fast to the general concept of knowledge as an intuiting that is clarified and analyzed in thinking. That is, every truth of thinking is necessarily directed toward being demonstrated and confirmed in intuition. We shall see that this is the central question of the *Critique of Pure Reason*, where the issue is the problem of ontological knowledge.

The second thesis concerns the finitude of knowledge. It is essential that the issue is not that of just any reason—a vagueness that is quite dominant today—but that Kant states clearly in the next sentence: "But intuition takes place only insofar as the object is given to us. This again is only possible, for us humans at least, insofar as the mind is affected in a certain way" (ibid.).

The addition "for us humans at least" stems from the second edition. What does it mean that in the *Critique of Pure Reason* finite knowledge or human knowledge as such is the object?

When Kant speaks of finite and human knowledge, then its distinction from infinite or absolute knowledge is in the background. Such is held to be God's knowledge, God thought in the sense of the Christian conception of God, according to which God is primarily creator. According to the traditional conception, which Kant further refined for the purposes of elucidating finite knowledge, God's knowledge is intuitive knowledge or pure intuiting, or "only" intuition. Already in Scholasticism, in Aquinas, for example, though perhaps on grounds that are not tenable, there is a generally accepted clarity regarding the fact that God cannot think, for all thought is an index of finitude. Aquinas grounds this as follows: In thought, judgment occurs, here I add a predicate to a subject. I thus run through definite steps in making determinations, that is, thinking, as predication, is necessarily successive and requires time. Yet God is not in time. Not being able to think is therefore no shortcoming. God's knowledge is pure intuiting, that is, he knows beings as a whole in one moment—"*totum simul*"—what was before and will be in the future. This absolute intuition is at the same time the intuition in which beings, both those that are factically actual and those that are possible, are known in their essence from the outset. God knows all beings in their essence because he is, after all, the creator, because he himself creates beings. His intuition is one that, insofar as it is accomplished, lends being in a certain sense to that which is intuited. To his essence there belongs an intuition through which things first of all come to be; they do not come to be for God, for God they always are; they come to be within time. This intuition that gives what can be intuited the origin of its being Kant calls *intuitus originarius*, which as intuition helps what can be intuited find its origin. Such knowledge, as absolute intuition, is completely independent of the content that is intuited. For the latter originates from the intuiting itself.

In contrast to this absolute intuition that defines God, the intuition of all finite creatures is an *intuitus derivatus*, that is, an intuition that, as intuition, is dependent on something; as finite intuition that does not always already exist, it is referred to the fact that these very beings are present at hand of their own accord and that what is intuitable must be given to finite intuition, because such intuition itself does not create it. This is why the second sentence states: "But intuition takes place only insofar as the object is given to us." Consequently, a creature that is finite, that possesses finite intuition, is determined in accordance with its essence in such a way that something can be given to it, that it is receptive of something. It must have receptivity. This receptivity for something Kant also designates as sensibility. He is the one who for the first time determined the concept of sensibility precisely in terms of this opposition between absolute and finite knowledge. In keeping with its essence, a finite intuition is characterized by receptivity. That which is to be given to it must announce itself of its own accord to a certain degree, or, as Kant says, the being must affect the receptive subject. It follows from the essence of receptivity that it is determined by affection. The receptive being must therefore be structured in such a way that it can be affected. The organs and structures of affection we call the senses. As we believe today, the human being has five senses. That the human being has eyes and ears precisely, is absolutely contingent. What is absolutely necessary for a finite being is that it has receptivity and possible organs. For this reason, the concept of sensibility is not to be determined in terms of the sense organs. We have sense organs only because our essence is finite. This state of affairs was seen clearly for the first time by Kant. One cannot say that this has been appreciated to this day in its full implications. Finite intuition is thus necessarily determined as sensibility, while the kind of affection is a secondary question.

We know that Kant says: knowledge is determined by intuition and thinking. Finite knowing not only is intuiting as sensibility but is also referred to thinking. Thinking is itself something finite and is so for an essentially deeper reason than that cited by Aquinas, namely that thinking is characterized by succession, that thinking and intuition too unfold in a succession. The intrinsic finitude of thinking, rather, consists in the following: all thinking is a judging or determining of something as something. When I determine something in thought, I cannot determine whatever is to be determined, that is, the object, in such a way that I merely stare at it as such but must instead determine it with respect to something. If I say that this thing is red, then I draw this feature of it being red from the thing itself as given in intuition. Yet I understand this knowledge only if I know what color is, without my having the concept of color. That is, when in intuition I explicate the statement, I select the aspect of color, of something as something. All determining in thought, as the determining of something as something, must necessarily have regard to something with respect to which the object before us can be determined. Thinking is not intuition, but must make a detour via the respect in terms of which the object is determined. According to Kant, thinking as predication is not immediate, but mediate. It makes detours by its very essence. We thus see in knowledge a dual finitude, not just the finitude of intuition and finitude of thought as such, but in unison with these, their being referred to one another.

Third thesis: What is that which is knowable itself, insofar as it can be known by finite knowledge, and what is the knowable object of finite knowledge as distinct from the knowable object of divine knowledge? We have on the one hand finite knowledge, on the other hand absolute knowledge. The object of finite knowledge is called appearance by Kant. The object of absolute knowledge he calls the thing in itself. This state of affairs reflects the fact that the thing is not relative to a finite being; rather, the thing in itself is relative to the absolute. The object of finite knowledge is appearance. This concept, however, brought about great confusion, especially since this thing in itself was appropriated by psychology.

Kant names the object of finite knowledge appearance because, for a finite being, beings are accessible only through their showing themselves. That the object of finite knowledge is appearance means that it is that which shows itself, that is, something that must necessarily show itself. This entails that a finite being is able to know beings to the extent that beings are able to show themselves, and in the way that they are able to show themselves for this particular being, the human being. The question of the relationship between appearance and thing in itself is important, however, for understanding the entire problem, and here the confusion first begins. The thing in itself and appearance may only be understood in relation to finite and absolute knowledge. If one omits this, then there is no hope of understanding anything. We see this in how we explain the relationship assigned to both. One usually speaks of appearances such as celestial phenomena, phantoms, comets. Behind the appearances there really lies the thing in itself. That we cannot get behind appearances is something Kant denied. This distinction is indeed not so self-evident. The decisive insight, however, lies in this: An appearance is the being itself that shows itself, not something that comes to the surface, therefore, but the being itself. Kant says: This piece of chalk is an appearance, something independently present at hand. It never occurred to Kant that the piece of chalk would not be real, but something imagined by the subject instead. This piece of chalk is something present at hand that shows itself, something that is appearing, an appearance. The thing in itself, then, is not something behind the chalk; rather, the thing in itself is this same chalk that we are seeing, only now thought as the object of an absolute knowledge. The distinction between the two concerns the distinction between the being in question becoming a possible object for God or for a finite creature. There are not two layers of beings, rather the same being as the object of finite knowledge is appearance, and as the object of absolute knowledge, the thing in itself.

β) The execution

We now wish to break down the execution of this laying of the ground into four steps. The issue is the essence of pure knowledge.

In the first stage, Kant must treat the elements of a pure knowledge.

At the second stage, he asks concerning the intrinsic connection or intrinsic unity of these elements of a pure knowledge. This is the question concerning the essence of this knowledge itself.

At the third stage, the question is raised concerning the ground of this essence or the inner possibility of an ontological knowledge.

At the fourth stage, Kant develops such ontological knowledge itself in its systematic character, or as he says, the transcendental, that is, ontological principles.

The positive laying of the ground in the *Critique of Pure Reason*, which in traditional terms is a laying the ground for *metaphysica generalis*, extends to this point. This is then followed by the critical laying of the ground for *metaphysica specialis*, which no longer has to do with transcendental truth, but with transcendental illusion, with untruth, which is necessarily linked to this transcendental truth.

We take up the first stage: The elements of pure knowledge. You can already see from these first steps of the problem why a general characterization is provided first. When we speak of knowing in connection with the three theses we are not yet discussing whether it is experiential knowing or knowing that is free of experience. But now the problem is that of a pure knowing, that is, a knowing that is free of experience; more precisely, the problem concerns the elements of such a pure knowledge. From the foundational thesis we know that intuition and thought belong to any knowledge. We said that intuition has the character of receptivity, that intuition is always a letting oneself be given something. This is why Kant also says receptivity in place of intuition, insofar as the issue is finite intuition. Thought is not a letting oneself be given that which shows itself but rather is a determining of that which gives itself, a determining that emerges spontaneously and freely from the acting subject. This is why thinking, as a free action, is called spontaneity. These two elements of knowledge Kant also calls the two stems of knowledge, which grow and emerge from a common root, a root, however, that is unknown to us.

At the conclusion of the introduction to the *Critique of Pure Reason* Kant points especially to the unknown root of the two. He designates these two faculties as two fundamental sources of our mind, where mind [*Gemüt*] is used for *mens* in the sense of Descartes, Leibniz, and Augustine. Now, the problem is not just any knowing but ontological knowledge, that is, an a priori, pure knowing. This means, therefore, that the problem is pure intuition and pure thought; more precisely, in keeping with the first sentence of the *Critique of Pure Reason*, the knowing is an intuiting that is determined by thinking. Determination by thought stands in service to intuiting. Knowing is always thoughtful intuiting.

The second stage asks concerning the unity or the essence of a pure knowledge, thus concerning the possibility of a pure intuition. Intuition, in Greek, αἴσθησις, is the object of the Aesthetic. The issue is a possible a priori intuition, that is, therefore, a transcendental investigation of intuition. Accordingly, the elaboration of a pure intuition is the object of a Transcendental Aesthetic. Correspondingly, the elaboration of pure thinking is the object of the Transcendental Analytic.

Insight into the essence of pure intuition is one of the most fundamental discoveries to which Kant may lay claim. Intuition means letting oneself be given something, such that whatever gives itself becomes intuitable in itself; intuition of what is received = reception. Reception is referred to affection, that is, to the fact that whatever I am to intuit announces itself in me of its own accord. Here the issue is the problem of a pure intuition, that is, an intuition a priori, or, as Kant says, without and prior to all experience. An intuition without receptivity is the problem that Kant failed to elaborate with full incisiveness, an intuition that is receptive as such because it is, after all, human intuition, and yet a priori, that is, springing from the subject, from its spontaneity, not referred to what can be intuited having to announce itself of its own accord. The idea of pure intuition has a dual character. In it lies the idea of a faculty in which the human being is in a certain way productive insofar as he is not referred to something that gives itself but rather to something that he gives himself in advance, so as to intuit it. There is thus an analogy to the creation intuition of the *intuitus originarius*.

What, then, is pure intuition? The two pure intuitions that belong to the finite creature are space and time. This is at first surprising, insofar as one cannot exactly see how space or even time are supposed to be an intuition. I shall just develop a brief characterization of the idea of pure intuition in terms of time, because according to Kant, time is a more comprehensive intuition than space; here, I shall go beyond Kant in my interpretation.

Time itself plays a central role in the *Critique of Pure Reason*. For Kant it is a pure sequence, pure succession as such, which in its peculiar flow is now, previously, and afterward, something that we do not find among the things before us. And yet, it is something that determines everything that we experience of things; everything intuitable, everything that gives itself in receptivity, is determined as given now, previously, or later. Everything that can be experienced is given in a temporal determination. Time, pure succession, is a form of givenness to which we always already look in advance whenever we experience objects, things, without our having an explicit awareness of it, without our making this succession into an object of contemplation. We are directed in advance toward pure succession in a nonobjective manner. Prior to all experience, and not on the basis of experience, that is, a priori, we intuit time, and time itself only is and only gives itself as pure succession in and for this intuiting. Time is therefore a pure intuition in a double sense: something intuited a priori, and at the same time something that in a certain way only is within intuiting itself. We thus have time as pure intuition that in a certain way embraces the pure intuition of space.

A corresponding consideration is directed toward pure thinking. For Kant, in keeping with the tradition, thinking is the same as judging. I think = I judge. I judge means: I connect a subject with a predicate. I think is thus equivalent to I connect; the action of thought has the character of synthesis. Now, for Kant the issue is that of pure thinking, that is, of a kind of thinking that, prior to all experience, nevertheless thinks something, is not simply the form of thinking but rather, as thinking, of its own accord assigns a determination to that which can be determined in thinking, to intuition.

The question is therefore this: Does there lie at the same time in this human action that we call thinking, in the possibility of judging, a source of knowledge that has content? If I formally connect a = b, then according to Kant a quite determinate knowledge already lies in this connecting, insofar as all connecting of something with something is referred to a unity with regard to which the connecting is undertaken. Now, Kant finds forms of having regard in the traditional table of judgments. In each of these forms of judgment there must each time be a corresponding having regard to a corresponding unity. In the proposition 'a = b' we find regard to a unity, that is, to an independently subsisting thing, a substance. The concept of such a unity Kant calls a category. Pure thinking is thus represented in categories or, to put it more precisely: I think a category, that is, I move within a form of connecting for which I must necessarily look toward a unity that provides me with a guideline for the kind of unifying being undertaken. Kant formulates this after the fact, at a hidden point where it is not the theme: "The Transcendental Analytic has given us an example of how the mere logical form of our knowledge may contain the origin of pure concepts a priori, which represent objects prior to all experience, or rather, indicate the synthetic unity that alone makes possible an empirical knowledge of objects" (A 321, B 377). For in order to know empirical objects, I must not only intuit empirically but think them as things with properties.

The fundamental problem of the *Critique of Pure Reason*, however, is the unity of a pure intuition with a pure thinking, that is, of a possible a priori unifying of time and category. At the second stage, Kant discusses the essence of such an inner possibility of pure intuition and category.

Synthesis a priori and the unity of a pure receptivity with a pure spontaneity must be possible. Pure intuition and pure thinking must become united. Each of the two must have an inner relatedness to the other. Pure intuition as receptivity must in a certain way have the character of thinking, it must be spontaneous. Conversely, if pure thinking is to become united with intuition, pure thinking must not only be spontaneous but have a relatedness to intuition, that is, be receptive. If, therefore, the two faculties are to have a relatedness to one another, and if a unifying is to be possible, then there must be an intermediary that has the character of spontaneous receptivity and at the same time that of receptive spontaneity. According to Kant, this is the transcendental imagination. It is the strange faculty of a spontaneous receptivity and a receptive spontaneity; and the essence of ontological knowledge lies in the transcendental imagination.

How far removed this interpretation is from the interpretation hitherto you can see from the fact that this faculty was consistently interpreted away by Neo-Kantianism, because one saw a remnant of psychology in it. In the Marburg school, the problem was unfurled in such a way as to develop everything out of pure thinking; Windelband and Rickert sought the unity of the two—intuition and thinking—without the imagination. We must show, however, that the transcendental imagination indeed has this character and that time therefore goes back to the transcendental imagination, as does the category. What we asked about at the beginning, the unknown root, as Kant calls it, is the transcendental imagination itself. It is characteristic that Kant became afflicted by a metaphysical anxiety in the face of the transcendental imagination and tried to excise it from his work.

This much is clear: under the heading of the transcendental imagination Kant encounters a phenomenon at the center of his own problem that—as he also remarked—runs completely contrary to something that according to the tradition and to his own conviction is to be regarded as a fundamental phenomenon of human Dasein. As soon as one introduces the imagination as a central faculty, the entire idea of philosophy hitherto collapses—whence Kant's evasion. What is important for us to see now is how this transcendental imagination looks.

According to traditional anthropology, the imagination is a faculty that, within the general classification, belongs to sensibility, a faculty that is subordinate to sensibility. And yet with the compelling force of the central problem of the *Critique of Pure Reason*, the imagination acquires a function that according to Kant's systematic viewpoints should not be attributed to it. Kant keeps to traditional psychology. He adopts literally the definition found in Wolff, which goes back to the Aristotelian concept of φαντασία (Kant's *Anthropology*, §28): "The imagination (*facultas imaginandi*), as a faculty of intuition even without the presence of the object, is either productive, that is, a faculty of original presentation of the latter, *exhibitio originaria*, which therefore precedes experience."[27] The imagination is a faculty of intuition, that is, a faculty that is capable of giving something, and what the imagination gives us is a view of something, without what we are viewing itself presenting itself in presence. This is the general and fitting definition of the imagination.

------

27. *Immanuel Kants Werke* (Cassirer), vol. 8. *Anthropologie in pragmatischer Hinsicht*, ed. Otto Schöndörffer (Berlin: B. Cassirer, 1923), §28, 54.

By virtue of this faculty, the human being becomes to a certain extent like God, that is, in this faculty, he has the possibility of giving himself something that can be intuited, purely of his own accord, though in such a way that what is given here as a view is not itself an existing object, in the way that with God the things not only are intuitable but become actual in their being things. That is the essential difference between the *exhibitio originaria* and the *intuitus originarius*. We must therefore understand our good German expression *Einbildung* [imagination] in a dual sense, in keeping with a dual signification of the expression *bilden: bilden* means, first, to produce; second, we can procure for ourselves a *Bild*, an image or view of something; image here not in the sense of a copy. *Einbilden* [to imagine] means to procure for oneself an image, such that this view is formed by us ourselves. This *Bilden* [forming of an image] is therefore a certain kind of shaping of synthesis. For this reason, Kant also calls the transcendental imagination *synthesis speciosa* in Latin terminology. *Species* means image, that is, the shaping that procures an image for us without what we are viewing being present. In the German way of expressing things he designates this *synthesis speciosa* as *figürliche Synthesis*, figurative synthesis. This is the general characterization of the transcendental imagination that he takes as his basis in working out the essence of the relation of a pure thinking to a pure intuition.

With this we arrive at the third stage: the ground of the inner possibility of knowledge. With this problem the issue can be none other than the question: How is pure thinking, that is, the pure concepts of the understanding, to be brought into relation to pure intuition? To relate oneself to an intuition or to function as determining a pure intuition means nothing other than presenting in pure intuition. The problem of a possible relation of the categories to the pure intuition called time is the problem of the possible a priori presentability of the categories in time. How can pure concepts of the understanding, that is, categories, be intuited a priori in time, or how can time be the pure image of the categories? This is the formula that the problem of synthetic knowledge a priori comes down to. This problem is solved by Kant in his chapter on the Schematism, in a section of ten pages. The operation of our mind in which something like the intuitive presentation of the categories in time is accomplished is the schematism. Schema = image = view. Schematism is the faculty of procuring an image for the pure concepts, of bringing them into a pure image. In other words, the innermost ground of the possibility of synthetic knowledge a priori is the transcendental imagination as schematism.

Kant calls time a pure intuition. As intuition, it is receptivity, it gives, lets receive. It is a pure intuition, that is, an a priori receptivity or a spontaneous receptivity, that is, a free giving to oneself; pure intuition freely gives itself time as pure succession. If one analyzes this context phenomenologically then it is immediately apparent that giving oneself the now, back then, after that, is possible only if this pure intuition is a free shaping in accordance with all three fundamental dimensions of time. Only the transcendental imagination comes into question for this free shaping.

A more penetrating interpretation must show that what Kant develops in the Aesthetic as pure intuition is fundamentally the transcendental imagination. Conversely, pure thinking is initially characterized as spontaneity but as one that, in the manner of unifying, must at the same time look to the guiding idea of unity. In thinking as spontaneity there necessarily lies a character of receptivity in the sense of an a priori receptivity. Now, the connection of pure thinking to the imagination is what is most obscure in Kant. Only a very little is found about it in the first edition. But everything remains rough and is not posed as the specific problem: How can one show the rootedness of pure intuition and thinking in the imagination? From here there arises the conclusion that was drawn by Jacobi. Time and thinking are traced back to the imagination; therefore, time is something imagined. The question here, however, is what this imagination itself is, whether it itself is something imagined or whether we do not have to name it the primordial reality of human being.

This interpretation of Kant's first acquires its meaning and legitimacy once it has been systematically shown that what Kant hits upon is time itself, though in a sense that was no longer accessible to Kant. This operation of the transcendental imagination is thus that whereby a pure intuition is procured for the categories. Insofar as the pure intuition of time is that determination that determines in advance every object of experience, the relatability of the categories to objects themselves is ensured with the possible relatability of the pure concepts of the understanding to time.

Thus, there arises the real question of the Transcendental Deduction: How can a priori concepts of the understanding have objective reality, that is, how can they belong a priori to the substantive content of an object? This schematism must in any case be analyzed by Kant to the extent where he attempts to show how for each category time constitutes the schema, that is, its possible presentability, in a determinate respect. In the Schematism chapter, he says (A 141, B 181f.): "This schematism of our understanding, with regard to appearances and their mere form, is an art concealed in the depths of the human soul, whose real operations nature is hardly likely ever to let us uncover, and to set openly before our gaze."

One can express things this way if, like Kant, one allocates the basis for questioning to psychology from the outset, something that the *Critique of Pure Reason* does not discuss further. If, however, one sees the problem of laying the ground for metaphysics in an essentially more radical way, then the question is whether one may address the transcendental imagination merely as an art concealed in the soul, or whether it is not precisely that with whose aid we attain the concept of a soul. I cannot go into this problem in detail here.

Fourth stage. Kant immediately adds to this fundamental discussion of the possibility of synthetic knowledge a priori and of its ground a systematic presentation of such forms of synthetic knowledge a priori, that is, of the synthetic principles of the understanding. He divides these principles into four classes, in keeping with the guiding thread of the table of categories:

1. Axioms of intuition
2. Anticipations of perception
3. Analogies of experience
4. Postulates of empirical thought in general.

What is important for us in this fourfold division is the separation of these principles into mathematical and dynamic principles. The mathematical principles concern intuition, the dynamic concern existence. Kant explicitly remarks (A 162, B 201f.): "But it should be noted that we are as little concerned in the one case with the principles of mathematics as in the other with the principles of general (physical) dynamics. We treat only of the principles of pure understanding in their relation to inner sense (all differences among the given representations being ignored). It is through these principles of pure understanding that the principles of mathematics and of dynamics become possible. I have named them, therefore, on account rather of their application than of their content." He wants to say: the table of principles embraces the forms of ontological knowledge, that is, the knowledge that in general determines what belongs to the ontological essence of nature. Now we know, however, that a being, for instance, nature, is determined on the one hand by its essence = what-being = *essentia*, and on the other hand by its particular way of being = *existentia*, in Kantian terminology, by existence. Corresponding to this duality of *essentia* and *existentia* the system of ontological principles must also be articulated into mathematical and dynamic principles.

Ontologically, these expressions mathematical and dynamic mean as much as essential and existential in Leibniz's sense. The reason I mention this division is that what emerges from it once again is the extent to which the table of principles is nothing other than the entirety of our ontological knowledge of nature, or the possibility of a nature in general. Yet just as nature is thought by Kant in correlation to that knowledge which he calls experience, so the elaboration of our knowledge of a nature in general is at the same time the delimiting of the essence of experience. With this uncovering of the possibility of experience and of the possibility of nature the positive part of the *Critique* as laying the ground for *metaphysica generalis* is completed.

Nevertheless, this phenomenon of the possibility of experience in two directions poses a peculiar new problem that we may formulate not so much negatively, as does Kant, but positively. To experience, that is, to finite knowledge there belongs the fact that that which is known affects us. To the essence of experience in the sense of affection and receptivity belongs contingency. Every experience is contingent, that is, referred to the emergence of the particular fact that we are affected by particular things in a particular situation. This entails that the unity of experience is always dependent on the empirical content of whatever has become accessible on each occasion. This empirical unity of experience, however, is itself only thinkable as a unity if it is determined by a higher one. The very possibility of experience as the unity of a determinate knowledge entails within it the question concerning with respect to what is the possibility of experience something contingent, restricted, and conversely the question of what the higher unity is within which every empirical unity of experience moves.

There is no a priori ontic knowledge but only ontological, and this under determinate conditions, which is to say that the legitimate and genuine knowledge that is related a priori to beings is ontological. Yet has the latter already been fully determined? Transcendental truth and transcendental illusion (untruth): something that pretends to be ontic a priori knowledge but is not.

c) Excursus: Kant's Dialectic

To be able to discuss the seat of illusion and of transcendental illusion in general, we need more than the Analytic that has preceded. In illusion itself there lies something positive that presents itself as . . . and that is not identical to synthetic knowledge a priori, but underlies such knowledge itself as its conditions.

The really central ontological problematic extends into the transcendental ideal, that is, it springs from there, that is, from the essence of finite human reason, "of this divine human within us" (A 569, B 597).

The task is to bring to light the entire basis for the whole of metaphysics and to see the latter in its inner entirety and movement. The fundamental ontology aims at this, but is initially ventured only with regard to the Analytic (not theory of knowledge). The result of the *Critique of Pure Reason* up to the Transcendental Dialectic is this: there is no general knowledge of beings a priori, no ontic knowledge a priori, but only an a priori knowledge as ontological. The essence of the *generalis* in *metaphysica generalis*, and thereby of metaphysics itself, is determined more primordially. With this, the concept of ontological knowledge is determined for the first time, even if it must be said that Kant did not pose the problem within the entire scope of the understanding of being. In any case, the possibility of a fundamental implication for the whole idea of metaphysics has now been given.

Kant now has a guiding thread in hand for his purposes in terms of which he can assess what kind of knowledge it is that is laid claim to in *metaphysica specialis*, namely an a priori ontic knowledge concerning the soul, world, and God. However, the issue is not that of now simply rejecting such knowledge as impossible but just as much that of indicating positively what is legitimate about the aim of such knowledge with respect to the nature of the human being to whom such questioning belongs. The task is not just to recognize the illusion of such a priori ontic knowledge; rather, we must become clear about the fact that where there is illusion—illusion as necessary, natural illusion—there is truth also.

Important though the negative rejection of the presumption of special knowledge remains for Kant, he must at the same time arrive at positive insights that are manifestly connected to the problem of metaphysical knowledge already treated.

Indeed, there is more: we shall see that what Kant discusses on the basis of the Transcendental Analytic as seemingly just a critical application for its part first opens the true foundations for his starting point. We thus see in Kant too how all philosophical laying the ground does not simply head in a straight line toward a foundation present at hand somewhere and settle there, but precisely constantly digs away the ground under its feet and moves increasingly on the edge of an abyss.

However, what makes difficult a central, inner understanding of the problematic of laying the ground for *metaphysica specialis* and above all its connection with *metaphysica generalis*, and indeed downright impedes it, is the architectonic that Kant gave his work and which is by no means merely a matter of a superficial arrangement. We have already pointed out how the framework is constructed: Transcendental Aesthetic, Transcendental Logic; and we pointed out that the scission between *metaphysica generalis* and *specialis* lies within the Logic itself, so that the latter therefore has a quite special priority within the entire problem of the *Critique of Pure Reason*.

For this priority of the Logic in the *Critique of Pure Reason*—and elsewhere too in Kant—we shall name two among a series of other reasons:

1. Logic is the most general knowledge of thinking, of *ratio*, of reason; it thus affords the broadest insight into the structure of reason.
2. As this knowledge of *ratio*, logic itself counts as the most rational and thereby most rigorous knowledge; accordingly, it is the most certain and most general knowledge of reason.

For these two reasons, which have almost become a matter of self-evidence, logic suggests itself without further ado as the suitable guiding thread for a critique of pure reason. Furthermore: knowing is judging, determining in thought.

Thinking is what is uppermost and ultimate and authentic. (And there is also no escaping it, however: psychological anthropology, even imagination.)

The elaboration and securing of the field within which Kant is moving is handed over to these traditional disciplines. Now, it is already an intrinsically questionable undertaking to adopt logic as the guiding thread in laying the ground for metaphysics, even if it must be, and is, corrected ad hoc at every step. The questionable character of this is essentially increased, however, when we consider that logic precisely in the form that Kant found it before him rests on completely unclarified metaphysical presuppositions that are connected to the historical origination of this logic from the metaphysics of antiquity. These presuppositions of logic, indeed its very concept, have never yet been made a problem and the fundamental problems have never been considered regarding the fact that, and how, logic as such is grounded in metaphysics, that is, how it only ever gives the illusion of letting itself develop purely out of itself, as it were. Despite this, we should not be blind to the fact that Kant has given his Logic a very transparent, systematic form.

Connected to this unclarified and unquestioned priority of logic itself in posing the problem of the *Critique of Pure Reason* is the fact that precisely the transition to laying the ground for *metaphysica specialis* must remain forced and artificial, however much essential issues are developed in detail with full clarity there. This is true in particular for the way in which the "idea" is introduced.

With the doctrine of the principles, the real task of how synthetic a priori knowledge is possible appears to be solved. For not only are the essence of such knowledge in general clarified and the ground of its inner possibility illuminated, but it itself is uncovered in its entirety as that knowledge which constitutes the possibility of experience. Such knowledge contains what belongs to the constitution of the being of those beings that are accessible to the finite human creature. Kant names the possible knowledge of accessible beings experience; "experience" is ambivalent: It means experiencing and also that which is itself experienced.

d) Kant's concept of 'idea'

Among the representations, the intuitions and concepts that belong to this possibility of experience, the concept of world does not appear. "World" is neither pure intuition nor pure concept (*notio*), nor category as the notion that can be presented in pure time. Nonetheless, the concept "world" is not an arbitrary one, but a necessary representation of a unique kind, an idea.

We must therefore now ask:

1. What does Kant understand by idea?
2. How does the necessity for ideas arise for Kant?
3. What does it mean for how the concept of world is conceived if it is determined as an idea?
4. What fundamental problems arise from this conception of the phenomenon of world?

Ad. 1 and 2. Experience and/or the being that gives itself in experience is necessarily determined in advance by the transcendental principles. For all its determinacy, all experience is still incomplete by its very essence, because it belongs to its essence that beings are encountered of their own accord, that they must be given, and the possibility of something being given that has not been experienced hitherto, the necessity of an individual, factical giving on each occasion, belongs to the essence of experience. Being given—a happening and operation at the same time, a *commercium* of the two, factical. Although experience itself as receiving is ontologically determined, it remains incomplete and contingent. The unity of what is given is only ever an empirical one, determining itself in terms of what precisely gives itself; this "conditioned" empirical unity can, however, at any time be represented in and through what is given.

The knowledge and synthesis of objects of possible experience is "at all times conditioned" (A 308, B 365). The concept of condition indeed lies analytically within the concept of the conditioned. Yet this is not yet to say that if the conditioned is given, the condition too is given—together with "the entire series of conditions, subordinate to one another, a series which is therefore itself unconditioned" (A 307f., B 364).

A statement that makes such an assertion is a synthetic statement and indeed purely from the idea of reason as the faculty of inference and of principles. Such a knowledge, however—synthetic and from pure reason—Kant calls a principle pure and simple. Now, "ideas . . . contain a certain completeness to which no possible empirical knowledge ever attains, and in them reason aims only at a systematic unity, to which it seeks to approximate the unity that is empirically possible, without ever completely reaching it" (A 567/8, B 595/6). "By a system I understand the unity of the manifold modes of knowledge under one idea. This idea is the concept provided by reason, of the form of a whole, insofar as the concept determines a priori not only the scope of its manifold content but also the positions which the parts occupy relative to one another" (A 832, B 860).

The idea represents a whole, the wholeness of a whole that as such can never be empirically fathomed or attained. The idea therefore leaps over every possible empirical whole in advance; the wholeness (totality) represented in the idea is such not just in one particular respect, but in every respect, with a view to every intent, that is, it is absolute. Kant uses the term "absolute" in keeping with the explicit elucidation of the concept, as signifying "in every relation," "altogether" (A 324f., B 380f.). An idea is the antecedent representation of an absolute totality. (Cf. what is said about "world" in Kant's dissertation; see p.176f.)

It is decisive to understand what it is that such an idea relates to. "The absolute whole of all appearances is only an idea, for we can never project such a thing in an image, and it thus remains a problem to which there is no solution" (A 328, B 384). The unity that lies in the representation of an absolute totality therefore never relates to what is given as such in intuition on each occasion; certainly, what is thus given always already stands within a unity of experience on each occasion, and this unity is determined by the principles of understanding. Accordingly, if the idea brings a yet higher unity, but one that cannot be presented in intuition, then this unity can only relate to the unity of the understanding, that is, its synthesis. Understanding is the faculty whereby I connect; I think = I connect = I judge.

The idea accordingly has the function of prescribing to the understanding "its direction toward a certain unity of which the understanding has no concept and that is directed toward uniting all acts of the understanding, in respect of every object, into an absolute whole" (A 326/7, B 383). Just as the understanding brings the manifold of intuition under concepts and thereby connects this manifold, so the idea brings the manifold of the rules of the understanding, and thereby the understanding, "into a thoroughgoing accordance with itself" (A 305, B 362). Ideas are therefore never related directly to intuition, but always to the understanding and to that which, as the faculty of concepts, of synthesis, it unifies, to the unity of understanding (A 307, B 363). This is essential for the way in which Kant further determines the idea.

These ideas, however—as representations of an absolute totality—"are not arbitrarily invented, but imposed by the nature of reason itself, and therefore relate of necessity to the entire use of the understanding" (A 327, B 384). They are "in no way to be regarded as superfluous and void" (A 329, B 385). The ideas are necessary concepts, specifically of reason. They belong to the nature of reason. (Cf. the serial arrangement on p.198.)

What is the essence of reason? Kant says: "In the first part of our Transcendental Logic we explained the understanding as the faculty of rules; here, we shall distinguish reason from the understanding by calling it the faculty of principles" (A 299, B 356). The way in which the understanding and reason are determined in the *Critique of Pure Reason* fluctuates. And what does "principle" mean? According to Kant, the expression is "ambiguous" (A 300, B 356). "Every general proposition, even one derived from experience (through induction), can serve as the major premise in a syllogism of reason, but it is not itself a principle on that account" (ibid.). Compare: All humans are mortal; A is a human; A is mortal. Every syllogism of reason is "a form of deducing knowledge from a principle" (A 300, B 357). The general premise functions as a principle from which a conclusion is drawn. That is, in the major premise of the syllogism, in the principle, what is established or sought is "the general condition of its judgment (the conclusion)" (A 307, B 364).

The intent of reason in these syllogisms is thus concerned "with finding for the conditioned knowledge of the understanding the unconditioned with which the unity of the understanding is completed" (ibid.). The syllogism as a mode of thinking is thus regarded as a formal, fundamental tendency toward the unconditioned. Not every general premise [*Satz*] is therefore entirely and properly a principle [*Prinzip*]. Even the fundamental principles [*Grundsätze*] of the pure understanding are not properly principles,[28] but only function as such, for example, the principle of causality: "That everything that happens has a cause cannot at all be concluded from the concept of what happens in general" (A 301, B 357). These principles, although a priori, are always related to pure intuition. "Absolute principles" are "synthetic knowledge from concepts" (A 301, B 358). These concepts must therefore contain the unconditioned a priori, that in which the unity of the knowledge of the understanding, which is in each case conditioned, completes itself entirely; these concepts of absolute totality, however, are the ideas.

The idea, as a pure concept of reason, is thus "none other than the concept of the totality of the conditions for any given conditioned. Now since it is the unconditioned alone that makes possible the totality of conditions, and, conversely, the totality of conditions is at all times itself unconditioned, a pure concept of reason can in general be explained by the concept of the unconditioned, insofar as it contains a ground of the synthesis of the conditioned" (A 322, B 379). "As is easily seen, what pure reason alone has in view is nothing other than the absolute totality of synthesis on the side of the conditions . . . and that it is not concerned with absolute completeness on the side of the conditioned. For the former alone is required in order to presuppose the whole series of conditions, and to present it a priori to the understanding" (A 336, B 393). "If they [the concepts of reason, the ideas] contain the unconditioned, they are concerned with something to which all experience is subordinate but which is never itself an object of experience: something to which reason leads in its inferences from experience and in accordance with which it estimates and gauges the degree of its empirical employment, but which never constitutes a member of the empirical synthesis" (A 311, B 367/8).

Because they are the concepts corresponding to inferences of reason as such, Kant therefore calls the ideas "inferred concepts," as distinct from the pure concepts of the understanding, which are "merely reflected"; they contain "nothing more than the unity of reflection upon appearances, insofar as these appearances must necessarily belong to a possible empirical consciousness" (A 310, B 367). "Ideas" are "inferred concepts whose object can in no way be given empirically" (A 333, B 390). Ideas—springing more originally and more purely from reason— themselves document reason more originally.

---

28. German has three different terms that can translate to "principle" in English. The word *Satz*, which can also mean statement, proposition, or propositional statement (as we have often rendered it in the context of "propositional truth" [*Satzwahrheit*]) is translated as "premise" in the context of syllogistic reasoning. But it can also mean principle, as in the principle of causality (*Satz der Kausalität*). A *Grundsatz* is a fundamental or foundational proposition, generally translated as "principle" in the context of the Kantian *Grundsätze des reinen Verstandes*, the principles of the pure understanding. As Heidegger elucidates here, both *Satz* and *Grundsatz* are to be distinguished from principles in the more restricted sense of the principles (*Prinzipien*) of pure reason, which are concerned with the unconditioned a priori.—Trans.

We may summarize this general characterization of the Kantian concept of the idea in five points.

1. Idea is a "species of representation" (A 319f., B 376f.). It is thus subordinate to the universal genus "representation in general" (*repraesentatio*). The species-character of the idea as a species of representation, its specific way of representing (ἰδεῖν), becomes manifest from the following "serial arrangement" that Kant concisely presents in this context.

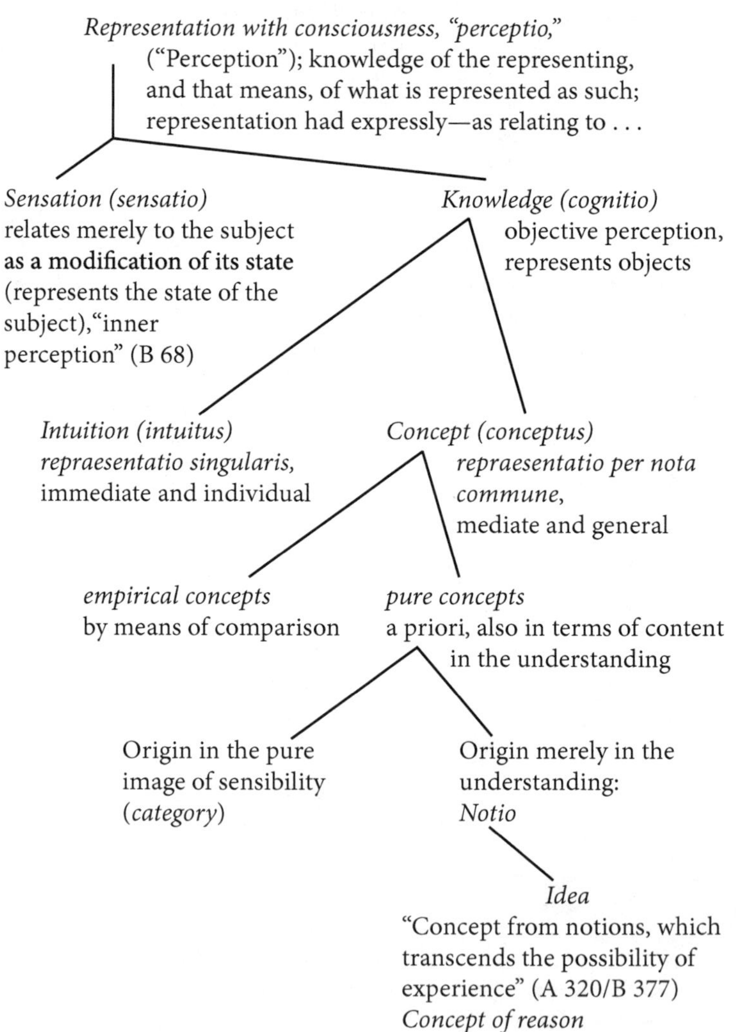

2. Idea with regard to what is represented in it as a representing: absolute wholeness, and specifically of the synthesis of the understanding, synthetic concepts.
3. As a concept of reason, it is an "inferred" concept, belonging a priori to the inference of reason as such, a concept that, as synthetic, provides the totality of the conditions of synthesis, that is, precisely the unconditioned.
4. This synthetic concept of reason is entirely a priori as a principle, prescribing a direction therefore, yet nevertheless intuitively unfulfillable in principle.
5. The reality of this concept is not an objective one, that is, not an empirical one, but a transcendental one, a concept that concerns the a priori condition of possibility of an a priori relatedness to objects (synthesis).[29] "Reality [substantiveness], in the pure concept of understanding, is that which corresponds to a sensation in general; it is therefore that whose concept in itself indicates being (in time). Negation is that whose concept represents not-being (in time)" (A 143, B 182); "transcendental material."

Kant's concept of idea therefore means: the conceptual representing of absolute totality as a ground of synthesis of the conditioned, that is, conceptual, transcendentally real representing of the un-conditioned. This representing is a priori, prescribing a direction, intuitively unfulfillable, giving unity to the synthesis of the understanding as such.[30]

Ad. 3. (Cf. p.194.) What does it mean for how the concept of world is conceived when it is determined as an idea? This question first demands a brief discussion of the extent to which a manifold of ideas results in general for Kant and the extent to which "world" is one among these.

---

29. *Realitas = determinatio (praedicativa) positiva vera*. Being real for Kant means making something into an object, something by which something is given that can be asserted (A 583, B 611, note). To be distinguished from this are "to hypostatize," "to personify." Reality: empirical (objective and subjective) reality (A 37, B 53), "inner experience"; reality: absolute, pertaining absolutely to things as a condition or property; reality: transcendental (A 36, B 53): "merely subjective."

30. Representation: Making present (presenting—in the more recent broad sense of something by way of something else) that which is composite, manifold within what is simple, one; cf. Leibniz, V. Letter to Clarke, n.85, *Principes de la nature et de la grâce*, n.2. Concentrating presentation is the fundamental power of representation. Unity simple with respect to objects (a) immediate, (b) mediate—and here this concept, scarcely ideated, is taken as equal to objective, objective so to speak: that is, indeterminate. The ontological [. . .]* of this being concentrating together with being presenting—without seeing the entire specific problematic of transcendence.

    Perceptio—a *repraesentatio* with consciousness, a concentrating presenting: independent, the kind that can relate itself or concentrate on itself. The presenting is not simply something known, but as such "with consciousness," a knowing becoming aware, "perceiving."

    *Editor's note: One word is missing in the manuscript, presumably *Grundkraft* [fundamental power].

According to their most general essence, the ideas as pure, inferred concepts are representations, and indeed *cognitiones*. As such, representations have "relations" to consciousness, "they relate to . . ."; that to which they relate itself presents itself in representations. Accordingly, Kant says: "The relations that are to be universally found in all our representations are: 1. relation to the subject; 2. relation to objects, either as appearances firstly or as objects of thought in general. If we combine this subdivision with the one above, all relation of representations of which we can have either a concept or an idea is then threefold: 1. the relation to the subject; 2. the relation to the manifold of the object in appearance; 3. the relation to all things in general" (A 333/4, B 390/1).

The universal aspect of any relation, that is, what such a relation can relate to in general, is threefold; yet the terms of this threefold are already different: (a) subject or object: the aspect of the what, the to what; (b) object qua appearance or qua thing in itself: the aspect of the possibility of finite or infinite representation, sheer productive representation or "reproductive." Three fields of possible synthesis, the fields of a possible totality. Correspondingly, our conceptual, ideational representing is threefold, and there are three classes of ideas. The first class of idea is concerned with the unconditioned unity of the thinking subject; the second, with the unconditioned unity of the series of conditions of appearances; the third, with the absolute unity of the condition of all objects of thought in general. This threefold is merely enumerated; it is no longer comprehended in terms of transcendence; cf. grounding.

"The thinking subject is the object of psychology, the sum-total of all appearances (the world) is the object of cosmology [*ens creatum*, finitude, "transcendental science of the world"], and the thing that contains the highest condition of the possibility of all that can be thought (the being of all beings) the object of theology" (A 334, B 391). The three disciplines of *metaphysica specialis* are thus developed from out of pure reason itself. "Pure reason thus furnishes the idea for a transcendental doctrine of the soul (*psychologia rationalis*), for a transcendental science of the world (*cosmologia rationalis*), and, finally, for a transcendental knowledge of God (*theologia transcendentalis*)" (A 334/5, B 391/2). "The mere project indeed" is not at all something that can be deduced from the understanding, "but is merely a pure and genuine product, or problem, of pure reason" (A 335, B 392). Pure reason = a priori synthetic reason.

With this, the concepts of world and cosmology have received their systematic justification; at the same time, however, the traditional concept of *metaphysica specialis* has been adopted and yet transformed. (Cf. *Critique of Pure Reason*, note added at B 395.)

"No objective deduction is possible" with regard to the ideas (cf. A 336, B 393), that is, the elucidation of their essence results from the essence of the relation to objects in general and whatever belongs to it. Among objects, the ideas have in principle no congruent object; there is no object for them; they run counter to the concept of object. How both, subjective and objective deduction, belong together—transcendence, and indeed ontic-ontological. Transcendence is at the same time and as such precisely the origin of the ontological difference.

Even if no objective deduction is possible, "we could," however, "undertake a subjective guidance [*Anleitung*] (*Akademie-Ausgabe*: derivation [*Ableitung*]) of them from the nature of our reason [ambiguous in relation to objects and to the function of making inferences] [cf. A XVII]" (A 336, B 393). Deduction of the three classes from the "function of reason in its inferences": categorical, hypothetical, disjunctive (A 321/2, B 378).

e) World as the idea of the totality of appearances: Correlate of finite human knowledge

World is on the one hand grasped by Kant as the "sum-total of all appearances" (A 419, B 447), and then as the "sum-total of all objects of possible experience" (*What Does it Mean to Orient Oneself in Thinking?*, 1786), which now means: the a priori general representation of the absolute totality of beings, insofar as they are accessible to a finite being. "Appearances are thus here regarded as given" (A 416, B 443). Appearances are constituted through ontological knowledge—principles—synthesis. "I name all transcendental ideas, insofar as they refer to absolute totality in the synthesis of appearances, concepts of world" (A 407/8, B 434).[31]

The concept of world as an idea is related not to an object in itself but to appearances, that is, to the unity of the conditions of synthesis, and this idea indeed concerns only "the ascending series of conditions" (A 409/10, B 436). These ideas as concepts of world—cosmos. The latter we also call "nature." An elucidation of the distinction between world and nature is therefore required (A 418/19, B 446/7). Even though Kant speaks of concepts of world in narrower and broader significations, all cosmological ideas are nevertheless concepts of world.

Concepts of world are indeed transcendental by contrast with categories, by contrast with appearances as a whole they are transcendent, that is, relatively transcendent; they are at the same time transcendent and transcendental; their reality is transcendental, because they are relatively transcendent in relation to appearances, yet nevertheless determine their unity as a totality. It is a subjective reality, yet cosmologically related to the world of the senses; what is thought in the concept of world is the empirically unconditioned totality of appearances

---

31. Concept of world—empirical synthesis, finitude of reception, experience. Concepts of world = ideas that have as their theme the doctrine of world, cosmology—cosmological ideas.

(objects), but not yet the unconditioned pure and simple. What gets expressed here is that the unconditioned totality qua world still has an essential relation to appearances after all, that is, to beings insofar as they are accessible to a finite being. Although it is an idea, it is still conditioned after all by its relation to finite knowledge. World is the idea of the totality of beings insofar as they are accessible to finite knowledge; it transcends appearances and yet is precisely related to them.

Decisive for the concept of world is the essential relation to finitude on the part of the noncreative being (the human being). This merely arrives at an ontologically more clarified expression of what the traditional concept of world always already indicates in referring to the *ens creatum*. Yet in Kant, the latter does not stand in itself, as it were—existent, finite things—but stands in its objectivity precisely for creaturely beings also. World is the totality of appearances, a still conditioned unconditioned totality. World is the idea of the totality of created beings in the possible perspective of a knowing being that is for its part also created. What we see emerge here at the same time is that the world as the idea of this totality itself owes its origin to finite reason—a Janus face: totality of appearances, of beings themselves, and nevertheless belonging to the nature of the finite subject. In the *commercium* of finite substances there exist those that represent the others through sensibility and reason, that is, know them as appearances within the totality of a world.

With the representation "world" as an idea what is indeed thought is an unconditioned totality with respect to appearances, but precisely with respect to these, not the unconditioned totality of beings insofar as they are also the object of an unconditional knowledge, that is, the creative intuition of God, *intuitus originarius*. World: the term for finite, human knowledge, the manner of knowing, the characteristics of the knowable—over against it: ideal.

f) Idea and ideal. The full determination of the concept of world as a transcendental ideal

When we posited the unconditioned totality of beings in themselves in this way, then we not only overstepped—as in the concept of world—the empirical unity of appearances, we not only absolutized in advance the objectivity of appearances; rather, we stepped altogether outside of appearance and its relation to beings and transposed ourselves entirely into the representation of the creative being himself in his creative unity and wholeness with whatever is known by him. With this representing of the properly unconditioned, however, we completely overstepped finitude, and "then the ideas become transcendent" (A 565, B 593) altogether; we not only, within finite knowledge, overstep what is given in it as such; rather, we step out of finite knowledge altogether, "out of all possible experience," not even concerned with appearances anymore, although overstepping in the manner of world. "As soon as we posit the unconditioned, however (with which we are really concerned) in that which is entirely outside the sensible world and therefore outside all possible experience, then the ideas become transcendent" (ibid.). We overstep not only objects of finite knowledge but rather finite knowledge as such together with its relation to beings; in positive terms: we not only posit beings in themselves but necessarily together with this the representation of an absolute knowledge. From this emerges an idea of a quite unique kind, which Kant calls the ideal and delimits from categories and ideas in the broader sense in the following way.

Categories have objective reality, that is, their substantive character can be presented *in concreto* and indeed a priori in objects (in the a priori intuition of time), that is, in terms of that to which these concepts are related in accordance with their full employment; regarded as pure concepts of the understanding, admittedly, in an isolated and logical manner, they too are already no longer presentable *in concreto*, but indeed as related a priori to appearances (A 567, B 595). "Ideas, however, are still further removed from objective reality than are categories; for no appearance can be found in which they could be represented *in concreto*" (ibid). "But what I call the ideal seems to be further removed from objective reality even than the idea. By the ideal I understand the idea, not merely *in concreto*, but *in individuo*, that is, as an individual thing, determinable or even determined by the idea alone" (A 568, B 596). Ideal: that which is represented itself, "the thing" re-presented absolutely as individual, determinate, that which corresponds to the full content of the idea, represented in thought as existing and indeed as individual.

The ideal is then: (a) idea *in concreto*, that is, the representational content of the idea is represented as the being itself pure and simple, in which the idea had to present itself; (b) this being as an individual thing determined solely by the idea: the correlate of an absolute intuition—archetypal image; the existing unconditioned whole, the whole of the being in itself in its existent totality.

The formal object of the ideal is therefore nothing other than the *intuitus originarius* as being, being in unity with what is intuited in it.—The character of the idea is exploded, not a concept, which is always "generality"; formally presented as *repraesentatio singularis*.

Already when characterizing the concept of world, Kant remarks that this concept is directed toward the synthesis of the conditions of appearances, "since on the contrary the absolute totality, in the synthesis of the conditions of all possible things in general, will give rise to an ideal of pure reason which is entirely distinct from the concept of world, although it may indeed stand in relation to it" (A 407/8, B 434/5). Accordingly, we see that here there is another, entirely different and higher idea than the concept of world, and yet the latter is related to it. It is thus first from the idea as ideal that we acquire the full determinateness and systematic place of the concept of world.

Compared to the category, the idea and especially the ideal have less and less objective reality and increasingly more subjective reality, to the extent that we may speak here of levels of degree at all. That the ideal has purely subjective reality, however, at the same time means that in it the innermost essence of the subject of pure, finite human reason makes itself known. In interpreting Kant, we must fundamentally heed the fact that those ideas represented by reason that must increasingly dispense with objective reality become increasingly decisive for the fundamental structure of finite reason. Kant must have intimated as much upon completion of the work, so that now, precisely in terms of the root that he must strive to expose, he had to develop the whole in positive terms in a more original elaboration (cf. A XVII).

It is no accident, therefore, that Kant comes to speak of "humanity," the essence of the human, when analyzing the concept of an ideal in general. "We must concede," says Kant, "that human reason contains not only ideas, but also ideals" (A 569, B 597); they indeed do not have "creative," but practical power, that is, related to and constitutive of the finite existence of freely acting beings; they underlie "the possibility of the perfection of certain actions" (ibid.). Virtue, human wisdom, for instance, are ideas. "The wise man (of the Stoics) is, however, an ideal, that is, a human being existing in thought only, but in complete conformity with the idea of wisdom," that is, as at once an individual and precisely the concretion of the idea. "Just as the idea gives the rule, so the ideal in such a case serves as the archetype for the complete determination of the copy; and we have no other standard for our actions than the conduct of this divine human being within us, with which we compare and judge ourselves, and so reform ourselves, although we can never attain to it" (ibid.). The a priori representation of such a thing is the ideal. Although ideals have no "objective reality (existence)," they are not mere figments of the mind, but rather "an indispensable standard for reason" (ibid.). Archetypal image, correlate of intuition. To the human essence belongs the "idea of perfect humanity" as an ideal, of the divine human being within us. In the ideal lies the thoroughgoing determination of everything that belongs to the idea. Thoroughgoingness, full concretion (Hegel).

Relying on this characterization of how the ideal belongs to the essence of the human being, and indeed as an acting, practical being, Kant now constructs the transcendental ideal with a speculative, theoretical intent. This appeal to humanity and its ideal as belonging to it signifies a certain subjective deduction of the ideal; certainly, the inner connection between this ideal and the transcendental ideal does not become visible, because what is not clearly developed is that in this, the idea of an absolute knowing and relation to unconditioned possibility is constructed. Ideal: unconditioned character of the human being as a whole.

The transcendental ideal in a speculative, theoretical intent constitutes the third class of ideas. The three classes correspond to the three traditional disciplines of metaphysics, that is, this third class is that of rational theology. The construction of the transcendental ideal is therefore nothing other than an interpretation of the concept of God in Christian theology with a view to the possibility of a knowledge of things in themselves in their totality.

Pointing to this cannot mean that on the basis of this connection, the problem drops out of the domain of philosophical discussion from the outset, but on the contrary indicates that the basis for the confrontation with this idea was a fundamental clarification of the basic problems of ancient philosophy and the way in which it impacted medieval Scholasticism. Yet this is true not only for Kant but much more comprehensively for the whole of German Idealism.

In the knowledge of God as the absolute, what is known is not only what is actually present at hand, created beings, but the entirety of what is possible, of that which comprises the essence of possible things, the whole of reality, *omnitudo realitatis*. Each thing is subordinate to this sum-total of all possible predicates. For this reason, each thing stands "as regards its possibility . . . subject to the principle of complete determination, according to which if all the possible predicates of things are compared with their opposites, then one of these opposites must belong to it" (A 571/2, B 599/600). There is also rationalism in this ideal, but ontological rationalism. "It is obvious that reason in achieving its purpose, that, namely, of merely representing the necessary complete determination of things, does not presuppose the existence of a being that corresponds to this ideal, but only the idea of such a being, and this only for the purpose of deriving from an unconditioned totality of complete determination the conditioned totality, that is, the totality of the limited. The ideal is for reason, therefore, the archetype (*prototypon*) of all things, which one and all, as imperfect copies (*ectypa*), derive from it the material of their possibility, and while approximating to it in varying degrees, yet always fall infinitely short of attaining it" (A 577/8, B 605/6). "The object of the ideal of reason [*intuitus originarius, intellectus archetypus*], an object found merely in reason, is therefore also called the primordial being (*ens originarium*). Insofar as it has nothing above it, it is also called the highest being (*ens summum*), and since everything conditioned is subject to it, the being of all beings (*ens entium*). None of these terms, however, are to be taken as signifying the objective relation of an actual object to other things, but only that of the idea to concepts, and we are left entirely without knowledge as to the existence of a being of such outstanding preeminence" (A 578/9, B 606/7).

The result is thus that world—as the idea of the totality of appearances—is incorporated into the higher idea of the transcendental ideal. Not in the sense of an ontic dependency of finite, created things upon an existing creator, but in the sense that the totality of the conditions of the possible entirety of experience shows itself to be a possible restriction of the absolute totality of possible things and their essence in general. Insofar as we are asking ontologically concerning the possibility of beings qua nature, and at the same time for finite beings, this question of possibility, as related to the contingency of experience as such, must lead to the emergence of a more far-reaching one concerning the absolute sphere of the possible, within which the fact of experience as such is possible. "For the ideal of which we are speaking is based on a natural, not a merely arbitrary idea" (A 581, B 609). "Owing to a natural illusion we regard this as a principle that must be valid for all things in general, although it is really valid only for those that are given as objects of our senses" (A 582, B 610). In accordance with this natural illusion we hold the empirical principle of possibility that relates to appearances to be a transcendental principle of the possibility of things in general.

With this, the situation regarding the concept of world in the *Critique of Pure Reason* has been characterized from every side. Precisely by considering the overarching idea of the transcendental ideal we have clarified, furthermore, that world expresses the totality of beings to which the human being comports himself as a finite being, and in such a way that he himself belongs to it. World and possibility (being and possibility).

We thus arrive at our fourth question: What fundamental problems arise from this conception of the concept of world in the *Critique of Pure Reason*? To see this, we must briefly once again focus more sharply on the peculiarity of the phenomenon of world. World is a determination of beings, where we must say that such being is thought in an undifferentiated manner, and nevertheless it does not belong to the ontic content of beings, as though it were a piece of them or a property present at hand in them, such as hardness or weight. World here belongs to what is present at hand and yet is not something present at hand. On the other hand, world is at the same time related to the human being, not only insofar as world—as an idea—arises from human reason, but insofar as it belongs essentially to reason as the idea of the totality of those beings that can be known by finite beings.

A series of questions arises from this:

1. How can world ontologically determine what is present at hand without being something present at hand?
2. How can it, as such a determination, belong to the essence of human Dasein?
3. How must this Dasein itself be such that, comporting itself toward beings, it is related to such a thing as world in so doing?
4. Is the connection between pure, idea-forming reason and pure intuition—the pure sensibility of space and time—clarified in any way by Kant in

general or even made a problem, so as to be able to show that and how the nature of human reason in its empirical comportment toward beings can necessarily be related to world? Is the essence of humanity illuminated and grounded in a sufficiently original way so as to posit the nature of the human being as the originating source of this forming of ideas?

5. If world is thus meant to determine necessarily the totality of beings knowable by the human being, and if these beings not only have the character of things of nature, but if history and thus the human being himself belong to such beings, is not the Kantian concept of world too narrow in principle, quite apart from the failure to clarify how it is rooted in Dasein?

6. How is an expansion possible? How can and must the problem of the concept of world be developed out of a radical dimension of metaphysical questioning, and in such a way that with a radical and explicit grounding of its origin the adequate breadth of the phenomenon can also be attained?

Precisely because the architectonic and unfolding of the problem of the *Critique of Pure Reason* places the problem of the concept of world into a seemingly unequivocal context it is necessary to point to what is problematic. The questions posed, however, are not to be answered individually now and with particular relation to Kant. Rather, following this historical orientation regarding the history of the concept of world, we shall now attempt to clarify the problem in connection with our leading question concerning the essence of Weltanschauung and the relationship of philosophy to it.

However, our characterization of the Kantian concept of world would be incomplete and one-sided if we neglected to point out yet another use of the expression "world."

g) The existentiell signification of the concept of world

Looking back at history, when we compare the Kantian concept of world with the concept *mundus* it becomes apparent initially that Kant, relying on traditional metaphysics, conceives of the concept of world in the sense of the first signification of *mundus = universum creaturarum*, the totality of existing, finite things, the specifically cosmological signification of the concept of world, but just essentially reworked by the transcendental form of questioning.

We saw, however, that from the New Testament onward to Augustine and Aquinas and others, a second signification of *mundus* develops according to which world means human beings and indeed in a peculiar position relative to the world in the first sense: *amatores mundi*, children of the world. Here we have the existentiell signification of the concept of world. World now signifies: human beings among one another in their relationship to one another. Worldly designates the conduct of human beings, and indeed the signification of worldly life determined in a specifically Christian way gradually erodes. We speak of the emergence of the man of the world; the expression *mondaine* characterizes a quite specific form of human existence.

Now this existentiell signification of the concept of world also emerges in Kant, admittedly without comprehending the problem of the connection between the two concepts and of thereby awakening the problem of a more radical grounding of the phenomenon. "But the most important object in the latter [in the world] for which he can employ the former [all human culture] is the human being: because he is his own ultimate end.—Knowledge of him, therefore, according to his species as a creature of the earth endowed with reason, especially merits being called worldly knowledge, even though he constitutes only a part of the creatures of the earth" (*Anthropology*, preface, first paragraph).[32] Worldly knowledge is here therefore knowledge of the human being with regard to how he stands and comports himself in the world. Kant therefore directly calls worldly knowledge anthropology, namely, pragmatic anthropology; as distinct from physiological anthropology, it contemplates the human being "with respect to what he, as a freely acting being, makes of himself, or can and should make of himself" (ibid.). "The inner principle of the world, however, is freedom. The vocation of the human being is therefore to strive for his greatest perfection through his freedom."[33] World stands for *habitator mundi*, for the human being with regard to his existence. Anthropology, doctrine of the human being = pragmatic knowledge of the world. This expresses in the most pointed form that world signifies precisely human beings. Knowledge of humans, anthropology = knowledge of world.

Worldly knowledge is contrasted with the schools, with scholastically acquired knowledge. The schools "make us skilled. Their main feature is to surpass others in the amount of knowledge. Such a scholar we call a scholastic. At most, he can usefully apply his erudition as a schoolteacher. One who is taught by schooling is passive."[34] Not only is scholastic knowledge material that is learned technically without practical purpose for life, but it is knowledge that by its very essence does not aim at what is essential for the existence of Dasein.

Worldly knowledge is drawn from experience of life and directed toward Dasein in turn. "Such an anthropology, as worldly knowledge that must follow schooling, is not yet properly called pragmatic if it contains an extensive knowledge of things in the world, for instance of animals, plants, and minerals in various countries and climates, but rather when it contains knowledge of the human

---

32. *Immanuel Kants Werke* (Cassirer), vol. 8, 1.

33. *Eine Vorlesung Kants über Ethik*, ed. Paul Menzer (Berlin: R. Heise, 1924), 317.

34. Immanuel Kant, *Anthropologievorlesung*, ed. Arnold Kowalewski (Munich and Leipzig: Rösl & Cie, 1924), 71.

being as citizen of the world" (*Anthropology in a Pragmatic Respect*, preface).[35] "The expressions *knowing the world* and *having the world* are still quite far apart in their signification; for the one merely understands the game he has watched, but the other has participated in the game.—To pass judgment on the so-called wide world, however, on the status of its undertakings, is a task for which anthropology finds itself in a very unfavorable standpoint; for these two are too close to one another, yet too far from others."[36]

What Kant means by "world," "knowing the world," and "having world," and that he understands "world" in an existentiell sense, becomes especially clear from the transcript of an anthropology lecture of Kant's from 1792 that was found among the lecture notebooks of Count Heinrich zu Dohna-Wundlaken. Worldly knowledge: "It makes one intelligent and clever, bringing the man his skillfulness. A man of the world is a participant in the great play of life."[37] World = the great play of life, = life-experience, human Dasein as such. Worldly knowledge = anthropology. Earlier *habitatores mundi*, now participant. "The majority of human beings educate themselves for the world through school, and are educated by the world for the world. The two mixed together is best: 1. scholastic knowledge and 2. education by dealings." "Man of the world means knowing one's relationships to other human beings and how things happen in human life." "Having world means having maxims and imitating great examples." "One can have a lot of world and yet be ignorant. World rests on formalities." "The word cleverness is taken in a twofold sense: on the one hand, it can bear the name worldly cleverness, in a second sense, that of private cleverness. The first is a human being's skill in influencing others, in order to use them for his ends."[38] World: being with one another. Furthermore: "A story is pragmatically written if it makes one clever, that is, instructs the world how to procure its advantage better than, or at least as well as, the previous world" (ibid.). "World" and "previous world" here quite clearly mean human beings themselves in their being with one another, and not, say, the cosmos or nature. World: the term for human Dasein, namely, with regard to how things happen in it, the play of humans with one another in their relationship to beings. World: a term for human beings, and precisely not as an element of the cosmos, a thing of nature, but in the historical relations of their existence. The concept of world here is grasped much more unequivocally in an orientation toward human Dasein.

This signification of "world" is intended when philosophy is called "worldly wisdom" and when Kant in particular characterizes philosophy as a whole in

---

35. *Immanuel Kants Werke* (Cassirer), vol. 8, 6.
36. Ibid., 7.
37. Kant, *Anthropologievorlesung*, 71.
38. Immanuel Kant, *Grundlegung zur Metaphysik der Sitten*, ed. Karl Vorländer, 6th ed. (Leipzig: Felix Meiner, 1925), 42n.

a dual respect: philosophy according to the scholastic concept, and philosophy according to its worldly concept. It is again the difference in knowing that we already encountered in the introduction to the *Anthropology*.

This characterization is found in a distinctive concluding section of the *Critique of Pure Reason*, where Kant makes a fundamental pronouncement about philosophy as a whole. He says here: "The mathematician, the natural philosopher, and the logician, however successful the two former may have been in their advances in the field of rational knowledge, and the two latter especially in philosophical knowledge, are yet only artificers in the field of reason. There is a teacher in the ideal who sets them their tasks and employs them as instruments to further the essential ends of human reason. Him alone we would have to call the philosopher; yet as he nowhere exists, while the idea of his legislation is to be found everywhere in that reason with which every human being is endowed, we shall keep merely to the latter and determine more precisely what philosophy prescribes as regards systematic unity in accordance with this concept of world from the standpoint of its ends" (A 839f., B 867f.).

Here we initially have the distinction between the "artificer of reason" and the "teacher in the ideal," that is, in what constitutes the divine human in us, in what is essential for each human being as existing and acting. Philosophy in this sense, that is, with a view to human Dasein as such, is philosophy in accordance with the concept of world. That is, world here means once again human Dasein in what is essential regarding its existence. In his note to this passage, moreover, Kant also provides an explicit elucidation: "Concept of world here means the concept that relates to that in which everyone necessarily has an interest; and accordingly, if a science is to be regarded merely as one of the skills toward certain arbitrary ends, I determine its intent according to scholastic concepts" (B 867–868n.). Cf. also the introduction to the *Lecture on Logic*, Section III.

We shall not discuss here as yet whether this division with respect to the concepts of philosophy can be made in general or whether logic is merely an affair for the artificer of reason. We simply see the signification of the concept of world emerge once more that is prefigured in the specifically transcendental concept in the *Critique of Pure Reason*, yet itself is manifestly influenced by the existential signification of *mundus, monde*.

This existentiell signification of the word "world" is meant in our expression *Weltanschauung*, even though the cosmological signification also imposes itself, indeed not by chance, but because nature and world too are embraced by the existential concept. For this concept is not the narrower one, but the broader, much more original one. Yet it is not our intention to determine the essence of Weltanschauung by pursuing the history of the meaning of the expression "world"; rather, this history of its meaning was intended merely to provide us with a concrete pointer to the fact that the concept of world is itself problematic. Our task now is to arrive at the central problem and thereby the basis for clarifying the essence of Weltanschauung in general.

The problematic character of the concept of world that has now emerged can be established in the following points:

1. The concept of world is in general problematic insofar as it vacillates back and forth between two significations, which, on the other hand, are not completely unrelated.
2. Viewed more closely, this vacillation has its grounds in the failure to clarify how what is understood by world here relates to Dasein.
3. On the one hand, world is the determination of the whole of beings, and is in this regard also related to the human being, yet not in a special way to Dasein; every being belongs to world: animals, plants, stones.
4. Nonetheless, this world is related to Dasein in an emphatic sense, insofar as it is supposed to be an idea that is said to spring from the nature of human reason.
5. Beyond this, however, the question concerning the special relation between world and Dasein becomes sharper not only with regard to the origin of the concept of world from human nature but with respect to the fact that precisely being human, its play and activity, is conceived as world.

Certainly, it would be a mistaken path and merely an escape if we wished to eliminate these difficulties by seeking to mediate dialectically between the various significations of world and the various relations between world and Dasein. For the lack of clarity concerning these relations would thereby still persist, and such dialectics are only ever—at most—the importing of obscurities into a system, that is, a violent eliminating of problems with the appearance of a transformative and strict conceptual mastery. The difficulty that opens up in the concept of world is instead something we must look in the eye, holding it before us without glossing over it or diminishing it, in bringing it to the bare question: What then is the relationship between Dasein and world in general?

As we shall see, it lies in the essence of the matter that we are inquiring after that the problem of the concept of world in general cannot be discussed without the question of its relation to Dasein. With the question concerning the essence of world, we are touching on a phenomenon that is especially multilayered. Above all, however, essential presuppositions are demanded for understanding the problem, not so much ones that concern the technical mastery of methods of interpretation, but specifically human presuppositions in the sense of being able to take a look into Dasein; and the sharper the drive to introduce philosophizing becomes, the more it intensifies, and the more urgent it becomes to awaken these presuppositions. In our ensuing discussion, the issue for you is therefore not to master the whole of the interpretation in every step and to be able to appropriate it in unequivocal conceptual knowledge but rather to be attentive to what the overall goal is.

2 Weltanschauung and Being-in-the-World

§35. Dasein as being-in-the-world

We speak of the nature of the human being and of its relation to the world without having decided whether we have yet determined this nature of the human being sufficiently to be able to ask concerning its relation to the world in general. Is it the case that on one side we have the relational point Dasein and on the other side what we call world? Is it the case that this Dasein on occasion also takes up a relation to the world, or does Dasein have a constant relationship to the world? Why is that so, and how?

What is notable is that so long as we pose the question as one concerning the relationship of Dasein on the one side to world on the other, we merely betray the fact that we have as yet no concept whatsoever of what makes these the allegedly secure anchor point and point of departure for this question. For Dasein does not, as it were, have a relation to the world just added on, rather the relation to world is an essential trait of Dasein itself, indeed the distinctive constitution of its essence. Dasein means nothing other than being-in-the-world. If we say Dasein, and are not merely pronouncing a word but understand what we mean, then we already mean being-in-the-world and it is pointless to ask whether and how Dasein, which as such is being-in-the-world, has a relationship to the world. Yet it then becomes all the more urgent to ask what being-in-the-world means.

Dasein means being-in-the-world. The very fact that in the long history of the concept of world precisely this relation of Dasein and world has remained unclarified, indeed has not even become a problem, must tell us that the connections at issue do not become visible without further ado, that they presumably belong to those connections that in themselves are just as simple yet also concealed, misinterpreted, and dissembled for the common understanding. The chief difficulty in understanding therefore lies in seeing through these distortions and misinterpretations, in thus breaking through them and attaining a free look into the simple. As everywhere in philosophy, here too it is not a matter of discovering unknown territory, but rather of liberating from semblance and from being shrouded in fog what is, and has long been, all too familiar.

Dasein means being-in-the-world, and this is meant to distinguish Dasein as the essential structure proper to it. Against this, important reservations now arise immediately that we shall briefly discuss. What is meant by being-in-the-world must thereby become clearer.[1]

The thesis is a statement of essence and refers to something quite elementary that, precisely for this reason, must indeed confront the difficulty and acuteness of the problem. What we are touching on, as it were, with this pointer to being-in-the-world is nothing less than the structure of transcendence that we already encountered on our first path. There we said: Dasein oversteps beings and in such a way that in this overstepping it is first able to comport itself toward beings and is thus first able also to comport itself toward itself as a being, that is, is first able to be itself, to be a self. Dasein transcends, oversteps beings, not occasionally, however, but rather as Dasein, and it oversteps not this or that select being but beings as a whole. Only because it oversteps beings as a whole can it comport itself within beings to this or that being selectively; here, the selection is essentially already decided with the factical existence of each Dasein. Within this sphere that has been decided, certainly, there is then a leeway or space in which freedom plays out [*Spielraum der Freiheit*].[2]

What does this "as a whole" signify that belongs to transcendence? It is that toward which the overstepping of beings occurs, that toward which transcendence transcends, and accordingly that from which Dasein, in its comportment toward beings, returns to these beings. That toward which the essentially transcending Dasein transcends we call world. In overstepping, however, Dasein does not step outside of itself in such a way that it would leave itself behind, as it were; rather, it not only remains itself but precisely first becomes itself. That toward which the overstepping occurs is that within which Dasein holds itself as such. Transcending means being-in-the-world.

At the end of our first path we saw the following: the understanding of being is transcending; but now we are saying: Transcending means being-in-the-world. Yet we also explicitly emphasized earlier that the understanding of being does not exhaust the essence of transcendence. We can now also express this as follows: To being-in-the-world, there belongs the understanding of being; the latter is not equivalent to the former, however, but is only one essential moment of being-in-the-world. This entails that being and its possible manifold, which we

---

1. Cf. Martin Heidegger, *Vom Wesen des Grundes*, section II. (For bibliographical details see §33 n.10.)
2. The German *Spielraum*, frequently translated as "leeway," has the more literal meaning of a space (*Raum*) where play (*Spiel*) can occur. Given the importance of the theme of play in this final part of the lecture course, we have tried to convey both senses here.—Trans.

understand, whether explicitly or not, in understanding being, is by no means equivalent to what the term "world" means, even though being and everything this expression means belongs to the content of the concept of world. Being-in-the-world is primarily codetermined by an understanding of being; but such being, as being-in-the-world, is not only an antecedent understanding of being. This understanding has a character of its own, not that of theoretical familiarity or knowledge.

Even though being and world, or understanding of being and being-in-the-world, are not equivalent, we can nevertheless now clear a path toward the further illumination of what "world" really means in the term "being-in-the-world," proceeding from the understanding of being, which is a necessary component of transcendence.

To put it more precisely, through this characterization of the understanding of being with respect to the phenomenon of world, not only does the latter come to be determined, but conversely the understanding of being as a whole becomes clearer in its belonging to transcendence. Despite this, however, transcendence is not exhausted by the understanding of being.

We shall proceed here starting from Kant's cosmological concept of world. It concerns the totality of what is present at hand, of nature in the broadest sense. The totality of the constitution of the being of nature is here the correlate of finite, and indeed theoretical-scientific experience, or more extensively of the knowledge pertaining to mathematical physics. That Kant's questioning moves in this direction of a narrowing of the concept of world to the totality of nature can be seen in the fact that he distinguishes between a narrower and a broader concept of world. The narrower concept signifies the mathematical whole of what is large and small in the world, thus an infinity in two directions, toward the infinitely large and the infinitely small, that is, a specifically mathematical, that is, quantitative idea.

Kant's existentiell concept of world is admittedly in no way worked out or made a problem philosophically, but it points in the direction of a problem insofar as precisely the whole of what Kant calls the play of life manifestly has a wholly different character in the constitution of its being than does this being called nature—and yet not sufficiently. As we saw earlier, the factical, historical Dasein of human beings among and with one another is always, and necessarily, not only a being alongside what is present at hand, but also alongside items of use. In other words, insofar as Dasein is by its very essence equiprimordially being with others in being alongside what is present at hand, and all of this as being a self, the whole of the constitution of being of these manifest beings as a whole is in principle richer and more primordial than what is thought in Kant's cosmological concept of world and is at least indicated in the anthropological concept.

Accordingly, if we take in a sufficiently primordial and broad way what is always already understood of being in Dasein, although not conceptually comprehended, and if we designate as world the whole of being thus understood, then we have already fundamentally gone beyond the Kantian concept of world, and not only in the sense of merely extending and completing the regions of being. World is not only the whole of the constitution of being of nature and of historical being with one another and of one's own being a self and of items of use but the specific wholeness of the manifold of being that is understood in a unitary way in being with others, being alongside . . ., and being a self. Yet precisely the wholeness of such a whole, essentially oriented toward Dasein, is a problem; it is not attained, for instance, by our simply adding alongside Kant's ontology of nature in the broadest sense an ontology of historical Dasein, of items of use, or of subjectivity; with all of this, the essential problem has already been hopelessly lost. What must be determined is the specific wholeness of the whole of being that is in each case understood within Dasein, the inner organization of this wholeness of being, which we may not grasp in terms of theoretically developed ontologies as a stratification or juxtaposition of regions.[3]

§36. World as "play of life"

We have seen that when Kant wants to elucidate the existentiell concept of world, or to characterize its significance in general in a more prephilosophical way, he speaks of the "play of life." In this, he follows the use of language, in which at all times philosophy is contained, philosophy that is still latent, as it were, if only we have an ear for it. And how should it be otherwise, if philosophizing belongs to the essence of Dasein and Dasein speaks itself out in language—if only about everyday matters? The expression "play of life" has certainly arisen from the fact that the historical being with one another of human beings offers the view of a colorful manifoldness and variability, contingency. Yet this entire visible surface can surely only be the reflection of the essence of Dasein that plays itself out factically and historically there. In other words, an aspect of play must lie within the essence of Dasein if it is to be capable of offering such a view.

We must now indeed say, with regard to the question concerning the wholeness of the whole of that which we call world: the wholeness of being that is in each case always already understood in Dasein, in particular the character of this understanding and the organization of what is understood, being-in-the-world in general—world has the character of play. For various reasons, I shall provide this initially somewhat bold characterization, but must refrain from offering a

---

3. The specific wholeness of these a priori metaphysical rules of play that in each case make possible a factical play of life.

detailed interpretation of the essence of what we are calling play. A few relevant pointers may suffice.

We speak of the playing of card games, of party games, of the lute, of pantomime, of playing in the sense of "playing a role." We say of a human being that he has a playful nature. We speak of mere play, which then has the character of semblance, of the nongenuine, the "as if."

This interpretation of play leads us to also regard the playing of children, which in its meaning is genuine, in a positivistic sense, that is, we see it in the horizon of a so-called serious occupation of adults. The questions of whether it is genuine or nongenuine, "for real" or merely "as if," concern distinctions in the factical function and effect of playing, but not this playing itself. Above all, the play of children cannot be understood in these terms. On the other side, one should also not think that something specifically childlike lies within play. If it is a prerogative of the child to play, this initially signifies only that play in some way belongs to the human being. Perhaps the child is only a child because in a metaphysical sense it is something that we adults no longer comprehend at all anymore.

Admittedly we also speak of a play of animals and take this as evidence that play is something belonging to biological existence [*Dasein*], something pertaining to the child but that the adult lacks. This argumentation rests on a mistaken inference, insofar as it presupposes that what we call the playing of animals is identical with what we call the child's playing. On the other hand, if it were possible to demonstrate a playing of the animal, this would prove only that play is a broad phenomenon and that if so-called adults no longer play in the sense of the games of children, but nonetheless procure a substitute for this, then this must have its reasons. What has been said thus far is only a hint about the ontic domains in which we commonly speak of play.

a) Being-in-the-world as the original play of transcendence

That we speak of the "play of life" is not just a figure of speech; on the other hand, we must guard against simply reading something into the mere word. The task, rather, is to clarify its being and in doing so to grasp the substantive phenomena themselves that we hit on and to keep them together, as it were, with what we mean by "world."

Play means, first, playing, in the way that we refer to the playing of a game; second, it means the whole set of rules according to which playing is to proceed. Yet as playing, play is indeed not just following the rules of the game and comporting ourselves accordingly. This does not hit on the essence of play. Not only do the rules of play and the players belong immediately together in play, but in play, there lies something more: It is something more originary from the outset. We speak vaguely of a certain pleasure in a game, not only in the game, however, but in playing itself. In accordance with its fundamental character, playing is a being-in-attunement [*In-Stimmung-sein*], being attuned; indeed, the reverse is even true: to every attunement there belongs play in a quite broad sense. Not only is pleasure to be found in playing, but in all pleasure—and not only in it—and in every attunement, there is found something like a play. For "games" are in each case only particular factical possibilities and manifestations of playing. We play not because there are games but the converse: there are games because we play and do so in a broad sense of playing that does not necessarily manifest itself in being occupied with games.

Playing is accordingly: 1. Not a mechanical sequence of events, but rather a free—and that always means, rule-bound—occurrence. 2. What is essential in this occurrence is not the action or activity. What is decisive in playing, rather, is precisely the specific state we find ourselves in, the peculiar way in which we find ourselves in playing [*Sich-dabei-befinden*]. 3. Because what is essential in playing is thus not our comportment, the way it is regulated also has a different character: The rules first form themselves in the playing. The way in which we are bound is a free one in quite special sense. The playing plays itself, and indeed on each occasion first plays itself into a game, which can then be detached as a system of rules. In this playing itself into . . . the game first arises yet does not have to develop into a system of rules or pre-scriptions. This entails, however: 4. The rule of play is not some fixed norm drawn from somewhere but can change in the playing and through the playing. It is the playing that each time creates for itself, as it were, the realm within which it can form—and that means at the same time, transform—itself.

It is in this original, broad sense, and ultimately in a metaphysical sense, that the expression "play" is to be taken when we now say: "World" is the term for the play played by transcendence. Being-in-the-world is this originary playing of the game that each factical Dasein must play itself into so as to be able to play itself out, in such a manner that it is factically played with in one way or another in the duration of its existence.

Now, it is essential that common understanding notices nothing, as it were, of this original play of transcendence, and it therefore at once becomes horrified when the suggestion is made that it is being played with—when after all every-thing has its fixed rules and norms, its comfortable security. To deliver human existence [*Dasein*] over to a game? To stake the human being on the play of Dasein?[4] Indeed!

---

4. The German used here, *auf das Spiel setzen*, literally "to put into play," also has the more idiomatic sense of something being put at stake. We have tried to convey the sense of both play and being at stake in this and following instances.—Trans.

Yet we should not forget, first, that play is being taken in a quite broad sense, and such play is anything but "playful," a mere game as opposed to reality—there is no such distinction at all within transcendence. Above all, however, it is not our respective factical comportment that is being characterized as play, but rather that which enables it. This is to say that such play is precisely concealed at first. Second, play is being taken as being intrinsically leapt over in overstepping, antecedently disclosed.

A game is not something playing itself out within a subject, but the reverse. In this play of transcendence every being toward which we comport ourselves is already embraced by play, and all comportment is attuned to such play.

Yet precisely if transcendence is supposed to be a play, then surely everything begins to vacillate. We said earlier that to transcendence there belongs an understanding of being.[5] Being that is understood there has become at least partly manifest in what Plato recognized as ideas and that we know, after all, to be beyond change and the flux of time—to be eternal; the system of categories, even if we are not yet completely familiar with it, is surely precisely the in-itself pure and simple.

Such arguments sound very convincing at first, and yet they are pronounced more for the appeasement of common human understanding than in terms of the question regarding what should become a problem here. What we must precisely learn to see is that what we call the understanding of being does not have

------

5. The question concerning the concept of being and everything entailed in this is the transition from the self-evident understanding of being to the radical will to conceptual comprehension.

What is the understanding of being? To where should we transpose ourselves in order to acquire the point of departure for the question? Well, we do not at all need to transpose ourselves there, we always already move within it, we, the being that we each are, that we call human being, and for which we have certain representations and concepts, even anthropology.

Understanding of being is something found in human beings, a property, a peculiarity; understanding of being is therefore one property of the human being, included in the essence of the human being. What follows here from this, however, is that if this question of being is indeed the fundamental question of metaphysics, the human being becomes the center of the problematic. Is there a more radical justification for the philosophical fact of anthropology than that, as has now surely been shown, it furnishes the basis for the point of departure and further development of the question of being?

But wait—is the understanding of being only a property that we simply [. . .]* to the human being as a determination of his essence that has perhaps been insufficiently heeded thus far, or is what we have tried to bring to light regarding the understanding of being what is most originary in the essence of the human being, such that conversely it is from here that the radical question concerning the essence of the human being must first of all proceed and that precisely anthropology must remain excluded? Yet—why exclude? At most, what follows from this problematic is that anthropology must be grounded anew from out of the central orientation toward the question of being. Therefore, the idea of philosophical anthropology as center remains and is in this way precisely grounded for the first time.

*[Two words illegible.]

the harmlessness of an analysis of categories that one assembles completely over time like a coin collection, but that the understanding of being and being itself forms itself, rather, with the formation of world.

Being-in-the-world as transcendence, as transcendental play, is always world-formation.

For the distinctly narrow horizon of common understanding, the categorial, if it is familiar at all, precisely appears stable, or—and this is just the flipside of this kind of insight—if this fixed thing comes to be in flux, then such understanding knows only one thing: to complain about relativism.

b) Transcendence qua understanding of being as play

We are using the word "play" in an originary and at the same time broad sense. We are grasping transcendence as play, and transcendence itself initially with respect to the aspect of our understanding of being, the latter therefore also having this character of play. When we speak of being-in-the-world as playing then we do not here mean playing a game in the ordinary sense, merely transferred and enlarged, as it were, to cover the whole of Dasein. Nor do we mean, however, playing with beings, nor even playing with being, but rather: playing being, attaining it through play, opening and forming it in such play. Our task is instead to grasp the specific occurrence and its vibrancy that we mean by playing in general.

Grasping the interpretation of what world means in its essential trait demands that we bring the phenomenon of world into an inner connection with Dasein itself, and that we bring into view a fundamental constitution of Dasein that, by way of anticipation, we are calling being-in-the-world. This fundamental constitution of Dasein, however, is simultaneously the fundamental structure of transcendence that we are to come to know.

Transcendence has been brought closer to us on the path of clarifying the understanding of being, that is, the fundamental fact that, in our comportment toward beings, we have already stepped over beyond beings and are able to understand them as beings only insofar as we have done so. This understanding of being we characterize as transcendence, with the qualification that transcendence is not exhaustively determined by the understanding of being. Nevertheless, the understanding of being is now to serve as our guiding thread for interpreting being-in-the-world and thereby the phenomenon of Weltanschauung, and for conceptually comprehending the latter as an essential aspect of philosophy itself.

To accomplish this, it is necessary to deviate more than hitherto from the previous questioning of the history of metaphysics and philosophy in general, and in order to make this step comprehensible, I have tried to clarify by way of anticipation a strange phenomenon that at first sight appears less than suited for characterizing the fundamental phenomenon of Dasein, transcendence:

being-in-the-world or world as play. This expression is not arbitrary, as our mention of the Kantian usage of the term already indicates.

That we are viewing life, being-in-the-world, world itself as play has its reasons. What is at stake is to move beyond the ordinary expression and its signification, not by working out a concept of play for ourselves and then applying it to Dasein, as though Dasein were an enlarged form of play, by contrast with habitual toys that we play with. The phenomenon of play, rather, is to direct us toward the unitary character of an occurrence that fundamentally determines transcendence.

We shall summarize once more in four points the fundamental aspects of what we seek to uncover as play, and do so now in order to emphasize the unitary character and vibrancy of the phenomenon.

1. Playing is a free forming that in each case has its own attuned accord [*Einstimmigkeit*] insofar as it forms such accord for itself in playing.
2. Although it is a free forming, playing is thereby precisely a binding, not a detached formation, however, but rather a formative binding oneself to and into the very forming at play.
3. Playing is therefore never a comportment toward an object; it is not at all a mere comportment toward . . ., but rather the playing of play and the play of playing at once as an originarily and intrinsically inseparable occurrence.
4. Playing in this sense we call being-in-the-world, transcendence, which initially we have always characterized as the overstepping of beings. Being-in-the-world has always already played beyond beings, embracing them in play in advance; in this playing, it forms for the very first time, indeed in an actual sense, the space within which we come upon beings.

c) The correlation of being and thinking. Its narrowing in the "logical" interpretation of the understanding of being

If, remaining within the limits of our discussion thus far, we now grasp transcendence qua understanding of being as play, we encounter the greatest difficulties precisely here. The understanding of being belongs essentially to the play of transcendence and is therefore itself a play.[6]

We may briefly recall that the understanding of being first explicitly emerged as a problem in Plato and that it found its solution in what one usually calls the doctrine of ideas. An idea is that which is sighted in a being as it itself, that which

---

6. Understanding of being as play; from here transcendence, being-in-the-world, world, Weltanschauung are to be conceptually comprehended. For this, it is necessary to explain "understanding of being" more clearly than before, how it has hitherto been grasped, in order to assess from this what our attempt is claiming. Now no longer hearing the reductive sense associated with play: "only," "mere"; looking at matters in reverse: there is power within play; but leave both of these aside.

is in a being, the what-being of things, or their essence. Here we see that the idea and the way it is determined are placed in correlation with the λόγος. It would certainly be going too far if we were to say that the idea is the origin pure and simple; nevertheless, this step that philosophy took here came to be of decisive significance. In short, it leaves its imprint in the subsequent history of philosophy in the fact that "being" becomes a correlate of the λόγος, of *ratio*, of reason.

This correlation found its most grandiose development in Hegel's *Logic*, which is meant to present nothing other than reason's absolute self-knowing with regard to itself; in terms of its content, and with a clear consciousness of this, this work is metaphysics, total knowledge of being; yet it is not without grounds that Hegel calls it *Logic*, so as to express the fact that the whole of being (substantiality) in the broadest sense is centered in reason (subjectivity). The essence of being therefore lies in the subject. Being, and the entire wealth of what this idea includes within itself, is thinking. If we consider that in Hegel's *Logic* all essential motives of Western metaphysics are concentrated in one grand idea, that the understanding of being, rational thinking in the lawfulness of that idea, and indeed in its early form, is subordinate to the dialectic, then it will seem strange to bring the understanding of being onto the vacillating ground of a play.

Nonetheless, it is necessary to ask in this direction for an essential reason, namely, because in metaphysics hitherto there lies an essential narrowing and trivialization of the problem of being.[7] This reason becomes clear to us, and receives its effective force, when we lay before us the question: How precisely do we arrive at this correlation of being and thinking, being and reason? One could point to the fact that ancient philosophy begins with a thesis that appears to express nothing other than this correlation of being and thinking. Parmenides: "For one and the same are thinking and being" (Diels, fragment 5), the two belong together. Yet this pointer is insufficient, if only because νοεῖν may not be equated without further ado with Kant's or Hegel's concept of reason; above all, however, because this unequivocal orientation of the problem of being toward the λόγος began only later, and indeed on the basis of two main motives. If being is being sought in its most graspable form, as it were, then it imposes itself in language, specifically in the "is," the copula; it is in a certain sense housed in the propositional statement—λόγος. This manifestation of being is seized upon all the more unhesitatingly because at the same time it also makes known being true, as distinct from semblance.[8]

---

7. Being, reason, *ratio*; all not specifically theoretical rational comportments: irrational; everything was contested using this distinction and indeed also became contestable, as with every dichotomy.

8. a is b signifies not only that b is attributed to a as a predicate but also: a is indeed and in truth b. a is b means, secondly, the being-true of a's being b.

On the grounds of this elementary state of affairs which we are unable to inquire about further here, the propositional statement, λόγος, attains an exceptional function within the problem of being and the discipline that has the λόγος as its theme: the role of logic in metaphysics.

As an aside: In this context, it is not to be disputed that there is a connection here; the question remains only whether it is an original one and the most original one for the question of being. What must be disputed is that the propositional statement is interpretive, foundational.

However, what first entrenched the dominance of the λόγος and of logic in metaphysics is something else and very difficult to discern, above all to ground it in its possibility and accordingly to overcome it.

All explicit questioning concerning being is a transition from the ordinary understanding of being to a conceptual comprehension; all comprehension [*Begreifen*], as the name says, is conceptual determining [*begriffliches Bestimmen*]. The conceptual comprehension of being is rational, logical determination (especially as experience is excluded). Now we see what is strange: that which functions as the way of determining being and its structures, conceptual, rational, logical knowledge, simultaneously becomes reinterpreted into that relation that originarily and solely opens up an access to being. The way in which being is conceptually determined becomes the fundamental manner of understanding being in general. The understanding of being, if one is familiar with it as such at all, is logical grasping. And in this way, the problem of being first shifts completely into the jurisdiction of logic and reason; to this is added the fact that this supreme problematic of being is sought after as the most rigorous and assimilated to mathematical rationality. It is not entirely wrong that the problem of being in Plato has been called "logic of being."

While interpreting the *Critique of Pure Reason* and Kant's position regarding the transcendental imagination we indicated briefly how difficult it is to free oneself from this sphere; that Kant shrinks back in the face of the transcendental imagination has its grounds in the self-evident supremacy of the concept of reason, not just in the particular form it takes in the age of Enlightenment.

The stubborn persistence of this approach to the problem can be seen above all, however, in the fact that if one wishes to dethrone this domination of reason within reason, then rationalism extends at most to an irrationalism, that is, to a position that shares its foundation with the former. Ir-rationalism: the latter only thrives from the former and is its guest in everything that comprises conceptual interpretation in determining. Nothing whatsoever is gained, merely greater precedence and more semblance; for it only seems as though one has now done justice to whatever rationality is unable to grasp. On the other hand, rationalism once more has the advantage of claiming for itself the clarity of the concept by contrast with the milieu of what one calls "life-philosophy." So too the spontaneous reaction against the attempt to ground the problem of being and transcendence in general in a form of play will thus be to see or to fear an irrationalism in this. Certainly one would have found a comfortable label with this, but indeed nothing more.

Yet one will say: Why not leave metaphysics in the safe and definite protection of logic? Why the struggle against rationalism, when it has provided such great incentives in the history of metaphysics?

However, what is at stake is not the struggle against rationalism, just as little as party membership with irrationalism, but solely the enabling of a more radical interpretation of transcendence, of the understanding of being, in view of the fact that the λόγος has a merely interpretive and determining function, which does not mean that it would have no role at all in the problem of being.

Our task is to see that understanding of being lies prior to all logical assertion and determining and also first makes this possible. We must ask what it is that we mean by understanding of being. We have indeed already said a number of important things about it (cf. first path: projections of the constitution of being, fundamental concepts). We also already pointed to the fact that understanding of being is manifestly a primordial fact of Dasein and that only on this ground is it able to comport itself toward beings. And yet this is not sufficient, not if we are setting about actually exposing various determinations of being. That is indeed possible via historiographical recollections: the doctrine of ideas. Yet precisely here we must give a pointer: It is indeed relatively easy to show that the what-being of something is to be thought as that in terms of which each individual "this" is determined. This unprecedented great insight, which we should never be allowed to diminish by its threatening to become all too familiar to us, also already forces the problem into dead ends. The insight was too fascinating to be able to press forward in an original way: χωρισμός, μέθεξις, ὄντως ὄν.

The transition was accomplished in the elementary simplicity of the initial seeing, without adequately securing the point of departure. Insofar as the result henceforth remained what dominated, the step back once again that would have allowed this move to be accomplished anew with greater lucidity and scope was ventured only incidentally and for the most part not at all. One followed the overstepping of beings that lies in the understanding of being without having the possibility of first keeping these beings uncovered with such scope that the transition in relation to them could be accomplished in its full scope and manifold character. In pursuit of the overstepping and fascinated by the vision of being (the ideas), beings were even demoted to being a mere springboard, the μὴ ὄν. (Even though there was a turning here in Plato, it failed to take effect.)

On the basis of a definite undifferentiated approach and in a particular direction the understanding of being was forced into the concept, and without it itself being sufficiently illuminated as that which should have been conceptually comprehended as a whole here, above all without securing that soil in which it has grown as such. For this reason, nothing emerged beyond the mere indication of a place (ψυχή) and the logical characterization we have described. Admittedly, Socrates is not the "inventor" of the concept and of definition.

Since then, the issue of what constitutes the point of departure and the space for all questioning concerning being has remained something unasked and unclarified: the characterization of the understanding of being precisely in its configuration and function prior to all logical-ontological judgment, in this pre-ontological configuration in its entire essential scope and multilayered character. This can be achieved, however, only if the understanding of being as a whole can be placed fully and explicitly into that context in which it essentially belongs: transcendence—being-in-the-world.

Yet because we are considering this problem in its entire incisiveness, there is no reason to act superior; for by the very essence of the matter, this is possible only on the path of a fundamental revision and radical retrieval of the first inception. We therefore necessarily remain indebted to our predecessors.

In order now to see this immediate whole of the understanding of being it is initially necessary to have Dasein in view with regard to the fundamental structures we have already named several times—what is present at hand, the Dasein-with of others, being a self—and this in the concrete unity of historical Dasein with the entire wealth of its essential possibilities. Above all, however, within factical Dasein, in its understanding of being, the task is to understand the manifold character of the being of this being in which, however, our understanding of being does not step out of one region and step over into another but rather directly oscillates back and forth, as it were, in its understanding of nature and history, for instance. The "and" is already misleading here: The fate of a human being or of a people is understood directly, just as a change in the weather, some sudden turn that nature takes, or the swaying and stirring of our own bodily Dasein, our fate in a natural catastrophe; by contrast, we are familiar with possible fields each separated out: natural science, science of history, ontology; and yet in this way precisely what is peculiar will fail to appear. It is this oscillating back and forth in the manifoldly attuned character of the whole of being that is central and essential to our understanding of being and is to be incorporated into the problem of the question of being from the very beginning and from the ground up.

To grasp this from the ground up, the phenomenon of transcendence must be brought to light and grasped in its full structure. This is to be enabled through the interpretation of transcendence as play. That means, however: we are not simply transferring a concept of play onto transcendence or onto the understanding of being in particular. Rather, via the guiding thread of this phenomenon and what it freely prefigures, with a view to transcendence and in terms of it, we shall attempt to grasp it in a way that is both fuller and more originary.

This, then, entails the following: Transcendence as play is not some property, not even just a fundamental property of the human essence; rather the human being is at stake in the play of Dasein—primarily an assertion for now indeed—in the play of the understanding of being. This means: The understanding of being is not some undifferentiated, though perhaps universal property of Dasein; transcendence is not some harmless structure that one can heed or not. Our task is now to show this. The play-character of world will thereby become clarified, being-in-the-world will thereby receive its own incisiveness as a fundamental determination of existence, and with this we shall attain the dimension into which the essence of what we call Weltanschauung must be integrated.

§37. Achieving a more concrete understanding of transcendence

a) Selfhood (for the sake of oneself) as determining the being of Dasein. Exposure as an intrinsic determination of being-in-the-world

Weltanschauung is a necessary component of being-in-the-world, of transcendence. The problem of world is originarily unified with the question of being, and the problem of being and the problem of world in their unity first determine the genuine concept of metaphysics. From here, we must then be able to see how Weltanschauung is linked in a peculiar way to the essence of metaphysics.

The understanding of being is not something that also appears in Dasein simultaneously with many other things, rather, understanding of being and/or being-in-the-world is precisely what makes this being, Dasein, altogether unable to be indifferent toward itself. A being to whose fundamental constitution the understanding of being belongs, rather, exists precisely from out of an understanding of being, and in terms of being as understood; a being that is staked on the play of the understanding of being—and this basically says the same thing—is delivered over to itself, or it is for the sake of itself, that is, it exists.

It is only because Dasein by its very essence comprises the ontological constitution in keeping with which the being that is constituted as Dasein is for the sake of itself that the factical human being can on each occasion be an end in himself, as Kant says. This "for the sake of itself" constitutes the self as such. Selfhood as determinative of the being of Dasein never consists primarily in this being simply being conscious of itself, rather, self-consciousness as reflection is only ever a consequence of selfhood, or more precisely: in being for the sake of itself, that being which we call Dasein is unveiled in such a way that it is always placed before its ownmost potentiality for being, and in being placed before it must decide what its ownmost being is capable of with respect to the possibilities of being essentially belonging to it: being with others, being alongside what is present at hand, being a self.

Brought before itself and full selfhood does not therefore mean drawn back on itself in an individualistic or egoistic manner. Aside from the fact that "being-with" essentially emphasizes this point, such an interpretation is the crudest misconception of the problem. Dasein must essentially be able to be itself and authentically be itself if it wants to appreciate itself as carried and guided by another, if it is to be capable of opening itself for the Dasein-with of others, if it is to engage itself for others.

Certainly, if one sticks with the traditional concept of the subject and the I, then the relation to self is egoistic. The degree and levels of knowing about it and the forms of this being placed before oneself are quite manifold in this respect.

If, therefore, we say that an understanding of being belongs essentially to Dasein, and that both the being of Dasein and the being of non-Dasein-like beings are understood together at the same time in this understanding of being, then we can now see the following: This understanding of being is not some harmless knowledge of categories or contemplation of ideas. Rather, what is entailed in the understanding of being is precisely the full trenchancy of Dasein's being placed before itself, and in such a way that this being that is placed before itself as such comports itself toward other beings that it is not.

Dasein is that being that is essentially entrusted with the task of being in whatever way it can be. The being of itself is given in advance and given as a task precisely because an understanding of being belongs to Dasein, which entails that the being of itself is placed before it as how and what it has to be. Being is expressly a given task and possibility for this being, and indeed essentially so; insofar as it exists, it cannot escape this, but must come to terms with it in one way or another in each case. Suicide is only an extreme form in which the essential task of existing given to Dasein can come to be settled.

The understanding of being as an essential moment of Dasein's transcendence, that is, of the fundamental constitution of this being, has already from the ground up brought into the being of this being that characteristic in relation to which we say: Dasein is at stake, put in play. Let it be well noted: This "for the sake of itself," itself being an issue, this trenchancy of its struggle, is not some after-effect arising because Dasein, insofar as it exists, factically appears among other beings. Rather, in the essence of existing, that is, of the being of Dasein, there lies the trenchancy of this "for the sake of itself."

It is only because Dasein is the kind of being that, in its being, has its very being as an issue that it is exposed to beings, and indeed by the necessity of its essence. For we heard that Dasein is disclosed; beings that it is not are manifest to it; yet now we see: not in the sense of a mere cognizance. Rather, because Dasein has essentially stepped out of itself, it is exposed to beings and to their superior power, not just to the superior power of the forces of nature, for instance, but also to the powers and forces that Dasein shelters within itself as a being.

Transcendence as the overstepping of beings in understanding being has thus completely lost the undifferentiated character that one is tempted to ascribe to it if one develops the problem of the understanding of being within the framework of traditional ontology. The antecedent understanding of the being of beings, coming back to beings in overstepping them, is not a harmless looking down at the contingencies of factical beings from the unendangered height of an a priori knowledge of essence. Rather, transcending beings, that is, being-in-the-world, means being exposed to beings. Only the exposure of Dasein to beings, including to itself, an exposure grounded in the "for the sake of itself," enables a confrontation and a held comportment [*Verhaltung*] toward beings. Only from such confrontational comportment does there arise the possibility of a factical defeat or else victory in each case, the possibilities of being unendangered, of appeasement and security, of faring well and of dominion over beings.

That a Dasein exists factically in this latter sense, and thus in factical existentiell terms knows nothing of such exposure, is no proof against it, if only for the reason that our respective factical existing, whether in fortune or misfortune, can decide nothing about what constitutes the metaphysical essence of Dasein. That essence must be sought at the place from where the very possibility of fortune and of misfortune becomes comprehensible. For this reason it is a superficial and crude misunderstanding if one thinks that by attributing to Dasein an exposure to beings we are giving voice to a pessimism.

In relation to this, the task is precisely first to learn that pessimism and optimism, as in each case taking up factical positions toward factical Dasein, themselves already presuppose Dasein, and indeed Dasein that can understand itself in one or other of these ways. Pessimism merely confirms the essential exposure of Dasein, namely, in such a way that it gives in to such exposure. Optimism, however, attests to it no less, insofar as it does not believe in it. Exposure is neither first proven by pessimism, however, nor refuted by optimism.

With regard to these determinations it must be comprehended that I have designated the being of Dasein as care. This has nothing to do with Schopenhauer or Christian asceticism and doctrine of original sin, nor with the fact that with the concept of 'care' one will come upon death and conscience, all of which sound severe to contemporary ears.—One has understood little of such things if against them one pleads for the cheerful Weltanschauung of Goethe and wants to see the general decency and niceness of Dasein preserved and even offers the wise advice that in life there is also such a thing as love. Who would deny this? Yet I doubt that what these philosophical philistines covertly believe or that what one calls love here hits the metaphysical essence of what is named. In the end, the petty feelings that are presented under this name are very far removed from it. It would need to be asked whether every great love, which alone makes known something of its essence, is not fundamentally a struggle, not only or in the first instance a struggle for the other but a struggle on his behalf, and whether it does not intensify to the degree that the sentimentality and agreeableness of feelings decrease. But enough of that!

To make the decisive point briefly once again: Dasein is not the harmless subject that gets posited in philosophy and that always finds itself embarrassed, as it were, if the demand is made even to think it as existing.

The whole in terms of which Dasein understands itself, the world, is not a free-floating system of ontological propositions, rather, understanding oneself means existing for the sake of oneself, and this is intrinsically a being exposed to beings. The world exposes Dasein, exposes it to the necessity of confronting those beings it is not, as well as itself. Dasein is not first exposed to beings through the fact that they are present at hand, rather, exposure is an intrinsic determination of being-in-the-world as such.

What results from this interpretation of transcendence is: 1. that Dasein as such is in each case already with and alongside beings; and 2. that this being alongside . . . and being with is not a having of objects standing over against it in an undifferentiated way but rather exposure. Yet the aspect of transcendence that we are indicating as "exposure" has still not been sufficiently grasped. For even now it still appears as though Dasein were, so to speak, a subject hovering over beings, albeit exposed to them.

b) Exposure as thrownness

Dasein is not, and essentially never, isolated from beings and then simply exposed "to" them, rather, as Dasein it finds itself in the midst of beings. This in turn does not mean that it too crops up among other beings; rather, the "in the midst" means: Dasein is pervaded by the beings to which it is exposed. Dasein is corporeal, a living body and life: it does not have nature simply or only as an object of contemplation, rather, it is nature; yet not in the sense that it presents a conglomerate of matter, body, and soul; it is nature as a transcending being, Dasein, pervaded and pervasively attuned by it. It is in the manner of a being attuned that Dasein in each case finds itself in the midst of those beings that pervade it.

We are here concerned with a fundamentally broader and more originary concept of nature: *natura, nasci*, of its own accord, something that Dasein, as a free self, does not have power over. Dasein does not first find itself by letting the thought occur to it to enter into a relation to nature; rather, prior to all free comportment toward nature, it is in its midst. It in each case already finds itself within it. This finding itself in the midst of such being pervaded by beings is something that Dasein as such does not have power over. We therefore say: Dasein is thrown into beings. To being-in-the-world there belongs thrownness. The index for this fundamental aspect of transcendence is what we are familiar with as attunement; we are in each case attuned in one way or another, even and especially when we are not held in the extremes of an elated or depressed attunement but in that strange, indeed mostly unremarked, yet fundamentally uncanny attunement of apparently not being attuned at all.

The authentic essence of exposure is determined only in thrownness. For exposure does not only concern Dasein's comportment toward beings, as it might seem initially—quite apart from the fact that what is not expressed in the concept of comportment toward beings is that whoever comports themselves is in each case essentially already in the midst of beings, pervaded by them. All comportment toward beings, rather, always grows out of an already being exposed to beings in the sense of thrownness; it is not within and on the occasion of a comportment toward beings that it is exposed to beings, rather, all comportment as a mode of Dasein occurs within thrownness. All comportment essentially finds itself; to the understanding of being that illuminates and guides every comportment toward beings, there belongs a being attuned. To put it fundamentally: the overstepping of beings occurs in and from out of a finding oneself in the midst of beings. To transcendence, to being-in-the-world, there belongs thrownness.

Only because Dasein is essentially pervaded by beings in whose midst it finds itself, yet Dasein as finding itself attuned also always comports itself freely toward beings in one way or another, do fundamental possibilities arise within Dasein's thrownness in accordance with which Dasein can know itself to be elated and buoyed or, on the other hand, depressed and burdened; both fundamental ways of finding oneself presuppose thrownness in the same way. Finding oneself is taken as something that Dasein does not have power over, that it fails to master, and that remains as an essential burden on itself, one that it can never be rid of so long as it exists, that it can only forget, so as thereby to confirm it all the more emphatically.

Thrownness can essentially pertain only to the kind of being whose being is determined by the "for the sake of itself"; only that which is intrinsically a self can be thrown.

In our previous meeting we gave a general characterization of the inner connection between the two paths to philosophy, the path through science and the path through Weltanschauung; they coalesce in the thesis: Philosophizing is explicit transcending.

Attaining an understanding of this requires the interpretation of transcendence, over beyond the understanding of being.

With respect to this task, we now pause at an important point, important in itself, but above all with respect to the tradition and in relation to possible misunderstandings, insofar as it becomes necessary to overcome the dominance of logic in metaphysics, where "logic" is the title for the science of reason as such. Here, we leave open the question of whether logic hitherto has penetrated into the meaning of what it fundamentally seeks. We are not yet determining its relationship to metaphysics.

Overcoming the dominance of logic does not signify defending irrationalism, nor affirming life-philosophy. If we orient ourselves historiographically, what should be said, rather, is this: The motives that in Western philosophy thrust themselves to the fore in determining the essence of philosophy are to be comprehended in their entire scope and equiprimordiality, not eclectically, that is, but rather to be developed from out of an exposition of the fundamental problems themselves, on the basis of transcendence.

The insight is essential that transcendence, as the fundamental constitution of Dasein, shares Dasein's being, codetermines it and for its part is codetermined by it.

In this regard we note three things: 1. Dasein for the sake of itself, its ability to be is placed before it itself; as bodies are essentially extended, so Dasein, in its being Dasein, is placed before itself. 2. Dasein, as for the sake of itself, has stepped out of itself, is exposed to beings. 3. Exposed in the midst of beings, being pervaded by them, is called thrownness.

c) Facticity and thrownness. The nihilative character and finitude of Dasein. Dissemination and individuation

We shall leave open the question of whether every self as such must necessarily be a thrown one or not. One need only pose the question to see that in every case the respective existence of a Dasein is expressed by thrownness with respect to its facticity. This means: 1. No Dasein comes into existence on the basis of its own decision or resolution. 2. No Dasein, if it exists, can ever discern that it must necessarily exist, thus could not not exist. Rather, every Dasein can also not be.

This is indeed not simply an objective proposition that we are stating about Dasein; rather, every Dasein understands more or less explicitly and in various forms and images that it not only could also not be at all but constantly may no longer exist. Insofar as understanding belongs to the essence of existing, this means that Dasein exists constantly on this verge of the "not." This means: in being placed before oneself with respect to its own possibilities, the possibility of not being always shows itself as well. This "not" is by no means something that lies outside of Dasein and is merely imputed to it; rather, this not-character belongs to the essence of its being. It has this not-character, is determined by this "not," "nihilative"; yet nihilative here does not mean "nothing" but rather the reverse: This nihilative character [*Nichtigkeit*], which has not remotely been exhaustively grasped through what has been said, constitutes the most positive aspect that can belong to Dasein's transcendence; indeed, precisely in this original determination the "for the sake of" and thrownness go together in one. We must characterize it in several directions, however, without posing the problem as a whole.

Uncovering this nihilative character lying within the constitution of Dasein's very essence in no way signifies a valuative declaring of this being as "null" [*nichtig*] in the sense of unimportant or even worth nothing. The issue, rather, is that of bringing to light the trenchancy that lies within Dasein, and of comprehending that what we call the "finitude" of Dasein is not something that simply adheres superficially to this being, first arising through its being compared with other things that it is not. For all too long, metaphysics has been made the fool of the positive, which on the basis of a seeming priority over the negative has posed as the absolute and original. Our traditional logic, ontology, and doctrine of the categories are built accordingly, and their concepts do not extend far enough to reach what we are referring to under the term "nihilative character." The depiction of "finitude" by createdness is only one particular way of explaining "finitude" and, indeed, one that rests on faith; it is not, however, a clarification of the metaphysical essence of finitude as such.

The not-character is therefore precisely the authentic force of Dasein's existence, and by no means does the nihilative character of Dasein lie only in its thrownness, which we can express concisely as follows: Dasein is impotent with regard to the fact that it exists at all and does not not exist.

The nihilative character is found already where we least suspect it. Earlier we showed that Dasein is equiprimordially being alongside . . ., being with . . ., and being a self. It is always in this way in a unitary and simultaneous manner. Up to now, we have placed weight only on the equiprimordiality of these constitutive moments by contrast with the traditional concept of the subject. But we have not provided a more detailed characterization of this equiprimordiality. If we attempt to do so, then what shows itself initially is this: Dasein as we say, is dis-persed [*zer-streut*] into the manifold of these relations. This dispersion [*Zerstreuung*], however, is in no way a dissolution of Dasein into disintegrating parts but precisely the reverse: In this dis-persion [*Zer-streuung*], Dasein has and wins the primordial, whole unity proper to it. We therefore speak in the first instance not of a dispersion into these relations but of an originary dissemination [*Streuung*]. It is this dissemination that is the condition for the possibility of a dis-persion in the sense that Dasein can on a given occasion transpose itself predominantly into one of these relations but always at the cost of existing in the others.

Dasein can dwell predominantly in being with one another; it can become absorbed predominantly in a preoccupation with things; it can predominantly lose itself in self-reflection. To the extent that Dasein essentially maintains itself as a unity within the whole of this dissemination, it must on each occasion decide for itself in this way or that, that is, it can never decide only for one relation except through compromise, through a trade-off. In this "never only for one" the nihilative character within the essential constitution of Dasein itself makes itself known once more. It is to be noted that Dasein is not first forced into what we call "compromise" in particular factical situations, but essentially and pervasively. Whoever, therefore, chooses and acts without compromise, decisively in one direction, in factical, concrete decisions precisely moves, from a metaphysical perspective, within the nihilative character of dissemination, insofar as he must take on board the severity and harshness of his endeavor, that is, must somehow come to terms with it.

In the inner necessity of a constant trade-off in this dissemination—whether it factically succeeds or not—the nihilative character of our understanding action accordingly makes itself known as well. It acquires its particular trenchancy, however, through the fact that each of these relations is determined by thrownness, that is, being with others is confined to a particular circle, being alongside what is present at hand is confined to a particular accessibility, kind, proximity, and scope of the manifestness of beings, the relation to oneself is confined to particular possibilities of understanding oneself and of confrontation with oneself.

As thrown, each Dasein must be individuated with respect to a particular situation. This individuation does not signify isolation, however, but rather brings Dasein in the whole of its relations into the midst of beings in each case. I am not able to discuss here how the problem of Dasein's individuation is connected to what one usually calls the principle of individuation, nor can I discuss the "position" in space and time—here purely a schema of ordering—that belongs to beings, yet is superficial. Here, by contrast, we are concerned with individuation in terms of the being itself: temporality.

What is important for us is that in individuation there necessarily lies a restriction in the truth of Dasein. The manifestness of beings is in itself at the same time concealment, un-truth in the essential sense, and not, say, merely in a quantitative sense of our not knowing and being familiar with everything and of our means and ways being limited. The limit does not so much come from the outside, from the plenitude of beings. The untruth is not so much that of mere concealment but rather the untruth that we properly name such—semblance, deception, being captivated, blindness. It is not the quantitative restriction of what is knowable, but rather the qualitative restriction with respect to what is factically accessible.

This untruth, and thus nihilative character occurring within Dasein itself can readily be demonstrated. I deliberately choose an example that certainly will not raise the suspicion that we are talking about old-fashioned things but that above all demonstrates the state of the matter in an extreme form.

The apparatus of the radio has displaced the limits of what can be directly known and experienced away from us in an unusual way; indeed, it has eliminated them altogether in a certain respect. The possibility of truth is increased, the chances of not experiencing are essentially diminished.

Now, how does someone who possesses a radio stand in relation to these possibilities? One will say that here too he must select; he must limit himself to one station and one station number; he cannot listen to everything, even if he devotes his entire day to this apparatus. We indeed see here the necessity of a restriction, the necessity of un-truth in the sense of the concealment of what cannot be heard. However, that is not what is decisive; we see, rather, that many—the number is completely irrelevant here—fail to choose any possibility of listening whatsoever but are intent on jumping from one wavelength to another. The possessor of the radio, who is given an extraordinary possibility of what can be experienced, makes himself the slave to his apparatus. He blocks his access to things in a manner completely impossible for one who does not possess such an apparatus. He brings an untruth and a semblance into his Dasein that can scarcely be conceived as greater. Indeed, in a certain way he deprives himself altogether of an understanding of truth and untruth. Yet this is an event that indicates something essential, namely, the insurrection of untruth and semblance from out of and within Dasein itself. On a large scale, the same thing can be seen, for example, in the fact that the sciences have today become a big-city business, human beings have become employees of science, but science is no longer a possibility of existence for Dasein.

One final point: Precisely those moments of Dasein in which we are able to exist as a whole and essentially not only are rare but are as it were like a narrow pinnacle that we dwell upon only fleetingly. Even if through genuine recollection they retain their effective force for Dasein, they thereby make known with all the more trenchancy that existence for the most part is not like this, even though it is indeed happening.

I have thus provided pointers from various sides to the fact that the finitude of Dasein does not rest on a restriction of properties but lies in the manner and way in which Dasein exists. This nihilative character within the essence of Dasein also attests to the fact that Dasein is constantly a weighing up and venturing, falling and rising, giving and taking—all this not as the result and product of a collision of beings with beings, but as the manner of being of Dasein itself, that is, as the play on which the human being is staked. This play is what is essential in what we call world, which, as world, worlds only in and as being-in-the-world.

It would be an error to take this nihilative character of Dasein as something negative, as the dark side of Dasein, and to oppose to it the cheerfulness of the positive, of that which elates. For none of the things we call such are opposed to its nihilative character but are at stake within it, that is, the nihilative character of Dasein depicted is the originary ground of the possibility for what is positive and negative in Dasein in the ordinary sense. Only in view of the originary nihilative character of Dasein does everything so-called positive acquire its force and singularity but not by our evading the nihilative character of Dasein and closing our eyes to the play that we are staked on. For in this way we deprive ourselves of the possibility of demanding something of ourselves. The individual is only ever what he demands of himself and can demand of himself.

d) The lack of hold pertaining to being-in-the-world

Dasein's being-in-the-world, its transcendence, makes itself known to us as a lack of hold [*Halt-losigkeit*]. It must in each case accomplish its being by way of a choosing in the essential sense and give itself a hold [*Halt*] in one way or another.[9] (I am deliberately avoiding speaking of freedom here.) This is to say: the being that is for the sake of itself is such within the nihilative character we have depicted. This nihilative character in itself directs us toward finding a hold, the necessity of decision. When we attribute this lack of hold to Dasein, then this is not a factical assertion, as though no Dasein could ever attain a hold, rather it is an assertion of essence that precisely entails that each factical Dasein, insofar as it exists, must in each case already have attained a hold in one way or another.

Being put into play and at stake, that is, being-in-the-world, is intrinsically a lack of hold, that is, Dasein's existing must procure a hold for itself. Expressed more pointedly: Being-in-the-world is not some property attached to Dasein but rather the constitution of its being, which by its essence demands that Dasein hold itself within it. Dasein has in each case in one way or another been brought into the how in which it exists, entered into it, of its own accord, through others, through circumstances and contingencies. Even what does not arise through its own explicit decision, as with most things in Dasein, must be retroactively appropriated in one way or another, if only in the mode of coming to terms with something or getting out of something; even those things about us that are not at all subject to freedom in the narrower sense, an illness or particular predisposition, are never simply something present at hand, but rather something that

---

9. From here, Heidegger unfolds a rich discourse built around cognates of the German root *Halt*, meaning "hold," but which, it should be noted, also has the temporal sense of a "stop" or "pause." The German *Halt-losigkeit*, which we render as "lack of hold," is frequently (though not consistently) hyphenated in the text; the hyphenation is presumably meant to suggest that the lack of hold is not the sheer absence of a hold but rather is intrinsically directed toward the possibility of acquiring or taking a hold (*Haltnehmen*). The sense of "hold" has in fact been present throughout much of the earlier part of the lecture course, implicit within Dasein's comportment (*Verhalten*) toward beings and dwelling (*Aufenthalt*) alongside beings, and more explicit in Dasein's holding itself (*sich halten*) within the uncoveredness and unconcealment of beings. The "fundamental stance" of the theoretical attitude earlier translated *Grundhaltung* (see §§22–24); from here on, we shall render *Haltung*—which Heidegger will relate to the Greek sense of ἦθος: see §43b)—as "held bearing" to convey the sense of "hold" that the German word contains. On philosophizing as a distinctive *Grundhaltung*, see §46.—Trans.

has been taken up into the how of Dasein or been rejected in one way or another. Being-in-the-world is through and through something in which we hold ourselves.

Holding oneself within being-in-the-world is what we mean by Weltanschauung. From this, we may directly surmise that a Weltanschauung factically forms itself in each case according to the way in which Dasein's lack of hold, being-in-the-world itself as such, is manifest for Dasein in each instance.

§38. The structural character of transcendence

a) Retrospect on the structural character of being-in-the-world attained

Our considerations serve to attain a more concrete understanding of transcendence. In this, we are pursuing a dual aim: 1. a more complete and richer characterization of transcendence, going beyond the understanding of being as characterized initially in a more traditional way; 2. a characterization, however, of the structural character of transcendence as such. Insofar as transcendence, however, is the fundamental constitution of Dasein, what has been said about it is true for all structures of Dasein, that is, for everything that is asserted about Dasein in a metaphysics of Dasein.

Negatively, the following must be said concerning the ontological constitution of Dasein: It is not some constructed framework simply pertaining to Dasein as a property that then first results in Dasein's way and manner of being; rather, these structures participate essentially in the way in which Dasein exists. This is to say that the distinction is not of such a kind that Dasein would merely know of the constitution of itself but that other beings would not, that Dasein is a being that, in its being, is accompanied by consciousness. Rather, the entire essential constitution of Dasein reaches into the manifestness of Dasein in such a way that it requires Dasein to take a position on each occasion. What determines the how of Dasein is essentially different; Dasein must necessarily respond to its how in one way or another. Even indifference is only one way among others of coming to terms with what decision—not random decision—demands.

In the direction of this characterization of transcendence we attempted to characterize the phenomenon of thrownness and that of its nihilative aspect. We pointed to the essential determination belonging to Dasein's facticity, namely, that Dasein does not owe, and never can owe, its existence to its own resolution or decision, and that the manifold of essential relations of Dasein is not something neutral, but rather that in this dissemination there lies an inner limitation of Dasein. We showed, furthermore, that Dasein is factically always determined by an individuation, that is, the manifold of these relations is always factically a concrete one, confined to Dasein's particular circle. An essential untruth thereby arises in Dasein: first, in the quantitative sense, insofar as there is so and so much that Dasein does not experience at all, and second, above all a qualitative untruth. From the characterization of this nihilative character we made a transition to depicting what we call the lack of hold pertaining to Dasein, so as from there to comprehend how Weltanschauung belongs to being-in-the-world.

Let us recall what we ultimately mentioned as a characteristic of thrownness in order to make visible the nihilative character of Dasein: no Dasein exists on the grounds of its own decision or resolution.

Admittedly, we have been blinded to such a degree by the centuries-long domination of psychology, logic, and epistemology that we have a difficult time accepting statements like the one just made as even equal in originality to, for instance, the statement that sense data are immediately given to a subject. We hold this latter statement to be evident and well-suited as a point of departure for further considerations about subjects, and see in the first statement merely metaphysical opinions that contain all too many presuppositions and therefore sound very grandiose when one presents them in the context of fundamental considerations.

It would be a mistake to want to deny such disconcertment, yet equally superficial to acknowledge it as a counterargument. We must ask ourselves, rather: From where does this disconcertment come? That such disconcertment exists precisely attests to the statement that asserts something about the essence of Dasein's facticity. The disconcertment exists, and this means: we do not think about it at all, it does not occur to us to take it into account; it is even questionable whether and how we should do such a thing, that is, we have already set about turning away from this impotence of our provenance and orienting ourselves, as it were, entirely in the forward direction of our Dasein and toward the present.

Dasein has, as it were, nothing to seek in the direction back toward its provenance. Let it be noted: the issue is not what we can bring into objective historical experience about our provenance after the fact—this can at most reinforce the fact that we are impotent with regard to our own Dasein—but rather whether Dasein, which is concerned with its potentiality for being, is able to ground the fact of its being, of its own accord and through its own decision. The fact that it cannot do so is not nothing or irrelevant but essential to the fact of Dasein.

That it has nothing to seek in the direction of its provenance by its own decision gives Dasein an essential thrust away from the darkness of its provenance into the relative brightness of its potentiality for being. Dasein always exists in an essential confrontation with the darkness and impotence of its provenance, if only in the predominant form of being habituated to a profound forgetfulness in the face of this essential determination of its facticity. This forgottenness comes to light in the disconcertment provoked by such statements and in the opinion that they presuppose too much. Yet may one make one's forgetful comportment the measure for how originally one apprehends oneself? This can be demonstrated by an example: a stone is also not present at hand on the grounds of its own decision. Yet here the "not" is to be understood in another sense. The stone is not, as it were, impotent in relation to its provenance, because it is altogether unable to be impotent. It is unable to be so because it bears no powerfulness or freedom—finitude—whatsoever within it. For something to be able to be impotent in relation to itself, it must be free. From this we see that this impotence and nihilative character of Dasein is an advantage that Dasein has over the stone. Nor is the stone even indifferent toward its being, because it has just as little the possibility of difference as that of indifference. Disregarding the fact that the stone is not at all determined by this impotence regarding its factual character, the stone can therefore not forget such a thing either, because being able to forget is possible only where there is a retaining—temporality. Everything in Dasein that belongs to it, but factically is not there for the most part, thereby receives an essential trenchancy with respect to its not being there, because this not being there is always determined from the manner of being of Dasein, that is, belongs to this manner of being.

A very penetrating reflection, repeatedly directed toward the whole, is required in order to see these elementary connections and to eliminate the opinion that statements about sense data would be more primordial than such statements, while matters lie precisely the other way around. It is a prejudice imported from science into philosophy that whatever is simple in the sense of scientific dissection is also what is essential and original in a philosophical respect.

b) Weltanschauung as holding oneself in being-in-the-world

This holding oneself belongs necessarily to transcendence because transcendence is essentially determined by a lack of hold. Transcendence—freedom! We have attempted to grasp this lack of hold in terms of its nihilative character and, in doing so, emphasized that the latter is not to be regarded as negative. We took lack of hold not in its ordinary signification of an "unstable human being" [*haltloser Mensch*] but as an essential structure of Dasein and indeed of transcendence. Even one who maintains a held bearing [*Haltung*] does so and can do so not because he is factically lacking a hold, but because he is so metaphysically in keeping with his essence, directed toward and free to give himself a held bearing. This means, however: the overstepping of beings that is pervaded by beings themselves, and indeed in the unity of dissemination, lacks a hold; in transcendence there lies being referred to a hold, yet not in the sense of an objective property. Rather, the being of Dasein in its happening is in itself a holding itself into possibilities within which it is meant to be able factically to take hold in each instance. Lacking a hold within dissemination is intrinsically the holding before oneself of possibilities for taking hold. Within the fundamental directions of Dasein's dissemination there lie, so to speak, glances cast ahead toward possibilities of being. Dasein's transcendence is nothing other than this glance of Dasein cast ahead as a whole, insofar as Dasein as a whole is indeed in each case a potentiality for being and remains placed before this potentiality. The lack of hold is not a mere void; rather, because it is constitutive of the being whose being is called potentiality for being, such lacking is a referral to possibilities of fulfillment; whether they are factically sufficient or not is a subordinate question. In this lacking there lies the "not yet" in the entire trenchancy of being referred to the choice that is necessary in each instance.

We showed earlier that Dasein is being disclosed, that is, the relations within the unity of dissemination have the character of making manifest. Within the unity of dissemination Dasein always holds itself in a manifestness. Being-in-the-world is always being-in-the-truth. This expresses the fact that truth belongs essentially to the concept of world. The lack of hold that lies in transcendence is accordingly always a referral to possibilities for holding oneself in the truth. From what has now been said regarding thrownness, we can see that our earlier characterization of being-in-the-truth could only be a provisional one. Being-in-the-truth as making manifest is not simply an indifferent uncovering of beings and contemplating them; rather, all making manifest of beings is intrinsically a being pervaded by beings. All making manifest is therefore a confrontation with beings, both in relation to what is present at hand (mastering) and in relation to Dasein-with (action) and being a self (resolute openness toward oneself). Yet because the interpretation of the being of beings, just as that of our access to beings, is oriented toward the λόγος, and the latter in turn as the λόγος that merely exhibits, the contemplating and intuiting of beings attains absolute priority among our relations to beings—science merely logically, and correspondingly the practical as nontheoretical.

3   The Problem of Weltanschauung

*§39. Fundamental questions regarding the principle
problem of Weltanschauung*

a) Weltanschauung as factically engaged being-in-the-world

It is precisely confrontation with them that makes beings in themselves accessible, and not mere contemplation. The latter is a subsequent form of possible appropriation of the truth, but is not what is essential in making manifest. Fundamentally, this is also the real signification that inheres in the term *Anschauung*. It is not at all a matter of self-evidence that the Western concept of knowledge is oriented precisely toward the idea of intuition, αἴσθησις, ἰδεῖν, νοεῖν, and that Kant establishes the idea of knowledge as *intuitus*. The "intuiting" of something seeks to express the immediate having of something as a whole; such having as an ideal one strives for intrinsically entails being oriented toward a not having, not possessing. Weltanschauung fundamentally means having world, possessing it, that is, holding oneself in being-in-the-world, something our lack of hold is deprived of, yet while precisely giving us the directive to bring this into our possession. In the expression *Welt-anschauung*, we are to hear the appropriated belonging of being-in-the-world to Dasein. Welt-anschauung as having world is being-in-the-world that is in each case factically engaged in one way or another. Strictly speaking, therefore, we should not say: Dasein has a Weltanschauung but rather: it is Welt-anschauung, and necessarily so.

Yet insofar as Dasein can and must explicitly trouble itself with regard to being-in-the-world, and insofar as definite knowledge, taking positions, habits, claims, and demands arise from such effort, and these can in turn be objectively communicated and presented, and insofar as what is made public in this way is what is initially graspable, the illusion arises that a Weltanschauung is something objectively present at hand, a product that Dasein can acquire, something found in books or that one can acquire from the lecture circles of the School of Wisdom in Darmstadt, something Dasein can then have or not have.

On the basis of this view that a Weltanschauung is a product that has been made public, albeit it one that has its own necessity and relative legitimacy, a further failure to recognize the essence of Weltanschauung arises, one that finds expression in the talk of a "natural Weltanschauung." By this is meant a kind of holding oneself in being-in-the-world that is natural for every Dasein and the same for each. If, however, each Dasein as factically existing must necessarily become individuated in a situation, then this entails that factically there is no such thing as a natural Weltanschauung. Each Weltanschauung, like each being-in-the-world, is in itself historical, whether it knows it or not. There is not a so-called natural Weltanschauung and then another one that is first created and packed on top, just as little as a Dasein can exist that would not in each case be the Dasein of a self and thereby necessarily dispersed into I-You relationships. The denial of a natural Weltanschauung, certainly, does not mean that there does not exist something like a common Weltanschauung, for instance, belonging to groups, tribes, clans, nations, peoples; in another direction, there is a common world belonging to particular ranks, castes, professions. Yet such commonality itself is historical, both in its form and in regard to its content.

The development of Weltanschauungen is initially a matter for science and for scholars, and has been so for a long time. Where such products are found, they are for the most part merely "world pictures" that are thought up, in which a particular knowledge about beings is compiled and furnished with bits of wholesome practical advice.

The manner and way in which Weltanschauungen are factically formed is subject to definite essential laws. Problems are:

1. What is in each case the mode whereby the lack of a hold pertaining to being-in-the-world is manifest to Dasein? (a) In which predominant direction within the whole of dissemination? (b) With what degree of originality of being-in-the-world? (c) The mode of clarification and interpretation in which the manifestness of the lack of a hold occurs.
2. What is the character of the hold that is prefigured in each case as possible within the manifestness of the lack of a hold?
3. What is the genuine form in which this hold is attained, the form in which it is preserved and transmitted?
4. What are the forms of degeneration and substitution that are put in place within the particular hold itself, as belonging to it?
5. To what extent does the degeneration of one particular hold at the same time provide the directive toward the possibility of a new one?

These are fundamental questions of the principle problem of Weltanschauung that must be preceded by a clarification of the essence of Weltanschauung in general and by the demonstration of its origin in being-in-the-world, in transcendence.

Our entire discussion of world, being-in-the-world, and Weltanschauung served to provide us with a basis for the question of the relationship between Weltanschauung and philosophy. More precisely: via a clarification of the essence of Weltanschauung, which current educated awareness always associates readily with philosophy, we seek to illuminate more incisively the essence of philosophizing.

b) The concept of Weltanschauung in Dilthey

Before we attempt this last step, we want to return to Dilthey's concept of Weltanschauung that we took as our guiding thread earlier (see p.167), and to briefly answer the seven questions that we raised with regard to Dilthey's way of determining the essence of Weltanschauung. Answering these questions will lead us directly to the guiding problem. In this summary discussion we shall at the same time bring before us the entire problem of interpreting the essence of what is called Weltanschauung and also assess the importance of discussing our first path in relation to the second, that is, in particular the fundamental significance of overcoming the psychological and epistemological concept of the subject in the sense of an interpretation of the essence of Dasein.

Dilthey says: "An inner relation between life experience and a world picture is always contained within the structure of Weltanschauung, a relation from which an ideal of life can always be derived."[1] World picture, life experience, ideal of life, and actuality, value, and determination of the will are, according to Dilthey, components of Weltanschauung "of various provenance" and of various kinds. This conception is decisive for the position Dilthey takes toward the possibility of a philosophical Weltanschauung, something he identifies with "metaphysics," and for his concept of philosophy. In light of the seven questions, we must now discuss:

1. Are these fundamental components defined in a sufficiently original way? For Dilthey, "world picture" means the objective causal nexus of what is present at hand, as uncovered by natural science in the broader sense. "Life experience" is also designated "appreciation of life" by Dilthey, or as the lived experiencing of meaning and sense; "ideal of life": principles of action. These are the three domains of beings.

    Yet does Dilthey mean that a Weltanschauung consists of objectively present at hand nature, of psychological subjects who experience, and of principles—that it is, so to speak, some kind of objective mixture of these three? By "world picture" he means, rather, nature as known causally, what is known in knowing; the psychological nexus of experience as lived, and the principles as that which binds action. Certainly, he means this, but he also means the former. In other words: we find here an essential indeterminacy in the way the component parts are characterized as such: on the one hand, objectively present at hand ontic domains (objective), but at the

---

1. Wilhelm Dilthey, "Das Wesen der Philosophie," in *Die Kultur der Gegenwart* I, 6, 38. *Wilhelm Diltheys Gesammelte Schriften*, vol. 5, 380.

same time with regard to the fact that they are known, felt, and willed (subjective); now the one, "now the other," now both in this relatedness (subject-object relation), where especially this relation remains indeterminate. The fundamental components are therefore not defined in a sufficiently original manner, but from the outside, in an ordinary way, in alternating and shimmering relations, now objectively, now subjectively, now in the subject-object relatedness itself. Yet only with regard to the fact that the three components refer, as it were, to three ontic domains can Dilthey say that they are "of various provenance."

Being	Value	Willing	Uppermost determination of thinking
The actual (world)	Life	Principles	objective
Knowledge	Feeling	Will	subjective
World picture	Life experience	Action	subjective-objective

Yet Dilthey himself vacillates in this ordering.

2. As components of Weltanschauung, are they of different provenance or not? If one regards them objectively, then indeed they are; nature is something independent, likewise psychic life and valid principles. No one domain can be traced back to another. If, by contrast, the components as such refer to Weltanschauung, and the latter as determining psychic life, that is, the three components as knowing, valuing, and willing comportment, then it is impossible to see how there should be talk of a different provenance of the component parts here; precisely the reverse: they have the same provenance in terms of the whole of psychic life. Dilthey himself says, contra the thesis of their different provenance: "The fundamental distinction between these component parts goes back to the differentiation of psychic life, which we have designated as their structure."[2] Not only the characterization of the component parts themselves is indeterminate, therefore, but also the way their provenance is determined; the latter has to be vacillating because the component parts themselves are under multiple pressures. A further difficulty now becomes entwined with this.

---

2. Ibid.

3. The question of the possible connection between the component parts. Fundamentally, Dilthey no longer enquires about this; he stops at the tripartite division of the faculties of knowing, feeling, and willing; certainly, he—and especially he—is not of the opinion that these three simply crop up alongside one another; he endeavors precisely to bring their unity to light, yet in such a way that he in each case points to how all three are factically linked— we never have one faculty without the other two—yet what is decisive, the possibility of this nexus, that is, the fundamental structure of Dasein itself from which such components may be taken, is not made a problem. It thus remains

4. indeterminate whether they have simply happened to come together, or whether an original unity within Dasein that is necessary to its essence makes itself known here. Dilthey says: "Their psychic relation [that of the component parts] is there for us in lived experience; it belongs among the ultimate attainable facts of consciousness. The subject comports itself toward objects in this diverse way, and one cannot go back to any ground behind this fact."[3]

Dilthey's fundamental position becomes clear from these statements. We shall simply highlight a few points in relation to clarifying the essence of Weltanschauung: The component parts are now grasped directly as psychic and in a psychic relation; he calls them at the same time "facts of consciousness," behind which we cannot go back to any ground. Here it becomes clear that despite all essential revision of psychology in the sense of naturalistic elementary psychology, Dilthey has not advanced beyond psychology as such in determining the essence of "life" (Dasein). The problem of Dasein is one of psychology, that is, the approach remains that of an ontic connection, psychic events, facts of consciousness. The question is not asked as to what the manner of being of the psychic is here or indeed whether the psychic thus determined is adequate even to make the essence of Dasein a problem and thereby to first attain the basis for determining the essence of Weltanschauung. Dasein, seen in terms of psychology and on the basis of psychology, then becomes a problem of knowledge, of theory of science and culture. Dilthey remains stuck in a positivism of a higher form and fails to understand the conditions he must satisfy in order to pose what he is asking as an actual problem at all. For precisely his important insight too, the historicality of life, remains fundamentally not understood, because it is not conceived in an ontological and metaphysical way. This is why the history of Dasein as such is not seen, but "culture," etc., is instead an expression, an objectivization of the psychologizing of life, an aesthetics of historicality and culture.

---

3. Ibid., 61 (405).

Yet one deprives oneself of the possibility of any substantive understanding and of actual problems if, as soon as there is talk of historicality, one thinks of the name Dilthey and is then of the opinion that the problem is thereby solved. This is a bad habit of so-called scholars of philosophy who are only able to pursue a problem so far as to be able to cite a list of author names and book titles. One is then unable to see the problem of historicality that Dilthey treated; just as little the problem of time that Bergson treated, the problem of the intuiting of essences that Husserl recognized; and even the problem of existence is of necessity impossible to see through the usual characterization. This way of furthering a lack of education like a market trader is in part responsible for the miserable state of philosophy.

Dilthey's thesis becomes evident in his second statement, where he says that it is impossible to go back behind the facts of consciousness to some deeper ground. This naturally means: to a substance, to a being that still underlies, in terms of which the psychological manifold of beings could be explained. That is, Dilthey is familiar only with the ontic awareness of facts, where it is questionable what "ultimate" facts is supposed to mean.

Dilthey fails to see, first, that precisely for his problem of determining the structure of psychology ontological knowledge is already presupposed and accomplished; and second, however, that the question concerning the ground of possibility of the unity of the said "facts" need not already be a question of ontic explanation but can be an ontological question of essence. He moves here in Kant's direction, who was equally unable to see clearly in this regard. When in his paralogisms Kant rightly points to the impossibility of an ontic-rational metaphysics of psychic life, nothing is thereby decided against the possibility of an ontology of the psychic or of the human being, so little, in fact, that it is precisely shown to be necessary—and Kant must constantly make use of it. Between, or prior to, the appearing of the psychic as an appearance and a dogmatic, theoretical metaphysics of the subject and concept of the subject an ontology of the soul is indeed possible and necessary. One may concede that for factically executing the Kantian problem of the *Critique of Pure Reason* such an ontology is not required; but it does not follow from this that the possibility of a metaphysical consideration of the psychic is excluded in principle. Had Kant pressed ahead to these fundamental questions and recognized them as problems in their own right, then German Idealism in its factical form would have become impossible.

Not only is it possible to inquire back to the ontological question of essence, but this has also always already occurred, whether explicitly or not. For the fact that Dilthey must necessarily make use of such a ground, even though he fails to see it and misconstrues it, can be seen precisely from the multiple senses in which he uses both the concepts of the individual components of Weltanschauung and the concept of Weltanschauung itself.

The multiple senses of the components: world picture, appreciation of life, ideal of life; actuality, value, purpose; knowing, feeling, and willing, as well as the multiple senses of the concept of Weltanschauung: that which is intuited, the intuitions, the intuiting of what is intuited—these are not accidental. Precisely because Dilthey presses toward an understanding of the structure of Weltanschauung in a vital way he must make use of these multiple senses, yet without succeeding in establishing the directions of their meaning or even of showing and of grounding the necessity of these multiple senses. Yet the fact that Dilthey is moving within these multiple senses is proof of the fact that he makes use of a primordial structure of Dasein—one not recognized as such—and that he does so because he must make use of it, if Weltanschauung indeed belongs to human Dasein.

5. This primordial structure is transcendence as being-in-the-world; Dasein as such is transcending; it has in each case always already leapt over beings, and done so in the threefold direction of dissemination, that is, as disclosed, not only does it comport itself toward beings as a whole in general, but this entails: it holds itself within the understanding of being, and the latter is even the condition of the possibility of the said comportment. It is not a psychic subject in an interiority of consciousness (something subjective) that then also has a relation to objects. Subjective and objective are component parts because, as comportments of Dasein, they hold and maintain themselves on the grounds of Dasein's transcendence, and the ontological already underlies prior to all such ontic comportment, something Dilthey does not see at all.

The possibility and necessity of Weltanschauung, that is, its essence, is grounded in Dasein's transcendence, and one not only can but must inquire back behind the facts of consciousness, insofar as a fact provides nothing whatsoever in the direction of the knowledge that Dilthey himself is striving for in wanting to understand the structure of the world in terms of the life of the soul.

Yet it is not enough to oppose Dilthey by merely pointing to the ontological clarification of essence by contrast with a positivistic, psychological description. Rather, what is required is the fundamental deliberation that we expressed in our sixth question:

6. How must Dasein be brought into view in principle in order to make visible the primordial structure? This has already been answered through the full interpretation of the essence of transcendence, where the task was to uncover the trenchancy, the nihilative character and lack of a hold lying within the being of Dasein; put negatively: the constitution of its being has neither ontic components and ultimate facts nor, however, simply a harmless, indifferent ontological structure; rather, Dasein's constitution thus essentially participates in its being. Its constitution is not some framework but rather the manner and way in which the being of Dasein temporalizes itself.

In conclusion, we may say vis-à-vis Dilthey, whose advance in the direction of clarifying the essence of world should not be diminished in its significance: Weltanschauung is not some psychic product constructed from heterogeneous components within a subject that is intrinsically encapsulated as a fact within consciousness but is rather an originally unified, although not simple, fundamental transcendental phenomenon, that is, belonging to Dasein's transcendence and determining Dasein's being in the manner of Dasein.

§40. How does Weltanschauung relate to philosophizing?

a) The ordinary form of the problem: Can and should philosophy construct a scientific Weltanschauung?

With this, we arrive at our seventh question, which everything is directed toward answering: How does this original structure of Dasein, Weltanschauung as holding oneself in being-in-the-world, relate to philosophizing, which, as we already indicated, occurs in transcendence as the fundamental constitution of Dasein? The thesis is as follows:

Philosophizing is explicit transcending. What this means must now let itself be determined more concretely through our elucidating how philosophizing relates to Weltanschauung, which after all constitutes an essential determination of being-in-the-world, of transcendence.

One could say: transcending means being-in-the-world. To being-in-the-world, however, there belongs on each occasion a particular mode of holding oneself within it, thus in short, a Weltanschauung. Explicit transcending is accordingly an explicit holding oneself within being-in-the-world or an explicit constructing of a Weltanschauung. If transcending means being-in-the-world and the latter is in each case a holding oneself within it, Weltanschauung, then explicit transcending, that is, philosophizing, is an explicit constructing of Weltanschauung. And since—according to the usual opinion that repeatedly surfaces—philosophy is scientific knowledge, indeed the highest and first, but scientific knowledge aims at universal validity, ultimate certainty, and the apodictic justification of knowing, then philosophizing must be the scientific construction of a universally valid Weltanschauung. Accordingly, Dilthey too speaks of the philosophical Weltanschauung as the "venture of raising the Weltanschauung to universal validity,"[4] and at the same time, he designates this venture as the essence of metaphysics. This is indeed the dominant opinion, except that Dilthey considers the factical fulfillment of this task

---

4. Ibid., 55 (399).

to be impossible, and indeed because metaphysics cannot satisfy the demands of science.[5]

The ordinary form of the problem of "Weltanschauung and philosophy" is accordingly: Can and should philosophy construct a scientific Weltanschauung or not? However, we do not want to keep to this problem, if only because it is a warped problem and altogether fails to identify what really demands to be clarified. Perhaps philosophy neither should nor can construct a scientific Weltanschauung; yet precisely because it neither should nor can, in the end it nevertheless stands in a unique relationship to Weltanschauung. We shall keep the ordinary problem in view, especially since it is coupled with the question of philosophy and science; but we shall now develop the answer to the question of the relationship of Weltanschauung and philosophy systematically on the basis of a more precise interpretation of Weltanschauung and transcendence.

Philosophizing is explicit transcending. At the outset of the lecture course, we said that Dasein as such philosophizes insofar as it exists. In the course of our first path, we saw that the essence of existence is transcendence. Nevertheless, explicit transcending is a free possibility of Dasein, not just belonging to Dasein, but freely springing forth from Dasein precisely with respect to its explicitness. For a connection between the essence of Weltanschauung and the essence of philosophizing to become visible, we must first briefly go into a fundamental distinction within the possibilities of Weltanschauung.

b) On the historicality of Weltanschauungen

We have already pointed to the fact that the forming of a Weltanschauung is determined by the kind of manifestness of the lack of hold pertaining to being-in-the-world, that is, by the manner in which being-in-the-world is itself experienced and the lack of hold interpreted. This manifestness of a lack of hold is not some theoretical knowing but rather precisely a mode of holding oneself within it. With the thrownness of Dasein a particular holding oneself within being-in-the-world has been decided initially, even if not definitively and in every respect. We emphasized moreover that being-in-the-world itself always determines itself in its manner of being from out of Dasein itself.

In keeping with their own essence in each instance, the fundamental possibilities of Weltanschauung also have a particular essential lawfulness among themselves with regard to their occurrence and their sequence. Certainly, one can arrange the main types of Weltanschauung in a freely created statistical analysis and typology according to some schema or other. This is mostly what happens. Initially the sole principle is that one seeks to order the manifold of Weltanschauungen in a logical manner, so as to get an overview of them. Yet in

---

5. Cf. ibid., 60 (404).

this, precisely one thing is forgotten, something essential to a Weltanschauung: its historical character, the fact that it is rooted in the happening of Dasein and at the same time determines it. The point is not to deduce possibilities from a formal concept; rather, from the insight that Dasein, insofar as it exists, is in each case already in a world, historical stages result that are determined from out of the essential historicality of Dasein.

If this historical character belongs to its essence, then the interpretation of the fundamental possibilities of Weltanschauung must also take this into account, that is, the essential connections in their sequence and in their interpenetrating laws.[6]

§41. Two fundamental possibilities of Weltanschauung

a) Weltanschauung in myth: Shelter as a hold amid overwhelming beings themselves

For our purposes, we must be satisfied with shedding light on two fundamental possibilities of Weltanschauung in terms of the essence of Dasein itself and its happening. The two, however, can factically never be separated: the first continues to be at work in the second, and the second is always already anticipated in the first.

We say that to being-in-the-world there belong the essential aspects of for the sake of oneself and thrownness. The less Dasein is initially permeated by "knowledge," learning, technics, organization, the more direct is its being pervaded by beings in its comportment toward them, the more primordial is its being at the mercy of beings, and this always within the whole of Dasein's dissemination. This means, however: beings at first manifest themselves exclusively in their overwhelming power and do so pervasively. Dasein becomes absorbed in them, captivated by the whole, not just by things. Even one's own soul, one's own self is so to speak an alien power, a daemon that takes care of the individual or threatens him. The idea of soul and spirit came about not by applying the concept of substance to inner mental phenomena but from this being pervaded by beings and being exposed to their overwhelming power. That Dasein, which does not recognize itself as such, manifests itself to itself as something alien is grounded in this being pervasively governed by beings in their overwhelming powerfulness. Beings as a whole have the character of overwhelming powerfulness.

The being of all beings is understood in this sense, being-in-the-world as this being at the mercy of the overwhelming power of beings, in the fundamental ways of being carried by them and being threatened by them. All of Dasein's

---

6. Here we are already touching on problems that we shall encounter on our third path. We must be reminded of this without being able to go into it in detail. Editor's note: The third path (Philosophy and History) was not realized.

relations and all beings it comports itself toward are interpreted out of this understanding of being as overwhelming powerfulness: space, time, number, causality, being with one another, and beings as a whole in their provenance and in their occurrence.

These connections have recently received greater attention in investigations extending to the knowledge of myth and of mythical Dasein. Cassirer has attempted to interpret mythical Dasein or, as he says, mythical thinking.[7] In so doing, he embarked above all on an interpretation of the ethnological knowledge that we today have of primitive peoples. In all mythologies, being signifies nothing other than overwhelming power, powerfulness. It is in this sense that the various words of primitives must be grasped: mana, wakanda, orenda, manitu. Cassirer has used extensive material from ethnology but in so doing focused too much on these domains and not at all on the great and richer mythology of the Greeks, for instance.

Myth marks one fundamental possibility of being-in-the-world; this means, however, that to such myth there belongs a quite determinate, though variable holding oneself within being-in-the-world, a quite determinate Weltanschauung. Insofar as Weltanschauung responds, as it were, to our lack of hold, the essential question is: How is Dasein's lack of a hold manifest to mythic Dasein in general? The response to this is: in the manner of an insecurity. Because mythic Dasein is at the mercy of the overwhelming powerfulness of beings, it is at the same time always captivated by beings in such being exposed. Exposure is essential for the understanding of existence. Dasein therefore has the tendency to become absorbed in beings themselves. For even one's own self is not yet understood as such, but delivered over to a power that is the same as that which pervasively governs the whole of beings. Being is unarticulated, yet in this indeterminacy beings are all the more powerful and more penetrating in a unitary manner. "Pantheism" and the like are all bad names and concepts, illuminating theologically, but not ontologically or metaphysically. This being captivated, however, is not to be regarded as something like a state of sleep or drunkenness. Rather, in the specific wakefulness of being at the mercy of the overpowering, the latter always makes itself known at the same time as threatening. Dasein is haunted by the overpowering. Its lack of a hold is a lack of protection in being exposed, and holding

---

7. Cf. Ernst Cassirer, *Philosophie der symbolischen Formen. 2. Teil: Das mythische Denken* (Berlin: Weidmann, 1925). Cf. *Deutsche Literaturzeitung*, vol. 21 (1928). [Cf. also Martin Heidegger, *Kant und das Problem der Metaphysik*, Gesamtausgabe Band 3 (Frankfurt: Klostermann, 1991), 255–70.] (The *Deutsche Literaturzeitung* reference is to Heidegger's 1928 review of volume 2 of Cassirer's *Philosophy of Symbolic Forms*, on mythical thought. The review is also reproduced in volume 3 of Heidegger's Complete Edition, *Kant and the Problem of Metaphysics*, trans. Richard Taft [Bloomington: Indiana University Press, 1997], 180–90. An earlier translation of Heidegger's review is available in *The Piety of Thinking: Essays by Martin Heidegger*, ed. James G. Hart and John C. Maraldo [Bloomington: Indiana University Press, 1976], 32–45.—Trans.)

oneself in such being-in-the-world is a holding oneself within an insecurity, that is, a taking shelter, procuring protection, strength, and power for oneself. From this comes the central significance of magic and enchantment and the corresponding forms of sacrifice and cult, of vegetation rites.

The lack of hold pertaining to being-in-the-world is manifest as an insecurity of Dasein. The character of the hold that constructs itself for holding oneself in this lack of hold is accordingly that of security, of a shelter amid those beings as a whole that pervade Dasein and toward which it comports itself. The first fundamental possibility of Weltanschauung is accordingly marked by the fact that the hold has the character of a shelter within beings. An entire fullness of essential connections is thereby given: The hold is found within beings themselves as overpowering; beings are that which provide the hold and security. Holding oneself, as taking a hold, is accordingly a placing oneself under the overwhelming power of beings while in need of protection; a terror in the face of these beings here goes hand in hand with appeasement, veneration, serving, and our relation to them—sacrifice; at the same time, the tendency manifests itself to somehow master them through magic, prayer, and the like.

Holding oneself within being-in-the-world as such shelter thus gives rise to an entire sphere of activities that are subject to quite definite kinds of regulation in rite and cult. Rite itself becomes deposited in prescriptions, statutes, doctrines that are recorded in sacred books or passed on in secret oral tradition. Dasein's shelter and whatever belongs to it itself becomes a power that is objectively present at hand, so to speak, becomes convention and custom, and the whole of Dasein in its happening indeed enters the jurisdiction of this shelter. This occurs with Dasein in such shelter. This can be seen above all in the regulation and function of day and night, of the seasons and festivals, in the rites relating to birth, marriage, death, sickness, war, hunting, the tilling of the fields, voyaging on the seas. Gaining a hold accordingly means fitting oneself into these regulations and statutes, participating in these magical actions, making use of and being thoroughly governed by their effects.

Through the various ways in which transcendence has been characterized we have seen that the being that we call Dasein becomes manifest in the face of the whole of beings. Dasein is this peculiar locale for the entirety of beings, which we can also call the unconditioned. In other words, Dasein in itself, in its existence, always has a particular idea of the divine, if only of the idol. When we say that Dasein is by its very essence this peculiar locale of the unconditioned then this is not saying that Dasein as this locale of the unconditioned is itself the unconditioned. One can only see these connections clearly and guard against psychological misunderstandings by speaking from out of the fundamental constitution of Dasein, transcendence. Insofar as we are dealing with Dasein as locale of the unconditioned, which one designates as the divine, one is tempted to interpret these connections, including the origin of religion, even mythical

Dasein, in terms of particular kinds of knowledge about God, in terms of theological theories.

Thus even Schelling, one of the few philosophers who developed a major, original insight into mythical Dasein, failed to avoid the danger of orienting his interpretation all too much around fundamental theological concepts. Schelling is in a certain sense correct when he says that at the beginning of mythical Dasein there stands a monotheism that does not exclude a plurality of gods, but indeed produces such a plurality. Polytheism then first arises from this plurality of gods through a process of decline, and within this polytheism arises a monotheism in the theistic sense. These problems, however, must be removed from the sphere of theisms and of a theological orientation in order to grasp the metaphysical character of these connections. What is at stake here is a happening of Dasein itself, and indeed one that subsequently occurs in and with every Dasein, even when the particular forms that come to mark it historically have become ineffective or even unknown.

The ground in which the origin of the myths of factical religions occurs and is rooted is to be seen in this fundamental form of being-in-the-world and its Weltanschauung, something we cannot go into here. Just one point needs to be made: Given all we have said in principle about Dasein, the issue here—with this and with every fundamental form of Weltanschauung—cannot be one of so-called psychological occurrences; it would be a misunderstanding if one wanted to see in what has been said a psychological explanation of the myth of religions.

The sole thing that we are concerned with here is seeing the essential character of this hold as shelter and seeing its kind of lack of hold as an insecurity. Insofar as being-in-the-world remains thoroughly governed by this insecurity, and being-in-the-world, however, is eo ipso a being-in-the-truth, truth also has a specific character here. What is essential for this kind of truth is the distinction between the holy or sacred, and the profane. All becoming manifest of beings springs not from one's own uncovering and investigating, nor is it appropriated as knowledge, but the reverse: what is newly manifest entails terror and danger and the necessity of protection, of making our comportment secure. Mythic Dasein has no science, not because human beings were too stupid for this, but because the kind of being-in-the-world that science entails is not possible at all within mythic Dasein.

The unconcealment of beings is in a specific sense oriented around an insecurity amid them, or in the care for shelter. So long as one fails to clearly survey this essential connection between insecurity and unconcealment in specifically mythic being-in-the-world, one will fail to have an adequate guiding thread for interpreting the specific truth of myth. One is then necessarily in the situation of either explaining the truth of mythic Dasein as superstition or else understanding it as the mere expression of a particular attitude of consciousness, that is, also in a fundamentally subjectivistic way. Cassirer too, in his presentation of mythic thinking, fails to escape the danger of such an interpretation. Although he takes up Schelling's recognition of the independent nature of mythic truth affirmatively, his specifically Kantian standpoint has prevented him from seeing these problems.

b) The degeneration of shelter: Weltanschauung that has become busyness

Our characterization of this one fundamental possibility of Weltanschauung whose hold has the character of a shelter within the beings to which Dasein comports itself was intended above all to provide us with a background, as it were, against which we can set into relief another fundamental possibility of Weltanschauung. Following what has just been discussed, this possibility too must let itself be determined by our asking once more about another possible kind of manifestness and accordingly another interpretation of our lack of hold. We already said, however, that these possibilities do not surface next to one another but have essential historical connections in which the forms of degeneration and substitution of Weltanschauung show themselves on each occasion in their peculiar function that proves productive.

Without now constructing this essential history in detail or saying anything about factical Weltanschauungen in the genuine sense or about religions, we can make one thing comprehensible: when a Weltanschauung develops as a shelter, then it lies within its most proper meaning to develop the entirety of ways and means to salvation in a definite and binding configuration and to incorporate this into every individual mode of comportment on the part of concrete Dasein, so as to pervasively govern and precisely thereby to secure it.

Now this necessary, objective securing and governing that lies within the most proper meaning of shelter, the public proffering and improved accessibility of means, carries within itself the seed of degeneration. We are here disregarding the cravings for power and domination and the lust for gain on the part of those who administer the organization of such a form of salvation; here, as in other domains of human existence, the consequences of such instincts are unavoidable; in themselves, however, they cannot endanger or disrupt the entirety of the very idea, means, and ways of salvation. It is these means and ways themselves, however, in their accessibility and in their use, that presumably thrust themselves before that which they themselves serve, as it were. For their dominance and their use gives them a public character, which means, however, that they present themselves as beings just like those that they relate to, and insofar as they are what is "nearest," one's interest is drawn to them. They become ends in themselves, attending to them and deploying them takes precedence over everything. What is essential is now no longer whether their magic works and its effect is experienced and believed but that it is carried out in accordance with what is prescribed, and its use demanded. Shelter loses its proper function of holding and of providing a hold; it becomes busyness.

What are the implications of this for the Weltanschauung in question? Holding oneself within being-in-the-world now becomes a particular configuration thereof; what is decisive is no longer the security of Dasein, but instead that its shelter function, that it remain in prominence and in power. This securing of the organization of shelter is accompanied by an ineffectiveness of the security it offers. The in-security disappears, not on the grounds of a sheltering, however, but together with the degeneration of such sheltering, that is, both are altered; they are seemingly neither a lack of hold nor the need for a hold, because they are neither insecurity nor sheltering. Yet precisely this indifference, that is, an inner emptiness of Dasein, is the uncanny situation in which a sudden change is being prepared. What is peculiar is that with the reign of busyness the insecurity of Dasein disappears and Dasein loses itself.

A new and altogether different lack of a hold announces itself, one that indeed is for the most part still suppressed, and will be for a long time, by the fact that the Weltanschauung that has become trivialized and become busyness seeks to renew itself, to improve itself, to assimilate itself to needs, and thus gives rise to mixed forms that in fact only accelerate the inner disintegration. The reign of busyness makes manifest a new lack of hold, and this means that despite itself, it provides a directive toward possibilities of taking up a hold that were not hitherto manifest. The indifference between hold and lack of hold, the reign of busyness, makes it evident that the means and ways of sheltering fall short when insecurity as such is itself no longer there within Dasein but is, as it were, covered over by busyness. The no longer being there of Dasein's insecurity means, however, that Dasein has lost itself. The awareness dawns that already within that being at the mercy of the overwhelming power of beings and within every so-called gaining a hold, that is, within insecurity as giving rise to sheltering, there lay a primordial being of Dasein for the sake of itself, one that was admittedly taken away from it, as it were, and indeed in a genuine way, by the sheltering that originarily arose.

Dasein henceforth indeed continues to be at the mercy but of busyness, and in such a way that its insecurity has seemingly disappeared. Being at the mercy of busyness means, however, that Dasein no longer authentically holds itself within itself at all, which means that prior to this, it did hold itself within itself, albeit obscurely, and despite everything had set itself upon itself. With the disappearance of insecurity and with sheltering becoming trivialized into busyness, what we designate as the emptiness of Dasein, as lostness, slipping away from oneself, necessarily sets in—Dasein itself becomes a victim of busyness: everywhere where busyness is what is essential, an emptiness of Dasein is covertly there, one that is precisely supposed to be constantly eliminated by the bustle of busyness.

Yet the question is once again: How can holding oneself within oneself become manifest here at all? It occurs through busyness itself; as bustle, such busyness makes known a certain free possibility of Dasein (to set itself upon itself) in its comportment, and this at the same time awakens the recollection of the possibility of holding oneself within oneself.

Busyness thus manifests the lack of Dasein's authentically being itself, which we designate as a stance, a held bearing [*Haltung*], and indeed in a dual way: 1. the becoming manifest of slipping away from oneself, the emptiness of Dasein, holding itself within itself. 2. together with this: being referred to one's own possibility of activity—the emphatic held bearing of comportment. In the no longer being there of a held bearing becoming manifest there lies the directive toward the possibility of an original appropriation thereof. In other words: From the manifestness of the lack of hold as lack of a held bearing there arises a new possibility of taking a hold, that is, of holding oneself within being-in-the-world. Hold is now manifest as a held bearing.

§42. *The other fundamental possibility: Weltanschauung as held bearing*

a) Weltanschauung as held bearing and the confrontation with beings arising from it

With this, we arrive at the second fundamental possibility of Weltanschauung, one essentially related to the first and that always remains related. A hold as sheltering has its hold primarily in that to which it holds, in the beings in which it is secure; hold as a held bearing has its hold primarily in holding oneself itself. Dasein itself—as such—lets the hold happen and be; yet Dasein is not, however, the being to which it holds itself, although the chief possibility of the degeneration of Weltanschauung as a held bearing lies in this direction.

As sheltering, the first hold is related to the lack of hold as original insecurity. Its necessary unfolding degenerates into busyness, which for its part—initially in the manner of semblance (being busily occupied) and of lack—makes manifest the possibility of a held bearing, and together with this, a new lack of hold. The latter is busyness itself; what is characteristic is that here the lack of hold is expressed positively. For the more Dasein in its happening distances itself from what is authentic, and "truth" becomes transformed in how it is, the more essential and "free" the semblance becomes. "Busyness" presents itself as semblance of the highest actuality, as action, "something is happening." Insofar as the lack of hold corresponding to a held bearing lies within busyness, yet the latter intrinsically functions as a mode of sheltering, the held bearing remains in an essential connection with sheltering itself, and thus with the lack of hold as in-security. In this essential alloy of held bearing and sheltering lies the essential ground for the necessity of confrontation and struggle between the two. Sheltering and held bearing are two fundamental modes of Weltanschauung, that is, of being-in-the-world, of the respective facticity of transcendence. They are essentially related to one another. By setting one possibility into relief against the other, both can be clarified, which is important for us with regard to the second possibility above all.

From the outset we must not forget: as Weltanschauungen, sheltering and held bearing always concern the whole of Dasein in the unity of its dissemination. This is all the more important since precisely in the two fundamental modes of transcendence, what transpires in each case is a displacement of the weight of transcendence, without the latter falling apart in the process, as it were. Displacement of its weight is an inner possibility of transcendence in its character of play. We can depict this only schematically, with the entire reservations of such a characterization.

In sheltering, the weight of Dasein lies in its being pervaded by beings, and in such a way that the truth of Dasein is determined primarily by insecurity. Dasein is to a certain degree taken into the whole of beings, yet nonetheless not lost but rather carried by them.

In Weltanschauung as a held bearing, by contrast, the weight of Dasein lies in comportment as Dasein comporting itself and itself acting. The "for the sake of itself," which even in mythic Dasein is not missing, as it were—otherwise sheltering would lack being—brings Dasein to itself. The "for the sake of itself" now expressly comes into a holding oneself. This means, however, that Dasein has taken hold of itself in its thrownness and in its factical possibilities. In being pervaded by beings, it holds itself into possibilities of itself that it holds before itself. A held bearing, as the second fundamental kind of Weltanschauung, expresses what is essential in the holding that occurs within Dasein. The Dasein that is determined by a held bearing is a holding itself into possibilities of its held comportments, possibilities held before it.

This formulation has been chosen intentionally in order to show how this second fundamental mode of Dasein is determined through and through by existing as acting in existence being set upon itself, which does not, however, mean that the thrownness of Dasein disappears—it cannot do so at all—but rather that it too is maintained within the held bearing. Dasein's own comportment attains a priority in such a held bearing, but it places itself into a comportment toward those beings that hitherto have not lost the aspect of powerfulness, even though its specifically mythic modification, powerfulness as sacredness, has already vanished. Explicit comportment toward superior powers, however, becomes a confrontation with them on the part of Dasein within its sphere and in all essential relations. In this fundamental way of a held bearing, Dasein becomes a confrontation with beings, and indeed in all essential relational directions of Dasein's dissemination. The whole of beings that was manifest within sheltering—within the way of sheltering—has not disappeared, but presumably the character of truth has changed. (Not only something else manifest, but uncovered for the first time, and with respect to what?)

The beings already manifest now show themselves in and for a Dasein determined as a held bearing, that is, a confrontational Dasein; they show themselves as that which is to be mastered, dominated, governed. By essential necessity, however, this intrinsically demands a knowing one's way around in beings with respect to what and how they are in themselves, irrespective of whether they offer security or refuse it. Knowing one's way around in beings must make these beings manifest in such a way that it becomes possible to govern, direct, and dominate them. Being able to govern them, however, presupposes that we understand in advance and can foresee how beings behave, so to speak, that is, we must have an insight in advance into how a sequence of events is ordered. We designate the constitution of beings in this regard as lawfulness. Insofar as laws are to be recognized, however, this means that beings must be uncovered in themselves. Knowledge of laws arises from and is borne by being-in-the-world as a held bearing in confrontation.

The idea of lawfulness, and correspondingly the way in which lawful connections are themselves determined, can be very basic and can develop. What remains decisive initially is that with the change in the character of truth that installs itself already in advance with a Weltanschauung as held bearing—it is not simply a late result—our fundamental position toward beings changes. To put it more correctly: with a held bearing, Dasein arrives for the first time at a fundamental position toward beings in such a way that only now are beings manifest in themselves. Only now that the "for the sake of oneself" expressly becomes a holding oneself, that is, holding oneself within being-in-the-world, which at the same time means within being-in-the-truth—only now is there such a thing as a for the sake of being-in-the-truth, for the sake of truth. Only in such a Dasein that is determined from the ground up by an expressly chosen held bearing of itself, and is essential in its confrontation with beings, can there be such a thing as research and science.

The making manifest of beings or of the things themselves is one aspect of scientific knowledge, but neither the only one nor the most original one, yet presumably the one that first catches our eye, the one from which one purposefully proceeds when characterizing science. Yet, it is an error to see the essence of such knowledge in this alone. Knowledge of beings in themselves and of their laws has a deeper grounding, in transcendence. The view that knowledge of beings in themselves is the essence of science, just because they are that which is in itself, is a belated invention on the part of scholars who still want to procure some significance for their craft in this way, now that the trivialities have become too great.

If earlier we said that scientific knowledge is positive knowledge for the sake of truth, of being-in-the-truth, what now becomes clear is this: Being-in-the-truth belongs to being-in-the-world and is therefore necessarily determined by Weltanschauung in each case and indeed by a held bearing; only within the latter is science possible.

Mythic Dasein has nothing like science and knows no such thing, not because the human beings of such Dasein would be too clumsy or even too stupid for this but because science has essentially no meaning at all within such Dasein. One of the greatest methodological errors that pervades the interpretation of mythic Dasein hitherto—as in the school of French sociologists and ethnologists—is therefore that one regards mythic thinking in some sense as a preform of modern European scientific thinking, and indeed of science, and interprets it from the perspective of this guiding thread. Yet even Cassirer has not mastered this fundamental error.

b) Weltanschauung as held bearing and the transformation of truth as such

With the development of Weltanschauung as a held bearing, an essential transformation of truth as such has necessarily occurred as well. The fact that in individual domains there are then other truths that cannot be reconciled with those of myth is merely a consequence but not the grounds for the essential transformation of truth itself. All making manifest is now primarily a confrontation with beings that regulates and seeks domination.

This, however, does not only concern the transformation of truth pertaining to science, for instance. Art too becomes detached from its specifically mythic or religious function, and religion acquires an essentially different function: a theology develops for the first time. What is now theology is in mythic Dasein what one can call theogony: an objective process of the very becoming of God, within which there stands the priest. The priest is not merely the functionary of a holy institution.

With this transformation of the various regions of beings, truth is transformed in its particulars, and only now does a technics arise in the authentic sense and a new structuring and ordering of society. Yet the transformation of truth is not, for instance, a consequence of the transformation of social relations. That is a profound error, whether in the sense of a crude Marxism or of a modern sociology of culture. In all of this we see only that transcendence lies at the foundation of all essential fundamental possibilities of Dasein and that the transformation of truth prefigures particular new possibilities and a transformation in forms of existence.

The confrontation with beings (transformation of being-in-the-world) that arises with Weltanschauung as a held bearing always concerns the whole of Dasein's dissemination, thus also the way in which Dasein is itself and expressly comports itself toward itself. "Soul" and "spirit" as indices of the self are now no longer experienced in an insecurity and sheltering within the overwhelming powerfulness of beings; rather, beings, Dasein itself, are likewise comprehended and taken hold of in this confrontation. In the confrontation of Dasein with beings as a whole, in these beings becoming manifest to it, Dasein—which was previously located within beings and captivated by them—at the same time detaches itself from these beings. It itself becomes something that can be governed, and indeed in an exceptional sense, as can be seen; it becomes manifest that Dasein is itself such a being. With this, the possibilities of choosing itself in a resolute decision with regard to itself and in a corresponding action are given.

In the conception and interpretation of Dasein in antiquity there is a word that, if correctly understood, expresses most originally what we mean by Weltanschauung: εὐδαιμονία. Δαιμονία is finding oneself within beings as a whole, within their overwhelming powerfulness (daemonic nature), while εὖ means finding oneself and holding oneself in the right way within the overwhelming powerfulness of beings. In the period when Plato and Aristotle were philosophizing—and already prepared earlier—εὐδαιμονία is sought in πρᾶξις, in free action that gives itself the goal, προαίρεσις.

Correctly understood, this word still preserves a recollection of this transition from mythic Dasein and its sheltering to a held bearing. In this fundamental way of Dasein, Dasein too remains in the midst of beings—this belongs to its essence—even though Dasein as such is now raised out of beings in a particular way. Such being raised out, however, is not isolation in the ontic sense of cutting it off; rather, this being raised out and coming to light together with the genesis of a held bearing merely signifies a transformed mode of the being of Dasein. This emergence is what we also designate as the explicitness of Dasein, which makes itself known as a newly penetrating character of Dasein within itself and its existence. This penetrating character of confrontation is one pertaining to the (ekstatic) dissemination of Dasein. It is nevertheless important for us, as in the case of the first fundamental kind of Weltanschauung as sheltering, to also make ourselves aware of the essentially associated forms of degeneration pertaining to the second fundamental possibility of Weltanschauung.

c) Forms of degeneration of Weltanschauung as held bearing

In Weltanschauung as a held bearing, the weight of transcendence diverts itself from being pervaded and into the "for the sake of." The potentiality for being a self becomes essential, and the being itself, the human being who is in the manner of Dasein, thereby moves into the center, and does so in accordance with three different respects, to which there correspond three forms of degeneration of the held bearing.

1. The held bearing gives Dasein a certain advantage among beings. The human being himself becomes important; everything becomes related to the human being and explained on the basis of his thoughts and efforts. The human being himself thereby becomes a distinct object of discussion and reflection. The held bearing as the becoming essential of one's own potentiality for being is now taken as occupying oneself with oneself. Busyness is now redirected, as it were, toward the human being. In the wake of the development of Weltanschauung as a held bearing, anthropologism always appears, a fastidiousness regarding the human being in the form of psychology and characterological analysis. The means by which this factically occurs are irrelevant. Where modern psychology exceeds its narrowly defined limits—as it usually does—there is nothing to distinguish it from ancient sophistry, except that the latter had an altogether different intellectual level.

2. Self-comportment in action is essential within the held bearing. The how of action has a certain priority over the what of doing and over that with which we are preoccupied. Here there lies the possibility that the how of the held bearing may inflate itself at the expense of a concrete and authentically effective action, and indeed the how of action can inflate itself in such a way that action itself becomes the object of its own kind of attention and cultivation. The held bearing now becomes essential as gesture; what is cultivated is the gesture, which mostly withdraws from actual action and, in keeping with its intention, gives precedence to art and its figuration. That is, it seeks out a corresponding content for presenting its gesture, a content that is then declared to be authoritative for everything, to be sacrosanct. What of necessity arises is an admittedly merely literary and aesthetic renewal of cults and myths; together with this goes the heroizing of particular human beings.

   Compared to the first form of degeneration, that of anthropologism, which on the grounds of its indiscriminate dissection of the human being and amassing of bits of knowledge about him readily leads to barbarism, there lies in the second form—which always goes together with a marked cultivation of literature—a distinct tendency opposed to all barbarisms, a sense for standards and for a held bearing in the specifically aesthetic sense of taste. This form too shows itself in the most varied forms; compared to psychological anthropologism, we may designate it as an aesthetic humanism.

3. In Weltanschauung as a held bearing, free choice, decision, plays a certain leading role. This entails that the one choosing reverts to himself as court of appeal. In the face of the external circumstances, affairs, and predicaments

of Dasein, reflection claims a certain precedence. Inwardness becomes something cultivated, not in psychological discussion, nor in being aesthetically shaped, but in the seriousness of one's way of thinking and of being concerned for oneself. Not only is the existence of the individual "I" the locus of decisions but it itself is what is decisive. This form of held bearing can readily become tied to, and indeed repeatedly arises in closest connection to, a particular religion, for example, to Christian religiosity. Here too we see the influence played by the first fundamental form of Weltanschauung; means and ways to salvation—the procurement of grace, sacraments—are indeed not employed but concern for the soul's salvation remains, indeed intensifies. Here there is no anthropologism, nor any humanism, yet the human being indeed stands in the center with respect to the salvation of his existence. The expression "existentialism" is beginning to become common today. This existentialism is for the most part religiously accented; with regard to what is decisive, it is promoted by a particular form of the renewal of Kierkegaardian thoughts.

We thus have three forms of the degeneration of Weltanschauung as held bearing: fastidiousness, gesture, and inwardness—subjectivism in various iterations. These three forms of the degeneration of Weltanschauung as held bearing factically always go together, can become mixed with one another in the process, and thereby can further intensify their lack of genuineness and their cluelessness. We find ourselves today in such a situation. We shall say no more about this here. Now, insofar as Dasein receives a distinctive function on the basis of entirely different motives [. . .]* in terms of the fundamental problem of philosophy and its knowledge, and this function has been concretely presented, it is inevitably—when converted into one of these forms—filed in a drawer and is then harmless.

What is important for us is that in these degenerate forms of held bearing a certain priority of Dasein makes itself known each time; this points to the fact that a becoming essential of the self belongs to the essence of this Weltanschauung as a held bearing. Yet something simple can be seen clearly, namely, that if the self becomes essential, it is initially of no importance whatsoever what kind of fastidiousness is staged with regard to the human being, which gesture is imputed [?] to him, or what existence is thought up for him. Rather, what is essential is manifestly the being of the self and the possibility of letting this happen.

In all these forms of held bearing, human life is basically understood as a business that is to be kept going either through psychological fastidiousness or neo-humanistic gesture or else through the absurd fretfulness of a so-called existentiell thinking. What remains important for the present context of a general characterization of held bearing is to see that it belongs to the essence of

---

* [One word illegible.]

Weltanschauung as held bearing that Dasein becomes explicit, "explicit" not primarily in the sense that it would be heeded, observed, and especially familiar, rather, explicitness as a characteristic of its being. The being of Dasein acquires a trenchancy for itself.

Where mythic Dasein determines the existence of the human being now only in faint recollection and painted over by a held bearing but no longer determines it explicitly, there human life holds sway only to the extent that it summons up Dasein within it on a given occasion.

The fundamental constitution of Dasein, however, lies in transcendence. In Weltanschauung as a held bearing, being-in-the-world as such comes to be more essential. Dasein itself takes hold of its possibilities of comportment toward beings as a whole. Transcending becomes explicit. In Weltanschauung as a held bearing there is an explicit transcending, which means, however, from what was said earlier: philosophizing. With the occurrence and development of Weltanschauung as a held bearing, philosophizing happens. Philosophizing is therefore the development of Weltanschauung as a held bearing, the held bearing is the philosophical Weltanschauung.

§43. On the inner relationship between Weltanschauung as a held bearing and philosophy

a) On the problematic of this relationship

Our problem is the relationship of Weltanschauung and philosophy, or more precisely, how the latter is determined by the former. In connection with a general clarification of its essence, which proved to belong to being-in-the-world, we proceeded to elaborate two fundamental forms of Weltanschauung: sheltering and held bearing. A priority of Dasein made itself known as a peculiarity of the second of these. This priority is initially given on the grounds of the confrontation with beings that belongs to the essence of a held bearing. In characterizing this confrontation, I pointed to the fact that in its fundamental tendency, all knowing aims at dominating, at becoming master over, and that the necessity of a thorough investigation of beings with respect to their lawfulness is thereby given. This has nothing to do with pragmatism, however, which equates being true with useful effect. It is not the useful effect, but rather beings themselves in their what and how that decide concerning the truth of knowledge. Beings can only do this, however, if they are interrogated in this regard, and such questioning, calling beings to account, is a confrontation with them. Merely staring at things is never able to uncover.

The peculiarity of Weltanschauung as a held bearing and the notable fact that in it Dasein receives a priority, was meant to display itself for us precisely in the fact that it leads to three forms of degeneration. The fundamental form of degeneration lies within the held bearing itself, insofar as Dasein becomes explicit in it. If we seek to grasp what is positive in what emerges in these forms of degeneration, it is the moment that belongs essentially to the held bearing, and which we designate as the gathering of Dasein. We know that to Dasein there necessarily belongs a threefold dissemination into its relations to beings or objects, to the Dasein-with of others, and to itself, and that Dasein has the tendency to lose itself in one of these relations, to become absorbed in it, to absolutize it. What is essential in Weltanschauung as a held bearing consists not only in attaining the whole of Dasein in accordance with these three directions but in holding them in a gathering. A held bearing is therefore intrinsically a gathering of dissemination into the primordiality of the Da-sein in the human being. Gathering is the primordial character that degenerates in the said forms of degeneration.

The issue is gathering, instead of subjectivism and individualism; however, the form of degeneration is not incidental but belongs to the essence of Dasein itself, here in its held bearing as there in mythic Dasein. I shall not go into the various other modifications of degeneration, especially not into individualism in all its shades and not into what one calls Enlightenment, or better, the Enlightenment spirit whereby one makes one's own understanding the standard of measure and master of everything. Kant: "Have the courage to use your own understanding."[8]

A held bearing is a gathering of the human being with respect to Da-sein in the process of confrontation. This does not merely entail asserting oneself and pushing through, simply securing oneself against . . ., rather a held bearing as Dasein is in itself the setting free of possibilities, it signifies "growth," but not "progress."

Held bearing as philosophical Weltanschauung is still a characterization that means a great many things, and above all is premature, superficial. This much indeed is clear: the held bearing, insofar as transcendence becomes more explicit in it, stands in a particular connection with philosophizing, if the latter is explicit transcending. Yet the inner relationship between Weltanschauung as held bearing and philosophizing is still completely problematic. We must beware here of wanting to find an all too easy solution.

We shall try to elucidate the problem by way of an analogy with the question from our first path. The problem there was: Is science the idea to which philosophy must be made subservient, philosophy as rigorous science, or is philosophy altogether not science, though for this very reason the ground of the possibility

---

8. Immanuel Kant, *Beantwortung der Frage: Was ist Aufklärung? Immanuel Kants gesammelte Schriften*, ed. Königlich Preußische Akademie der Wissenschaften, vol. 8 (Berlin: De Gruyter, 1920), 35.

of science? What we saw was that the idea of a scientific philosophy is like the thought of a roundish circle. Now, how do things stand correspondingly with regard to the relationship between Weltanschauung and philosophy? Is Weltanschauung that which should serve as the standard for philosophy? Is philosophy a Weltanschauung, or does, conversely, this Weltanschauung have philosophy as its presupposition?

As we explicitly emphasized, we have now asked about an analogy with our first path, that is, placed Weltanschauung in correlation with science. However, even that is impossible, for Weltanschauung is something essentially more primordial and belonging to Dasein, whereas science is not. It thus becomes questionable whether even here, on our second path, we may simply reduce the problem to this either/or, or whether what is peculiar to our present problem does not thereby indeed fall through the cracks and become ungraspable. This is indeed the case.

To this, we must add something else. It already emerged more or less clearly that philosophizing as explicit transcending has a special relation to the one fundamental form of Weltanschauung as a held bearing, and thus to a particular possibility, something that certainly does not exclude but includes that an essential relation to Weltanschauung as sheltering is also to be found here. Yet the general question concerning the relationship between philosophy and Weltanschauung thereby becomes more complicated already. In general, we may only say: philosophy and Weltanschauung both concern transcendence, being-in-the-world; but how remains the question.

b) Philosophy is Weltanschauung as held bearing in an exceptional sense

We want initially to anticipate the answer in a certain direction by saying: Weltanschauung, specifically as a held bearing, is a "presupposition" of philosophy. Yet what does "presupposition" mean here? Being-in-the-world as a held bearing must happen if there is to be able to be philosophizing. With the happening of Weltanschauung as a held bearing, philosophizing has also already awakened. Philosophy is already Weltanschauung from its very ground, and indeed necessarily in the manner of a held bearing, which includes a particular relation to sheltering. Philosophy "is" Weltanschauung. Because philosophy by necessity of its essence is Weltanschauung in this yet to be determined manner, it cannot then be the task and goal of philosophy to develop a Weltanschauung, and to distribute and claim this building thus fortified as a dwelling place for everyone.

Philosophy is Weltanschauung as a held bearing and is so in an exceptional sense. For held bearing, the Greeks have the word ἦθος—precisely for this reason, however, it is not the proclamation of an ethics. Yet if philosophy is neither science nor the development of a Weltanschauung nor the proclamation of an ethics, what does it accomplish, then, and what does it do? Philosophy philosophizes. This simply says: it can and must be comprehended in terms of itself; only in philosophizing is philosophy understood.

Philosophy is of its own essence, which does not preclude us from saying that it is Weltanschauung qua held bearing. (Cf. p.268.) For this assertion does not provide a definition in the sense that "Weltanschauung" would define the universal, uppermost genus for philosophy, as though we now wanted to substitute "Weltanschauung" for the universal genus "science," just as in the customary view science represents the idea of a genus. We are not saying: Philosophy is one form of Weltanschauung among others. This "is" has its own signification here.

In what sense, then, and in what way is a philosophy Weltanschauung, specifically as a held bearing? The answer cannot be all that difficult, one might reply, and above all we are surely not so clueless when faced with the question of what philosophy accomplishes; for after all, on our first path we assigned to it the question of being, the problem of being, working out the possibilities of being and the constitution of the being of the various domains of beings. That is enough of a task. So the only question now would be: How does philosophy as the question concerning being relate to the fact that it is Weltanschauung? Cannot the manner and way in which philosophy is Weltanschauung ultimately be discerned from the fact that it poses the question of being and from how it poses it?

However, we are not allowed to proceed in this manner, that is, we may not derive the result of our second path from the result of our first path. Rather, the second path is meant to bring us independently to philosophizing, and that indeed means that it is supposed to run together with the first. We can and must indeed orient ourselves toward the first (cf. transcendence and the problem of being) but not in the sense of deriving "results." We may not, therefore, ask: How can the manner and way in which philosophy is Weltanschauung be disclosed from the nature of the problematic of the problem of being; rather, we must initially proceed the other way around and ask: Can it be made clear from the essence of Weltanschauung as a held bearing to what extent that which we called philosophizing necessarily occurs with it? Can we, from the essence of a held bearing, shed light on the fact that in it the problem of being necessarily becomes awakened, and in what way? To what extent does there lie within Weltanschauung as a held bearing, and essentially and necessarily in it alone, the free possibility of the explicit working out of the problem of being, that is, the possibility of explicit philosophizing?

In sheltering, Dasein diverts itself into the whole of beings and finds its security therein. Beings as a whole are that which hold and provide a hold. In a held bearing, by contrast, the hold is not in the whole of beings, but in Dasein, the latter certainly as disseminated, yet not, for instance, in a manner corresponding to sheltering, as though the held bearing were a kind of sheltering, only now within itself. Attaining a hold in a held bearing does not at all have the character of sheltering. Taking hold does not occur in or with a being, not even Dasein, rather the held bearing is distinguished by the fact that here that which grants the hold has a different character: The hold occurs in the being of Dasein. The occurrence of holding oneself within being-in-the-world is not a taking hold in something else on the part of Dasein.

Because the occurrence of holding oneself as being-in-the-world is now essential, the confrontation with beings comes into play. Comportment toward beings in themselves becomes decisive, overcoming the overwhelming powerfulness of beings in such a way that in so doing, proceeding from Dasein, these beings in themselves are to be taken into Dasein's rule. Even if the issue is not yet at all that of expressly developed science, let alone a science comprehended as such, the comportment toward beings, as comportment toward . . ., is out to make manifest what and how beings are. It is not a matter of merely registering and collecting a bunch of values for knowledge, rather this truth is a direct moment of factically holding oneself in the midst of beings. In it, being-in-the-world is also accomplished.

This wanting to know one's way around in what and how beings are in each case does not begin somewhere in some random little corner of the wide realm of manifest beings, but engages simultaneously in all regions that are essential for Dasein, that is, in the whole of the relations of its dissemination. Each particular investigation in a single direction arises out of the whole and within the whole. This entails, however, that it is at the same time the whole of beings themselves that wants to be understood in what and how it is.

§44. In Weltanschauung as held bearing the problem of being irrupts

The held bearing, which is always a confrontation with beings as a whole, must if possible become master of the whole of beings in themselves in such confrontation. Beings as a whole in themselves become a question with regard to what they are. With this question concerning beings as beings, the problem of being explicitly irrupts. In Weltanschauung as a held bearing, that is, in the confrontation with beings, there necessarily lies an awakening of the problem of being, that is, of that which we called philosophizing.

Now precisely here, with respect to this origin of the problem of being from the origin of Weltanschauung as a held bearing, it is important to preserve the original shape of the problem of being in its entire originality, scope, and greatness, and not to shatter it from the outset through some later one-sided and diminished form of development.

A universal law pertaining to the essence of genesis holds here, namely, that what is originally inceptive is not, as positivistic science claims, what is simple, lowly, and impoverished but instead what is complex, supreme, and richest, and that all genesis is only ever a development in a particular direction, one that, at the expense of its determinacy, can never again regain the greatness of the origin. This means that the essential fullness of a problem must be sought precisely at the inception and so to speak at the birth of philosophy. And so too here with the problem of being.

If the problem of being necessarily awakens with the occurrence of a held bearing, that is, with the genesis of this second form of Weltanschauung from the first, from sheltering, and if the latter is not simply disposed of, but retains its specific force as a possibility that has been, then it is clear that the first concrete form of the problem of being too must be determined by the genesis of the confrontational held bearing from out of sheltering. People have always already been attentive to the origin of philosophy from myth—we are dealing with nothing else—especially the Greeks themselves; yet this means only that all philosophizing itself, commensurate with its own possibility, must time and again assure itself of this essential origin, that is, impart to itself its full essence from there. It cannot be said that this always happened or happens where the origin of philosophy from myth is discussed.

a) The awakening of the problem of being from Weltanschauung within myth as sheltering

We know little and only fragments from the earliest philosophers of antiquity but enough to recognize some essential things. When they ask concerning beings as a whole and for the first time raise their arms toward beings, as it were, and toward the overwhelming powerfulness that still continues to radiate from them in order to win beings in themselves, then with such questioning they themselves still stand, as it were, entirely in the midst of beings and ask about them in inquiring after their primal origin. For the overpowering as a whole is what they always already encounter pure and simple. This "always already" can for them only mean: powerful and happening since primal times, of an unfathomable age. When they enquire concerning beings in themselves, their question must be directed toward the primal origin of beings, their primal history, toward the ἀρχή. In the question concerning the primal origin of the happening of beings, pure mythology has already been abandoned, insofar as a confrontational question has come to life. Mythology is still there, to the extent that the orbit of this questioning is still prefigured by mythic Dasein. The answer is given in some kind of theogony or cosmogony.

We see already, however, that the confrontation with beings is neither restricted to a small corner nor simply of the kind that we just now characterized. The confrontation dominates Dasein through and through, that is, precisely in its most proximate undertakings and possibilities, in dominating nature, in voyaging on the sea, in working the land, or in city building. In such confrontational comportment toward beings, beings manifest themselves in a new way.

By contrast with what previously appeared by way of magic and enchantment without the human being knowing or wanting to know how, beings are now encountered that, in being freely produced, procured, and worked upon, become precisely the beings that were needed. In free production in the broadest sense, it becomes more or less clearly manifest, in a way that is conceptually still almost undetermined, that beings are something that are set forth and that stand at our disposal as set forth, present at hand before us. And conversely: the whole of those beings that make themselves known there in their overwhelming power is present at hand and as such somehow produced. If, accordingly, within this held bearing toward beings that unfolds in confrontation and setting forth, the question is raised explicitly about beings as a whole in themselves, then they are understood in advance as present at hand as a whole, produced, as having somehow come forth. When the general question thus awakens of what beings are and how they are, then this question follows these lines: What is it produced from, what does it consist of, what are its primordial components, and through what has it arisen? The question concerning what beings are is necessarily directed once more toward a whence, an ἀρχή, but ἀρχή now not in the sense of a mythic primal beginning but in the sense of what they consist of, prime matter, and through what, primal force—not, of course, taken in terms of a theoretical materialism and chemism of the nineteenth century.

The second form of questioning concerning beings as a whole, concerning the ἀρχή in its second signification, remains directly entangled with the first. Only because there is this connection, that is, because even the direction of questioning that seemingly arises purely from the confrontational comportment still remains bound up with the first, yet the first has its former legitimacy and power as mythic—only for this reason can the second be initiated and assert itself in the first instance.

With the development of Weltanschauung as a held bearing, because it is confrontation, a running up against beings as a whole thus transpires, running up against them in the now unyielding question of what beings are and how they are. Because this questioning belongs to Dasein as such, yet Dasein in an explicit sense comports itself toward itself in its held bearing, this questioning itself is also inserted into the general question concerning beings. To put it another way: Because the concern is expressly with the manifestness of what beings are, the manifestness of beings as a whole in themselves, this manifestness itself is thrust into the sphere of questioning, in the first instance not at all in the sense of a formal reflection on the method of questioning concerning beings, but in the still almost mythic form that truth as goddess provides the paths of questioning for decision and points the correct one—thus in Parmenides. The questioning confrontation with beings as a whole is placed securely on its own path and runs its course in the midst of these beings. However, with the becoming manifest of the path and of the position of questioning, a clearer light is at the same time shed on what is being asked after in the sense of the question concerning the ἀρχή, what it is that is being sought in beings as beings when the question is asked concerning what beings were from time immemorial and that through which they became possible. Beings were always already determined as beings by being; they were intrinsically possible through being. Only slowly, with difficulty, and with constant setbacks does this confrontation with beings as a whole attain a relative clarity about itself, that is, about what is being asked about, what the being of beings itself is, about Plato's seeking, the problem of being, ὄντως ὄν.

b) Historical forms of development of philosophy from Weltanschauung as sheltering and held bearing

We now return to the point of departure of our question. What does it mean: philosophy is Weltanschauung as a held bearing? It means: philosophy in its inner possibility is grounded in such Weltanschauung. Yet the converse is not the case: the held bearing does not exhaust itself in being philosophizing; to the contrary, it is for the most part not that at all, and if it is, then a peculiar modification. (Cf. §46 on held bearing in relation to ground.) With Weltanschauung as a held bearing, philosophizing happens. We sought to show this by demonstrating that the problem of being necessarily awakens with the occurrence of a confrontation. This means at the same time, however: This problem of being as such is itself intrinsically possible only in a Dasein whose being-in-the-world is determined primarily through a held bearing. In other words, there is no so-called philosophical problem in itself that just anyone can randomly grasp at. (If such a thing seemingly occurs, this does not yet guarantee that whoever holds forth within the framework and necessary technicality of such questioning is "doing philosophy," philosophizing in the sense of questioning.) An extreme view of the stock of problems in themselves can today be found in Nicolai Hartmann.

The problem of being has the intrinsic possibility of itself as a problem in Dasein as a held bearing. The fact that this is not understood, or that if such a thing is pointed out it is said that this is psychological explanation of problems in themselves and thus a linguistic [?] watering down of things, is not accidental. It has its grounds in the fact that the problematic of philosophy is not understood in terms of its original ground but instead within the framework and in the orientation toward the technical means of developing philosophy. Architectonic of disciplines.

In the confrontation with beings, there necessarily arises the making manifest and determining of beings in themselves, the determining of beings as this and that; a conceptual knowing arises. With this, however, the language that is already occurring gains new weight in the direction of a differentiation in its stock of significations. The whole of language itself functions, as it were, as an objectively occurring depository of the truth of beings. Language, word, signification, sense, what is meant, beings themselves are in a certain sense one and the same, exchangeable. The λόγος is the representative of beings themselves. The fundamental form of language, the word and sentence formation, nouns and propositional statements become the guiding thread for determining beings as such, the guiding thread for the problem of being characterized just now.

We must keep in view here that the problem of being is still entirely immersed in the task of a knowing confrontation with beings as a whole, not set into relief against sciences, but the reverse: the sciences arise now for the first time; they are a consequence of this held bearing as confrontation. The latter is directed toward the most immediate and great regions of beings: nature, the heavens, space, number, the human being himself (medicine); indeed it only now acquires regions.

With Weltanschauung as a held bearing, there thus necessarily occurs a confrontation with beings as a whole, philosophizing. This, however, necessarily lets two things emerge: 1. specially directed attempts to master and determine beings according to individual regions, positive knowledge, science. 2. general reflection upon beings as such, and in such a way that the *logos* enters the foreground as the milieu and guiding thread of the problematic.

In the wake of philosophy, the sciences and logic are formed; in themselves, however, these have precisely the tendency to serve as tools for directing and working, that is, to make the confrontation with beings on the part of knowing a "technical" one. Here we see the same law as in the first fundamental form of Weltanschauung, in mythic Dasein. There, sheltering makes itself public in pursuing the means and ways of salvation; here, philosophizing makes itself public in these forms of a confrontation on the part of knowing and does so necessarily. These forms are indeed necessary in all concrete investigation of beings; yet it is not necessary that these forms that have been made public as such now conversely determine primarily that in whose wake alone they are possible and necessary. Through logic and science, the inner form of philosophy now not only itself becomes superficial but is held at a remove from itself. Yet this does not happen by chance, as a peculiarity of philosophy or of Weltanschauung as held bearing, it also happens with sheltering; to Dasein as such there thus belongs falling, diverse variations—yet the essential determination of Dasein (care).

All great accomplishments of Western philosophy are concerned with the effort to master this power of logic itself,[9] but this happens in such a way that logic itself is admitted into its house, so to speak, and full dominion is extended it—Hegel. There is only one quite sporadic attempt to be found in Kant, denied

---

9. Logic: *ratio*—Descartes's mathematics and care for certainty—from here the *cogito*. Consciousness—reason of the a priori—two motives for the idea of the science of reason as philosophy.

by Kant himself, and that can be seen only if one approaches the Kantian problematic from a more radical questioning to the extent possible, which must be a principle of interpretation.

What is decisive in these considerations, however, is this: the task is to see the peculiarity, problematic, and limits of what I call the Aristotelian situation, that is, the form taken by the philosophizing of antiquity at this, its acme. The problem of being as a question concerning beings as a whole, this at the same time, however, as a question concerning beings as such: this problematic is that of first philosophy, that is, of philosophizing in the first instance, that is, of the original and whole confrontation with beings on the part of knowing. Here, the fate of Western philosophy is decided, it becomes metaphysics, as we then encounter it in Kant. Essential to its history is the incursion of Christendom into philosophy, or philosophy's serving the former. (Soul, world, God, sheltering.) This form of sheltering determines the inner shape of the metaphysical problem, of the question concerning beings as a whole. The problems are forced into this systematics; they thrive only to the extent that this framework leaves space for them, and they are only ever posed in terms of it; endless variations, programs, deracinated.[10]

Even the concrete, historical shape of the history of Western philosophy thus documents the fact that philosophizing, if we understand it from the perspective of the problem of being, is grounded in its very possibility in Dasein, whose being-in-the-world is determined primarily by a held bearing. We express this by saying: philosophy is Weltanschauung as held bearing. Do we with this now have the complete answer to the question that has guided us on our second path? Has the relationship between Weltanschauung and philosophy been thoroughly clarified? However, let us carefully recall; for we did not want to ask concerning the relationship between two quantities pregiven in themselves but rather—via a clarification of the essence of Weltanschauung—to introduce philosophizing more concretely, and that means, to gain an understanding of it as a whole.

On our first path, we came to see: philosophizing is the posing, development, and coming to terms with the question of being; we experienced, as it were, what is treated within philosophy. Now, we hear: philosophizing is Weltanschauung as held bearing, that is, such treatment is possible only on the grounds of Weltanschauung as a held bearing. We are not hearing anything about what is being dealt with but rather how such dealing is possible in its accomplishment, what it intrinsically presupposes for its accomplishment, or, if we grasp it quite formalistically, one might say: on our first path, we found the "content" of philosophy, the problem of being, and now we have found the form, Weltanschauung as

---

10. Here too, admittedly, there is still a directive pointing to the original problematic. Structuring of metaphysics; but not to be deduced from this itself.

held bearing. We did not stop, therefore, at characterizing philosophy as posing the question of being. We gave it a richer determination.

However, apart from the fact that such formulae are always subject to the suspicion of doing premature violence, we should not forget that we said that the paths were meant to lead independently to the whole of philosophy in each case; thus, the second path too must tell us the content of what happens in philosophy. Above all, however, we said already at the end of our first path, by way of anticipation: Philosophizing is explicit transcending. What that means was supposed to be illuminated precisely by our second path.

To what extent does our second path procure for us an original insight in this direction? The very fact that in our interpretation of the phenomenon of world we necessarily encountered the need to characterize transcendence, as suggested by the exclusive orientation toward the problem of being, in a fundamentally more original way points to the fact that the problem of being does not exhaust the whole problematic of philosophy or, to put it better, that we have not yet unfurled the whole that lies within it in its full import.

4 The Connection between Philosophy and Weltanschauung

§45. The problem of being and the problem of world

Our second path, shedding light on philosophizing by passing through a clarification of the essence of Weltanschauung, itself gives us a determination of philosophy in terms of its content. On this path, we encountered the phenomenon of world and made it into a problem, admittedly only to the extent demanded by our initial task. Yet the few things that we were able to discuss—play, thrownness, its connection to the problem of being—had to indicate that here we are faced with a problematic that is unique and extensive, one that is not identical to the problem of being, yet is not without an intrinsic connection to it. The problem of being—taken in its primordiality—necessarily unfurls into what we are calling the problem of world.

On our first path, it was not possible, and not directly our task, to analyze the problem of being. We merely outlined a few main questions. And we must proceed the same way now in relation to the problem of world. We have indeed already experienced a number of things in connection with our characterizing the essence of world as play, but we now wish to make that essence visible from a context that should at the same time indicate how the problem of being unfurls itself into the problem of world and forms a whole with it.

a) The question of being as a question concerning ground and the problem of world

In characterizing the question of being, we encountered the problem of the distinction between beings and being in general (ontological difference). We said that the distinction occurs and irrupts in the process of distinguishing, and this is transcending itself. We let the problem rest in this form, even though a quite essential question stands behind it. We placed special weight on the point that in our comportment toward beings, being is understood in advance. "Being," however, is itself not something that is, although even with this assertion we cannot avoid saying: Being "is" not something that is. We also already indicated: If being is not something that is, is it then nothing in the end? In a certain way, yes, if "nothing" does not mean *nihil absolutum*, sheer nothingness, but means not a being.

If beings indeed are, but not being, then what "is" it about it? How can one then ask concerning it or make being a problem at all? Being as such thus poses an altogether peculiar question to us, one that in part constitutes the core of the problem of being, yet in such a way that the problem of being thereby unfurls into the problem of world. The question of how things stand concerning being as such has its special trenchancy in the fact that it must at the same time also be asked in advance in this question how one can still question at all here. Here, it becomes manifest: When we are asking concerning being itself, we are asking concerning ground. Asking concerning being means "grounding." In traditional philosophy, the problem of ground [*Grund*] is familiar only as the principle of reason [*Satz vom Grunde*],[1] whose ambiguous position within logic and metaphysics is well known. Here, however, the issue is the essence of ground, the question of how such a thing as ground is connected to transcendence, and to what extent being-in-the-world as such is related to grounds.

The task is therefore first to analyze the essence of ground in general and the original ways of grounding. With this, however, we encounter the problem of world anew, and the essential forms of being-in-the-world in which transcendence is a grounding must become apparent. With this, however, we have attained the origin of the possibility of the question in general, the possibility of the why? The why, however, is not a free-floating form of questioning in general, but belongs in part to the essence of transcendence, of being-in-the-world. If, however, ground and the question concerning the why belong to the essence of transcendence, then it lies within transcending itself to ask concerning the why. Transcending, however, insofar as it is determined by a held bearing, is always a confrontation with beings as a whole. The original form of the question concerning the why in the understanding of being (of the nothing) is thus: Why are there beings at all, and not nothing?

If, however, beings are and this is said, then beings are thereby manifest. Yet what must be, so that beings can become manifest? The nothing must be given. What must be for the nothing to be given? The world or transcendence. This problem of the nothing is entangled with the problem of ground, and it then becomes concentrated on the question of what it means that such a thing as the irruption into beings of Dasein, of transcendence, occurs, and in such a way that only now can beings become manifest in themselves and be as a whole in each case.

Together with this question concerning beings and their ground, the question arises concerning the fundamental powers of beings, concerning the prevailing of nature within the happening of history. The issue here is not the region

---

1. *Der Satz vom Grunde*, generally translated and understood as "the principle of reason," is literally "the principle of ground" in German.—Trans.

of nature and the region of history in the specifically ontological sense in each case but rather the being of nature within the happening of history, the intrinsic connection of the fundamental powers of being itself. How is such a thing as nature within the whole of beings, which is at the same time historical? What does it mean that within beings, such a thing as time temporalizes itself and space spreads itself out? All these questions—the problem of ground, and that means, of freedom, the problem of the nothing, of the irruption of transcendence into beings, beings as a whole according to their essential powers (not regions) that pervade the whole in each case—are concentrated in what we call the problem of world.

In the order of approach and of developing the problematic, the problem of world can only be posed in such a way that it is led to unfurl itself from out of the problem of being. This means, however: the problem of being indeed requires a concrete grounding and working out of its possibility; the problem of world, however, cannot simply be added on; rather, in the fundamental consideration of the problem of being, the horizon must already form into which the problem of world can unfurl itself. The problems that are concentrated in the problem of world are, just like the problem of being, all familiar in a certain way and have already emerged in some distorted, misshaped form or other wherever there is philosophizing.

Nevertheless, it must be said that until now, we have been groping entirely in the dark in relation to the problem of world, not only with regard to answers, as it were, but above all with respect to the specific structure of the problematic that is demanded. Admittedly, this also holds true for the problem of being, even though the tradition gives more pointers and forms of recollection here. The fact that the problem of being is historically more familiar is at the same time an indication of the fact that it precedes the problem of world, and in such a way that the latter is also always already there too. The problem of world for its part, once unfurled, cannot be isolated but rather for its part bores itself back once again, so to speak, into the construction of the problem of being. The problem of being unfurls into the problem of world, the problem of world bores itself back into the problem of being—that is to say, the two constitute the intrinsically unitary problematic of philosophy.

b) In the problem of being and the problem of world, transcendence brings itself to conceptual unfolding

What irrupts here as the unitary problematic of the problem of being and of world is the problem of transcendence. Accordingly, our second path likewise leads to a concrete understanding of the problematic of philosophy itself in terms of content and does not merely concern the formal relationship between philosophy and Weltanschauung in the first instance. The true understanding of philosophy, however, now also makes clearer what it means to say that philosophizing is explicit transcending. In the problem of being and that of world, transcendence brings itself to conceptual unfolding.

Yet this does not now mean that in philosophizing, transcendence expressly becomes a theme in the way that a science makes a particular domain lying before it, such as that of plants, the object of investigation. We do not say that philosophizing is the investigation of transcendence, but rather: Philosophizing is explicit transcending. Working out the problem of being and the problem of world does not describe transcendence as something present at hand; it does not describe, because it cannot describe, and it is unable to do so because transcendence does not let itself be described, insofar as transcendence is not something that could lie before us like an object of science.

The conceptual working out of transcendence is an understanding unfolding of transcending itself, it is in itself the accomplishing of transcending, and indeed one of a properly primordial kind. For transcendence is occurring in every Dasein as such. The issue here, however, is that of a letting happen of transcendence from out of, and in, its ground. It is to "show itself," not like a present at hand painting that can be described. Rather, bringing transcendence to a phenomenon, to self-showing, means letting it first of all form itself in the ground of its essence.

This is the properly philosophical-transcendental concept of phenomenon. It is a superficiality when, in relation to the discussions in *Being and Time* and what is presented about phenomenon there, one says that a phenomenon is basically just like stuff and things. It is a superficiality because the section that develops the concept of phenomenon and of phenomenology there is explicitly titled: The "preliminary concept" of phenomenology, and because a major discussion of understanding as a fundamental determination of transcendence subsequently follows. The inner content in the central significance of understanding as projection lies in the fact that the original understanding of transcendence as projecting has the character of construction. In other words, philosophizing, in accordance with its innermost essence, is construction.

Philosophizing is this conceptually comprehending letting happen of transcendence from out of its ground, indicated by way of the problem of being and of world; philosophizing is explicit transcending. Now, we saw that the problem of being is itself possible only on the grounds of Weltanschauung as a held bearing; for only a being-in-the-world that is determined from the ground up as a confrontation with beings as a whole can, and must, pose the question of being. At the same time, we saw that the problem of being unfurls into the problem of world. From this it now becomes quite apparent that such a problematic of world is itself possible only where being-in-the-world as such, Dasein itself, also draws itself into the confrontation, that is, becomes explicit in its being.

Philosophizing as the unity of the problematic of being and of world, as explicit transcending, happens only on the grounds of Weltanschauung as a held bearing. Philosophizing is Weltanschauung as a held bearing. Yet given what we have now seen, we must say essentially more: Philosophizing as explicit transcending is a letting happen of the transcendence of Dasein from out of its ground, that is, in philosophizing there occurs the most original possible held bearing.

§46. *Philosophy as held bearing in relation to ground: Letting transcendence happen from out of its ground*

Philosophizing is not one Weltanschauung among others as a held bearing, but rather is the held bearing pure and simple in relation to ground.[2] Only in letting transcendence happen explicitly, in the irrupting of the inner expanse and primordiality of transcendence, do the concrete possibilities of a held bearing open up. These concrete possibilities, however, are not determined on the path of philosophy, but from out of each respective Dasein itself. Yet precisely because philosophizing as explicit transcending is a held bearing in relation to ground, it is not philosophy's essence or its task to develop a particular held bearing so as to proclaim it as authoritative or even supposedly to transplant it into others. The more purely philosophy understands itself, the more purely it is concerned solely with letting transcendence happen from out of its ground, the more purely and directly it satisfies the only thing it can be with respect to the factical forming of a Weltanschauung, namely, to be an occasion for factically existing human beings in each case for the emergence of possibilities of a held bearing in them. The more originally philosophy philosophizes, that is, is a letting happen of transcendence, the more freely and nonbindingly it is in each case the concomitant letting happen of a held bearing in the Dasein of the other. For philosophical Dasein is by its very essence being with others. The more nonbinding the held bearing in relation to ground is in itself, however, the more its happening can be an awakening.

From this, the relationship of philosophy and Weltanschauung first becomes fully clear. That philosophy is a held bearing in relation to ground means: 1. only in a Weltanschauung as a held bearing is philosophizing possible; 2. philosophizing itself develops, in the manner characterized, the "presuppositions" for the possibilities of a concrete Weltanschauung as a held bearing; 3. philosophizing itself, however, is neither an exemplary, thematic construction of a Weltanschauung

---

2. "Held bearing in relation to ground" attempts to translate *Grund-haltung*. The term *Grund-haltung* was earlier rendered as "fundamental stance" in the context of the discussion of the ascendancy of the theoretical life (see §§22–24). *Haltung*, previously rendered as "stance," has meanwhile acquired the sense of a "held bearing." Heidegger initially hyphenates the term *Grund-haltung* in this final section in order to convey the essential relation to ground, *Grund*, embodied in the distinctive held bearing or fundamental stance of philosophizing.—Trans.

nor indeed the proclamation of one but rather the letting happen of transcendence from out of its ground. Philosophizing means precisely the unfolding of that transcendence of Dasein that we call freedom, in which everything essential is staked on freedom. The essence of philosophy consists in the fact that it unfolds the leeway, the space of play, for the irruption of a concrete, historical Dasein determined by a held bearing; it is thereby futural, however, in a primordial and precise sense. Just as myth is an essential recollection for philosophy, so is the future its authentic force, every present, however, only the pinnacle of the moment, which draws its power and its wealth from futural recollection. It is essential that the present by itself alone is blind toward itself and therefore thinks that it alone is what is real and actual, when it precisely is not.

The relationship of philosophy and Weltanschauung was indeed to be clarified on all sides, but it is much too rich and complex to be reduced to a simple, neat formula. In any case, the ordinary representations of this relationship and the questions and desires arising from such representations fail to enter the sphere of what is essential.

One thing becomes clear, however, namely that philosophy has a distinct relationship to Weltanschauung as a held bearing. From this, however, there arises a new difficulty, if we consider that earlier, at the beginning of the lecture course, we said: Dasein as such philosophizes; philosophizing belongs to Dasein insofar as it exists. Yet now we are saying: Philosophizing is possible only on the grounds of Weltanschauung as a held bearing, thus only in one grounding form of Weltanschauung and so not in the Dasein whose being-in-the-world is determined primarily as sheltering.

Before we go into our opening thesis by way of conclusion, we must briefly point to the relationship between philosophy as a held bearing in relation to ground and Dasein as sheltering. The interpretation of these two fundamental possibilities already showed that a held bearing arises from sheltering, stands and always remains in an essential historical connection with it. This means: on the one hand, sheltering, mythic Dasein as prephilosophical in the strict sense, is by the necessity of its essence an enduring recollection on the part of philosophy as a held bearing in relation to ground; precisely because this bearing is intrinsically something else on the grounds of a history, philosophy remains related back to myth. What that means in detail is not to be discussed here.

On the other hand, however, philosophy as a held bearing in relation to ground is necessarily an annoyance for every Weltanschauung as sheltering. One may neither veil nor weaken this relationship; if one attempts to do so, then one is neither understanding oneself as existing within a sheltering nor is one understanding philosophy. Only if philosophy as a held bearing in relation to ground becomes a real annoyance and stumbling block for Weltanschauung as sheltering, only then can philosophy take on the role of performing a service for sheltering in the free, nonbinding manner of occasioning, if only that of recollecting that it has a hold in something essentially other than every held bearing. Yet how do things then stand with regard to the more precise clarification of the essence of philosophizing concerning our initial thesis that philosophizing belongs to Dasein as such? Must we not now retract this thesis, if indeed philosophizing is possible only as a held bearing? Indeed, we must retract the thesis; it was proposed so that we could now explicitly retract it. For in this explicit retraction, we see something essential: that the one philosophizing must explicitly transpose himself into the way of existence determined by a held bearing, that philosophizing does not just happen in general somewhere indeterminately or in itself. If, then, we said too precipitously at the beginning that philosophizing belongs to Dasein, in doing so we forgot that fundamentally we meant our Dasein as codetermined by a held bearing at any rate.

We say: to the essence of philosophizing there belongs the explicit leap into Weltanschauung as a held bearing and only in this way the possibility of letting transcendence happen from out of its ground. This leap of philosophizing into transcendence from out of its ground is necessarily, however, the leap into one's own historicality. The more historically and primordially the philosophizing Dasein attains its concrete transcendence, the more essential it becomes. This is what ordinary understanding—including when it degrades philosophy to a science—comprehends least of all about philosophy: that the unfolding of the highest and most universal problems such as being and world must necessarily be accompanied by a leap into the concrete historical situation.

Together with this, however, the leap enters into a passion for the concept, for the construction of transcendence, for a primordiality and rigor of knowledge such as science can never have. To fight for the science of philosophy means not only to misunderstand oneself as a supposed philosopher but to degrade philosophy itself, thereby, however, robbing Dasein itself of one of its supreme possibilities and putting a fantasy in its place.

That we are so little able to comprehend this essential character of philosophy has to do not only with the fact that the problematic of being and world has not been sufficiently clarified but with the fact that we fail to see that here, with this question, it is not at all a matter of a private and personal affair of the philosopher, but of nothing less than the problem of the truth of philosophy.

It is evident, however, that this problem can first concretely arise from the problem of being and the problem of world in their unity. This problem of truth, however, is the problem of truth as a whole, that is, the question of the essential belonging of truth to transcendence. (Only on the grounds of this original problem of truth can the question of scientific truth be posed and a philosophical interpretation of science become possible.)

The problem of truth in this original scope was supposed to emerge for us on our third path. What is commonly treated as logic has its place here, as does mythic truth as goddess (cf. p.267). We would have to show that each of these problems, the problem of being, the problem of world, and the problem of truth constitutes the whole of philosophy, and that it is an inner corruption of philosophy when one orients it around rigidly formed, traditional disciplines and lets the problems arise from these, instead of attaining the inner necessity of the architectonic of philosophy from the inner content of its fundamental problematic.

The two paths that we have traversed were meant to help us shed light on the essence of philosophy, and to do so with regard to the two powers that determine our Dasein at the university, whether we want it or not, science and leadership or Weltanschauung.

Science is only possible as philosophy; the latter, however, as explicit transcending—a held bearing in relation to ground—provides the original possibility for the occasion to interrogate one's own being-in-the-world in each case with respect to its hold and to its held bearing. Philosophizing as the letting happen of transcendence is the freeing of Dasein. What is freed is the freedom of Dasein, and freedom is only in being freed.

In the letting happen of transcendence as philosophizing, there lies the original releasement of Dasein (cf. earlier: letting be), the entrusting of the human being to the Da-sein in him and to its possibilities. From here alone, there arises the genuine force of the turning toward beings that all held bearing as a confrontation with beings intrinsically demands. With philosophizing, the ascent to the peaks of the summits of the greats begins. And if at times we are surprised that the greats have no effect or no longer have an effect, then we are forgetting that what is great acts only upon what is great. If we understand that, however, then we recall that it is inessential whether or not we triumph over contemporaries or others, but that we must instead procure inner greatness for ourselves by vanquishing our own demons.

Editors' Epilogue

The lecture course *Introduction to Philosophy*, published here for the first time, was held by Martin Heidegger for four hours per week in the winter semester of 1928–29 at Freiburg University.

This edition has been compiled from three sources: a photocopy of Heidegger's handwritten manuscript; a largely reliable, typewritten copy by Frau Hildegard Feick; and a transcript of the lecture course produced by Simon Moser that was authorized by Heidegger. A handwritten record of Eugen Fink's, which is incomplete, was consulted in a few cases of uncertainty.

The manuscript of *Introduction to Philosophy* comprises 106 quarter sheets written in landscape format. On the left is the main text; on the right are additions, insertions, and references that were in part presumably written after the lectures were held. Between the numbered pages are numerous sheets containing supplements, summaries, or recapitulations. A notebook with additional loose notes supplements the materials available for the edition.

The editors' task was to produce a coherent text from the divergent sources while incorporating the separate notes. Whereas Heidegger's manuscript is composed in a concise, concentrated style and for some passages consists only of keywords, the transcript of the lecture course is more detailed and extensive. From it, we can see how Heidegger endeavored to elucidate his thinking.

It thus could not be entirely avoided that the text of this edition displays different stylistic features, depending on whether it is based on the original diction of Heidegger's manuscript or on the more extensive oral lecture as preserved in the transcript. Where the manuscript consists only of keywords, or where thoughts are developed in the transcript that are not contained in the manuscript, recourse was had to the transcript.

Heidegger had structured the *Introduction to Philosophy* in three sections—"stages" or "paths": Philosophy and Science, Philosophy and Weltanschauung, Philosophy and History. The second section increased in scope due to a detailed discussion of Kant's concept of world, more than twenty pages of which, however, were not delivered. The third section was not realized.

In keeping with Heidegger's guiding principles for the edition of his lecture courses, a detailed sectioning of the text was undertaken, as reflected in the table of contents. Apart from the aforementioned division of the lecture course, the titles of the sections stem from the editors. Punctuation was adapted to the rules current at that time. Citations and references to literature were verified and made complete.

My sincere thanks to Herr Dr. Hermann Heidegger, Herr Professor Dr. Friedrich-Wilhelm von Herrmann, and above all Herr Dr. Hartmut Tietjen for his willing support and advice. I thank especially the staff of the *Studium generale* at the University of Mainz for their tireless assistance. I thank also Herr Peter von Ruckteschell, Cand. Phil., for his careful proofreading.

Mainz, July 1996 Ina Saame-Speidel[1]

---

1. Although just one name appears at the end of this Epilogue, the front matter of the German edition indicates two editors, one of whom (Otto Saame) was deceased when the volume was published.—Trans.

German–English Glossary

der Abgrund	abyss
die Abkehr	turning away
die Abwehr	warding off
alltäglich	everyday
der Anfang	beginning, inception
die Anschauung	intuition
der Aufenthalt	dwelling
das Aufgehen	dawning, emergence
aufgehen in . . .	to be absorbed in . . .
die Aufhellung	elucidation
aufweisen	to exhibit
der Augenblick	(temporal) moment
die Auseinandersetzung	confrontation
ausgeliefert	at the mercy of
ausgesetzt	exposed
die Aussage	assertion, statement
das Ausweichen	avoidance
die Barbarei	barbarism
bedeuten	to signify, mean
die Bedeutung	significance, meaning
die Bedeutungseinheit	semantic unity
sich befinden	to find oneself
die Befindlichkeit	finding oneself
begreifen	to comprehend conceptually
der Begründungszusammenhang	coherent grounding
benommen	captivated
die Bergung	shelter, sheltering
der Beruf	vocation
die Besinnung	reflection
betrachten	to contemplate, observe
die Betrachtung	contemplating, contemplation

der Betrieb	busyness
die Betulichkeit	fastidiousness
die Bewandtnis	involvement
der Bewandtniszusammenhang	nexus/context of involvement
die Bewegtheit	vibrancy
die Beziehung	relation
der Beziehungszusammenhang	relational nexus
die Bildung	education
die Bindung	commitment
der Bruch	fracture
der Dämmerzustand	state of latency
durchwalten	to pervade
die Einfühlung	empathy
die Einleitung	introduction
die Einstellung	attitude
die Einzigkeit	singularity
die Empfindlichkeit	susceptibility
die Endlichkeit	finitude
die Entartung	degeneration
entdecken	to uncover
das Entdeckendsein	being uncovering
die Entdecktheit	uncoveredness
die Entdeckung	discovery
enthüllen	to unveil
die Enthülltheit	unveiledness
die Entschlossenheit	resolute openness
der Entschluß	resolution, resolute decision
entwerfen	to project
der Entwurf	projection
erfassen	to apprehend
die Erhöhung	elevation
die Erinnerung	recollection
die Erkenntnis	knowledge
die Erläuterung	elucidation

erschließen	to disclose
die Erschlossenheit	disclosedness
die Existenz	existence
existenzial	existential
existenziell	existentiell
faktisch	factical
die Faktizität	facticity
fassen	to grasp
die Führerschaft	leadership
in Gang bringen	to get underway
die Gebärde	gesture
die Geborgenheit	security
gebrochen	fractured, broken
die Gelassenheit	releasement
gemeinsam	common
die Gemeinsamkeit	commonality
die Gemeinschaft	community
die Gerichtetheit	directedness
die Geschlechtlichkeit	sexuality
das Geschlechtsverhältnis	sexual relationship
das Geschehen	occurrence, happening
geschichtlich	historical
die Geschichtlichkeit	historicality
das Gesetz	law
die Gesetzlichkeit	lawfulness
das Gestimmtsein	being attuned
die Geworfenheit	thrownness
die Gleichheit	being identical
gleichursprünglich	equiprimordial
die Gleichursprünglichkeit	equiprimordiality
der Grund	ground
die Grund-haltung	held bearing in relation to ground
die Grundhaltung	fundamental stance
die Grundstellung	fundamental position

der Halt — hold

sich halten — to hold oneself

die Haltlosigkeit — lack of hold

das Haltnehmen — taking a hold

die Haltung — held stance, held bearing

die Haltungslosigkeit — lack of a held bearing

handeln — to act

die Handlung — action

die Helle — lucidity

die Herkunft — provenance

die Herrschaft — reign, governance, rule, dominion

hingerissen — enraptured

historisch — historiographical

die Identität — identity

der Inbegriff — sum-total

inmitten — in the midst

die Innerlichkeit — inwardness

die Macht — power

die Mächtigkeit — powerfulness

das Mitdasein — Dasein-with

das Miteinandersein — being with one another

das Mitsein — being-with

die Mitteilung — communication, sharing-with

der Mythos — myth

die Neutralität — neutrality

das Neutrum — neuter

nichtig — nihilative

die Nichtigkeit — nihilative character

das Nichts — the nothing

die Not — exigency

offenbar — manifest

die Offenbarkeit — manifestness

die Ohnmacht — impotence

ohnmächtig	impotent
ontisch	ontic
die Ontologie	ontology
ontologisch	ontological
der Ort	locus, locale
die Philosophie	philosophy
das Philosophieren	philosophizing
preisgeben	to expose
die Preisgegebenheit	exposure
die Sammlung	gathering
der Satz	statement, propositional statement
die Satzwahrheit	propositional truth
der Schein	illusion, semblance
die Seele	the soul
das Seelenleben	psychic life
seelisch	psychic
das Seiende	a being, beings
das Seiende im Ganzen	beings as a whole
das Sein	being
das Sein bei …	being alongside …
das Seinlassen	letting be
die Seinsart	manner of being
die Seinsverfassung	constitution of being
das Seinsverständnis	understanding of being
die Seinsweise	way of being
die Selbigkeit	sameness
die Sorge	care
das Spiel	play, game
der Spielraum	leeway, playing field, play space
die Stimmung	attunement
die Streuung	dissemination
sich teilen in …	to share, share in …
die Teilhabe, Teilhaberschaft	partaking
teilhaben an …	to partake in …, have a share in …

die Teilnahme	taking part
transzendental	transcendental
die Transzendenz	transcendence
transzendieren	to transcend
die Übermacht	overwhelming power, superior power
die Übermächtigkeit	overwhelming powerfulness
der Überschritt	transition
übersteigen	to overstep
der Überstieg	overstepping
das Überwältigende	the overwhelming
der Umschlag	changeover, sudden change
das Umwillen	the "for the sake of"
die Ungeborgenheit	insecurity
der Unterschied	distinction, difference
unverborgen	unconcealed
die Unverborgenheit	unconcealment
die Urhandlung	originary action
der Ursprung	origin
ursprünglich	originary, primordial
das Urteil	judgment
verborgen	concealed
die Verborgenheit	concealment
die Vereinzelung	individuation
das Verfallen	falling
das Verhalten	comportment
sich verhalten	to comport oneself
das Verhältnis	relationship
die Verknüpfung	association
die Verpflichtung	obligation
verschieden	diverse
die Verschiedenheit	diversity
das Verständnis	understanding
die Verweisung	reference
vorbegrifflich	preconceptual

vorgängig	antecedent
vorhanden	present at hand
vorontologisch	preontological
das Vorverständnis	preunderstanding
vorwissenschaftlich	prescientific
die Wahrheit	truth
das In-der-Wahrheit-sein	being-in-the-truth
das Walten	prevailing
der Wandel	change
die Welt	world
das In-der-Welt-sein	being-in-the-world
die Weltanschauung	Weltanschauung
die Weltbildung	world-formation
die Wissenschaft	science
wissenschaftlich	scientific
das Wortlaut	word-sound
sich zeitigen	to temporalize
die Zeitlichkeit	temporality
die Zerstreuung	dispersion
zuhanden	ready to hand
Der Zusammenhang	nexus, context

English–German Glossary

to be absorbed in . . .	aufgehen in . . .
abyss	der Abgrund
to act	handeln
action	die Handlung, das Handeln
action, originary	die Urhandlung
antecedent	vorgängig
to apprehend	erfassen
assertion	die Aussage
association	die Verknüpfung
attitude	die Einstellung
attuned, being attuned	das Gestimmtsein
attunement	die Stimmung
avoidance	das Ausweichen
barbarism	die Barberei
bearing, held bearing	die Haltung
bearing, held bearing in relation to ground	die Grund-haltung
bearing, lack of held bearing	die Haltungslosigkeit
beginning	der Anfang
being	das Sein
being alongside . . .	das Sein bei . . .
being, constitution of	die Seinsverfassung
being, manner of	die Seinsart
being, understanding of	das Seinsverständnis
being, way of	die Seinsweise
being-with	das Mitsein
being with one another	das Miteinandersein
beings, a being	das Seiende
beings as a whole	das Seiende im Ganzen
busyness	der Betrieb

captivated	benommen
care	die Sorge
change	der Wandel
changeover, sudden change	der Umschlag
coherent grounding	der Begründungszusammenhang
commitment	die Bindung
common	gemeinsam
commonality	die Gemeinsamkeit
communication	die Mitteilung
community	die Gemeinschaft
to comport oneself	sich verhalten
comportment	das Verhalten, die Verhaltung
to comprehend conceptually	begreifen
concealed	verborgen
concealment	die Verborgenheit
confrontation	die Auseinandersetzung
to contemplate, observe	betrachten
contemplation	die Betrachtung
context	der Zusammenhang
Dasein-with	das Mitdasein
dawning	das Aufgehen
degeneration	die Entartung
difference	der Unterschied, die Differenz
directedness	die Gerichtetheit
to disclose	erschließen
disclosedness	die Erschlossenheit
discovery	die Entdeckung
dispersion	die Zerstreuung
dissemination	die Streuung
distinction	der Unterschied
diverse	verschieden
diversity	die Verschiedenheit
dominion	die Herrschaft
dwelling	der Aufenthalt

education	die Bildung
elevation	die Erhöhung
elucidation	die Aufhellung, die Erläuterung
emergence	das Aufgehen
empathy	die Einfühlung
enraptured	hingerissen
equiprimordial	gleichursprünglich
equiprimordiality	die Gleichursprünglichkeit
everyday	alltäglich
to exhibit	aufweisen
exigency	die Not
existence	die Existenz
existential	existenzial
existentiell	existenziell
to expose	preisgeben, aussetzen
exposed	preisgegeben, ausgesetzt
exposure	die Preisgegebenheit, die Ausgesetztheit
factical	faktisch
facticity	die Faktizität
falling	das Verfallen
fastidiousness	die Betulichkeit
to find oneself	sich befinden
finding oneself	die Befindlichkeit
finitude	die Endlichkeit
fracture	der Bruch
fractured, broken	gebrochen
gathering	die Sammlung
gesture	die Gebärde
to grasp	fassen
ground	der Grund
happening	das Geschehen
historical	geschichtlich

historicality	die Geschichtlichkeit
historiographical	historisch
hold	der Halt
hold, lack of	die Haltlosigkeit
hold, taking a hold	das Haltnehmen
to hold oneself	sich halten
identical, being identical	die Gleichheit
identity	die Identität
illusion	der Schein
impotence	die Ohnmacht
impotent	ohnmächtig
inception	der Anfang
individuation	die Vereinzelung
insecurity	die Ungeborgenheit
introduction	die Einleitung
intuition	die Anschauung
involvement	die Bewandtnis
involvement, nexus/context of	der Bewandtniszusammenhang
inwardness	die Innerlichkeit
judgment	das Urteil
knowledge	die Erkenntnis, das Wissen
latency, state of	der Dämmerzustand
law	das Gesetz
lawfulness	die Gesetzlichkeit
leadership	die Führerschaft
leeway	der Spielraum
letting be	das Seinlassen
locus, locale	der Ort
lucidity	die Helle
manifest	offenbar
manifestness	die Offenbarkeit

at the mercy of	ausgeliefert
midst, in the midst	inmitten
moment (temporal)	der Augenblick
myth	der Mythos
neuter	das Neutrum
neutrality	die Neutralität
nexus	der Zusammenhang
nihilative	nichtig
nihilative character	die Nichtigkeit
the nothing	das Nichts
obligation	die Verpflichtung
occurrence	das Geschehen
ontic	ontisch
ontological	ontologisch
ontology	die Ontologie
origin	der Ursprung
originary	ursprünglich
to overstep	übersteigen
overstepping	der Überstieg
overwhelming, the	das Überwältigende
part, taking part	die Teilnahme
to partake in . . ., have a share in . . .	teilhaben an . . .
partaking	die Teilhabe, Teilhaberschaft
to pervade	durchwalten
philosophizing	das Philosophieren
philosophy	die Philosophie
play	das Spiel
play space, playing field	der Spielraum
position, fundamental position	die Grundstellung
power	die Macht
power, overwhelming, superior	die Übermacht
powerfulness	die Mächtigkeit
powerfulness, overwhelming	die Übermächtigkeit

preconceptual	vorbegrifflich
preontological	vorontologisch
prescientific	vorwissenschaftlich
present at hand	vorhanden
preunderstanding	das Vorverständnis
prevailing	das Walten
to project	entwerfen
projection	der Entwurf
proposition	der Satz
propositional truth	die Satzwahrheit
provenance	die Herkunft
psychic	seelisch
psychic life	das Seelenleben
ready to hand	zuhanden
recollection	die Erinnerung
reference	die Verweisung
reflection	die Besinnung
relation	die Beziehung
relational nexus	der Beziehungszusammenhang
relationship	das Verhältnis
releasement	die Gelassenheit
resolute openness	die Entschlossenheit
resolution, resolute decision	der Entschluß
rule	die Herrschaft
sameness	die Selbigkeit
science	die Wissenschaft
scientific	wissenschaftlich
security	die Geborgenheit
semantic unity	die Bedeutungseinheit
semblance	der Schein
sexual relationship	das Geschlechtsverhältnis
sexuality	die Geschlechtlichkeit
to share, share in . . .	sich teilen in . . .
share, to have a share in . . .	teilhaben an . . .

shelter, sheltering	die Bergung
significance	die Bedeutung
to signify	bedeuten
singularity	die Einzigkeit
soul	die Seele
stance, fundamental stance	die Grundhaltung
stance, held stance	die Haltung
statement	die Aussage
statement, propositional	der Satz
sum-total	der Inbegriff
susceptibility	die Empfindlichkeit
temporality	die Zeitlichkeit
to temporalize	sich zeitigen
thrownness	die Geworfenheit
to transcend	transzendieren
transcendence	die Transzendenz
transcendental	transzendental
transition	der Überschritt
truth	die Wahrheit
truth, being-in-the-truth	das In-der-Wahrheit-sein
turning away	die Abkehr
unconcealed	unverborgen
unconcealment	die Unverborgenheit
to uncover	entdecken
uncoveredness	die Entdecktheit
uncovering, being uncovering	das Entdeckendsein
understanding	das Verstehen, das Verständnis
underway, to get underway	in Gang bringen
to unveil	enthüllen
unveiledness	die Enthülltheit
vibrancy	die Bewegtheit
vocation	der Beruf

warding off	die Abwehr
Weltanschauung	die Weltanschauung
word-sound	das Wortlaut
world	die Welt
world, being-in-the-world	das In-der-Welt-sein
world-formation	die Weltbildung

WILLIAM MCNEILL is Professor of Philosophy at DePaul University, Chicago. He is author of several books on Heidegger, most recently *The Fate of Phenomenology: Heidegger's Legacy* (2020), and has translated or cotranslated a number of Heidegger's works, including his three lecture courses on Hölderlin.

For Indiana University Press

Tony Brewer, Artist and Book Designer
Brian Carroll, Rights Manager
Gary Dunham, Acquisitions Editor and Director
Anna Garnai, Editorial Assistant
Anna Francis, Assistant Acquisitions Editor
Brenna Hosman, Production Coordinator
Katie Huggins, Production Manager
David Miller, Lead Project Manager/Editor
Dan Pyle, Online Publishing Manager
Stephen Williams, Marketing and Publicity Manager
Jennifer Witzke, Senior Artist and Book Designer